STUDIES IN BAPTIST HISTORY AN[D]
VOLUME 25

Baptist Sacramentalism 2

STUDIES IN BAPTIST HISTORY AND THOUGHT
VOLUME 25

A full listing of all titles in this series
appears at the close of this book

STUDIES IN BAPTIST HISTORY AND THOUGHT
VOLUME 25

Baptist Sacramentalism 2

Anthony R. Cross

and

Philip E. Thompson

Foreword by Francis Schüssler Fiorenza

Paternoster:
thinking faith

MILTON KEYNES · COLORADO SPRINGS · HYDERABAD

Copyright © Anthony R. Cross, Philip E. Thompson and the Contributors 2008

First published 2008 by Paternoster

Paternoster is an imprint of Authentic Media
9 Holdom Avenue, Bletchley, Milton Keynes, MK1 1QR, UK
1820 Jet Stream Drive, Colorado Springs, CO 80921, USA
OM Authentic Media, Medchal Road, Jeedimetla Village,
Secunderabad 500 055, A.P., India

www.authenticmedia.co.uk
Authentic Media is a Division of IBS-STL UK, a company limited by guarantee
(registered charity no. 270162)

15 14 13 12 11 10 09 08 7 6 5 4 3 2 1

The right of Anthony R. Cross and Philip E. Thompson to be
identified as the Editors of this Work has been asserted by them
in accordance with the Copyright, Designs
and Patents Act 1988

All rights reserved. No part of this publication may be reproduced, stored in a retrieval system, or transmitted in any form by any means, electronic, mechanical, photocopying, recording or otherwise, without the prior permission of the publisher or a license permitting restricted copying. In the UK such licenses are issued by the Copyright Licensing Agency, 90 Tottenham Court Road, London W1P 9HE.

British Library Cataloguing in Publication Data
A catalogue record for this book is available from the British Library

ISBN 978-1-84227-325-8

Typeset by A.R. Cross
Printed and bound in Great Britain
for Paternoster
by AlphaGraphics Nottingham

Studies in Baptist History and Thought

Series Preface

Baptists form one of the largest Christian communities in the world, and while they hold the historic faith in common with other mainstream Christian traditions, they nevertheless have important insights which they can offer to the worldwide church. Studies in Baptist History and Thought will be one means towards this end. It is an international series of academic studies which includes original monographs, revised dissertations, collections of essays and conference papers, and aims to cover any aspect of Baptist history and thought. While not all the authors are themselves Baptists, they nevertheless share an interest in relating Baptist history and thought to the other branches of the Christian church and to the wider life of the world.

The series includes studies in various aspects of Baptist history from the seventeenth century down to the present day, including biographical works, and Baptist thought is understood as covering the subject-matter of theology (including interdisciplinary studies embracing biblical studies, philosophy, sociology, practical theology, liturgy and women's studies). The diverse streams of Baptist life throughout the world are all within the scope of these volumes.

The series editors and consultants believe that the academic disciplines of history and theology are of vital importance to the spiritual vitality of the churches of the Baptist faith and order. The series sets out to discuss, examine and explore the many dimensions of their tradition and so to contribute to their on-going intellectual vigour.

A brief word of explanation is due for the series identifier on the front cover. The fountains, taken from heraldry, represent the Baptist distinctive of believer's baptism and, at the same time, the source of the water of life. There are three of them because they symbolize the Trinitarian basis of Baptist life and faith. Those who are redeemed by the Lamb, the book of Revelation reminds us, will be led to 'fountains of living waters' (Rev. 7.17).

Studies in Baptist History and Thought

Series Editors

Anthony R. Cross	Centre for Baptist History and Heritage, Regent's Park College, Oxford, England
Curtis W. Freeman	Duke University, North Carolina, USA
Stephen R. Holmes	University of St Andrews, Scotland
Elizabeth Newman	Baptist Theological Seminary at Richmond, Virginia, USA
Philip E. Thompson	North American Baptist Seminary, Sioux Falls, South Dakota, USA

Series Consultants

David Bebbington	University of Stirling, Stirling, Scotland
Paul S. Fiddes	Regent's Park College, Oxford, England
† Stanley J. Grenz	Carey Theological College, Vancouver, British Columbia, Canada
Ken R. Manley	Whitley College, The University of Melbourne, Australia
Stanley E. Porter	McMaster Divinity College, Hamilton, Ontario, Canada

*In loving memory of our
friend, colleague and teacher
Stanley J. Grenz
(7 January 1950 – 12 March 2005)*

Contents

Foreword by Francis Schüssler Fiorenza xi

Contributors xv

Introduction: Practicing Sacramentality in Baptist Modality
Philip E. Thompson xvii

Chapter 1
Embodied Grace: Exploring the Sacraments and Sacramentality
Christopher J. Ellis 1

Chapter 2
'We have an altar': A Baptist View of Sacrament and Sacrifice in Hebrews
J. Ramsey Michaels 17

Chapter 3
The Sacrament of Fearful Intimacy
Jim Purves 30

Chapter 4
The Church as Sacrament: A Mediating Presence
John E. Colwell 48

Chapter 5
Re-Thinking a Sacramental View of Baptism and the Lord's Supper for the Post-Christendom Baptist Church
Michael F. Bird 61

Chapter 6
Ambiguous Genitives, Pauline Baptism and Roman *Insulae*: Resources from Romans to Support *Pushing the Boundaries of Unity*
Sean F. Winter 77

Chapter 7
A Feast for All? Reflecting on Open Communion for the Contemporary Church
Anthony Clarke 92

Chapter 8
Penance
Paul Sheppy 117

Chapter 9
Can a Baptist Believe in Sacred Space? Some Theological Reflections
Graham J. Watts 135

Chapter 10
Baptismal Regeneration: Rehabilitating a Lost Dimension of New Testament Baptism
Anthony R. Cross 149

Chapter 11
The Lord's Supper and the Spirituality of C.H. Spurgeon
Peter J. Morden 175

Chapter 12
Southern Baptists, Sacramentalism, and Soul Competency
Sean A. White 197

Chapter 13
Ex Opere Operato: Re-thinking a Historic Baptist Rejection
Paul S. Fiddes 219

Chapter 14
The Sacramentality of the Word in Gregory of Nyssa's *Catechetical Oration*: Implications for a Baptist Sacramental Theology
Steven R. Harmon 239

Chapter 15
Baptists and Churches of Christ in Search of a Common Theology of Baptism
Stanley K. Fowler 254

Index 271

Foreword

In the last decades, the theological interpretation of the sacraments, especially baptism and the Lord's supper, has been at the center of ecumenical dialogues. These dialogues have produced a vast array of official declarations. One finds the statements of the dialogue that the Anglicans have had with Lutherans, Orthodox and Reformed. Likewise there are the dialogues that the Roman Catholic Church has engaged with Lutheran, Evangelical, and Orthodox, and equally the dialogues between the Reformed Church and the Disciples of Christ, as well as between Baptists and the Lutherans. The scope and number of these statements are as vast as they are diverse. What is striking about these dialogues is not only the concern for the unity of the church and for ecumenical outreach, but also their reflections on the significance of the sacraments for the meaning of ministry and mission, the role of the churches and their ministry in the world, and the interrelationship between the Christian believer's faith in God's saving action in Jesus and the believer's commitments to God's creation and to the social world. These statements point to a new context and call for a deeper theological reflection. It is this call for further theological reflection that these essays answer.

Today, the term 'postmodern' has become very popular, though its meaning is often ambiguous and diverse. The appeal to the 'postmodern' often spans quite distinct attitudes, ranging from a traditional return to the pre-modern to a relativistic playfulness and radicalization. Nevertheless, the term can be applied in a meaningful way to the theological dialogues that have been taking place around the sacraments for various reasons. The birth of the modern European West took place as a convergence of diverse forces and conflicting movements. The struggle to reform Christianity by returning to its biblical roots led not only to a renewal of Christianity and to a rich diversity of Christian faith, but also to the religious wars that followed. These wars led to the attempts to develop religious tolerance within the modern West. The Enlightenment period witnessed attempts to bring a cessation to religious strife in various ways. It individualized faith as a private choice leading as a consequence to the privatization of religion. This privatization took place within the dominance of a certain kind of rationality: a technocratic scientific rationality that had scant regard for tradition and saw itself as alone fit for the public sphere. This rationality favored a deistic conception of the divine in which God's activity was excluded from the confines of a Newtonian and mechanical view of nature.

Today, one sees a strong push back against many of these modern and western trends. In this sense the term 'postmodern' has its validity. Against the Enlightenment emphasis on progressive rationality, there is an emerging respect for tradition and against its emphasis on the objectivity of reason, there is an increased awareness that rationality is embodied and that it must be open for the aesthetic, for feelings, and for religious belief. Against the privatization and individualization of religious faith, there is renewed awareness of the public and communal significance of a believer's faith. Against the deistic conception of God, far removed from a Newtonian world, there is the renewed retrieval of the Christian belief of the trinitarian and its emphasis on God's presence in the world and the Christian community. In this context an understanding of God's saving presence in creation and redemption opens the way for a renewal of theological reflection on the sacraments. Since the individualism and mechanical view of nature of the modern West has infected the attitudes and convictions within the Christian communities, the theological reflection on the sacraments seeks to overcome this individualism and to explore how creation is also a theater of God's activity.

The essays in this book, remarkable in their scope and depth, greatly contribute to this important and corrective direction. They represent in many ways the very best of evangelical Baptist scholarship. They all seek to be faithful to both the biblical witness and to Baptist traditions and beliefs. They demonstrate that theological reflection and reform takes place in the return to biblical witness that is complemented with attention to the tradition of the reception and interpretation of this witness and with an openness to other Christian denominations and communities. They squarely face the widespread skepticism that a robust sacramental theology can easily degenerate into a form of sacramentalism and ritualism or become a form of crypto-Roman Catholicism. The natural tendency would limit as much as possible language about the sacraments. In this respect they take up trends of the postmodern push back against aspects of modernity. In addition, rather than searching for the latest novelty, they display a remarkable erudition in their knowledge of the scriptures, their familiarity with patristic and reformation writing as well as their knowledge of contemporary theology, including Roman Catholic theology.

What is striking for me is the convergence among these essays despite significant differences. Several themes range through these essays. There is a consistent insistence on rejecting any mechanical or instrumental understanding of the sacramental that undercut or minimizes God's freedom or views the sacraments as some type of 'intermediary medium' between God's grace and humans. Expressed positively, this entails a thinking of the sacraments in ways that underscore God's freedom and human faith. Second, the essays not only explore further the meaning of the sacraments of baptism and the Lord's supper, but they also broaden and expand the notion of 'sacrament' so that it can include the practices of proclamation, ministry, and the coming together as communities of Christian believers. In this regard, they contribute to an understanding of Christian faith and life in a way that undercuts the individualism of much of modern life and brings to the fore the communal and social dimensions of Christian faith.

These essays take up with boldness controversial issues in theological reflection about the nature of sacraments. Is there any place for baptism as regeneration? For infant baptism? Can one make sense of '*ex opere operato*' in a way that does not posit an instrumental mediation between God and the believers? It is especially fascinating for me as a Roman Catholic theologian to read these theological reflections on the sacraments and to observe how theologians from diverse traditions and from different standpoints are moving in directions that lead to some convergence. One example is the notion of the church as a sacrament. This concept is a relatively new concept within Roman Catholic theology, even though some roots or traces exist within patristic thinking and some explorations took place in early nineteenth-century theology (Johann Adam Möhler). It was brought into prominence in twentieth-century Roman Catholic theology by Otto Semmelroth and, above all, my teacher Karl Rahner, and then adopted in Vatican II. Rahner emphasized the conception of the church as a sacrament in order to underscore the function of the Christian community as a symbol of God's grace and to emphasize the corporate, communal, and embodied aspects of grace. Directed against more mechanical and institutional conceptions of the church that developed in post-reformation controversial theology, it shifted the emphasis away from the church's human organization and structures to God's symbolic presence and activity in the community. In this volume the discussion of the church as a sacrament seeks to avoid individualistic conceptions of divine grace and to take seriously God's gracious presence in creation. At the same time, it strives to speak of the embodiment of God's grace in creation and in the Christian community in a way that preserves the primacy of God's grace and the uniqueness of baptism and the Lord's supper as unique events of God's grace. When Rahner's first publication on the church as a sacrament appeared it met with criticism fearing that it brought the church and Christ too closely together. I am sure that just as there have been critics of Rahner's conception as perhaps giving too much emphasis to the church and not separating sufficiently the Christian community from God's presence in Jesus, some of these essays might also find their critics. But what is most important is that they affirm the primacy of God's grace and conceive of God's grace in a way that takes seriously God's creation and the community of disciples. They move away from the individualist view of the human person and the mechanistic view of the world that has come to dominate in order to take community and creation seriously and thereby they create a space—may I say a sacred space—for Christian sacraments.

 These essays are dedicated to the late Stanley Grenz as a way of honoring him and his contributions to theology. Knowing Stanley for a long time as a personal friend, I am confident that he would have been pleased and delighted with this dedication. However, these essays serve the memory of Stanley Grenz in a stronger way than a dedication. They incorporate the breadth and depth of his approach to theology. They emulate his faithfulness to scriptures and tradition, and they explore new ways and new horizons to express the Christian faith. In one of his last works, he described the situation of the modern world as postmodern, he examined the possibilities of the understanding of the self within this world, and he sought to develop an appropriate Christian spirituality. These essays take this task a step further, when they seek to reflect on the meaning of sacraments within the Baptist tradition. They continue the very theological work and goals that Stanley exemplified in his teaching and writings. They would make him proud of having these essays dedicated to his memory.

Francis Schüssler Fiorenza,
Charles Chauncey Stillman Professor of Roman Catholic Studies,
Harvard Divinity School,
November 2008

Contributors

Michael F. Bird is New Testament Lecturer, Highland Theological College, Dingwall, UK

Anthony Clarke is Tutor in Pastoral Studies and Community Learning, Regent's Park College, University of Oxford, UK

John E. Colwell is Tutor in Christian Doctrine and Ethics, Spurgeon's College, London, UK

Anthony R. Cross is a Fellow of the Centre for Baptist History and Heritage, Regent's Park College, University of Oxford, UK

Christopher J. Ellis in Minister of West Bridgford Baptist Church, Nottingham, UK

Paul S. Fiddes is Professor of Systematic Theology in the University of Oxford, and Director of Research at Regent's Park College, Oxford, UK

Stanley K. Fowler is Dean and Professor of Theology, Heritage Theological Seminary, Cambridge, Ontario, Canada

Steven R. Harmon is Associate Professor of Divinity at Samford University's Beeson Divinity School, Birmingham, Alabama, USA

J. Ramsey Michaels is Professor of Religious Studies Emeritus, Missouri State University, Springfield, Missouri, USA

Peter J. Morden is Tutor in Church History and Spirituality, Spurgeon's College, London, UK

Jim Purves is Pastor of Bristo Baptist Church, Edinburgh, UK, and Lecturer in Theology, International Baptist Theological Seminary, Prague, Czech Republic

Paul Sheppy is a Fellow of the Centre for Baptist History and Heritage, Regent's Park College, University of Oxford

Philip E. Thompson is Professor of Systematic Theology and Christian Heritage, Sioux Falls Seminary, Sioux Falls, South Dakota, USA

Graham W. Watts is Minister of Albany Road Baptist Church, Cardiff, and Associate Lecturer, Cardiff University School of Religious and Theological Studies, Cardiff, UK

Sean A. White is the Associate Pastor of Fountain City Presbyterian Church, Knoxville, Tennessee, USA

Sean F. Winter is Professor of New Testament Studies for the Uniting Church Synod of Victoria and Tasmania and in the Uniting Church Theological College, Melbourne, Australia

Introduction:
Practicing Sacramentality in Baptist Modality

Philip E. Thompson

This, a second volume bearing the title *Baptist Sacramentalism*, is evidence that Baptist engagement with, and articulation of, sacramental theology is not a passing fancy, a strange aberration, something that will run a quick course and pass quietly out of sight and mind. Indeed, it cannot be because sacramental theology has never been any of those things among Baptists, even if numerous Baptists have lost awareness of it (see the essay by White). It cannot be because it is too vital a subject, too pressing a concern. Publication of this volume does, however, provide an occasion to orient ourselves to this phenomenon by asking critical questions. Not all see a sacramental move as a salutary development for Baptists. Southern Baptist Tom Nettles, for instance, has voiced concern over what he believes is a 'corrupting influence' in Baptist thought about the church and salvation arising from sacramentalist understanding of the church's rites. It could even lead Baptists, he claims, into 'real idolatry'.[1] Obviously, not all share such a dim view, or volumes such as this would not appear. Yet we need to take the concern seriously and ask what we then have in this phenomenon of Baptists writing sacramental theology. What leads Baptists toward sacramentalism, and what constitutes a distinctive modality of Baptist sacramental thought and practice?

Do we have, for instance, a certain liturgical aesthetic dominating theology; the sense that Baptists need a richer liturgical life, and that in turn requires more than mere symbolism? No. I will suggest below that ritual is not unimportant and is something to which Baptists should pay attention. But a more formal liturgical practice seems neither to lead Baptists ineluctably to a more robust sacramental understanding nor to bring about calls for one.[2] Is, then, this renewed interest in sacraments a sign of thinly veiled yearning for Rome (or Byzantium, or Canterbury, or Wittenberg, or Geneva)? No, though without doubt ecclesiological concerns are bound up with concerns sacramental. We see this in the way these essays are

---

[1] T. Nettles, *The Baptists: Key People Involved in Forming a Baptist Identity: Volume 3. The Modern Era* (Fearn, Rossshire: Christian Focus, 2007), pp. 310-11.

[2] See, e.g., C.W. Gaddy, *The Gift of Worship* (foreword by M. Marty; Nashville, TN: Broadman Pres, 1992); and C.W. Gaddy and D.W. Nixon, *Worship: A Symphony for the Senses*. Volume 1 (Macon, GA: Smyth & Helwys, 1998). Though the authors provide extensive discussion of the sensuous and aesthetic dimensions of worship there is no corresponding discussion of sacramentality or sacrament. Indeed, a sacramental understanding of the Lord's supper is at most obliquely indicated. See Gaddy, *The Gift of Worship*, pp. 145-49.

strikingly consistent in their orientation to Baptist life and thought, and not in order to encourage readers to abandon it. Indeed, essays in this volume (see the essays by Bird, Clarke, Cross, Ellis, Fowler, Morden, Sheppy, and White) as well as the first volume either demonstrate in various ways that a sacramental move by Baptists is not lacking historical precedent.[3] Then is this sacramental turn, we must ask, a form of antiquarianism? 'Baptists were sacramentalists and thus should be?' C.W. Mönnich commented some four decades ago, 'A foolish mistake in A.D. 600 is still no holy law in A.D. 1966.'[4] Certainly the same applies to the seventeenth and twenty-first centuries. Mere historical precedent is inadequate warrant for a theological move. Could Baptists have carried forward a sacramentalism from those from whom they emerged, only with time to come to a sounder understanding that led them to abandon them? Again, no. Examination of our past will help us take our bearings on this question.

What, then, have we here? I do not presume to speak for the contributors of the essays here assembled, to know what hopes and goals motivate their work. I will rather speak with an eye to Baptist history and thought. Baptist sacramentalists were not, as they are not, naïvely unthinking in their espousal of sacramental theology. Quite the contrary; Baptist sacramentalists seem historically to manifest quite clear and careful thought. Baptists in their first two centuries practiced something akin to Gordon Lathrop's idea of 'antiliturgica', inspired by Mönnich's 1966 title. That is, they practiced critique of worship for the sake of more faithful practice of worship.[5]

In the first *Baptist Sacramentalism* volume, I explored the way ecclesial practices function to 'legitimate' and 'delegitimate', in Peter Berger's terminology, socially constructed worlds.[6] Baptists of the seventeenth century concluded on the basis of their theological convictions that the state church engaged in various ways in what Lathrop calls 'the ritual making of false worlds'.[7] The Baptists thus professed and engaged ecclesial practices in such a way as to subvert the state church's claims about its rituals and hierarchy. It was with the Baptists, not the Anglicans, that the word was rightly preached and sacraments truly administered, and thus with them was found the true church 'to which church and not elsewhere, all persons that seek for

---

[3] See A.R. Cross and P.E. Thompson (eds.) *Baptist Sacramentalism* (Studies in Baptist History and Thought, 5: Carlisle: Paternoster, 2003), essays by Cross, Fowler, Haykin, Grass and Randall, and Thompson.

[4] C.W. Mönnich, *Antiliturgica: Wnige aantekeningen bij de viering van de kerkelijke feesten* (Amsterdam: Ten Have, 1966), p. 19, in G.W. Lathrop, *Holy Ground: A Liturgical Cosmology* (Minneapolis, MN: Fortress Press, 2003), p. 180.

[5] See Lathrop, *Holy Ground*, p. 182.

[6] P.E. Thompson, 'Sacraments and Religious Liberty: From Critical Practice to Rejected Infringement', in Cross and Thompson (eds.) *Baptist Sacramentalism*, pp. 40-49.

[7] Lathrop, *Holy Ground*, pp. 179-97. See too J.B. Elshtain, *Sovereignty: God, State and Self* (New York, NY: Basic Books, 2005).

eternal life, should gladly join themselves...'[8] Anglican practices, located as they were within a hierarchical order, reflected an erroneous understanding of 'church' and, Lathrop would have us understand, an erroneous cosmology as well.[9]

We find an antihierarchical ecclesiology at the beginning of the Baptist movement, with a theology of ministry and sacraments that continued even as Baptist polity developed over the decades. John Smyth declared in *Paralleles: Censures: Observations*, that Christ alone has monarchical power, and this is not communicable. Christ also has ministerial power, and this he delegated to the churches.[10] Smyth meant this strictly. The church is the true successor to the apostles '& no one man or Minister whatsoever, ...hath power to perform al offices of all officers and members, which notwithstanding the whole Church joyntly hath'.[11] Smyth granted that certain persons receive the gifts of preaching, administration of the sacraments, and governing. Yet the office and the officers are alike given to the church, and ministers receive their office and power from the church. Why? Because, Smyth argued, the power of Christ is given to the church, 'being the next Lord thereof under Christ the Monarch'.[12] All of Smyth's words could have been applied to the church conceived hierarchically, legitimating the *status quo*. That very *status*, however, was delegitimated as Baptists used the word 'church' to name 'a company of visible Saints, called & separated from the world, by the word and Spirit of God, ...and joyned to the Lord, and each other, by mutuall agreement, in the practical injoyment of the Ordinances, commanded by Christ their head and King'.[13] In this context we find the subversive modality of early Baptist sacramental practice. We glimpse the force of this subversion, and the force of reaction to it, in the words of Thomas Grantham, 'Let us give Precedency to Christ's Church which doth live this day in Jayls, in holes and dens of Thieves...'[14] It was in and with this assembly, the Baptists argued, that the grace of God was known because this assembly in humility embodied the character of Christ. Grantham provided a careful discussion of the centrality of humility to the corporate formation of the church, and oriented his treatment explicitly to the supper.[15] It is not saying

---

[8] *An Orthodox Creed*, in W.L. Lumpkin (ed.) *Baptist Confessions of Faith* (Valley Forge, PA: Judson Press, rev. edn, 1969), pp. 318-19.

[9] Lathrop, *Holy Ground*, pp. 183-84.

[10] J. Smyth, *Paralleles: Censures: Observations*, in W.T. Whitley (ed.) *The Works of John Smyth Fellow of Christ's College 1594–8* (2 vols; Cambridge: Cambridge University Press, 1915), II, p. 410.

[11] Smyth, *Paralleles: Censures: Observations*, p. 420.

[12] Smyth, *Paralleles: Censures: Observations*, pp. 423-24.

[13] Lumpkin, *Baptist Confessions,* p. 165. These words are from the *London Confession* of 1644.

[14] T. Grantham, *The Prisoner Against the Prelate...* (n.pl.: n.d. [c.1662]), p. 76. The words reflect his experience.

[15] See T. Grantham, *Christianismus Primitivus, or The Ancient Christian Religion*, Book II (London, 1678), pp. 87-91. 'This Holy Table of the Lord', he declared, 'is excellently fitted to help [believers] forward in the path of Godliness' (p. 91). Thus he

too much to claim that for him the supper was a school of humility, precisely because it held forth Christ in his perfect humility:

> It teacheth Humility because it setteth forth Christ in the greatest of his self-abasement, yea the depth of his Humility shewed forth in his bearing the revilings, contradictions, and murther of his enemies… *He humbled himself and became obedient unto death, even the death of the Cross*, Phil. 2.5 & c.[16]

Indeed, the formation in the likeness of Christ Paul encouraged in Philippians was the substance of communion's spiritual nourishment. Thus he could claim, 'this [rite] is no less efficacious to teach this duty of humility, than the word preached'.[17]

'If the liturgical assembly has anything to do with the Jesus of the Gospels, then above and below must be radically reconceived', comments Lathrop.[18] This the Baptists manifestly did, as Grantham's statement demonstrates, breaking the symbols of the state church hierarchy in the process. Might we ask, however, whether their critique was pushed too far? By this I most assuredly do not mean our forebears were somehow in error in their critique of the state church. Early Baptists were correct to insist that the state cannot legitimately impose religious ritual and doctrinal conformity. Yet human beings are inevitably ritualistic; and we know God, ourselves, and the world ritually.[19] We need to be clear that ritual itself should be, not rejected, but considered all the more carefully. Yet this has not been the case through much of the history of Baptist existence. Early Baptists, furthermore, were correct to lodge moral and political protest against presumed state control over sacraments and worship. Yet they did not reject sacraments as such simply because they had been distorted in Anglican practice. They did not reject sacraments as such, that is, until later.[20] Even then it was not complete. Throughout Baptist history, there have been pastors and theologians both in England and North America who have continued to affirm a sacramental understanding of the rites of baptism and the Lord's supper (see Morden).[21] And there was long what we might call a residual liturgical presence of sacramentality.

This residual presence is more important for us to see at this time than is the more formal presentation of theology. Articulations of a formally sacramental theology were important; but they were not particularly developed on the whole. Nor were they widely influential, as evidenced by the continued erosion of sacramental views, certainly in North America, even if not exclusively there. Yet Baptists prayed

---

was able to make the surprising assertion, 'no Ordinance (no not preaching of the Word) is of greater use to establish God's People in the Faith than this…' (p. 90).

[16] Grantham, *Christianismus Primitivus*, Book II, p. 90. Italics original.

[17] Grantham, *Christianismus Primitivus*, Book II, p. 90.

[18] Lathrop, *Holy Ground*, p. 186.

[19] See E.B. Anderson, *Worship and Christian Identity: Practicing Ourselves* (Virgil Michel Series; Collegeville, MN: The Liturgical Press, 2003), pp. 64-81.

[20] See Thompson, 'Sacraments and Religious Liberty'.

[21] See, e.g., Samuel L. Caldwell, 'Church Worship' in *The Madison Avenue Lectures* (Philadelphia, PA: American Baptist Publication Society, 1867), p. 302.

and sang a richly sacramental theology. We lack the space for adequate discussion, or even demonstration, of this and must allow a few representative examples to suffice.[22] Our focus will be baptism, the rite to which Baptists have given the greater attention over the years. As the latter quarter of the eighteenth century drew near, Morgan Edwards suggested a pattern for prayer at baptism for churches in the Philadelphia Association:

> Is baptism a symbol of the death, burial and resurrection of Christ; of the resurrection of the body; and of death to sin, and rising in the newness of life? ... Let us pray, Hear, O Lord Jesus! for he that is risen to be baptized and maketh no tarrying from obedience, calleth upon thy name! *Thou that didst come from Galilee to Jordan come now also from heaven to _____ and meet us on the banks of this river*; for we repair hither for the sake of fulfilling all righteousness! Lamb of God, which takest away the sin of the world meet thy disciples! ... *Thou that comest by water, and art witnessed to of the water come by this water. Let this laver of regeneration bear testimony to thee. And afford us communion with thee in thy baptism; for in the water and in the floods thy presence is promised!*[23]

The sacramental *lex credendi* of this *lex supplicandi* is evident. Likewise, we find numerous baptismal hymns and chants in nineteenth-century Baptist hymnbooks that manifest a sacramental understanding of baptism. A hymn appearing in several collections during that century was the sung epiclesis,

> Eternal Spirit, heavenly Dove,
> On these baptismal waters move;
> That we, through energy divine,
> May have the substance with the sign.[24]

Well into the nineteenth century, then, Baptists could affirm in song the possibility of mediation of grace in and through material elements by the power of the Holy

---

[22] I provide more thorough discussion of sacramental theology among nineteenth-century Baptists in the United States in P.E. Thompson, *The Freedom of God: Toward Baptist Ecclesiology in Pneumatological Perspective* (Studies in Baptist History and Thought, 20; Carlisle: Paternoster, forthcoming 2009).

[23] M. Edwards, *The Customs of Primitive Churches* (Philadelphia, PA, 1774), p. 81. Emphases mine.

[24] W.C. Buck, *The Baptist Hymnbook* (Louisville, KY: Monsarrat, 42nd edn, 1847), #801. We find this verse also in B. Stow and S.F. Smith, *The Psalmist: A New Collection of Hymns For the Use of The Baptist Churches* (Philadelphia, PA: The American Baptist Publication Society, 1847), #816; and a slightly modified form in *The Baptist Hymn Book* (Philadelphia, PA: American Baptist Publication Society, 1871), #757:

> Eternal Spirit, heavenly Dove,
> On these baptismal waters move;
> And grant that we, through grace divine,
> May have the substance with the sign.

Spirit (for affirmations of mediation, see the essays by Colwell, Ellis, Fiddes, Purves, and Watts).

While we could offer numerous other examples, were there no constraints of space, one further item must suffice. Congregations using *The Baptist Praise Book* were provided a chant to intone during baptismal services. It made clear, in words drawn from scripture, a connection between the rite of baptism and salvation, as well as the ethical dimension of the sacrament:

> Buried with Christ unto death,
> We rise in the likeness of his resurrection.
> If ye then be risen with Christ,
> Seek those things which are above, where Christ sitteth at the right hand of God.
> For as many as have been baptized into Christ, have put on Christ.
> Therefore glorify God in your body, and in your spirit, which are God's.
> Reckon ye yourselves to be dead indeed unto sin,
> But alive unto God through Jesus Christ our Lord.
> If we be dead with him, we shall also live with him;
> If we suffer with him, we shall also reign with him.
> Blessed is he whose transgression is forgiven, whose sin is covered.
> Blessed is the man to whom the Lord imputeth not iniquity.[25]

We are reminded by the conjunction of element, rite, and congregational chant of the lapidary statement of St Augustine, 'The word comes to the element and so there is a sacrament.'[26]

Baptists, even into the nineteenth century, had what we could call an embodied and practiced sacramental theology. They lacked to a significant degree, though not entirely, the formal theology to support and be supported by it (see essays by Morden and Cross for exceptions in the United Kingdom). The result of this lack was an erosion of both sacramental practice and understanding. Now we happily have a recovery of formal sacramental theology. The recovery is a happy one, or at least there is strong evidence that it is, because the scholars engaged recognize that recovery of the sacraments is not isolated from all other dimensions of Baptist life and thought. Rather, everything else is implicated. Sacramental theology is bound up with questions of the church (see the essays by Clarke, Colwell, Ellis, Purves,

---

[25] R. Fuller, E.M. Levy, S.D. Phelps, H.C. Fish, T. Armitage, E.T. Winkler, W.W. Everts, Geo. C. Lorimer, and B. Manly, Jr. *The Baptist Praise Book For Congregational Singing* (New York, NY: A.S. Barnes, 1872), p. 290. This chant was not numbered, and was placed between hymns #731 and #732. On the relation of ethics and worship, see E.B. Anderson and B.T. Morrill, SJ, *Liturgy and the Moral Self* (Collegeville, MN: The Liturgical Press, 1997).

[26] Augustine, *In Johannis Evangelium*, tractatus 80.4, *Opera 8, Corpus Christianorum 36* (Turnhout: Brepols, 1978), cited in G.W. Lathrop, *Holy Things: A Liturgical Theology* (Minneapolis, MN: Fortress Press, 1993), p. 164.

Michaels, and Winter), christology (see the essays by Bird, Ellis, Purves, and Watts), the Trinity (see the essay by Colwell), soteriology (see the essays by Cross, Fiddes, Morden, and Sheppy), scripture and catechesis (see the essay by Harmon), anthropology (see the essay by White), creation (see the essay by Watts), the Christian life (see the essays by Harmon, Morden, and Winter) and we could continue our list.[27] Throughout Baptist history, we can see reciprocity between the health or infirmity of sacramental thought and that of the other subjects.[28] It is important to devote sustained and careful attention, and these essays contribute to that end.

Doing so, however, for the sake of better practice, will necessarily entail a sort of 'antiliturgica' written against stunted and distorted practices among Baptists over the years of theological inattention. Sacramental theology in a Baptist mode will encourage changes in and critique of Baptist practices as they now stand. By this, I do not mean that more grace will be mediated in the practices. That is always the divine prerogative, and if we do not acknowledge that at every turn reflection on our practices risks a perverse *ex opere operato* logic. Still, though '[b]etter words in the sermon and a shared loaf in the eucharist do not make the grace larger …they are more fitting signs of the significance they carry'.[29] This striving for more fitting forms of liturgical and other ecclesial practices will differ by context, and need not be polemical in nature. Indeed, the essays of this volume constitute a form of irenic and deeply practical 'antiliturgica' for Baptists in the United Kingdom, North America and Australia (see the essays by Bird, Clarke, Cross, Ellis, Fiddes, Harmon, Purves, Michaels, Sheppy, White, and Winter). The undertaking needs to continue as this latest iteration of sacramental theology and practice in Baptist modality continues to take shape and come to increasing maturity as a theological movement among Baptists.

A concluding word about the order of the essays is in order. They are set into two broad groups, though the distinctions are not always hard and fast, and there are common themes, concerns, and topics across them. The first nine essays are predominantly biblical and theological explorations of sacraments and sacramental questions. The first two continue reflection on the larger question of how Baptists may and should think of sacramentality. Chris Ellis attends to considerations of materiality and mystery that always exist in, ideally, fruitful tension in sacramental thought. Ramsey Michaels utilizes a rigorously biblical logic to make explicit certain sacramental convictions latent in Baptist life and thought. Jim Purves and John Colwell provide arguments in some degree of tension, both exploring the church as a sacramental reality in christological (Purves) and trinitarian (Colwell) perspectives. Michael Bird provides further biblical reflection on the church as a

---

[27] Other works meriting mention in this regard are J.E. Colwell, *Promise and Presence: An Exploration of Sacramental Theology* (Milton Keynes: Paternoster, 2005); and B.A. Harvey, *Can These Bones Live? A Catholic Baptist Engagement with Ecclesiology, Hermeneutics, and Social Theory* (Grand Rapids, MI: Brazos Press, 2008).

[28] And certainly not just Baptist history!

[29] Lathrop, *Holy Things*, p. 169.

sacrament, focusing on Christ. Sean Winter, Anthony Clarke, Paul Sheppy, and Graham Watts apply sacramentally-oriented biblical and theological reasoning to questions that have been asked in Baptist circles with varying degrees of intensity (and even at times acrimony) over the course of Baptist history. Just as Lathrop has identified hierarchy to be the liturgical bane of the Catholic (Roman and Anglican) western communions, so he identifies the 'closed circle' as the Protestant bedevilment.[30] Winter addresses the classic Baptist form of this seen in questions of baptism and re-baptism. Clarke explores the corollary, closed communion. Sheppy and Watts, in their turn, raise questions for Baptist practice and thought that arise from sacramental theology. Sheppy considers the rituals of penance and the connection to forgiveness, and Watts attends to the question of holiness of place.[31]

The final six essays arise from engagement with ecclesial traditions' sacramental reflection. Anthony R. Cross, Peter Morden, and Sean White consider various aspects of Baptist witness, though with wholly different foci. Cross plumbs the Baptist past, as well as scripture and the witness of the catholic church as well, for guidance in articulating a position on baptism's regenerative function. Morden listens to the witness of the great Charles Haddon Spurgeon on communion. White's attention is on more recent Southern Baptist thought, finding resources for a more sacramental understanding of the supper as enactment, denials of sacramental efficacy of the rite notwithstanding.

Paul Fiddes, Steven Harmon, and Stanley Fowler receive the witness of other Christians. Fiddes provides a fascinating study, the fruit of his participation in the Baptist World Alliance dialogue with the Vatican. Whereas Baptists have regularly rejected out of hand, and without nuance, *ex opere operato* sacramentalism, Fiddes calls Baptists to reconsider with greater attentiveness to what is actually affirmed in that doctrine. Harmon, another dialogue participant, orients Baptist sacramental thought, appropriately, to the word. He draws assistance in thinking about this orientation from the 'Great Cappadocian' theologian, Gregory of Nyssa. The concluding essay is Fowler's exploration of convergences between two communions that had at one time converged and then diverged with some rancor, Baptists and the Christian Churches/Disciples of Christ. This leads him to give further attention to the question of baptismal regeneration.

That is not the end, however. This volume does not speak a final word on the subject, but is a step along the way toward recovery and reconstruction of a robust sacramentalism in a Baptist modality.

---

[30] Lathrop, *Holy Ground*, pp. 188-92.

[31] This is another topic that is perhaps latent in Baptist consciousness. As I was reading Watts's essay, I received word that the sanctuary of the church I served as pastor from 1995–2001 was on fire. It turned out to be a near total loss. In speaking with friends in the church, I reflected that while Baptists do not speak of holy places as do Catholics, shrines as the sites of pilgrimage, when a church burns we understand that there is a holiness of place. Indeed, many of the church members stayed and watched the fire to the bitter end. To have left, they said, would have been like abandoning a loved one on her/his deathbed.

CHAPTER 1

Embodied Grace:
Exploring the Sacraments and Sacramentality

Christopher J. Ellis

Baptist life has seemed to contain, in most generations, voices which have in debate or dialogue argued for and against what we might call a sacramental theology. The exception is probably the Victorian period when the reaction to the Oxford Movement, combined with the spirit of an entrepreneurial and scientific age, led to a prizing of individual faith and a suspicion of anything which smelled of magic. For example, at the beginning of the nineteenth century, Robert Hall was able to write of the Lord's supper,

> it is a feast upon a sacrifice, by which we become partakers at the altar, not less really, though in a manner more elevated and spiritual, than those who under the ancient economy presented their offerings in the temple. In this ordinance, the cup is a spiritual participation of the blood, the bread of the body of the crucified saviour... In its secondary import, it is intended as a solemn recognition of each other as members of Christ, and consequently in the language of Paul, 'as one body and one bread'.[1]

At the end of the nineteenth century, Silvester Horne tried to gather material for a *Manual of Church Fellowship* intended for use in both Congregational and Baptist churches. He tried to discover Baptist views of baptism but drew a blank:

> I visited Dr Clifford, but could not get from him any manual that contained a statement of their view of baptism. I wrote to Dr Angus, but received nothing more definite from him... So I am left to try and make some principles for this degenerate denomination.[2]

It is ironic that this should have been the situation for a denomination that has gained its identity from its stand on baptism. Probably that prophetic position *vis à vis* the wider Christian church—in which baptism has been resolutely defined, on the one hand, as requiring faith on the part of the one being baptized, and, on the other

---

[1] Quoted in E.A. Payne, *The Fellowship of Believers: Baptist Thought and Practice Yesterday and Today* (London: Carey Kingsgate Press, enlarged edn, 1952), p. 67.
[2] Quoted in Payne, *Fellowship of Believers*, p. 83.

hand, requiring a quantity of water such that the symbolism of burial can be enacted—resulted in most Baptist energy going into the polemics of mode and subject. There was, perhaps, insufficient energy remaining for a reflection on the meaning of baptism.

Yet in 1948, the council of the Baptist Union of Great Britain made the following statement:

> We recognise the two sacraments of Believers' Baptism and the Lord's Supper as being of the Lord's ordaining. We hold that both are 'means of grace' to those who receive them in faith, and that Christ is really and truly present, not in the material elements, but in the heart and mind and soul of the believer and in the Christian community which observes the sacrament... We believe it is important not to isolate the sacraments from the whole action of divine grace, but to see them always in the context of the total activity of the worshipping, believing and serving fellowship of the church.[3]

The second half of the twentieth century saw a considerable increase amongst British Baptists in writing about baptism in particular. Anthony R. Cross' study which charted this movement had plenty of material to work with.[4] From R.E.O. White and George R. Beasley Murray on the New Testament material, through Neville Clark on sacramental theology, to the group of authors who produced *Reflections on the Water* in the mid1990s, and beyond—interest has flourished.[5]

I have attempted to make my own contribution by at times addressing my fellow Baptists and at other times my ecumenical friends.[6] What I want to do here is rather

---

[3] See 'The Baptist Doctrine of the Church: A Statement approved by the Council of the Baptist Union of Great Britain and Ireland, March 1948', in R. Hayden, *Baptist Union Documents 1948–1977* (London: Baptist Historical Society, 1980), pp. 5-11.

[4] A.R. Cross, *Baptism and the Baptists: Theology and Practice in Twentieth Century Britain* (Studies in Baptist History and Thought, 3; Carlisle: Paternoster Press, 2000).

[5] R.E.O. White, *The Biblical Doctrine of Initiation* (London: Hodder & Stoughton, 1960); G.R. Beasley-Murray, *Baptism in the New Testament* (London: Macmillan, 1962); N. Clark, *An Approach to the Theology of the Sacraments* (Studies in Biblical Theology, 17; London: SCM Press, 1956); and P.S. Fiddes (ed.), *Reflections on the Water: Understanding God and the World through the Baptism of Believers* (Regent's Study Guides, 4; Oxford: Regent's Park College/Macon, GA: Smyth & Helwys, 1996). See also S.E. Porter, and A.R. Cross (eds), *Baptism and the New Testament Church: Historical and Contemporary Studies in Honour of R.E.O. White* (Journal for the Study of the New Testament Supplement Series, 171; Sheffield: Sheffield Academic Press, 1999); S.K. Fowler, *More than a Symbol: The British Baptist Recovery of Baptismal Sacramentalism* (Studies in Baptist History and Thought, 2; Carlisle: Paternoster Press, 2002); and S.E. Porter, and A.R. Cross (eds), *Dimensions of Baptism: Biblical and Theological Studies* (*Journal for the Study of the New Testament* Supplement Series, 234; Sheffield: Sheffield Academic Press, 2002).

[6] See Christopher J. Ellis, 'Relativity, Ecumenism and the Liberation of the Church', *Baptist Quarterly* 29.2 (April, 1981), pp. 81-91; 'Baptism and the Sacramental Freedom of God', in Fiddes (ed.), *Reflections on the Water*, pp. 23-45; and 'The Baptism of

different as I wish to reflect on the notion of 'sacramentality' or 'embodied grace'. I will explore a number of movements and authors who can illuminate our discussion of sacramental theology, reflect on the notion of sacramental practice as an embodiment of faith, and illustrate it with some examples concerning baptism. Then I will reflect on the notion of embodiment and its usefulness in understanding the relationship of worship to the whole of life.

Sacramental Theology and Sacramentality

In the often arid debate amongst Baptists of sacrament versus ordinance, people are often reacting against something which others are not saying. I have found it helpful, in the interests of saying as much as possible about, for example, baptism, to avoid 'sacrament' language and instead to ask a simple question, 'What is God doing in baptism?' The answers I receive are often close to what I would call a 'high theology' of the sacraments, yet often from people who would be shocked to hear such a libellous suggestion.

Related to this desire amongst many to affirm what God is doing in baptism, is the way in which Baptist and evangelical thinking has been influenced not only by ecumenical exposure but by charismatic renewal. In ecumenical discussions it can be helpful to acknowledge a number of potential polarities which express divergent approaches to viewing reality in general and, therefore, the sacraments in particular.[7] We could, for example, speak of polarities between creation and redemption, between the material and the spiritual, and between the internal and the external. In addition, we could speak of polarities between the visible and the invisible, the concrete and the abstract, or even the symbolic or the sacramental! How people view the world on the basis of these alternatives will inevitably affect how they view baptism or the Lord's supper and this may, in part at least, be affected by cultural distinctives as much as by confessional differences.

Baptists need to remind themselves that their community developed during the Reformation which was influenced by Renaissance concerns, and at the beginning of that period in western cultural development known as the Enlightenment.[8] At times they may have been overly rationalistic and even reductionistic, and this is particularly true in relation to how worship and ritual actions are to be understood. In my own survey of Baptist writings on the nature and practice of worship a particular spirituality becomes evident. While non-Baptist writers on worship may be concerned with the *way* in which, or the order in which, certain liturgical activities

---

Disciples and the Nature of the Church', in Porter and Cross (eds), *Dimensions of Baptism*, pp. 333-53.

[7] I first made this proposal in a contribution to a World Council of Churches Faith and Order consultation on 'The Sacramental Dimension of Baptism' in Prague, June 2000. The original paper was later published as C.J. Ellis, 'A View from the Pool: Baptists, Sacraments and the Basis of Unity', *Baptist* Quarterly 39.3 (July, 2001), pp. 107-20.

[8] See A.E. McGrath, *The Intellectual Origins of the European Reformation* (Oxford: Basil Blackwell, 1987).

are carried out, Baptist writers are primarily concerned with whether or not the worshippers are sincere—the integrity of heart and behaviour are seen to be more important than the mode of liturgical operation.[9] This signals an important Baptist distinctive, namely the concern for personal religion and the relationship of each worshipper to the God who sees and knows all. Indeed, the most important reality is that spiritual relationship with God which may be *expressed* through outward actions in worship but which is not dependent upon them.

This last point is important. Often the concern for personal spirituality has converged with a suspicion of ritual actions. However, the result has sometimes been to downgrade the scope of God's activity—faith becomes wholly inward and private, and no place is given for God's use of the community which God has gathered or the material media which God has created and seemed to use persistently: embodied grace.

This Baptist reductionism isn't only a rejection of *things* as media of divine grace, but becomes also an apparent agnosticism to God working in the worship actions of the community of faith. However, charismatic renewal has, in recent decades, given many Baptists a sense that God is at work *now* and that events can happen in worship in such a way that they want to affirm that things are different afterwards from what they had before been before. In particular, ritual actions such as the laying on of hands have come to increased prominence and offer, I believe, a model for divine–human synergy which could have fruitful possibilities for sacramental theology.

The rise of liturgical theology in the second half of the twentieth century has challenged the way in which sacramental theology was previously undertaken. The historic approach, at least since the scholastics, has been to treat sacramental theology as a subsection of Christian doctrine, in which a pre-existent system of theology was used to explain the nature of the sacraments. The Orthodox pioneer of modern, liturgical theology,[10] Alexander Schmemann, criticized this approach and argued that the explanation of what happens in the sacraments needs to be an exposition of the liturgical practices themselves.[11]

A similar view is found in an early work of Neville Clark, *An Approach to the Theology of the Sacraments*, though Clark argues more from the perspective of post war biblical theology. In particular, I am struck by his insistence that we should not construct a generic theology of what constitutes a sacrament in order to provide an

---

[9] See C.J. Ellis, *Gathering: A Theology and Spirituality of Worship in Free Church Tradition* (London: SCM Press, 2004), pp. 81-89.

[10] Arguably, the methods and insights of *modern* liturgical theology are a development of the mystagogy methods of catechesis practised in the fourth and subsequent centuries.

[11] See A. Schmemann, *Introduction to Liturgical Theology* (Crestwood NY: St. Vladimir's Seminary Press, 1966); and T. Fisch, *Liturgy and Tradition: Theological Reflections of Alexander Schmemann* (Crestwood NY: St Vladimir's Seminary Press, 1990).

interpretive filter for understanding baptism or the supper.[12] Rather, we should ask about the meaning of baptism and the meaning of the Lord's supper and from our subsequent reflections draw conclusions about sacraments. Schmemann wants to do this from the study of the liturgy, as he sees the divine liturgy as the embodiment of the faith which is 'traditioned' in the church. Clark wants to develop a theology of the sacraments from a study of the biblical material in relation to baptism and the Lord's supper. Yet each argues that our understanding of sacrament needs to be determined by the specific liturgical and biblical material rather than some separately developed notion of sacrament.

However, it is possible to have a 'both/and' approach if we distinguish between a pre-existent definition of 'sacrament'—which I also would prefer to avoid—and the notion of 'sacramentality' which is the principle underlying the use by God of material media—or 'embodied grace'.

It is at this point that the contribution of the Roman Catholic theologian Edward Schillebeeckx, and his book *Christ the Sacrament of the Encounter with God*, is particularly relevant. He uses the notion of sacramentality as a way of linking God's activity in Christ to his activity in and through the church.[13] He claims that the *incarnation* is the primordial sacrament of God's saving encounter with humanity:

> The man Jesus, as the personal visible realization of the divine grace of redemption, is *the* sacrament, the primordial sacrament, because this man, the Son of God himself, is intended by the Father to be in his humanity the only way to the actuality of redemption... Human encounter with Jesus is therefore the sacrament of the encounter with God.[14]

Schillebeeckx argues that the word 'sacrament' should operate in three distinct, though related ways. The first is to denote Jesus Christ as the bodily, sacramental presence of God, coming in saving power and inviting a human response. The second is to speak of the church, the body of Christ, as a sacrament of encounter in which Christ is manifest in the people of God, graciously accessible in saving power. The third use is the traditional one, which refers to '*the* sacraments' celebrated by the church, which he claims are in reality the action of Christ. If the incarnation of the eternal Word in the historic Jesus of Nazareth is the primordial sacrament of

---

[12] Clark, *An Approach to the Theology of the Sacraments* 71. As an historical footnote, it would be interesting to know whether Clark had any awareness of Schmemann's early work. I think the date of his book makes it unlikely, but its publication followed his postgraduate studies at Union Theological Seminary in New York in the mid-1950s and Schmemann arrived in New York from Paris in 1951.

[13] Although Schillebeeckx, or at least the English translation of his work, doesn't use the term 'sacramentality', he does use the adjective 'sacramental' and his developing argument examines this concept through pagan religion and the Old Testament in such a way as to suggest an underlying principle of God encountering us in grace through material media. See E. Schillebeeckx, *Christ the Sacrament of the Encounter with God* (London: Sheed and Ward, 1963), pp. 7-13.

[14] Schillebeeckx, *Christ the Sacrament*, p. 15.

the encounter with God, these sacraments of the church become, for Schillebeeckx, the earthly vehicle of this encounter in the present.[15]

Because they are centred in Jesus Christ, who is the primordial sacrament of the encounter with God, the Lord's supper and baptism enable the contemporary church to encounter Christ in the present and to *become* the church, the body of Christ. This is, I believe, of great importance: the incarnation is the basis of any understanding of how God might work through bread and wine. In the word made flesh God has demonstrated a willingness to work through the stuff of creation in order to achieve our salvation.

Historically, the churches of the Reformation have rejected the Lombardian synthesis of seven sacraments and spoken of the two 'dominical sacraments'. This has normally been understood in terms of the two which scripture explicitly describes as commands of Jesus, though some, such as the General Baptists, may well have been right to add foot washing on this criteria![16] Be that as it may, the notion of a dominical sacrament carries more meaning than simply that which is commanded—in other words, dominical 'ordinances'. Yet it is also possible to argue that the sacraments are dominical because they convey Christ through references to the institution in the upper room and his command to go and baptize or, indeed, to his own baptism. Furthermore they enable participation in Christ as believers are buried in union with him (Rom. 6.3) and as Christian community is created in Christ though the sharing of bread and wine (1 Cor. 10.16).

The Practice of Baptism

In preparing the baptismal section of *Gathering for Worship*,[17] I was concerned that the worship material itself should embody and express the meaning of baptism. My commitment to the insights of liturgical theology—that worship expresses the belief of the worshipping community—were to find expression in the structure of the service as well as in the words.[18] Thus the book recommends that candidates be baptized and received into membership, with prayer and the laying on of hands, in the same service. This was offered as an embodiment of the conviction that baptism is into Christ and that 'into Christ' includes the corporate reality of baptism into the

---

[15] Schillebeeckx, *Christ the Sacrament*, pp. 43-45.

[16] Raymond Brown, *The English Baptists of the Eighteenth Century* (A History of the English Baptists, 2; London: Baptist Historical Society, 1986), p. 18, includes foot washing in a list of General Baptist practices which exemplify their concern to restore what they saw as New Testament practices or injunctions. Roger Hayden, *English Baptist History and Heritage* (Didcot: Baptist Union of Great Britain, 2nd edn, 2005), p. 39, notes that the Fenstanton church practiced foot washing in the middle of the seventeenth century.

[17] C.J. Ellis, and M. Blyth, *Gathering for Worship: Patterns and Prayers for the Community of Disciples* (Norwich: Canterbury Press, 2005), pp. 64-90.

[18] For a fuller treatment of this concept see Ellis, *Gathering*, especially pp. 13-24 and 225-44.

body of Christ: 'For in the one Spirit we were all baptized into one body' (1 Cor. 12.13).

This ecclesial emphasis had in fact been present in preceding British Baptist service books, though to lesser degrees. Payne and Winward in 1960 expressed the uniting of baptism and reception into church membership in one service as 'desirable'.[19] The editors of *Praise God* in 1980 offered the whole sequence of baptism and reception into membership, but were rather muted in their commendation that all this should happen in one service, perhaps aware that at the time of publication such a practice was still a minority one.[20] Eleven years later the editorial group of *Patterns and Prayers* was also hesitant in its recommendations because of the continuing variety of British Baptist baptismal practice, and provided material in such a way as 'To accommodate these variations'.[21] The message is fairly clear: in each case the editors were convinced of the integrity of keeping baptism and reception into membership liturgically united, yet the widespread practice of splitting of the two, not just in time but by church membership not always following baptism in many churches, left the editors with a dilemma. This dilemma could probably be considered 'par for the course' for those editing denominational service books amongst Free Churches where there is no centralized enforcing of liturgical practice. Should editors robustly present a model of liturgical 'best practice' and, as a result, either alienate or offer material which would not be regarded as useful for those who do not choose to follow such practice? There is little point in offering material which, however commendable, is not going to be widely used—or purchased.

However, by 2005, not only were there more Baptist sacramental voices in print,[22] but a report of the Doctrine and Worship Committee of the Baptist Union of Great Britain, in a section entitled 'Baptism and the journey of new life: or Pilgrim's Progress', had declared,

> this baptismal beginning will include initiation as a member of the whole Church of Christ, since the Church is inseparable from the 'Body of Christ' into which the person has been baptized (1 Cor 12:12-13). **There should thus be no baptism without membership in a church which is a local manifestation of the universal Body of Christ.**[23]

---

[19] See E.A. Payne and S.F. Winward, *Orders and Prayers for Church Worship: A Manual for Ministers* (London: The Carey Kingsgate Press, 3rd edn, 1965), p. 168.

[20] A. Gilmore, E. Smalley, and M. Walker, *Praise God: A Collection of Resource Material for Christian Worship* (London: The Baptist Union of Great Britain and Ireland, 1980), pp. 137-40.

[21] *Patterns and Prayers for Christian Worship* (Oxford: Oxford University Press, 1991), p. 93.

[22] See n. 4 above.

[23] *Believing and Being Baptized: Baptism, So-called Rebaptism and Children in the Church* (Didcot: Baptist Union of Great Britain, 1996), p. 12, bold type in the original.

While the report was not received by the constituency with unanimity, it encouraged a move from simply reflecting the variety of current baptismal practices to advocating what it considered to be best practice. Here is often a dilemma for the editors of service books, or, indeed, hymnbooks—how much should the resource simply reflect current practices and how much should it exercise leadership in encouraging developments in those practices? The practical issue which confronts editors and their publishers is not merely a matter of pragmatics, but reflects a deeper issue with regard to the relationship between theology and liturgical practice. Schmemann, as a Russian Orthodox, took the view that worship did not change, but was the 'given' which expressed the church's faith. However, in the churches of the Reformation the *lex orandi* is always available to be critiqued by the *lex credendi*, so current practice is open to be challenged on the basis of theological, pastoral or other considerations.[24] In the case of the relationship between baptism and church membership it can be argued that the separation of baptism and membership reflects a certain ecclesiology. The desire to unite them is not simply in order to improve liturgical practice but to encourage a holistic understanding of faith in which its communal dimension is properly valued and in which that communal dimension is embodied in the membership of a local covenanted community.

I have dealt at some length with the unity of baptism and church membership as an example of how the worship *practice* of the church embodies that community's convictions with regard to the nature of faith and the nature of the church as a specific, local community. Space does not permit equal treatment to be given to the other meanings of baptism and how its practice embodies the convictions of the community. An exposition of the understanding of baptism which undergirds the baptismal material in *Gathering for Worship* opens the respective chapter and contains a section entitled 'Fullness of Meaning and Fullness of Practice'.[25] It highlights four dimensions which need to find expression in the baptismal practice of a congregation:

> repentance, faith and commitment
> testimony, proclamation and evangelism
> renewal of life, receiving the Spirit and commissioning for service
> union with Christ and incorporation into the Church

What actually happens in a baptismal service should be an interactive component in any sacramental discussion. What do we believe that God is doing in the act and how is it expressed? What does the Christian community believe about beginning the Christian life and how is that expressed? What do we believe about the saving acts of God in Christ to which baptism points and how do these find expression in worship?

One more example must suffice for the present. In the Baptist Union report, *Believing and Being Baptized*, there is a section entitled, 'Dimensions of believers'

---

[24] G. Wainwright, *Doxology: The Praise of God in Worship, Doctrine and Life* (London: Epworth, 1980).

[25] Ellis and Blyth, *Gathering for Worship*, pp. 64-66.

baptism not present in infant baptism'. It explains that the very nature of a sacrament means that the amount of water used embodies some part of the spiritual reality of the sacrament. It argues,

> In baptism, God takes an element in his creation—water—and uses it as a place where he meets us with his grace... To call something a 'sacrament' means that God uses some material stuff of creation (water, bread, wine) as a means of grace, that is as a way of deepening his relationship with us. The 'sacramental impact' of believers' baptism, preferably by immersion into water as a symbol of death and rising from death...is necessarily reduced when the recipient is an infant with undeveloped consciousness, and when the amount of water used is minimal.[26]

This not simply a repeat of the time-honoured Baptist polemic about the appropriate mode and recipient of baptism, but an ecumenical argument which attempts to engage with the materiality of the sacrament and in which embodied grace assumes an embodiment appropriate to the grace which is proclaimed and conveyed.

I will conclude this section with a further extract from the introduction to the baptismal section of *Gathering for Worship* which continues from the section which has argued for the unity of baptism and church membership:

> Christian discipleship is embodied living and needs to be continually embodied in the local body of Christ.
>
> In all this, Jesus Christ is central. The saving work of cross and resurrection, the identity of Christian community under the Lordship of Christ, and the discipleship character of life in the Spirit should all feature in baptism. Here is a patterning of the believer and the Church into the image and likeness of God which is our human destiny and Christ's revelation. This pattern is focused in baptism but is a continuing process of entry and re-entry into the way of Christ and the life of the Church.[27]

Such a statement about baptism affirms that the agents of baptism are the candidate, the church and God. This is a communal event in which material stuff, water, is used as a means of grace and this observation leads us to reflect further on the spirituality of embodiment.

Embodied Worship

That God uses the physical universe to achieve his purposes seems to me incontrovertible. The questions is not If? but Why? and How?

We have seen how one of the consequences of the doctrine of the incarnation is to provide a basis for understanding how God works in the world. The fleshiness of

---

[26] *Believing and Being Baptized*, p. 19.
[27] Ellis and Blyth, *Gathering for Worship*, pp. 65-66.

Jesus was shocking when John affirmed it in his prologue—and was even more so seconds later when he asserted that this is where we see his glory (Jn 1.14).

In the iconoclastic controversy of the eighth and ninth centuries, the church made strong connections between the place of the icon in devotion and the doctrine of the incarnation. It was argued that the prohibition in the Old Testament commandments was not being breached, not only because the icons were being venerated and not worshipped, but because there was a new dispensation from the time of the incarnation of the Son of God. The incarnational principle was affirmed: God had used material means, flesh and blood, in the great work of redemption and so who now might call unclean what God has used. Thus the Old Testament suspicion of images was replaced by an almost sacramental use of material media (especially wood and paint) through which God's grace was encountered.[28] As John of Damascus expressed it,

> Of old, God the incorporeal and uncircumscribed was never depicted. Now, however, when God is seen clothed in flesh, and conversing with men, I make an image of the God whom I see. I do not worship matter, I worship the God of matter, who became matter for my sake, and deigned to inhabit matter, who worked out my salvation through matter. I will not cease from honouring that matter which works my salvation. I venerate it, though not as God... I honour all matter besides, and venerate it. Through it, filled, as it were, with a divine power and grace, my salvation has come to me. Was not the thrice happy and thrice blessed wood of the Cross matter? Was not the sacred and holy mountain of Calvary matter? What of the life-giving rock, the Holy Sepulchre, the source of our resurrection: was it not matter? Is not the most holy book of the Gospels matter? Is not the blessed table matter which gives us the Bread of Life? Are not the gold and silver matter, out of which crosses and altar-plate and chalices are made? And before all these things, is not the body and blood of our Lord matter?[29]

---

[28] I am not aware of a connection being made in that debate between the incarnational argument and the story of Peter's dream in the house of Simon the Tanner. Yet the arguments have a certain symmetry: God has created all beasts, therefore all flesh, as 'clean' and suitable for eating, while God has made all matter and, in Christ, inhabited the material world so that all matter may be deemed able to mediate the divine glory. In each case, such arguments lead to a renegotiated relationship with the Old Testament commandments. In the case of icons, Orthodox spirituality has continued to view their use as far more than devotional aids, but rather a guarantor of certain theological affirmations, namely: they affirm the incarnation of the divine Word made human flesh; they affirm the goodness of the material world which is created by God; and they affirm that this same physical world has the potential for God to transfigure it and draw it into the new creation. Such arguments could also be made in the realm of sacramental theology, as bread and wine, for example, may be seen as signs of the new creation made possible in Christ and through the contemporary work of the Holy Spirit.

[29] From St. John Damascene, *On Holy Images* (trans. by Mary H. Allies; London: Thomas Baker, 1898), Part I.

Thus the incarnation is affirmed as the primordial sacrament but, as such, it is in part a revelation of how God deals with the world and how redemption happens from within creation as well as from within history. Schillebeeckx claims that 'every supernatural reality which is realized historically in our lives is sacramental'[30] and, underlying this and his arguments which flow from it, is what we might call 'a principle of sacramentality'; that God uses material media to encounter us in saving grace. Yet this general principle does not degenerate into some kind of vague idealism because of his affirmation that Christ is the primordial sacrament. Each sacrament, and each sacramental moment outside the church's worship, gains its reference point in Christ. It is true that this focus is the cross and resurrection, yet none of this would be possible without incarnation—either in the flesh of Jesus of Nazareth or in bread and wine, water or whatever. Those Baptists and others who resist the notion of God meeting them through material means need to consider what such a restriction of grace implies with regard both to grace and a taking seriously of the doctrine of the incarnation. Docetism often lurks just below the surface of some spiritualities and recourse must constantly be made to that 'became' (ἐγένετο) in order to counter any avoidance of the earthy and fleshly nature of God's saving action.[31]

I am not arguing that Baptists tread the road to Constantinople—or the road to Rome. Yet there is much to learn here of a spirituality in which creation is taken seriously and the principle of incarnation is seen not only as an explanation for what God did in Jesus, but the principle of why *the* incarnation was necessary. God is committed to creation, and the incarnation of the second Person of the Trinity is evidence of that, but this commitment to creation and to history is the context in which *we* live and believe and seek to be faithful and obedient. The Christian church has rejected those approaches to theology which have said that the spiritual matters so much that what you do in history doesn't. We are created in this world, we live in this world, we are called to follow Jesus in this world and we worship in this world.

So it is not surprising that our materiality can have a part to play in our communion with God and our encounter with God's word—whether it be bread and wine, or water, whether it be visual images or architectural space, ritual action or dramatic presentation. In all these it is the doctrines of creation and incarnation which undergird what we do and they challenge those Free Church sensibilities which suspect that to experiment in such things is to sell out a birthright.

Some of the positive eclecticism of church life in recent decades has resulted in banners appearing in many Baptist church buildings, yet often these visual symbols are 'controlled' by accompanying biblical texts. It was Edwin Muir, the Scottish poet, who wrote,

---

[30] Schillebeeckx, *Christ the Sacrament*, p. 5.

[31] I do not wish to argue that God's grace is restricted to the sacramental use of material media. I have argued elsewhere for 'the sacramental freedom of God' (Ellis, 'Sacramental Freedom of God') and would now want to develop what might be a called 'a mystical and sacramental mixed economy' based on the sovereignty of God.

> How could our race betray
> The Image, and the Incarnate One unmake,
> Who chose this form and fashion for our sake?
>
> The Word made flesh is here made word again,
> A word made word in flourish and arrogant crook.
> See there King Calvin with his iron pen,
> And God three angry letters in a book,
> And there the logical hook
> On which the Mystery is impaled and bent
> Into an ideological instrument.[32]

I wonder whether it is possible to overcome this fear of symbols enough to allow the Holy Spirit to reach us through them? Why does mystery always need to be controlled by theological parameters? If the response to this plea is an appeal for the necessary safeguarding of orthodoxy, then the dialogue might continue though an exploration of the δόξα (glory) which leads not to conceptual and linguistic formulation but adoration and love. In worship we are invited to practise being Christian, rehearsing the values and attitudes which we then take into the world in our living 'Christianly'. If our rhetoric and practise of baptism and eucharist can encourage an anticipation of divine glory, then it is a small step from the experience of worship to expecting to be met by the glory of God in God's world in many and varied ways. Here sacramental theology and a theology of aesthetics have much to say to one another.

Embodiment and Focus

To see the embodied grace of sacramental events as an anticipation of encountering the divine glory in everyday life, is to find in the sacraments a fruitful way of understanding the relationship between worship and the whole of life. Whenever I ask a group of people what they consider to be the meaning of worship, a number of suggestions will be made. However, at some stage there is likely to be at least one person who will chime up with something like, 'But the whole of life is worship.' At this point, which is often a disclosure moment for the group, we begin to explore the 'double meaning' of the notion of 'worship'.

On the one hand we can recognize the root meaning of worship in the cultic activity of the gathered community:

> Christian worship is a gathering of the church in the name of Jesus Christ in order to meet God through Scripture, prayer, proclamation and sacraments and to seek God's Kingdom.[33]

---

[32] E. Muir, 'The Incarnate One' in R.S. Thomas (ed.), *The Penguin Book of Religious Verse* (Harmondsworth: Penguin, 1963), p. 55.

Whether this working definition is adequate of not, it does at least attempt two things. It describes what event is being defined and it gives some indication as to the purpose of that event. Descriptively, it locates the meaning of worship in the gathering of the faith community and the pattern of predictable actions (rituals) which comprise the event. Normatively, it identifies an encounter with God and an alignment with God's will (seeking the kingdom) as the purpose of the gathering.

On the other hand, real dangers hover around this understanding of worship if it is not informed by another, more expansive perspective. The danger is to expect that encounters with God will *only* happen in the worship gathering, or that the desirable apex of Christian commitment is to spend more and more time in such cultic activity. This is when the whole-life perspective becomes an important corrective in which the whole of life may be seen as an offering to God of who we are, what we believe and what we hope for. In writing to the Romans, Paul speaks in these terms:

> I appeal to you therefore, brothers and sisters, by the mercies of God, to present your bodies as a living sacrifice, holy and acceptable to God, which is your spiritual worship. Do not be conformed to this world, but be transformed by the renewing of your minds, so that you may discern what is the will of God—what is good and acceptable and perfect. (Rom. 12.1-2)

In the verses which follow, Paul offers a series of ethical injunctions which relate to life in community and how to respond to others who are behaving badly. They are to love one another (v. 10), bless those who persecute them (v. 14) and treat their enemies with compassion (v. 20). 'Do not be overcome by evil, but overcome evil with good' (v. 21). So Christian living is itself seen as a worship response to God in which the Christian behaves in a Christ-like way. Now clearly, this presentation of life as worship is a metaphorical one and therefore derivative of the cultic meaning. Yet more must be said, because while conceptually the *image* of an offering is derivative, the *reality* is more dialectic. The prophetic invective against cultic sacrifices which were not accompanied by justice or mercy is well known (see, e.g., Amos 4.4; 5.21; Isa. 1.10-17; Jer. 7.9-26), but how are we to negotiate the relationship between these two areas of discourse?

Our starting point must be to see the two spheres of cult and life as mutually interdependent. Without the encounter with God in worship life is likely to become secularized and lacking in any perception of the transcendent, and ethical behaviour will be autonomous and without Christian direction.[34] Unless the whole of life is seen as an offering to God, the gathering for worship is likely to be 'ghettoized' as

---

[33] Ellis, *Gathering*, p. 250.
[34] This is not to say that ethical behaviour will be 'un-Christian', but rather that its basis and norms will have a reference point which does not necessarily coincide with God's revelation in Jesus Christ.

worshippers turn their back on God's world in search of increasingly intense, but spiritually suspect, mystical experiences.[35]

I offer two models which can illuminate this relationship of mutual interdependence. The first is the notion of *rehearsal* where we can see what happens in worship as a rehearsal for what happens in everyday life. In this model we can identify many of the practices of worship as opportunities for practising living Christianly.[36] So to offer a prayer of thanksgiving is not only an act which expresses gratitude to God, but is an affirmation that all of life is a gift and a rehearsing of attitudes which will affect how we view, and indeed how we *act* in relation to, wealth, justice or the use of time. Similarly, testimony can encourage us to see God at work in our lives, and sharing at the Lord's table or the sharing of the peace can shape our attitudes to community and relationships in a significant way. This formational function of worship should be an important consideration in any liturgical or pastoral planning, but it cannot be the primary purpose of the worship gathering. This formational function only succeeds if the worship is first the worship of God and any attempt to use the worship gathering in an instrumental way for the benefit of the worshippers will undermine its integrity and it will cease to be worship and will, in turn, fail to have the formational effect which is being sought.

The second model to illuminate the relationship between the gathering for worship and the whole of life is that of a lens in which worship focuses to an intense degree that which is always true but often not perceived or explicitly expressed. So in worship we are enabled to see and affirm what is true all the time, not only in worship, and we see more clearly into all reality, not only a supposedly *spiritual* reality.

It is at this point that our discussion of worship in general returns to the more specific question of the sacraments and the principle of embodiment. The God who meets us in the baptismal pool is the same God who in faithfulness meets us when the waters of chaos engulf us or when the shadow of death darkens the valley in which we walk. The God who is made known to us in the breaking of bread is the same One who is present at every meal, the giver of nourishment and the creator of community.

These things are generally true, yet in the sacraments they are embodied in a way which enables us to recognize them. The predictability of grace embodied in bread and wine, themselves a proclamation of the death of Christ, encourages us to be open to the everyday God who graciously accompanies and meets us in the midst of a troubled world. This is where the dominical nature of the sacraments becomes theologically and spiritually crucial. The connection between the sacraments and the whole of life is not so much an idealistic resonance as a means of grace. It is precisely because the Word has been made flesh in Jesus Christ that the sacramental

---

[35] For a more extended, journalistic treatment of this dichotomy, see C.J. Ellis, 'Worldly Worship', *The Baptist Times* 27 September 2007, p. 12.

[36] See D.C. Bass, *Practicing our Faith: A Way of Life for a Searching People* (San Francisco CA: Jossey-Bass, 1997), and other subsequent books which have come from the Practices of Faith project.

elements minister God's grace. And it is the continual journey back into the salvation story of this Jesus that communicates God's gracious and life-giving presence. The embodiment of grace is not only an embodiment in bread and wine but an embodiment in the crucified and raised body of our saviour. It is because the elements open us to God and enable us to participate in and receive grace that they also embody and disclose God's transformation of the whole of life. Just as the incarnation resulted in the revelation of God's glory in material flesh, so that glory was not some general brilliance but the glory of God's only Son, 'full of grace and truth' (Jn 1.14). While we might reflect that the enfleshment of the Word was only possible because of the creation of humanity in the image and likeness of God,[37] so it was only because that incarnation took place that the transfiguration of all things became a possibility. Similarly, the embodiment of bread and wine become life-changing precisely because they embody Christ the giver of life and they give new meaning to every meal because they point to the presence of Christ at each table.

Embodiment and Grace

So the language of embodiment offers a number of possible benefits in the area of sacramental theology. First, it provides a framework whereby we can relate the spiritual meanings of the sacraments to the material media themselves: 'This is my body which is for you' (1 Cor. 11.24). Secondly, it encourages us to ensure that our liturgical practices in fact embody what it is we believe and, at the same time, to critique our sacramental body language in such a way as to make our practice a true embodiment of the faith of the worshipping community. Thirdly, it offers a way of understanding the relationship between the sacraments and the whole of life as we affirm the principle of embodiment or incarnation as a means which God has elected to use in the redemption of all things. And, finally, it enables us to see that the incarnational principle is good news precisely because it is Jesus Christ who is embodied in Bethlehem and wherever his people break bread in his name. *The Divine Liturgy* of St John Chrysostom offers prayer after communion:

> Master, Lover of mankind, who died for our sake and rose again, and gave us these your awe-inspiring and life-giving Mysteries, for the well-being and sanctification of our souls and bodies, grant that these gifts that bring me also healing of soul and body, the repelling of every adversary, the enlightenment of the eyes of the heart, peace of my spiritual powers, faith unashamed, love without pretence, fullness of wisdom, the keeping of your commandments, increase of your divine grace and the gaining of your Kingdom; that preserved through them by your sanctification, I may always remember your grace, and no longer live for myself but for you, our

---

[37] See C.J. Ellis, 'Imago Dei: A Study of its Meaning and Implications for Environmental Ethics and Christology' (MPhil thesis, University of Sussex, 1977), especially chapter 6.

Master and Benefactor... For you are the true desire and inexpressible joy of those who love you, Christ, our God, and all creation hymns you to the ages. Amen.[38]

---

[38] John Chrysostom, *The Divine Liturgy of our Father among the Saints John Chrysostom* (Oxford: Oxford University Press, 1995), pp. 53-54.

CHAPTER 2

'We have an altar':
A Baptist View of Sacrament and Sacrifice in Hebrews

J. Ramsey Michaels

To the contributing authors of the recent volume, *Baptist Sacramentalism*,[1] that term means one of two things: either that Baptists should pay more attention to the two so-called 'sacraments' of baptism and the Lord's supper as true 'means of grace', or that the term 'sacrament' itself should be defined more broadly so as to embrace other practices that are also important to Baptists, such as ordination, preaching, or simply working and worshiping together as communities of believers in Jesus Christ. The first is what might have been expected. The second is quite unexpected.

Clark Pinnock's opening essay[2] is the clearest example of the second approach. Pinnock distinguishes between 'natural and ecclesial sacraments', suggesting that 'Just as general revelation underlies special revelation and prefigures it, so general sacramentality underlies Christian sacramentality and heralds it.'[3] Or, as Gerard Manley Hopkins put it, 'The world is charged with the grandeur of God', and 'the Holy Ghost over the bent world broods with warm breast and with ah! bright wings.'[4] Another Catholic writer, Flannery O'Connor, hinted at something similar in describing how Francis Marion Tarwater, the young hero of her novel, *The Violent Bear It Away*, was 'afraid that if he let his eye rest for an instant longer than was needed to place something—a spade, a hoe, the mule's hind quarters before his plow, the red furrow under him—that the thing would suddenly stand before him, strange and terrifying, demanding that he name it and name it justly and be judged for the name he gave it. He did all he could to avoid this threatened intimacy of creation.'[5] The passage is strangely similar to another in the same work in which the godless schoolteacher Rayber 'would feel himself overwhelmed by the horrifying

---

[1] Anthony R. Cross and Philip E. Thompson (eds), *Baptist Sacramentalism* (Studies in Baptist History and Thought, 5; Carlisle: Paternoster Press, 2003).

[2] Clark H. Pinnock, 'The Physical Side of Being Spiritual: God's Sacramental Presence', in Cross and Thompson (eds), *Baptist Sacramentalism*, pp. 8-20.

[3] Pinnock, 'The Physical Side of Being Spiritual', p. 11.

[4] 'God's Grandeur', *The Poems of Gerard Manley Hopkins* (London: Oxford Paperback, 4th edn, 1970), p. 66.

[5] Flannery O'Connor, *Collected Works* (New York: Library of America, 1988), p. 343.

love. Anything he looked at too long could bring it on… It could be a stick or a stone, the line of a shadow, the absurd old man's walk of a starling crossing the sidewalk. If, without thinking, he lent himself to it, he would feel suddenly a morbid surge of the love that terrified him—powerful enough to throw him to the ground in an act of idiot praise. It was completely irrational and abnormal.'[6]

Pinnock, writing from a Baptist (or as he puts it, 'baptist') perspective, moves on from the sacramentality of all creation to the sacramental structures of Israel in the Old Testament, to Jesus Christ and the incarnation, 'our primordial sacrament', to the church as sacrament ('If Jesus is the sacrament of God, the church is a sacrament of Christ'), and finally to baptism and the Lord's supper, and beyond those two to 'many individual sacraments and many effective symbolic events', including 'singing and prayer, praise and thanksgiving, greeting and fellowship, teaching and instruction, loving acts and the holy kiss, footwashing.'[7] Whatever may be the strengths and weaknesses of Pinnock's view, it is from some such perspective as his that it is best possible to speak of 'Baptist Sacramentalism'. Sacramental purists will doubtless object that if everything is sacramental, nothing is. They may have a point, but if we are going to try to bring Baptist life and thought together with sacramentalism, it is not enough to say that Baptist life and thought[8] must to that extent be modified or redefined. Sacramentalism itself must also be modified or redefined. This has begun to happen from the sacramentalist side, not only in the two Catholic writers cited above, but in certain catechetical or creedal statements of the Roman Catholic Church, acknowledging that the church itself is a sacrament.[9] For committed sacramentalists to acknowledge such a thing is not a great step, but for Baptists it is not only a window of opportunity, but is borne out by the biblical witness.[10]

---

[6] O'Connor, *Collected Works*, p. 401.

[7] See Pinnock, 'The Physical Side of Being Spiritual', pp. 11-13.

[8] There is no single convenient word for 'Baptist life and thought'. One can hardly say 'Baptism', as one would say 'Methodism', 'Lutheranism', 'Catholicism', or even 'Anabaptism.' So unless we go with 'Anabaptism', which would somewhat cloud the issue, 'Baptist life and thought' will have to do.

[9] See Pinnock, 'The Physical Side of Being Spiritual', p. 13: 'Vatican II speaks of the church as "sacramentum mundi" (*Dogmatic Constitution on the Church* 1.1) because she mediates God's presence and lives to bring humans into relation with God.' According to the *Dogmatic Consitution Lumen Gentium* 1, the church is 'in Christ a sign and instrument, or as it were a sacrament [seu veluti sacramentum] of intimate union among all humankind, and with God' (see Timothy George, 'The Sacramentality of the Church: An Evangelical Baptist Perspective', in Cross and Thompson (eds), *Baptist Sacramentalism*, p. 21 n. 1). See also *Catechism of the Catholic Church* (Rome, Libreria Editrice Vaticana, 2nd edn, 2000), pp. 204-205.

[10] Timothy George, 'The Sacramentality of the Church', p. 21, comments, 'As an evangelical and a Baptist, I belong to an ecclesial tradition for whom the language of the church as sacrament is problematic, or at least not so congenial.' While this may be true, the notion of the church as sacrament is likely to be *less* problematic to Baptists than the notion of baptism and the Lord's supper as the two specific and unique 'means of grace'.

The Sacraments in Hebrews

In this essay I will try to show how this is the case with respect to just one New Testament witness, the anonymous letter 'To the Hebrews'. On the face of it, Hebrews appears to be one of the least likely places in the New Testament to find sacramentalism, Baptist or otherwise. The author's repeated insistence that the sacrifice of Jesus Christ on the cross was 'once for all'[11] seems to argue against any kind of re-enactment of that sacrifice in the believing community, whether in the waters of baptism or at the communion table. The Lord's supper is never mentioned explicitly in Hebrews,[12] nor is 'baptism' (βάπτισμα), although the author does speak (see NIV) of 'instruction about baptisms' (βαπτισμῶν διδαχῆς, 6.2, from a related word βαπτισμός, 'washing' or 'cleansing'), and 'various ceremonial washings' (διαφόροις βαπτισμοῖς, 9.10).[13] It is odd that in a document accenting the 'once-for-all' character of Christian initiation, such 'illumination' (see Heb. 6.4) is never explicitly identified as 'baptism', nor are believers said to be 'baptized'.[14] While Christian baptism is likely presupposed (see 10.22, 'and the body washed with pure water'), it is not singled out for special emphasis among other practices

---

[11] 'Once for all' in Hebrews is either ἅπαξ or ἐφάπαξ. Ἅπαξ is used of Christ's sacrificial death on the cross in Heb. 9.26, 27, and 28, and ἐφάπαξ is so used in Heb. 7.27, 9.12, and 10.10. In related or derivative senses, ἅπαξ is used of Jewish sacrifices on the Day of Atonement ('once a year,' Heb. 9.7), of Christian initiation or illumination (6.4), of God's 'shaking' of the earth and sky at the last day (12.26-27), and negatively, of what spiritual cleansing under the old covenant was not (10.2).

[12] This is not surprising, inasmuch as only Paul, in only one Epistle, speaks explicitly of the Lord's supper as a continuing practice in the early churches (see 1 Cor. 10.16-17, 11.23-27). Yet in retelling the story of Abraham's encounter with Melchizedek (Heb. 7.1-3), the author had a perfect opportunity to mention that Melchizedek ministered to the patriarch by bringing him bread and wine (Gen. 14.18). This detail might have drawn attention, at least implicitly, to the Christian eucharist, but (unlike Philo in *Allegorical Interpretation* 3.82) the author ignores it, focusing instead on two other aspects of the narrative: first, that Melchizedek 'blessed' Abraham, and second that he collected from him a tithe, both proving Melchizedek's superiority (see 7.6-10).

[13] While βαπτισμός does mean 'baptism' in the manuscripts in which it occurs in Col. 2.12, this meaning is virtually excluded by the plural forms in Heb. 6.2 and 9.10 (see Eph 4.5, 'one baptism'). See, however, the argument of Anthony R. Cross that the 'baptisms' of 6.2 might include both Christian baptism and the 'baptism of blood' in martyrdom ('The Meaning of "Baptisms" in Hebrews 6.2', in Stanley E. Porter and Anthony R. Cross (eds), *Dimensions of Baptism: Biblical and Theological Studies* [JSNTSup, 234; Sheffield: Sheffield Academic Press, 2002], pp. 163-86).

[14] To make the case, one must read Heb. 6.4 ('once illumined') through the glasses of Justin Martyr's *First Apology* 61.12: 'And this washing [τοῦτο τὸ λουτρόν] is called illumination [φωτισμός], because they who learn these things are illuminated [φωτιζομένων] in their understandings' (in A. Roberts and J. Donaldson [eds], *The Ante-Nicene Fathers*: Volume 1: *The Apostolic Fathers with Justin Martyr and Irenaeus* [Edinburgh: T&T Clark, 1996 (1885)], p. 183).

that might have gone on, such as footwashing (see Jn 13.1-11; 1 Tim. 5.10), or daily ritual cleansing before or after meals (see Mk 7.3-4). The latter, in fact (διαφόροις βαπτισμοῖς), are relegated in Hebrews to the status of mere 'regulations for the body [δικαιώματα σαρκός] imposed until the time comes to set things right' (9.10, NRSV).

Grace or Food?

Such 'gifts and sacrifices' (δῶρά τε καὶ θυσίαι, 9.9) of the old covenant fare even less well in Hebrews when they involve 'food and drink' (ἐπὶ βρώμασιν καὶ πόμασιν, 9.10). Food, the author insists, is of secondary importance, and those who make it primary endanger their salvation. Esau was an immoral and profane man who 'for a single meal' (ἀντὶ βρώσεως μιᾶς) gave up his birthright (12.16; see Gen. 25.29-34). Even more pointedly, the author warns his readers not to be 'carried away by varied and strange teachings. It is good for the heart to be strengthened by grace [χάριτι], not by foods [οὐ βρώμασιν], which do not benefit those who practice them' (13.9). It is unclear what the author of Hebrews is opposing here. In one sense he seems to be merely reaffirming the views of both Jesus (Mk 7.15) and Paul (Rom. 14.17; 1 Cor. 6.13, 8.8) that food, while necessary for physical life, has nothing to do with salvation or eternal life. But what 'kinds of strange teachings' (διδαχαῖς ποικίλαις καὶ ξέναις) about food is he warning his readers against? Are they the Jewish dietary laws that Jesus had overturned (see Mk 7.15)? Were some carrying those laws to the extreme of vegetarianism in order to guard against eating meat that had been sacrificed to idols (see Rom. 14.2, and perhaps 1 Tim. 4.3-4)? Something of the kind may be the case in chapter 9, where 'food and drink and various ceremonial washings' (9.10, NIV) belong to the old covenant, but in chapter 13 it seems that the opponents were laying down requirements as to what one must eat rather than what one must not eat. When the author says, 'It is good for the heart to be strengthened by grace, not by foods' (13.9), he implies that some were claiming that believers must be strengthened precisely by 'foods' (βρώμασιν), that is, presumably ritual meals of some sort.[15] Such 'foods' or 'meals', he counters, 'do not benefit those who practice them' (v. 9b). 'Grace' (χάριτι) is what strengthens us, he insists, not 'foods'.

In the next verse he goes a step further: 'We have an altar from which those who offer worship in the tabernacle have no right to eat' (13.10). The verse bristles with difficulties. What group is meant by 'we'? To what 'altar' (θυσιαστήριον) is the author referring? Who are 'those who offer worship in the tabernacle' (οἱ τῇ σκηνῇ λατρεύοντες)? And what is it exactly that they 'have no right to eat' (φαγεῖν οὐκ ἔχουσιν ἐξουσίαν)? The first question is the easiest. This author likes to remind his audience repeatedly of what 'we have' (ἔχομεν, or the participle ἔχοντες), whether 'a great High Priest who has passed through the heavens' (4.14), or 'not a High Priest

---

[15] Contrast the NRSV, which translates βρώμασιν as 'regulations about food'. But nothing is said here about 'regulations' (as in 9.10, δικαιώματα).

who is unable to sympathize with our weaknesses' (4.15), or 'hope...like an anchor of the soul, safe and secure, and entering that which is behind the curtain' (6.19), or 'such a High Priest, who sat down at the right hand of the majesty in the heavens' (8.1), or 'boldness to enter the Sanctuary by the blood of Jesus' (10.19) and (again) 'a great High Priest over the house of God' (10.21), or 'such a cloud of witnesses surrounding us' (12.1), or 'no continuing city here' (13.14). In every instance, 'we' embraces both author and readers, implicitly urging Christian believers to act on the immeasurable blessings and privileges that 'we have'. The same is true here. 'We' refers to the Christian community, whether local or universal, and its 'altar' to a place, and perhaps a manner, of worship. But what is the Christian 'altar', and in what sense, if any, is Christian worship at this altar 'sacramental'?

Surprisingly, the word 'altar' (θυσιαστήριον) occurs in only one other place in Hebrews, where it refers simply to the Jewish altar of sacrifice (whether in the desert tabernacle or the Jerusalem temple), where Jewish priests customarily officiated. No one from the tribe of Judah, the author remarks 'has ever served at the altar' (7.13, NIV). Here a different altar is in view, a Christian altar whose High Priest quite emphatically is from the tribe of Judah (see 7.14, NIV: 'For it is clear that our Lord descended from Judah, and in regard to that tribe Moses said nothing about priests'). But what is this altar that 'we have'? If Jesus is the 'great High Priest' of Christian believers, then is the 'altar' the cross on which he died as a sacrifice for sins, or is it a heavenly altar to which Christians now have access through his sacrificial death? While the book of Revelation speaks freely of an 'altar' (θυσιαστήριον) in heaven (see Rev. 6.9; 8.3, 5; 9.13; 14.18: 16.7), Hebrews does not, although such an altar could be inferred from the author's references to 'heavenly things' that served as models for their counterparts on earth (8.5) and 'had to be purified with better things' than the blood of animals (9.23).[16] But more likely, the 'altar' here is the cross, for it was on the cross that Jesus as High Priest offered himself as a sacrifice.[17] From this 'altar', we are told, 'those who offer worship in the tabernacle have no right to eat'. If the Christian 'altar' is indeed the cross, what would it mean to 'eat' (φαγεῖν) from this altar? Is it, as some have suggested, a reference to the Lord's supper?[18] If so, it is strange that the reference is not to 'eating' but quite explicitly to having 'no right' to eat. If some have 'no right to eat', do others have such a right? More

---

[16] For this interpretation, see, e.g., F.V. Filson, *Yesterday: A Study of Hebrews in the Light of Chapter 13* (London: SCM Press, 1967), p. 48.

[17] This is the most widely-held interpretation. See, e.g., F.F. Bruce, *The Epistle to the Hebrews* (NICNT; Grand Rapids, MI: Eerdmans, 1979), p. 379; H. Attridge, *The Epistle to the Hebrews* (Hermeneia; Philadelphia, PA: Fortress Press, 1989), p. 396; W.L. Lane, *Hebrews 9–13* (WBC, 47B; Dallas, TX: Word, 1991), p. 538; P. Ellingworth, *The Epistle to the Hebrews* (NIGTC; Grand Rapids, MI: Eerdmans, 1993), p. 711; C.R. Koester, *Hebrews* (AB, 36; New York: Doubleday, 2001), pp. 568-69.

[18] This has been somewhat traditional in Roman Catholic exegesis (for a recent example, see J. Swetnam, 'Christology and the Eucharist in the Epistle to the Hebrews,' *Biblica* 70 [1989], p. 90).

specifically, who are 'those who offer worship in the tabernacle' and have 'no right to eat'?

These questions bring us to the heart of the issue of sacramentalism, particularly the Lord's supper, in Hebrews, and to that extent also in Baptist thought and practice. On this issue, interpreters are divided. Most argue that 'those who offer worship in the tabernacle' are the Jewish priests under the old covenant, and that their 'tabernacle' is either the tabernacle of Moses or the temple in Jerusalem. On this reading, the author's point is that 'we [Christians] have an altar from which Jewish priests [and therefore Jews in general] have no right to eat'. This could mean either that Jewish priests or unbelieving Jews are excluded from the Lord's supper, or that they have no right to 'eat' of Christ's sacrifice metaphorically, in the sense of partaking by faith in its benefits.[19] The difficulty with this is that the Jewish 'tabernacle' (σκηνή; see 8.5; 9.2, 3, 6, 8, 21) was a thing of the distant past, replaced long ago by Solomon's temple and then by Herod's temple in Jerusalem. Even Herod's temple may have been destroyed by the time Hebrews was written. And even if 'those who offer worship in the tabernacle' are not temple priests but simply unbelieving Jews, their exclusion from the Christian 'altar' (understood as the cross) would seem to go without saying.[20]

More likely, therefore, 'those who offer worship [οἱ...λατρεύοντες] in the tabernacle' are Christian believers, whether the 'leaders' of the community (see vv. 7, 17, 24) or the Christian community as a whole. While this is a minority view among commentators,[21] it has much in its favor. The 'tabernacle' (ἡ σκηνη) *par excellence* in Hebrews is not Moses' tent in the desert, but rather its archetype in heaven, 'the true tabernacle [τῆς σκηνῆς τῆς ἀληθινῆς] set up by the Lord, not by man' (8.2, NIV). It is further described as 'the greater [μείζονος] and more perfect [τελειοτέρας] tabernacle that is not man-made, that is to say, not a part of this creation' (9.11, NIV). Just as Moses' temple housed an inner as well as outer sanctuary (see 9.1-5), so this tabernacle in heaven houses the 'Sanctuary', or 'Most Holy Place' (τὰ ἅγια), into which Jesus entered as High Priest (see 8.2, 9.12), and into which Christian believers too 'have boldness to enter...by the blood of Jesus, as a new and living way which he renewed for us through the curtain, that is, his flesh' (10.19-20). While 'offering worship', or 'serving' (λατρεύειν) under the old covenant was a priestly activity (8.5), it was also the duty of all the people of God,

---

[19] See Bruce, *Hebrews*, p. 378; Attridge, *Hebrews*, pp. 396-97; Lane, *Hebrews 9–13*, p. 539; Ellingworth, *Hebrews*, p. 710; Koester, *Hebrews*, p. 569.

[20] Another consideration is that if a contrast were intended between Christians and Jews, one would have expected the emphatic 'we' (ἡμεῖς) with ἔχομεν: that is, 'we [Christians]' in contrast to 'those [Jews] who offer worship in the tabernacle'. But those on the other side argue that the author would not have used the first person ἔχομεν ('we have') and the third person οὐκ ἔχουσιν ('they do not have') in the same sentence with reference to the same group (see Lane, *Hebrews 9–13*, p. 539). The two arguments may fairly be seen as canceling each other out.

[21] See, however, J. Moffatt, *A Critical and Exegetical Commentary on the Epistle to the Hebrews* (New York: Scribner's, 1924), pp. 233-35.

as the author assumes in making the point that the sacrifices offered did not succeed in perfecting 'the worshiper' (τὸν λατρεύοντα, 9.9) or freeing 'the worshipers' (τοὺς λατρεύοντας) from a consciousness of sin (10.2). We too, the author of Hebrews insists, are a community 'offering worship' (λατρεύειν), worshiping God not in a desert tabernacle or a temple in Jerusalem, but in a heavenly tabernacle, our 'altar' the cross of our 'great High Priest', Jesus. Having spoken of ritual cleansing under the old covenant, the author asks, 'How much more will the blood of Christ, who through the eternal Spirit offered himself blameless to God, cleanse our conscience from dead works so as to worship [εἰς τὸ λατρεύειν] a living God?' (9.14). Three chapters later, he concludes his main argument: 'Therefore, as we receive a kingdom that cannot be shaken, let us have grace, through which we offer worship [δι' ἧς λατρεύωμεν] pleasing to God, with reverence and awe, for our God too is a consuming fire' (12.28-29). That this 'worship' is in some way sacrificial is evident from the words 'pleasing to God' (εὐαρέστως τῷ θεῷ; cf. 13.16, 'for with such sacrifices God is pleased'). Hence the translation, 'offer worship'. In both passages, the 'worshipers' are the author's own Christian community—not a special priesthood among them, but the whole community seen as a priesthood.

The same is true in the next (and final) chapter of Hebrews, where the verb λατρεύειν, to 'offer worship', surfaces again in the phrase 'those who offer worship in the tabernacle' (οἱ τῇ σκηνῇ λατρεύοντες, 13.10). Here too, it appears, 'those who offer worship' are not Jewish priests, and not Christian priests either, but the whole Christian community.[22] The two passages (12.28-29 and 13.9-10) are further linked by an emphasis on 'grace' (χάρις). 'Let us have grace' (ἔχωμεν χάριν), the author urges in the first instance, 'through which we offer worship pleasing to God' (12.28), and in the second (before introducing the Christian 'altar') he states the principle that 'It is good for the heart to be strengthened by grace [χάριτι], not by foods' (13.9).[23] 'Grace' and 'foods' do not go together.[24] This principle then seems

---

[22] The 'leaders' (οἱ ἡγούμενοι) of the community, past and present (vv. 7, 17, 24) are said to 'stay awake on behalf of your souls' (v. 17), probably implying intercessory prayer (see my article, 'Finding Yourself an Intercessor: New Testament Prayer from Hebrews to Jude', in R.N. Longenecker [ed.], *Into God's Presence: Prayer in the New Testament* [Grand Rapids, MI: Eerdmans, 2001], p. 231). Yet nothing in the text suggests that their ministry rises to the level of a special priesthood.

[23] The use of the same word in the two passages is significant even though ἔχωμεν χάριν in the first instance, 'let us have grace' (12.28), probably means 'let us be grateful [to God]' (see W. Bauer, W.F. Arndt, F.W. Gingrich and F.W. Danker, *A Greek–English Lexicon of the New Testament and Other Early Christian Literature* (Chicago, IL: University of Chicago Press, 2nd edn, 1958), p. 1080; G. Kittel and G. Friedrich (eds), *Theological Dictionary of the New Testament* (10 vols; Grand Rapids, MI: Eerdmans, 1964–76), IX, p. 398), while 'grace' (χάρτι) in the second instance (13.9) probably refers to the grace God bestows (as elsewhere in Hebrews; see 2.9; 4.16; 10.29; 12.15; 13.25) rather than to 'grace' as it is sometimes used today of a prayer of thanksgiving over a meal.

[24] That is, 'grace' has nothing to do with 'saying grace' (see preceding note). Notice also the contrast between 'grace' and 'food' in 12.15-16, where the author first warns

to lay the basis for the assertion that 'those who offer worship in the tabernacle have no right to eat' of Christ's sacrifice (v. 10). The point is not that Jewish priests, or Jews in general, have 'no right' to eat of it, but Christians do. It is rather that no one has that 'right' [ἐξουσίαν] because it is not that kind of sacrifice. As the author is quick to point out, it is comparable rather to the Jewish sacrifices on the Day of Atonement, which were never eaten. Instead, 'the bodies of the animals whose blood the High Priest brought into the Most Holy Place for sin were burned outside the camp' (v. 11; see Lev. 16.27). This comes as no surprise, for throughout Hebrews the Day of Atonement has been the author's dominant point of comparison to the sacrifice of Jesus Christ on the cross (see, for example, 9.7, 11-14, 25-28). The Jewish people obviously ate of the Passover sacrifice (see Ex. 12.8-11), and Jewish priests and their families were permitted, even instructed to eat, at least in part, from various other sacrifices under the old covenant (for example, the grain, sin and guilt offerings, Lev. 6.16, 29; 7.6; Num. 18.10). Yet this was never permitted in connection with the Day of Atonement, for the sacrificial animals were consumed by fire.

How then, if not by eating, do Christian believers benefit from Christ's sacrifice? The author goes on to press the analogy between the Day of Atonement and the death of Christ: 'Therefore Jesus too, that he might consecrate the people by his own blood, suffered outside the gate. So then, let us go out to him, outside the camp, bearing his disgrace' (13.12-13). Instead of 'eating' of Christ's sacrifice by participation in a ritual meal of some kind, believers are called to follow in his steps, 'outside the camp' (ἔξω τῆς παρεμβολῆς), subjecting themselves to the same 'disgrace' or 'reproach' (τὸν ὀνειδισμόν) that Jesus himself faced.[25] The analogy between Christ's sacrificial death and the Day of Atonement can be expressed in the form of a chiastic, or a–b–b–a, pattern (vv. 11-12):

> a The blood [τὸ αἷμα] of animals was 'brought into the Most Holy Place for sin',
>
> b while their bodies were burned 'outside the camp' (ἔξω τῆς παρεμβολῆς, v. 11).
>
> b¹ Jesus suffered 'outside the gate' (ἔξω τῆς πύλης),
>
> a¹ so as to 'consecrate the people by his own blood' (διὰ τοῦ ἰδίου αἵματος, v. 12).

The analogy is not perfect because Jesus' body was not burned. The author is content to say that he 'suffered' (ἔπαθεν), but the analogy lies in the phrase 'outside the

---

'lest any come short of the grace of God' (ἀπὸ τῆς χάριτος τοῦ θεοῦ, v. 15), and then introduces as an example Esau, who 'for a single meal' (ἀντὶ βρώσεως) gave up his birthright (v. 16).

[25] A further point of comparison is Moses, who 'considered the disgrace of Christ [τὸν ὀνειδισμὸν τοῦ χριστοῦ] a greater wealth than the treasures of the Egyptians' (11.26).

gate' (that is, of Jerusalem),[26] corresponding to the biblical prescription, 'outside the camp' (Lev. 16.27). It follows that Christian believers appropriate the benefits of Christ's sacrifice not by ceremonial meals, or even by 'eating' of Christ metaphorically by faith (as some read Jn 6.53-56), but rather by faithful discipleship. This should come as no surprise at this point in Hebrews, because the author has already urged his readers to 'run with endurance the race that is before us, looking to the pioneer and perfecter of our faith, Jesus' (12.1-2). Here he adds only that they must 'bear his disgrace', that is, 'disregard shame' just as he did (see 12.2), and that they must do so 'outside the camp' (v. 13). The accent in Hebrews is not on a specific identification of 'the camp', whether as Judaism, or a particular city, or a Christian ghetto of some kind, but simply on what it means to be subject to public ridicule, abuse, or even martyrdom. The call to 'go out to him, outside the camp' is in effect the same as Jesus' call to any would-be disciple to 'deny himself and take up his cross and follow me' (Mk 8.34).[27] If sacramentalism is defined simply as the eating of ceremonial meals, the author's point seems to be that Christian discipleship trumps sacramentalism. If sacramentalism is defined rather more broadly, one might conclude instead that Christian discipleship is itself the kind (or at least one kind) of sacramentalism that this author recognizes, and in fact commands.[28]

Sacrament and Sacrifice

So which is it? How should sacramentalism be defined, whether in Hebrews or anywhere else? In defining sacramentalism more broadly so as to make room for it in Baptist theology, are we in effect defining it out of existence? The question is made more difficult by the fact that the New Testament has no word for 'sacrament', no umbrella term embracing baptism and the Lord's supper and whatever else one might want to include.[29] In Hebrews, such words as 'symbol' (ὑποδείγμα, 8.5, 9.23),

---

[26] This can be inferred from Mk 15.20; Lk 23.26; Jn 19.17, 20 (also Mt. 21.39). This was in keeping with Jewish custom regarding stoning (e.g., Lev. 24.14; Num. 15.35; 1 Kgs 21.3; Acts 7.58). While this tradition was not universal among early Christians, even the one major exception to it makes the same point: that is, that Jesus was executed *publicly*, within sight of everyone. In the second century, Melito of Sardis placed it 'in the middle of the main street, even in the center of the city, while all were looking on' (*On the Passover* 94; see G.F. Hawthorne, 'A New Translation of Melito's Paschal Homily', in G.F. Hawthorne [ed.], *Current Issues in Biblical and Patristic Interpretation* [Grand Rapids, MI: Eerdmans, 1975], p. 171; see also Rev. 11.8-9). Such public humiliation, whether outside or within the city, would have meant 'disgrace' (ὀνειδισμόν, v 13), or 'shame' (αἰσχύνης, 12:2), and that is where the emphasis lies.

[27] See Attridge, *Hebrews*, p. 399.

[28] This is a possible interpretation of John 6.53-56 as well; see my commentary, *John* (New International Biblical Commentary, 4; Peabody, MA: Hendrickson, 1989), pp. 116-17.

[29] The Vulgate's use of *sacramentum* for the Greek μυστήριον (Col. 1.27; Eph. 3.3, 9; 5.32; 1 Tim. 3.16; Rev. 1.20, 17.7) hardly qualifies. Of these, only Eph. 5.32 is

'shadow' (σκιά, 8.5, 10.1), and 'copy' (ἀντίτυπος, 9.24) are as close as one comes to 'sacrament', and those words without exception refer to the tabernacle and the sanctuary of the old covenant, not the new, with all the old covenant's trappings: 'the lampstand and the table and the presentation of the loaves...the golden incense stand, and the ark of the covenant, covered all around with gold, in which was the gold jar of manna, and Aaron's staff that budded, and the tablets of the covenant, and above it the cherubim of glory overshadowing the mercy seat' (9.2-5). These were the material artifacts, the 'sacraments' if you will, of the old covenant, pointing to 'the heavenly things' (τὰ ἐπουράνια, 8.5, 9.23) of which they were mere copies or shadows or symbols. If there are 'words of institution' in Hebrews, they are Moses' words to Israel, 'This is the blood of the covenant [τοῦτο τὸ αἷμα τῆς διαθήκης], which God commanded us' (Heb. 9.20, from Ex. 24.8), not Jesus' words in the Gospel tradition, 'This is my blood of the covenant [τοῦτό ἐστιν τὸ αἷμά μου τῆς διαθήκης], which is poured out for many' (Mk 14.24; see also Mt. 26.28). But with the coming of Christ, 'sacrament' gives way to reality, as believers are granted 'boldness to enter the Most Holy Place by the blood of Jesus' (ἐν τῷ αἵματι Ἰησοῦ, 10.19). His blood, not the blood of sacrificial animals, is now 'the blood of the covenant' (τὸ αἷμα τῆς διαθήκης, 10.29; see also 13.20), for his covenant is 'new' (καινήν, 9.15), making Moses' 'first' covenant 'old and near to vanishing' (8.13), with its tabernacle, its sanctuary, and all its 'sacraments'. They existed for only one purpose, the offering of sacrifices, and once the perfect sacrifice has been offered they are obsolete. Their heavenly counterparts remain (see 9.23-24), but are now accessed differently, 'by the blood of Jesus, as a new and living way which he renewed for us through the curtain, that is, his flesh' (10.19-20).

In short, to the extent that 'sacrament' is in any way a meaningful concept in Hebrews, it is simply a corollary of sacrifice. The proper question is not, 'Does Hebrews recognize the Lord's supper and baptism as sacraments?', but rather 'Given the finality of Christ's sacrifice on the cross, what sacrifices if any do Christian believers continue to offer according to Hebrews?' The answer comes in two closely related passages near the end of the letter which we have already examined in part, 12.28-29 and 13.9-16. Both passages speak of sacrifices offered by Christian believers, the first implicitly, as we have seen ('grace, through which we offer worship pleasing to God' [εὐαρέστως τῷ θεῷ], 12.28), but the second quite explicitly: 'Through him, let us offer up a sacrifice [ἀναφέρωμεν θυσίαν] of praise continually to God, that is, the fruit of lips confessing his name. And don't forget doing good and sharing, for with such sacrifices [τοιαύταις γὰρ θυσίαις] God is pleased' (εὐαρεστεῖται ὁ θεός, 13.15-16). The two passages also have in common a reference to fire. Just as the sacrifices of the Day of Atonement ended not with a sacrificial meal, but with the bodies of the sacrificial victims being 'burned [κατακαίεται] outside the camp' (13.11), so we who follow Christ, the author

---

translated as 'sacrament' (rather than 'mystery') in the English Douai version (understandably, because of its reference to marriage).

insists, must offer up our sacrificial worship 'with reverence and awe' (12.28, NIV), because 'our God too is a consuming fire' (πῦρ καταναλίσκον, 12.29).

The last clause comes from Deuteronomy 4.24, 'The LORD your God is a consuming fire, a jealous God', just after Moses has warned Israel 'not to forget the covenant of the LORD your God that he has made with you' (4.23). The notion of God as 'consuming fire' (see also Ex. 24.17; Dt. 9.3) comes from the same world of 'flaming fire, darkness, gloom and whirlwind' as the author's vision of Mount Sinai in the preceding paragraph (see Heb. 12.18), so that the reader will naturally think first of the fire of judgement (see also 6.8, 10.27)—surely the best of all possible reasons for 'reverence and awe' (v. 28b). Yet at the same time the image follows appropriately on the preceding reference to offering 'worship pleasing to God' (v. 28a). A 'consuming fire' can be the fire of divine judgement, but can just as easily be God's response to the 'sacrifices' we offer in worship (see 13.15, 16), signaling God's pleasure and satisfaction with them, and consequently with us. We need only remember God's response to Elijah's offering in his contest with the prophets of Baal, when 'the fire of the LORD fell and burned up the sacrifice, the wood, the stones and the soil, and also licked up the water in the trench. When the people saw this, they fell prostrate and cried, "The LORD—he is God! The LORD—he is God!"' (1 Kgs 18.38-39, NIV). God as 'consuming fire' stands here as a threat, but perhaps also as a promise—a threat to those who approach him without 'reverence and awe', but a promise to all who by grace 'offer worship pleasing to God' (v. 28a), 'a sacrifice of praise continually, that is, the fruit of lips confessing his name. And...doing good and sharing, for with such sacrifices God is pleased' (13.15-16).

To the author of Hebrews, these Christian sacrifices are the only present-day 'sacraments' that count. In this respect, he agrees in principle with Paul's appeal to the Romans to 'present your bodies [τὰ σώματα ὑμῶν] a living sacrifice [θυσίαν ζῶσαν], holy, pleasing to God [εὐάρεστον τῷ θεῷ], which is your spiritual offering of worship' (τὴν λογικὴν λατρείαν, Rom. 12.1). Just as the 'bodies' (τὰ σώματα) of sacrificial animals were burned 'outside the camp' (Heb. 13.11), so Christian believers are called to suffer Christ's disgrace 'outside the camp' (13.13), where (metaphorically speaking) God's 'consuming fire' awaits, signaling his acceptance of their sacrifices.[30]

What about the Lord's Supper?

Does any of this prove that the author of Hebrews knows nothing of the Lord's supper, or worse, that he is forbidding his readers to practice it? Not at all. As we have seen, the author leaves little doubt that his readers were in fact baptized (see

---

[30] An interpretation of a well-known reading found in 1 Cor. 13.3 along this line is an intriguing possibility ('and if I give up my body, that I should be burned'). Yet the reading is probably a later one (see G.D. Fee, *The First Epistle to the Corinthians* [NICNT; Grand Rapids, MI: Eerdmans, 1987], p. 629 n. 1, 634-35); it is doubtful that such a subtle notion, and one so distinctive to Hebrews, would have occurred to later scribes.

10.22), even though he never refers explicitly to Christian 'baptism' (βάπτισμα). Similarly, he never mentions the Lord's supper, or eucharist, as a Christian practice, yet his silence is fully in keeping with every other New Testament document but one (see above, n. 12). His polemic, if we may call it that, is not against Christian believers eating together as a religious practice, but against the notion that such meals are sacrificial meals, that is, that the benefits of Christ's sacrifice on the cross are appropriated by eating, or by a ritual meal of any sort, as might have been the case in certain Hellenistic religions.[31] 'We have an altar', he insists, 'from which those who offer worship in the tabernacle have no right to eat' (13.10). Yet at the same time, he insists on the absolute necessity of 'meeting together' regularly as a believing community. Believers must 'provoke one another to an outburst of love and good deeds, not neglecting to meet together [τὴν ἐπισυναγωγὴν ἑαυτῶν], as some are accustomed to do, but encouraging each other, and all the more as we see the day drawing near' (10.24-25).

Nothing in Hebrews is more central to the author's purpose than this. Evidently it was in the context of such regular 'meetings' that he expected them to offer the 'worship pleasing to God' of which he speaks later (12.28), the 'fruit of lips confessing his name', and the sacrifices of 'doing good and sharing' with which, he promises, 'God is pleased' (13.15-16). He implies as much here, in speaking of 'love and good works' and mutual encouragement, and goes on to commend his readers for their faithfulness in time of persecution and their compassion toward those who had been imprisoned (10.32-34). These are the 'sacrifices', or 'sacraments', that really count so far as this author is concerned. While he says nothing of common meals in connection with the practice of 'meeting together' (τὴν ἐπισυναγωγὴν ἑαυτῶν, v. 25), such meals may well have been an integral part of what went on.[32] Paul, for example, can speak of 'coming together' either in

---

[31] A question that deserves further attention is whether or not the perspective of Hebrews can be reconciled with that of Paul in 1 Cor. 10.16: 'The cup of blessing that we bless, is it not participation [κοινωνία] in the blood of Christ? The bread that we break, is it not participation [κοινωνία] in the body of Christ?' To be sure, the inconsistency is mitigated somewhat by Paul's next sentence, in which (like the author of Hebrews) he focuses attention on the assembled community: 'Because there is one loaf of bread, we the many are one body, for we all partake of the one bread' (10.17). The relationship between Paul and Hebrews on this point (as on others) deserves further study.

[32] See the second-century *Didache* 14.1, where 'coming together' (συναχθέντες) involves 'breaking bread' (κλάσατε ἄρτον) and 'giving thanks' (εὐχαριστήσατε), after 'having confessed your transgressions, so that your offering [ἡ θυσία ὑῶν] might be pure'. This command is supported by a citation of Mal. 1.11: 'In every place and time offer me a pure sacrifice [θυσίαν καθαράν], for I am a great king.' This is perhaps the earliest reference to 'the eucharist' as a sacrifice, yet only in the sense that 'the eucharist' (ἡ εὐχαριστία; see *Didache* 9.1) is understood in its literal meaning of 'thanksgiving' (see R.A. Kraft, *The Apostolic Fathers: A New Translation and Commentary. Volume 3: Barnabas and Didache* [New York: Thomas Nelson, 1965], pp. 165-66). As we have seen (n. 22), 'thanksgiving' in Hebrews is subsumed under the broader heading of 'grace' (and therefore not of food).

connection with the Lord's supper (συνερχόμενοι, 1 Cor. 11.33; συνέρχησθε, 11.34), or in connection with the exercise of spiritual gifts in a setting of worship (ὅταν συνέρχησθε, 1 Cor. 14.26), so that there is little reason to imagine much of a distinction between the two. Moreover, Paul's comment that when his Corinthian readers eat the bread and drink the cup they 'announce the Lord's death until he comes' (1 Cor. 11.26) is not so different from the exhortation in Hebrews to continue meeting together 'all the more as we see the day drawing near' (10.25).

In short, while not mentioned explicitly, the Lord's supper (or something like it) may well be presupposed in Hebrews, just as Christian baptism is presupposed, but if so the accent is not on the bread and the cup or on the act of eating, but on the gathered people of God. Sacramentalism ('Baptist' or otherwise) cannot be found in Hebrews by looking for veiled references to baptism or the Lord's supper, but only by viewing the church itself as a sacrament (see above, n. 9), whether 'meeting together' in worship and sharing with those in need, or in the world 'outside the camp', suffering persecution for Christ publicly as his faithful disciples. Sacramentalism means embodiment, but in Hebrews God's grace finds embodiment not in objects or rituals, but in a pilgrim people, in all the concreteness of their daily lives. Perhaps in acknowledging this, we Baptists are simply rediscovering and appropriating what we have known all along.

CHAPTER 3

The Sacrament of Fearful Intimacy

Jim Purves

Will a Real Sacrament Please Step Forward?

This essay is an attempt at constructive theology, written by a full-time stipendiary pastor who is trying to think through issues that face him, as he seeks to steer and guide a local church in a manner that is both true to Christ and relevant to the missional challenges of the twenty-first century. As well as writing from the context of the local pastorate, my approach is in large measure influenced by colleagues who constitute the learning community of teachers and researchers based at the International Baptist Theological Seminary in Prague. All shortcomings in what follows are mine and mine alone.

What Does a Sacrament Do?

Sacraments have always been problematic for me. In the 1970s, whilst studying and preparing for ministry in the Presbyterian Church of Scotland, I was attached to a parish church in the centre of Edinburgh. I remember listening to the parish 'minister of Word and Sacraments', as he explained how the significance of the bread and wine had always been a mystery to him, until the day he came to understand. I was suddenly on the edge of my seat: at last, an explanation would come to me! And then he stopped. He said nothing more. I was left, sitting on the edge of my seat, with my mouth open. The mystery remained.

Granted, I had only been a Christian for two years. And I was only a first year theology student. But now, nearly thirty years later, I'm not sure if I'm much clearer. True, I now appreciate that for John Calvin the essence of the Lord's supper lay in that very sense of mystery. But I also realize that other traditions, ranging from the sacrificial symbolism of the Catholic Mass, through to simple acts of communal celebration and sharing among some Free Church traditions, bring different perspectives. And that's not to mention baptism, this 'sacrament'[1] that can separate Baptists from other Christian traditions; or further practices other radical traditions consider important, such as Mennonite footwashing.

---

[1] I treat 'sacrament' and 'ordinance' as synonyms, in recognition of that simple association in the mind of most Christians.

But what are the real sacraments? More fundamentally, what are they for? The issue becomes complicated further should we seek to engage with an age where a climate of postmodernity calls for deconstruction. The foundationalism of yesterday has faced, in an environment of scepticism and relativism, an aggressive challenge leading to an iconoclastic shattering of many traditional certitudes. Readily acceptable dogmatic truths allowed earlier generations of Baptists to affirm that the truth of God is found in the scriptures and that a believer should be baptized and then become a regular participant in the Lord's supper. Now new questions in epistemology and hermeneutics illumine an underlying review and loss of confidence in such unassailable foundations, questioning attitudes that present Christian faith in terms of unchallengeable certitudes. This is an age of uncertainty and reconstruction. But reconstruction of what?

A good illustration of this crisis, born out of the postmodern environment, is found in Ian Stackhouse's recent work, *The Gospel-Driven Church*.[2] Stackhouse argues for a fresh appreciation of the classical sacraments, supplemented by the preached word[3] and 'baptism in the Holy Spirit'.[4] Sacraments, as Stackhouse understands them, mediate God's grace and affirm transcendent realities.[5] Stackhouse views himself as responding to a slavish reduction in contemporary charismatic and evangelical circles to legitimizing the gospel by means of phenomenology.[6] As he puts it, he is searching for 'an understanding of sacrament, which moves beyond the Zwinglian memorialism of frontier revivalism to embrace the notion of sacrament as instrumental in the transmission of grace to the church'.[7] His advocacy of a range of sacraments is therefore intended as an antidote to this demand for phenomenological immediacy.

Our conundrum lies in this attempt to offer a sacramental alternative to phenomenological immediacy. Where the inherited focus of sacramental theology brings us to speak of 'mediated' grace are we in fact focusing on the essential heart of the Christian gospel? Stackhouse does place a strong emphasis on church as transformed community, with the power and potential to have a transformative influence on society around;[8] and he does identify the ontological[9] nature of the church, as the body of Christ.[10] But the problem arises in the very act of bringing the focus of grace's impartation onto mediating agencies: the sacraments. For who is

---

[2] Ian Stackhouse, *The Gospel-Driven Church: Retrieving Classical Ministry for Contemporary Revivalism* (Deep Church series; Milton Keynes: Paternoster Press, 2004).

[3] Stackhouse, *The Gospel-Driven Church*, p. 106.

[4] Stackhouse, *The Gospel-Driven Church*, p. 168.

[5] Stackhouse, *The Gospel-Driven Church*, p. 127.

[6] Stackhouse, *The Gospel-Driven Church*, p. 175.

[7] Stackhouse, *The Gospel-Driven Church*, p. 137.

[8] Stackhouse, *The Gospel-Driven Church*, p. 271.

[9] In this essay we define ontological as 'that which pertains to or derives from the essential Being (Greek *ontos*) of God'.

[10] Stackhouse, *The Gospel-Driven Church*, p. 265.

to decide what can legitimately mediate grace? Stackhouse advocates two additional 'sacraments'; but if neither the seven sacraments of the medieval Council of Trent nor that dominically inspired brace beloved of the Reformers[11] are to be affirmed on the basis of modernity's foundationalism, who is to say that such sacraments are anything other than mediating agents of existential fantasy? And what do we say about the place of liturgy, or the iconography of the Orthodox? Are we to be left with an understanding of sacraments that is no more than a Christian equivalent to New Age crystals, mediating an awareness of the divine?

The fundamental challenge before us in this essay, in looking to elucidate the dogmatic heart within an applied theology of sacrament, is to discern and affirm the essence of Christian sacrament as revelation from and centripetal to the life that God embraces us with, in and through Jesus Christ. Are we, with Stackhouse, to reiterate the axiom of traditional sacramental theology, thereby risking the introduction of a dichotomy between the transcendent and the immediate? Or should we be looking elsewhere?

In this essay we challenge the fundamental tenet of Christendom's axiom: that the transcendent God has to somehow communicate mediated grace to human beings. We will argue that a baptistic appreciation of the gospel is a predicate of the ontological immediacy of the incarnation, rooted in a *de facto* communion with the resurrected Christ. And we will seek to demonstrate that a perception of the church, the body of Christ, as the primary sacrament of God to the world, is not only a predicate of the incarnation but is the primary and necessary means of communicating the veracity and pertinency of the gospel in a postmodern world.

The Problem with Church

In discussing this topic with a colleague serving with a national evangelical agency, my friend opined, 'Church as sacrament? I don't know if I can go that far!' There is an irony here. For many evangelicals, the entity of church is too human, too fallible, to be entrusted with the stewardship of truth and grace. Certainly, the Bible might be entrusted as exhibiting eternal verities; but the church? From the first century through to the present day, the dynamics of church have proven to be quixotic and volatile. Can such a catalyst truly represent the presence and power, let alone the truth, of God among us?

Further, when I speak to friends and colleagues in pastoral ministry, it is hard to avoid conversations that reveal either unresolved hurt or deep cynicism over the practical possibility of living as committed and fully involved participants in church. Why is this? There are two reasons that I meet with repeatedly, one dynamic and one conceptual. The first relates to the difficulty of being community. The second to the tension between communicated grace and the immediacy of God's kingdom presence.

---

[11] Baptism and the Lord's supper.

The Difficulty of Being Community

Why is it that Christians struggle so hard with the possibility of the gathered community of believers being the primary sacrament of God to the world? Is there not a place of commanded blessing?[12] Did not Jesus speak of this gathering as being both exemplary and paradigmatic?[13] As a pastor, I have to acknowledge that one of the factors that works against viewing church as the primary sacrament is that church as community is so difficult to sustain. And this is partly because church as community is a *relative* reality: there is always a deeper level of community to be entered into, if we choose. It is a teleological ideal that seems barely realizable in this present age of consumer immediacy.

So it is easier to make secondary indicators and instruments of community the focus: the vehicle of initiation into community (baptism) and of the sustaining symbol of Christ in the midst (eucharist). Or perhaps, with Stackhouse, we might choose to add punctuating points: 'baptism in the Spirit' or 'the preaching of the Word'. There is a seductive attraction to such *foci*, in that they take our eyes beyond the frailty and fallibility of human beings who cause us hurt and pain.

The essence of the problem here is dynamic, not conceptual, in that we experience pain in the pursuit of community. We find it hard to pursue church as community, because it brings suffering: it is a cross-bearing activity. It is difficult and costly, forcing challenge and change upon us. In the words of Jean Vanier, the founder of the first L'Arche community,

> community is a terrible place. It is the place where our limitations and our egoism are revealed to us. When we begin to live life full-time with others, we discover our poverty and our weaknesses, our inability to get on with people, our mental and emotional blocks, our affective or sexual disturbances, our seemingly insatiable desires, our frustrations and jealousies, our hatred and our wish to destroy.[14]

To speak of church as sacrament, this wound-inflicting community that gathers in Christ's name, is not easy. Is it perhaps easier to pursue more transcendent, noetic alternatives?

The Confusion of Communicated Grace and the Immediacy of God's Kingdom Presence

Traditional sacramental thinking[15] invites an understanding of grace that is implicitly ontological, albeit Aristotelian in construction.[16] Such sacramental grace infers, at

---

[12] Psalm 133.

[13] John 13.35; 17.22-23.

[14] Jean Vanier, *Community and Growth* (London: Darton, Longman and Todd, 1981), p. 5. This quote was introduced to me by Lina Andronoviene in her master's thesis, 'Involuntarily Free or Voluntarily Bound: Singleness in the Baptistic Churches of Post-communist Europe' (Prague: IBTS Occasional Publications, 2003), p. 52.

[15] Here I speak of western traditions, both Catholic and Protestant.

the popular level, a sense of something transmitted, for is it not grace that births faith, the 'substance' of things hoped for?[17] Therefore grace becomes something substantial to be imparted, even mediated. And through the mediating efficacy of the sacraments, grace is received. An alternative perspective, stressing that biblical grace carries an attitudinal rather than a substantial connotation—grace as the disposition or intent of God to give to mankind an undeserved or unmerited gift—is easily lost sight of.

It is not without significance that church traditions that own and support the notion of Christendom are more likely to speak of the impartation of grace than the present power of the kingdom; and conversely, that Nonconformists or radicals, especially charismatic or neo-pentecostal groups, are more likely to focus on the language describing the presently realized, eschatological immediacy of the kingdom of God.

How can we properly speak of communicated grace and the immediacy of God's kingdom presence, possessed of one focus and expressed among us? And how can we overcome the fear of community that so many have? We will be in a better position to address these challenges if we first address the challenge of determining the sacramental significance of the gathered community, the church.

Where it Begins: The Word Became Flesh

Christ Alone

On what basis might we argue that church, as gathered community, is God's primary sacrament? Can there be a dogmatic foundation that withstands reductionist or deconstructionist demands?

> The Word became flesh and made his dwelling among us. We have seen his glory, the glory of the One and Only, who came from the Father, full of grace and truth.[18]

Without the incarnation there is neither full giving of grace from God to people, nor full expressing of the love of God towards humanity.[19] The confessing of Jesus Christ as come '*in the flesh*' distinguishes worship of God[20] from service to the antichrist.[21] Without the incarnation there is no atoning sacrifice, no bodily resurrection, no hope of ascension and no pentecostal outpouring. Whether we look

---

[16] The Roman Catholic doctrine of grace communicated in the sacrament of the bread and wine, and the doctrine of transubstantiation, exemplifies an Aristotelian understanding of grace. It depends on Aristotle's notion that the visible *substance* is an expression and not simply a symbol of invisible *form*.

[17] 'Sperandorum substantia rerum' (Hebrews 11.1 Latin Vulgate).

[18] John 1.14.

[19] John 3.16.

[20] 1 John 4.2.

[21] 2 John 1.7.

to a Petrine,[22] Pauline[23] or this Johannine pericope, the incarnation predicates all that we can say and know of God, in Jesus' name. He is the confessional centre of the disciple's life: Christ alone.

But can we properly speak of church as the predicate of the incarnation? In answering 'yes', our justification wholly lies in that the *'Word became flesh'*. We cannot escape the ontological character of this affirmation whereby the being of God, the eternal Word, becomes conjoined to the fabric and substance of our humanity. It is this fusion of the Son of God to our createdness, in becoming flesh with us, that predicates in Christ Jesus a community of humanity rooted in intimacy with God our Father, enabled by the Holy Spirit. Human persons are properly defined in an identity that is found in Christ alone,[24] to the extent that the church can properly be named 'the body of Christ'.[25] The incarnation is the *primal* sacrament, in that it births the realization of God's full disposition of grace towards humanity. The incarnation actualizes God's reign in and among our corporate personhood through the physical personhood of Jesus Christ. In this sense, we can then speak of church, a community of personhood that is defined by Jesus Christ, as *primary* sacrament; because it is the ontological predicate of God's *primal* sacrament, the incarnation of the eternal Word.

God's grace, the disposition of his nature towards us, finds its fullest and complete expression through the coming of Jesus Christ, in the incarnation of the eternal Word. It is through the incarnation that the kingdom of God is brought to earth, communicated to us in and through the person of the Word become flesh. The presence of God is brought to us through personhood expressed in human physicality.

The Primal Sacrament: The Incarnation

The incarnation is a primal, physical sacrament. Through this demonstration and sign of God's love, we are confronted with God's willingness to identify himself with us, and his desire to identify us with himself. In and through the humanity of Jesus Christ, we can see and recognize that God shares in our humanity with us.

Indeed, it is the priority of the incarnation that makes the cross of Christ such an offence. God's embrace of all humanity is so complete. In Christ, all die.[26] And it is in and through the activity of the Holy Spirit, active in our lives, that we are brought to life, joined with Christ in the reality of his resurrection.[27] This reality is now rooted, because of his body's physical resurrection, in the eternal being of God, outwith the constraints of temporal and spatial definition. The challenge of faith is to root our physical lives in this reality, looking for the atemporal reality of God's

---

[22] E.g., 1 Peter 2.4-9.
[23] E.g.: Colossians 1.15-18.
[24] Galatians 2.20.
[25] Romans 7.4; 1 Corinthians 10.16; 1 Corinthians 12.27; Ephesians 4.12
[26] 2 Corinthians 5.14.
[27] 2 Corinthians 5.15.

presence in Christ's physical humanity to be translated into our own temporal and special context.

How Christians have wrestled with the immensity of this grace. The completeness of God's forgiveness proffered to all humanity in and through the atoning death and resurrection of Jesus Christ can seem, well, a little too generous? For if the death and resurrection of Christ is truly sufficient, then there is no more to be added as a means of communicating God's grace to humanity. All that is required is an environment whereby humanity is gathered in Christ to enjoy that which has been freely given to us. Full forgiveness, full acceptance, fulness of life. The community of humanity embraced by and joyfully celebrating the embrace of God: the church.

Yet is the simplicity of this truth too great to bear? Witness the ease with which this profound reality of God's grace come through the primal sacrament of the incarnation is lost. We see this, for example, in the confusion that we find in reconciling the relationship between the practices of love-feast and eucharist in the early church. The formalization of the latter, and the diminution in practice of the former, betrays a movement of focus that loses sight of church as primary sacrament, founded upon a common humanity shared in communion with Jesus Christ. Instead, a form of mediation is looked for. Why? We would not deny that derived, secondary sacraments such as the Lord's supper and baptism are effective in calling us into deeper participation with Jesus Christ. However, these sacraments surely can only be understood when they are perceived as secondary to the primary sacrament of shared communion, the physical community of church. Why? Because of God's prior embrace of us in and through the incarnation, life, death, descent, resurrection and ascension of Jesus Christ. The totality of God's unilateral mercy and utter love is given to us in the physicality of Jesus Christ's body.

Too much focus on secondary sacraments carries the danger of diminishing proper appreciation of church as primary sacrament, predicated out of the incarnation. The church is a physical entity born of grace and expressing grace. Our existence is dependent on the present humanity of Christ, hidden in the heavenlies. Our salvation is assured in and through the surety of our humanity's physical resurrection in and through Jesus Christ. So it is that the church is truly 'the body of Christ'.

The Completeness of God's Embrace in Christ

Over the years, I have been both impressed and depressed by how often Christians at prayer can be heard pleading to God for forgiveness of sins. I find it increasingly hard to understand this. But I have come to realize that, in evangelical circles, it is not uncommon to find an attitude that circumnavigates the shared, physical humanity of Christ, extrapolating from the teaching of Christ principles that take little or no account of what was accomplished in and through his atoning death and physical resurrection. Does not the physicality of the cross fundamentally change our relationship to God? Is it not the case that at the cross Christ Jesus *became* sin for us, enabling us to become the righteousness of God through our physical participation in him?[28] We are called to live our physical lives in the light of God's love towards all humanity; the blotting out of all our sin; the complete acceptance of every sinner through Christ's atoning sacrifice; the universality of the atonement. All of this has to be completely absorbed by us.

Choosing to Enter In

Of course, the corollary to universal atonement for humanity is God's universal invitation to humanity. And the contingency upon a faith-response in this universal invitation underlines the individual's responsibility and creative right to choose. God delights when we make a responsive investment of faith in Christ.

But the choice of faith is, at its heart, a choice for physical community and shared personhood. To recognize the body of Christ is to recognize the community of faith in which the presence of the Spirit of resurrection is found.[29] A baptistic understanding of church life must centre on the sacrament of relational community, for the *sacramentum Corpus Christi* is the true *sacramentum ecclesiae*. Who we are as church lies at the heart of who we are in our identity as Christians. The key to church lies in choosing to live in the dynamic of interpersonal relationality that God calls us to enter and enjoy through Jesus Christ. Emphasizing a relationality that commands forgiveness and reconciliation, and a corporate discernment in resolving issues and challenges, lies at the heart of being church together. And this relationality and corporate discernment can only be rooted where meaningful interpersonal engagement is possible: in the life of the local congregation.

In the first section of this essay we suggested that a fear of community, together with a failure to grasp the ontological fulcrum of the kingdom come in Christ, can work against a proper appreciation of the church community as primary sacrament. It is appealing to distance the release of the immediacy of God's grace from the stark, painful reality of our failure to develop sustained, interpersonal relatedness. Yet to allow a disjunction between the existential and the known, the heavenly and the earthly, the triune God and our human interconnectedness, can be a denial of all that God brings to us through the incarnation. This theophany of incarnation, on which all our Christian understanding of the trinitarian God depends, declares that our knowledge of God as Father and the Holy Spirit as Sanctifier comes only through our participation in the body of Christ. That is, we pronounce God's invitation that all mankind should surrender to the absolute reality of interconnected humanity embraced and recapitulated in the humanity of Jesus Christ. In Jesus is our knowledge of God. In Jesus is our acceptance and affirmation by God. In Jesus is our worship of God. In Jesus is our life. And that life is life in the physical community of his body.

The development of institutional, sacramental theology forged a path that diminished the initial importance and emphasis on the local congregation as the body

---

[28] 2 Corinthians 5.21.
[29] 1 Corinthians 11.27–12.20.

of Christ as primary sacrament. Why? Because the desire to distinguish between the impartation of God's grace and the challenge of relating together as the body of Christ is always present. It can be seen in many congregations, Sunday by Sunday. That people are able to enter a gathering of Christian people and to leave again without being greeted, welcomed and introduced by name to others, is an appalling denial of the affirmation of the physical interrelatedness of humanity and the nature of church that comes to us through Jesus.

What needs to be emphasized is Christian life *in* Christ Jesus. How do we do this? One important aspect is to focus more on the reality of his bodily resurrection.

Surrendering to the Power of Bodily Resurrection

The Pauline scriptures tell us that our lives are hidden in Christ in the heavenly places.[30] The Johannine book of Revelation speaks of our participation in a city that is coming out of heaven to the earth,[31] repeating Isaiah's vision of reconstruction and renewal.[32] And the Petrine Epistles speak of us as sharers in the divine nature,[33] royal priests and a holy nation.[34]

We cannot, in the light of Christ, escape or retreat from the importance of our physicality in identifying who we are. We need to embrace the physical reality of the Christian life, and interpret our physicality in the light of the bodily resurrection. The bodily resurrection of Jesus is a vindication of his life and ministry as a human person. It is the fruit of what he has undertaken. It is the outcome of a life consecrated to God and fulfilling humanity's calling.

Bodily resurrection is what we are brought into, in and through Jesus Christ. Following on the power of what Christ has accomplished on our behalf, this power of resurrection is not negated by our ongoing propensity to sin. The bodily resurrection of Jesus Christ is the ontological foundation for our sanctification. The power of resurrection working in us is not contingent upon our success in honing holiness.

All of the Holy Spirit's present dealing with us, in our humanity, is as the Spirit of resurrection. The Christian life is not about seeking grounds for our justification, but about living in harmony with the Spirit of resurrection. It is the Holy Spirit, as the power of resurrection working in us and through us, that actuates in us the reality of Christ's physical humanity, lifting us up into the transformative communion of the Son with the Father. Sanctification is about learning to live in the power of the Holy Spirit, who is the enabler of the age to come.

In this sense, resurrection is both a *present* and a *future* experience. *Present* experience of resurrection is experimental, in that it involves our humanity being quickened and enabled, resourced and empowered by the Spirit of resurrection. So it

---

[30] Ephesians 2.6.
[31] Revelation 21.
[32] Isaiah 54.
[33] 2 Peter 1.4.
[34] 1 Peter 2.9.

is that Christians have to learn to surrender into, rather than earn, intimacy with God. From there, God wants us to share in the intentionality that the Holy Spirit calls us into. It is through learning what it means to live 'keeping in step with the Spirit'[35] that ethical integrity grows and develops within us.

The resurrection is *future* experience in that its full effect on our lives is teleological, belonging to the time of fulfilment when Jesus Christ fills all in all. The call to sow the perishable, natural body[36] is about acceding to the presence and power of the Holy Spirit who would arrest us and harmonize us with Jesus Christ. Our experience of resurrection is of physical resurrection in Jesus Christ.

The Sacramentality of Resurrection

The church is God's sacrament to the world, because the community of the church alone manifests, through the working of the Spirit of resurrection, the physicality of Christ's resurrection. The church is not a corporation, nor simply a structure. She is an organic, physical being, existing to display in her physicality the transformative power of Christ's death and resurrection; a community that manifests the rule of God realized among us. The sacramental nature of the church is predicated by her physicality, rooted in the humanity she shares with Jesus Christ.

In the next section we go on to review the implications of this in the way we address church as a society of physical, human interconnectedness.

Holistic Health: Modelling Jesus

The Divine Dance: Choreographed by Jesus?

The personhood of Jesus Christ appears in and through the act of the incarnation: there is no constituted human personhood of Jesus Christ prior to that conjoining of the divine and human in his physicality. We may properly affirm the pre-existence of the Logos as the second person of the Trinity; but the human personhood of Jesus Christ does not occur until the virgin conceives and gives birth. And as Jesus Christ defines and renews our humanity through his life, physical death and resurrection, the personhood of each human being finds proper definition in and through him alone. We share in his relationship with Father because he shares his humanity with us. We can know resurrection power in our bodies because he is resurrected.

If the personhood of Christ is founded in his physicality, then the revelation of Jesus Christ is expressed through the physical community: the community of persons whose personhood is defined as the body of Christ. In this sense we might say that our human interconnectedness mirrors the interconnectedness of God himself. Man is truly made in God's image. As the Cappadocians sought to explain the unity of God constituted in the interrelatedness[37] of three persons, so we can

---

[35] Galatians 5.25.
[36] 1 Corinthians 15.42.
[37] Greek *perichoresis*.

understand our humanity in unity: a unity constituted by a plurality of persons, who discover the true identity of their personhood through their interconnectedness with one another.

This understanding of the interconnectedness of our humanity, mirroring the *perichoresis* of God's triune being, has been perceptively explored in recent times.[38] And of course, it is with this triune God that our communion occurs. What is equally important to us is the understanding that our communion, or conversation, with the divine is rooted in the event of *the Word became flesh.*

But in what way does this impinge on the reality of congregational life? If we are to be, collectively, the body of Christ, the community of the local church should reflect the personhood of Christ, whose personhood validates and defines us. How? The answer to this question requires us to establish what is shared in common between the personhood of Jesus and the plurality of persons that constitute the gathering of believers in the local church. I want to suggest that we look to identify what is truly expressive of the body of Christ in terms of the tripartite indicators of the cognitive, affective and volitional aspects of our physicality.

A Physical Body

To identify three distinguishing aspects to our humanity is not a novel idea.[39] What is introduced here is an understanding that such a tripartite division is aspective and not partitive,[40] with the cognitive, affective and volitional aspects of faith corresponding to areas of orthodoxy, orthopathy and orthopraxy: understanding, sensing and choosing to behave in a manner that is representative of the faith of Jesus Christ.

It is important that our starting point lies in this physicality of Jesus of Nazareth, the man in and through whom God makes himself fully known. This must be our starting point in both a doctrine of Trinity and in our understanding of God mediating himself to us. There can be no looking behind the back of Jesus Christ, as if this might show us what God is really like. He meets us in the physicality of the incarnation. It may be a subtle distinction to say that there is one God *in* three

---

[38] Paul Fiddes, for example, seeks to discern pastoral implications arising from an appreciation of *perichoresis*. See Paul S. Fiddes, *Participating in God: A Pastoral Doctrine of the Trinity* (London: Darton, Longman and Todd, 2000).

[39] I am grateful to Nancey Murphy for pointing me towards a tripartite division of 'knowing, feeling and doing' being traced to the eighteenth century in the work of Emmanuel Kant, in Nicholas Lash, *Theology on the Way to Emmaus* (London: SCM Press, 1986), p. 153. My adaptation is to replace the function of 'doing' with that of 'choosing'.

[40] A distinction introduced by Dunn when differentiating between characteristics of the human person: 'it was more characteristically Greek to conceive of the human person "partitively", whereas it was more characteristically Hebrew to conceive of the human person "aspectively"'. James D.G. Dunn, *The Theology of Paul the Apostle* (Grand Rapids, MI: Eerdmans, 1998), p. 54.

Persons, rather than a God who *is* three persons, but the distinction is a vital one. The ontology of the triune God must not be reduced to a 'personology'.[41] The Father is met with in the Son incarnate, just as the Holy Spirit leads us to the Son incarnate. It is in this One, in the physicality of Jesus of Nazareth, that mediation of God to humanity fully takes place.

The move towards recognizing human beings as integrally unitary beings, characterized by their physicality and without reference to a dualist or tripartite, partitive divisions of 'body and soul' or 'body, mind and spirit', is a growing feature of contemporary life and thought. Physicalism, or the conviction that we are what we are as human beings without reference to dualistic or tripartite categories, is of growing importance in addressing the relevance of the gospel to secular, material cultures.[42] A focus on the physicality of community gives us proper opportunity to emphasize God's saving interest in people as people.

God's Self Mediation

To insist that the primary sacrament is the physical community, focusing on the incarnation and the physicality of Jesus, prevents our focus from drifting towards an abstracted Nicene reflection upon the immanent Trinity. By seeing that the primary sacrament of the church demonstrates the physicality of Christ, our focus remains on the manifestation of God in his economy as we are drawn into communion through the Son, brought to the Father, by the Holy Spirit. Certainly, there are potential dangers in focusing on the economy of the triune God towards us. By stressing God's dynamic becomingness and his ontic actuality towards us might risk an over-emphasis on the humanity of Christ, at the expense of his divinity. The danger of implying subordinationism within the triune God is real. Yet the danger with having our starting point in the immanent Trinity rather than the incarnation is that we reduce or lose sight of the critical focus that this God has fully met us in and through the physicality of his Son. We should not forget that the developed model of an immanent Trinity among the church Fathers was subsequent to their appreciation and embrace of the dynamic of the economic Trinity. A developed doctrine of the immanent Trinity from the fourth century would enable the church to affirm that God is truly God within his own, triune being. At the same time, it remains the case that priority within early, pre-Nicene theology lay with appreciating that God is met with in his economy that comes *from* the Father, *through* the Son and *by* the Holy Spirit.[43]

---

[41] This point is well made by Emil Bartos, *Deification in Eastern Theology: An Evaluation and Critique of the Theology of Dumitru Staniloae* (Paternoster Biblical and Theological Monographs; Carlisle: Paternoster Press, 1999), p. 143.

[42] For a fuller development of this thesis see Nancey Murphy, *Bodies and Souls, or Spirited Bodies* (Cambridge: Cambridge University Press, 2006).

[43] For a fuller exploration of this theme, see Jim Purves, *The Triune God and the Charismatic Movement: A Critical Appraisal of Trinitarian Theology and Charismatic Experience from a Scottish Perspective* (Carlisle: Paternoster Press, 2004).

So it is that we need to be wary of attempts to explain a pre-incarnate personality in the Son of God, other than through our knowledge of him in the incarnation. At best, such attempts to speak of a relationship between the Father, Son and Holy Spirit draw us away from physicalism into an emphasis upon the abstracted, cognitive and rational facility of humanity, diminishing our appreciation of the affective and volitional aspects of our humanity; at worst, they lead us into a dualist or tripartite anthropology or theology. One of the lessons to be learnt from the development of patristic understanding of personhood is that the Persons of the Trinity are not defined in isolation from one another, but are to be construed in terms of their dynamic relationality. Where early, economic models of the Trinity emphasized this as a dynamic that exists in God's ontic actuality towards us, later Nicene and post-Nicene speech relating to the Trinity preserved the vital emphasis that the personhood of Father, Son and Holy Spirit could only be understood in terms of their perichoretic relatedness. Any drift, in contemporary, popular theology, towards a notion that we can speak of the Trinity as the 'divine dance' of three separate persons was, in the fourth century, anathema. It is no less problematic today.

We can see something of the tensions that arise from a theological hermeneutic that has its starting point in the immanent Trinity in the writing of John Colwell, of Spurgeon's College. Colwell describes our engagement with God's presence and action as 'grace'.[44] He views the transcendent, immanent Trinity as a self-mediating reality, predicating an economy whereby 'means of grace' mediate the immediacy of God. Colwell makes clear his distaste of 'the prioritising of the unmediated, of private rationality, of felt experience',[45] choosing instead to speak of a 'sacramentally defined'[46] church, where the church's job is 'to point away from itself to [Christ]; to announce that which is future by proclaiming that which is past'.[47]

Is there, underlying Colwell's thesis, an implicit rejection of what we have sought to affirm as the necessary physicalism of church? Certainly. Colwell has difficulty in naming groups such as the Salvation Army or the Society of Friends as church, because of the absence of sacraments as means of mediating grace.[48] He is uneasy with any 'idealizing of the community of the Church'.[49] Colwell's focus on the immanent Trinity and rejection of an integral experientialism causes him to reject a definition of church that roots our communion with God simply in our

---

[44] 'God is named as Father, Son and Holy Spirit; he is perfect love eternally in himself. His love for that which is other than himself therefore is not arbitrary. His love for that which is other than himself is not necessitated. His love for that which is other than himself therefore is grace', John E. Colwell, *Promise and Presence: An Exploration of Sacramental Theology* (Milton Keynes: Paternoster, 2005), p. 28.

[45] Colwell, *Promise and Presence*, p. 11.

[46] Colwell, *Promise and Presence*, p. 79.

[47] Colwell, *Promise and Presence*, p. 82.

[48] Colwell, *Promise and Presence*, p. 125.

[49] John E. Colwell, *Living the Christian Story: The Distinctiveness of Christian Ethics* (Edinburgh: T&T Clark, 2001), pp. 120-21.

shared, corporate physicality with Jesus himself. Colwell looks instead to the secondary sacraments and implicitly rejects the contention that it is only through the unmediated presence and power of the Holy Spirit that we are drawn into a deeper realization of our physicality, in the plural personhood of our humanity, which is rooted in Christ alone.

Furthermore, Colwell insufficiently engages with the Spirit's work as proleptic and anastatic, meeting us as the Spirit of resurrection. When we see the work of the Spirit upon us in this way, there is no idealization; but there is a recognition that in the midst of our humanity God can be enabling us in a direct and unmediated manner; because the very humanity we know and live with is the humanity shared by Christ Jesus himself. Secondary sacraments are indeed useful; but they do not define us as church. What defines us is the immediate, present work of the Spirit in our midst, active in our human physicality, affirming us as the very body of Christ upon earth.

The baptistic ethicist James William McClendon, Jr, wrote 'that ecstasy and fellowship are the distinguishing marks of the Spirit of God—the gifts of God who is the Spirit and who in coming to us brings us into intimate relation with the Spirit and with one another'.[50] We should not fear the Spirit's embrace of us, in the frailty of our humanity. We are affective, volitional, cognitive beings. Rather than reject the central importance of experiencing God, we should seek to ensure that our experience is contained within the bounds of an orthopathy held together with an orthodoxy and orthopraxis that is recognized and encouraged by the local community of Christian disciples, God's primary sacrament to the world.

Rooting for the Metanarrative

Beyond Orthodoxy Alone

In standing over against our thesis that the church should be viewed as primary sacrament, Colwell is in part reacting to what he views both as a false triumphalism and a belief in immediacy that featured in liberal, Enlightenment thought as much as in modern, charismatic experience. In this, is he possibly echoing the scepticism of a post-Christendom culture that appears to have rejected the centrality of the physical community of church? Colwell is sceptical of any argument that seeks to treat the church as primary sacrament.

How do we overcome such scepticism? It can only be done if we can guide the church in its local expression towards an appreciation and affirmation of its physicality and shared humanity that properly represent the affective, volitional and cognitive dimensions of the life of Jesus Christ. In this sense, we can sympathize with both Colwell and Stackhouse's theses, in that both call us to focus on an orthodoxy grounded in the practice of the church, in the celebration of sacraments. This would surely allow us a foundation that avoids the caprice of both the affective

---

[50] James Wm McClendon, Jr, *Systematic Theology:* Volume 2. *Doctrine* (Nashville, TN: Abingdon Press, 1994), p. 438.

and volitional aspects human nature and church practice, whether expressed in the style of worship or through social projects.

But is there no sharing for us in the affective and volitional dimensions of the life of Jesus? What is it that Jesus felt and expressed in and through his humanity? What were the feelings that compelled him, the choices that drove him? In seeking to stress the priority of the local congregation as an expression of the life of Christ, there can sometimes appear little apparent confidence that the virtues that compel the life of the local congregation can or should be reflective of virtues that drove Jesus himself. Virtues become contextually and culturally defined. We see this is the work of ethicists Stassen and Gushee, who whilst arguing in their work *Kingdom Ethics*[51] for expression to be given to Jesus' teaching of the Sermon on the Mount, do not go on to develop any understanding of universal, core convictions that can belong to every local church. On the other hand, there seems to be no end of advocates of special causes, whether political or social, who are keen to proselytize and win to their position pastors and members of local churches.[52]

Can there be a place for virtues, exemplified and modelled in the local body of Christ, that express universal values? Can the local church, in its physicality, model not only in its orthodoxy but also through its orthopathy and orthopraxy something that is true of the physicality of Jesus Christ himself, validating the thesis that the local community of Christians is truly God's primary sacrament to the world?

In his recent work, *Bible and Mission: Christian Witness in a Postmodern World*,[53] Richard Bauckham contends for a hermeneutical approach that moves from the particular towards the general. He believes that we can seek to deduce universal Christian truths, yet these must begin with an examination around the particularity of the way God deals with us, through the coming of his kingdom into the world.

Bauckham argues for an interpretative approach that acknowledges the temporal, geographical and societal factors in the narrative of scripture, observing the centrifugal nature of God's kingdom intent as he makes himself known through Israel and her Messiah, Jesus Christ. This allows us both to acknowledge the particularity of circumstance in the narrative, whilst going on from there to deduce implications for this beyond the primary context.

What features of the biblical text allow for the temporal, geographical and societal factors? We would contend that there are two essential features in the biblical

---

[51] Glen H. Stassen and David P. Gushee, *Kingdom Ethics* (Downers Grove, IL: InterVarsity Press, 2003). In this work, Stassen and Gushee advocate that Christian ethics should be grounded not in a static set of rules or framed abstractly through 'decisionism', but be moulded in order to express the dynamic commitment we have, in and through Jesus Christ, to serve and express the reality of Kingdom of God.

[52] The present writer painfully recalls a visit from such a 'biblical position on...' parachurch campaigner, who on the pretence of discussing a biblical perspective, subjected this pastor to a forty minute monologue without soliciting either opinion or comment.

[53] Richard Bauckham, *Bible and Mission: Christian Witness in a Postmodern World* (Carlisle: Paternoster Press, 2003).

narrative that arise from the physicality of Jesus Christ expressed in and through the local church. These are features that are affective and volitional, allowing universal values that allow us to speak of orthopathy and orthopraxy. These are found in the manifestation of the glory and goodness of God.

Foundations of Orthopathy and Orthodoxy

In 2 Peter 1.3 it is written that God's 'divine power has given us everything we need for life and godliness through our knowledge of him who called us by his own glory and goodness'. Significantly this pericope does not proceed from and our response in faith towards God's glory and goodness. Rather, the promises of God and faith in them is a predicate of and not a foundation for a meeting with God in his manifest glory and goodness. Cognition follows God's communication of himself to us through affective (glory) and volitional (goodness) expression.

This passage is significant in its Old Testament allusion to the theophany that occurs in the giving of the law to Israel at Sinai, as Moses meets with God on the mount, craving to see God's glory; and where God's response to Moses is to declare to him God's goodness. What follows is distinctive in the Old Testament, in that we hear God describing himself in volitional terms that can be directly associated with our humanity:

> And he passed in front of Moses, proclaiming, "The LORD, the LORD, the compassionate and gracious God, slow to anger, abounding in love and faithfulness, maintaining love to thousands, and forgiving wickedness, rebellion and sin."[54]

Where does this lead us? A dangerous presumption is that theological enquiry and construction should begin with precepts that are propositional in style and structure. Indeed, it seems to the present writer that much of the debate over how Christian theology can engage meaningfully with contemporary, postmodern culture hinges on what sort of reasoning we should invoke. What happens, though, when we follow the physicalist supposition that our humanity and personhood are integral, not divisible into parts? It may be argued that one consequence is that our appreciation of personhood is not measurable solely by cognitive means, thereby marginalizing or ignoring affective or volitional aspects of our personhood. If God is truly a God who reveals himself to our humanity through his glory and goodness, and if our humanity is truly reflective of him, then this similitude cannot be structured merely in cognitive terms or identified purely by cognitive means. If our pericope is representative of God's revelation to us, then we see that God reveals himself by addressing first our affective and volitional senses, only then reinforcing this with our cognitive facility. We might then expect that the manner of God's reflection in and through our physicality would first be in affective and volitional ways, reinforced by cognitive appreciation:

---

[54] Exodus 34.6-7a.

> Through these he has given us his very great and precious promises, so that through them you may participate in the divine nature and escape the corruption in the world caused by evil desires.[55]

Secondary sacraments can reinforce this sense of present participation in the body of Christ, participating in the community of his presence on earth. But they cannot express the full dynamic of glory met with, desired and experienced; goodness received in renewal and transformation; and purposeful promises focused upon, trusted in and pursued. Yes, they can reinforce these. But the primary focus can be found only among the physicality of men and women seeking to move forward in relationality with each other and with God: meeting with him, receiving from him, believing in him. Reflecting that reality in the physicality of their life with one another.

Here is another reason why church must be embraced as the primary sacrament given from God to mankind. It is in and through the manifestation of our physical personhood and corporal relationality that the manifestation of God is made known. Through touching us with the presence of his glory and the healing character of his goodness, he reinforces this revelation of his purpose by expressing and arousing not only the church's affective, volitional and cognitive appreciation of him, but reaching out through us to touch the lives of those around.

The Sacrament of Fearful Intimacy

The Call to Identity

What does it mean to say that our life is 'in Christ'? What does it mean for us to share in his affective, volitional and cognitive awareness? If we are truly one with his body, we must surely share in his physical experience, in all these three aspects of his personhood.

> Going a little farther, he fell to the ground and prayed that if possible the hour might pass from him. '*Abba*, Father,' he said, 'everything is possible for you. Take this cup from me. Yet not what I will, but what you will.'
>
> Then he returned to his disciples and found them sleeping. 'Simon,' he said to Peter, 'are you asleep? Could you not keep watch for one hour? Watch and pray so that you will not fall into temptation. The spirit is willing, but the body is weak.'[56]

Effective service in ministry, pursuing a path that gives continued expression and enables ministry through the physical body of Christ, is not easily purchased. To turn church into either a comfortable classroom or an ecstatic event, seeking to attract crowds that will have either their cognitive or affective senses sated, is not his way.

---

[55] 2 Peter 1.4.
[56] Mark 14.35-38.

The way that ensures the authentic physicalism that conveys the reality of Jesus, the way that risks rejection and desertion by others, touches us deeply in every part of our being as we wrestle with the call to focus on a way forward that is true to Jesus Christ. Being church together involves consecrating ourselves when surrounded by the dysfunctionality of others. It is painful. A struggle. For it will take us, paradoxically, into a sense of isolation even as we give ourselves to serve the continued expression of a humanity marked by love in relationality. A life laid down for the forming and expression of community. We are called to an identity that embraces the affective, volitional and cognitive struggles of Christ himself. This is where the sacrament of fearful intimacy leads us.

The Pain of Community

The sacrament of fearful intimacy begins in the upper room. The secondary sacrament, instituted there, is present.

> When evening came, Jesus arrived with the Twelve.[1] While they were reclining at the table eating, he said, 'I tell you the truth, one of you will betray me—one who is eating with me.'[57]

The secondary sacrament reinforces the call to journey and also to participation. It calls and directs our attention towards applying ourselves to celebrate the primary sacrament, the sacrament of fearful intimacy and to join with Christ in his way and in his ministry. The call is to be a people who come together recognizing Christ in the midst. To realize that it is in our journeying together as a community of sacramental intimacy, where uncomprehending questioning and betrayal by brothers and sisters are close at hand, that the authentic expression and reflection of Christ is found.

---

[57] Mark 14.17-18.

CHAPTER 4

The Church as Sacrament: A Mediating Presence

John E. Colwell

[I pray] ...that all of them may be one, Father, just as you are in me and I am in you. May they also be in us so that the world may believe that you have sent me.[1] (Jn 17.21)

In writing this present paper I have a threefold purpose: firstly it is my intention to revisit and to develop a theme previously explored in my book on sacramental theology (and, in this respect, this paper could be viewed as a shameless piece of advertizing);[2] secondly, and more simply, I intend to develop this theme through a reading of Christ's high priestly prayer as witnessed in the seventeenth chapter of John's Gospel, focusing on what is attested there with respect to the identity of the church and its mission as this is established through its trinitarian indwelling; and finally, through this focus, I hope to offer some limited response to an account of Free Church ecclesiology in the work of Miroslav Volf:[3] concluding a review of Volf's book at the time I opined that '[p]erhaps what is required is not so much a 'Free Church ecclesiology' as an ecclesiology that is inclusive (though not uncritical) of the phenomenon of the Free Churches...', and I offer this discussion as a contribution to that end.[4]

To identify the church as 'sacrament', of course, implies a prior and assumed definition of sacramentality: such definition was my purpose in the book to which I have already referred but, for the purposes of this present paper I will begin with a brief summary of what was there argued and is here assumed. As a properly theological notion, sacramentality ought not to be considered merely as the nature of signs that are both sacred and visible as means of grace, but ought to be grounded in an understanding of God as narrated in the gospel story. This prayer recorded in John

---

[1] ἵνα πάντες ἓν ὦσιν, καθὼς σύ, πάτερ, ἐν ἐμοὶ κἀγὼ ἐν σοί, ἵνα καὶ αὐτοὶ ἐν ἡμῖν ὦσιν, ἵνα ὁ κόσμος πιστεύῃ ὅτι σύ με ἀπέστειλας.

[2] John E. Colwell, *Promise and Presence: An Exploration of Sacramental Theology* (Milton Keynes: Paternoster, 2005).

[3] Moroslav Volf, *After Our Likeness: The Church as the Image of the Trinity* (Grand Rapids, MI: Eerdmans, 1998).

[4] John E. Colwell, review of 'Moroslav Volf, *After Our Likeness: The Church as the Image of the Trinity*', Ashland Theological Journal 32 (2000), pp. 153-154, p. 154.

17 begins with reference to the glory shared by the Son and the Father before the world began (v. 5) and, accordingly, the church has heard the witness of the gospel story as the narration of God as the one who is Father, Son, and Holy Spirit, in eternal communion of intimate and perichoretic love. From this understanding of God's eternal triune identity, the church has inferred that God's relatedness to all that is not God is entirely gratuitous and unnecessitated; a matter of grace rather than a matter of necessity. God is eternally loving as Father, Son, and Spirit without the need for any reality external to God as the object of God's love. That God loves that which is other than God, creates that which is other than God, relates to that which is other than God, and purposes to redeem that which is other than God, is therefore entirely gratuitous, an outcome of divine freedom. Consequently, since God's relatedness to all that is not God is a matter of grace rather than necessity, this external divine relatedness cannot be presumed upon or manipulated; God's presence and action within the world can never become our possession or a matter at our disposal.

Moreover, that God is narrated through the gospel story as the one who is Father, Son, and Holy Spirit suggests that, even within this eternal communion of intimacy, God's love for God-self is a mediated love, a love mediated by the Spirit between the Father and the Son. This mediating function of the Spirit is not explicit in this high priestly prayer but it is explicit elsewhere both in this Gospel and in the Synoptics.[5] At key points within the gospel story the relatedness of the Father and the incarnate Son is identified as mediated by the Spirit and this narration can be heard as a reiteration of a mediated relatedness in eternity. If then mediated relatedness is of the essence of God we should expect God's relatedness to that which is other than God to be similarly mediated, to be a reiteration of the manner of that internal relatedness. That God, as Irenaeus attested, relates to created reality through the agency of Word and Wisdom, of the Son and the Spirit, may consequently be perceived as an outcome of this eternal mediateness.[6] But that God also mediates his presence and action within creation through the instrumentality of created reality may similarly be perceived as a consequence and reiteration of this eternal mediateness; a mediated immediacy is a coherent reflection of the triune life as rendered in the gospel story;[7] God, who mediates his presence within creation through the agency of

---

[5] So Jürgen Moltmann, *The Trinity and the Kingdom of God: The Doctrine of God*, trans. Margaret Kohl (London: SCM, 1981), p. 64, comments that '[t]he history in which Jesus is manifested as 'the Son' is not consummated and fulfilled by a single subject. The history of Christ is already related in trinitarian terms in the New Testament itself'.

[6] Irenaeus, *Against Heresies* IV.xx.1 and 3, in Alexander Roberts, James Donaldson and A. Cleveland Coxe (eds), *The Ante-Nicene Fathers* (Grand Rapids, MI: Eerdmans, 1987), I, pp. 487-88: 'For with Him were always present the Word and Wisdom, the Son and the Spirit, by whom and in whom, freely and spontaneously, He made all things... [T]he Son, was always with the Father; and that Wisdom also, which is the Spirit, was present with Him, anterior to all creation...'.

[7] I believe this phrase, 'mediated immediacy', was first coined by John Baillie, *Our Knowledge of God* (London: Oxford University Press, 1939), p. 181.

the Son and the Spirit, ultimately mediates his presence through the materiality of Christ's flesh. This ultimate and archetypical sacramentality which is Christ himself again is made explicit in this prayer: the Father is glorified in the Son (v. 1); to know the Father is to know the Son (v. 3); all that the Son receives is given by the Father (v. 7); we are sanctified through the sanctification of the Son (v. 19).

An affirmation of the mediated manner of God's presence and action within creation, together with the affirmation of the graciousness of God's presence and action within creation, consequently militates against any presumptuous notion of sacramentality as implying a presence and action of God at our disposal, falling under our control, liable to our manipulation. But an affirmation of this mediated manner of God's presence and action within creation also militates against any similarly presumptuous notion of an unmediated immediacy, of a presence and action of God within creation which, by virtue of its intangibility, reduces that presence and action to the vagaries of felt experience, rendering grace subject to subjectivism. Claims to a grace at our disposal or to an unmediated immediacy—twin aspects of a single delusion—should be resisted, not just with a view to their ecclesiological outcomes, but primarily because they offend a Christian doctrine of God: grace at our disposal or grace ultimately subject to the subject is no grace at all.

To define a sacrament as a means of grace, then, as a mediation of God's presence and sanctifying power, is not at all, for Thomas Aquinas any more than for the Reformers, to imply a grace at our disposal. For Thomas it is God alone, rather than the priest, the rite, or the elements, that is and remains the efficient cause of grace in the sacrament.[8] For Martin Luther[9] and for John Calvin[10] a sacrament is a matter of promise, and for Calvin explicitly a promise realized through the mediating action of the Spirit.[11]

---

[8] Thomas Aquinas, *Summa Theologica* (trans. by Fathers of the English Dominican Province; Westminster, MD: Christian Classics, 1981), III.62.1: '...the instrumental cause works not by the power of its form, but only by the motion whereby it is moved by the principal agent: so that the effect is not likened to the instrument but to the principal agent... it is thus that the sacraments of the New Law cause grace: for they are instituted by God to be employed for the purpose of conferring grace.'

[9] Martin Luther, *The Babylonian Captivity of the Church* (1520), in *Luther's Works* (ed. Helmut T. Lehmann; Philadelphia, PA: Muhlenberg Press, 1959), XXXVI, pp. 3-126, p. 42: 'For God does not deal, nor has he ever dealt, with man otherwise than through a word of promise...'

[10] John Calvin, *Institutes of the Christian Religion* (ed. J.T. McNeill; trans. F.L. Battles; Philadelphia, PA: Westminster Press, 1960), IV.xiv.3 [hereafter referred to as *Institutes*]: '...a sacrament is never without a preceding promise but is joined to it as a sort of appendix, with the purpose of confirming and sealing the promise itself, and of making it more evident to us and in a sense ratifying it.'

[11] ' Calvin, *Institutes*, IV.xiv.9: '...the sacraments properly fulfill their office only when the Spirit, that inward teacher, comes to them, by whose power alone hearts are penetrated and affections moved and our souls opened for the sacraments to enter in. If the Spirit be lacking, the sacraments can accomplish nothing more in our minds than the splendor of the sun shining upon blind eyes, or a voice sounding in deaf ears. Therefore, I

That God mediates his presence to Moses through a burning bush, then, may be a sacramental dynamic in a limited and general sense, a presence and power mediated through a material object, but it is not itself a sacrament; there is no promise of God that constitutes bushes as means of God's gracious presence and action. Moreover, a sacrament ought never to be misconstrued as God's 'prison', and this in two respects. That God has promised to mediate his presence and sanctifying power in certain places, through certain people, and through certain liturgical rites does not confine God; '...the whole earth is full of his glory' (Isa. 6.3); he can freely and graciously mediate his presence elsewhere and through other means—he simply hasn't promised to do so. But neither does this promise constrain God; his presence is not captured within the sacrament, becoming an object at our disposal; his promised presence here remains his gracious presence here, a dynamic of being given rather than a static givenness. A sacrament, therefore, is an enacted prayer; a hopeful seeking of a promised presence. A deluded presumption of possession and manipulation reduces prayer to incantation, sacrament to sacrilege, mystery to magic.

For *Lumen Gentium* to identify the church as 'in the nature of sacrament' was hardly innovative,[12] Catholic writers[13] had spoken of the church in this manner previously,[14] but, as others have noted, the definition can be read as in some tension with the hierarchical definition of the church that the same statement perpetuates.[15] Robert Jenson, a Lutheran theologian, perhaps compounds this tension by relating

---

make such a division between Spirit and sacraments that the power to act rests with the former, and the ministry alone is left to the latter—a ministry empty and trifling, apart from the action of the Spirit, but charged with great effect when the Spirit works within and manifests his power.

[12] *Lumen Gentium*, in Gregory Baum (ed.), *De Ecclesia: The Constitution on the Church of Vatican Council II with commentary* (London: Darton, Longman & Todd, 1965), I.1 [hereafter *LG*]: '...the Church, in Christ, is in the nature of sacrament—a sign and instrument, that is, of communion with God and of unity among all men...'; cf. *LG* II 9: '...God has gathered together and established as the Church, that it may be for each and everyone the visible sacrament of this saving unity'.

[13] Following convention, I use the term 'Catholic' to refer to the Roman Catholic Church, and the term 'catholic' to refer the church in its universal and continuing connectedness.

[14] E.g., Henri de Lubac, *Catholicism, Christ and the Common Destiny of Man* (London: Burns and Oates, 1950), p. 2: 'If Christ is the sacrament of God, the Church is for us the sacrament of Christ; she represents him, in the full and ancient meaning of the term, she really makes him present'; or Karl Rahner, *The Church and the Sacraments* (Tunbridge Wells: Burns & Oates, 1963), p. 19: '...the Church is the primal and fundamental sacrament'.

[15] For instance, Basil Butler, 'Preface' in Gregory Baum, *De Ecclesia*, p. 9, in his preface to this edition of the statement sees this emphasis, together with the emphasis on the church as a pilgrim people as identifying the church '...first and foremost as the spiritual fellowship of her baptized members, and only secondarily, and as it were consequentially, as a hierarchized communion.'

this identification of the church as sacrament with the New Testament imagery of the church as the 'body of Christ', and as a means of taking this imagery with 'ontological seriousness while avoiding the kind of identification of Christ and church that underlies ecclesial triumphalism'.[16] But can it be coherent to take a metaphor with 'ontological seriousness', or is Professor Jenson suggesting that the imagery of the church as Christ's 'body' is other than metaphorical, is a matter of ontological description (and, if this is the case, how might he avoid the 'ecclesial triumphalism' he repudiates)?

Notions of the church as the continuation of Christ's incarnation are not uncommon, particularly amongst Lutheran and Catholic authors, but the definition of the church as sacrament, at least as sacramentality has been defined earlier in this paper, militates against this too simple and direct identification. That the church functions, metaphorically, as Christ's body is an outcome of the Spirit's mediation of God's presence and sanctifying power, an outcome of the Spirit's distributing of gifts of grace 'just as he determines' (1 Cor. 12.11).[17] The church witnesses to Christ in common with the Spirit (Jn 15.26-27); the church mediates Christ's presence and power through the agency of the Spirit; but the church is not Christ and Christ is not the church.

As you sent me into the world, I have sent them into the world.[18] (Jn 17.18)

The sending of the church into the world by Christ is in the likeness of his being sent into the world by the Father, but it is not a simple continuation or repetition of that prior and definitive sending: the church is sent as Christ is sent; it is not sent as Christ. It is precisely this too simple and direct identification of the church and Christ, an assumption of givenness rather than a prayerful expectation of a being-givenness, that issues both in the sacerdotalism which, as I argue elsewhere,[19] marks an abandonment of Thomas' caution and precision, and in that institutional conception of the church that comes to expression in hierarchical structures. That the church truly exists on the basis of promise, as a living sacrament, militates against all such static conceptions and outcomes. The church is sent into the world as Christ was sent into the world and, as Karl Barth famously observes, there is a veiledness as much as an unveiledness in God's self-revelation in Christ.[20] The scribes and

---

[16] Robert W. Jenson, 'The Church and the Sacraments', in Colin E. Gunton (ed.), *The Cambridge Companion to Christian Doctrine* (Cambridge: Cambridge University Press, 1997), pp. 207-25, p. 212. Note that Karl Rahner also speaks of Christ's 'abiding presence' in the church, *Church and the Sacraments*, pp. 18-19.

[17] πάντα δὲ ταῦτα ἐνεργεῖ τὸ ἓν καὶ τὸ αὐτὸ πνεῦμα διαιροῦν ἰδίᾳ ἑκάστῳ καθὼς βούλεται.

[18] καθὼς ἐμὲ ἀπέστειλας εἰς τὸν κόσμον, κἀγὼ ἀπέστειλα αὐτοὺς εἰς τὸν κόσμον·

[19] Colwell, *Promise and Presence*, pp. 7-10.

[20] Karl Barth, *Church Dogmatics* (trans. G.W. Bromiley and T.F. Torrance; Edinburgh: T&T Clark, 1956–75), I/1, pp. 162-86; cf. pp. 320-33.

Pharisees saw Jesus as the carpenter's son from Nazareth, a Sabbath-breaker, a blasphemer, a disturber of the peace; the disciples gradually came to see Jesus as the making visible of the glory of God. And when Peter, like Martha, confesses Jesus as the Christ, the Son of God, Jesus does not commend him for being sufficiently perceptive to work this out; he rather attests that this could only be made known to him by the Father: 'No one knows the Son except the Father, and no one knows the Father except the Son and those to whom the Son chooses to reveal him' (Mt. 11.27). And just as a recognition of Christ was a matter of revelation, of being-givenness rather than simple givenness, so also the recognition of Christ's mediated presence and action in and through the church is dynamic rather than static, a being-givenness rather than a simple givenness, an outcome of promise rather than an institutionalized possession. The world may not recognize this mediated presence—the world did not recognize Christ—but the church's identity as the promised mediation of Christ remains nonetheless.

Of course the church, as the living sacrament of God's presence and sanctifying power, is not God's prison: he can mediate his presence and power otherwise and through other means—through bushes and flowers, through wind, earthquake, and fire, through human joy and human tragedy, through literature and music, through desolation and darkness—he can and does, but he has not promised to do so; his promised means of presence and grace within the world is the church, the people gathered to him through baptism and in eucharistic communion, the people who are one with each other because firstly they are one with him.

Moreover, it is not just that the church is not recognized by the world unless that recognition is imparted; it is more profoundly that the world is hostile to the church as it was hostile to Christ: there is that about the church which, as with Christ, is other than the world. Ultimately this is, of course, an inverted truth: the world is Christ's, it was brought into being through him, its materiality is ontologically grounded in the materiality of the flesh he assumes, when he comes to the world he comes to his own even if his own do not receive him and fail to recognize him. This otherness of Christ to the world, then, as with the otherness of the church to the world, is an ontological contradiction. But here and now, as there and then, this contradiction is actual as is its consequent hostility. And this otherness of the church to the world is identified in this prayer as an outcome of the church's sanctification, a sanctification deriving from the sanctification of Christ:

> They are not of the world even as I am not of it. Sanctify them by the truth; your word is truth... For them I sanctify myself, that they too may be truly sanctified.[21] (Jn 17.16, 17 and 19)

Quite understandably we tend to hear words such as sanctification and holiness as overwhelmingly negative notions—this, after all, is their predominant significance

---

[21] ἐκ τοῦ κόσμου οὐκ εἰσὶν καθὼς ἐγὼ οὐκ εἰμὶ ἐκ τοῦ κόσμου. ἁγίασμον αὐτοὺς ἐν τῇ ἀληθείᾳ· ὁ λόγος ὁ σὸς ἀλήθειά ἐστιν... καὶ ὑπὲρ αὐτῶν ἐγὼ ἁγιάζω ἐμαυτόν, ἵνα ὦσιν καὶ αὐτοὶ ἡγιασμένοι ἐν ἀληθείᾳ.

within the Old Testament; holiness seems to be a matter of separation from the ordinary, the everyday, and the common—but finally this cannot be the case: since holiness is properly a perfection of God's eternal nature, without prejudice to that which is other than God, holiness ultimately must be a positive rather than a negative quality. Here Christ prays specifically that we will be sanctified by (or in) the truth which is the divine word. The Word of God as it is heard through the reading of scripture and the hearing of Christian proclamation is itself sacramental; it is an instrumental means of God's presence and sanctifying power, but, specifically in this Gospel, I suspect we miss the point if we understand this prayer simply in this manner. This Word of God has become flesh as Jesus of Nazareth: Jesus himself is the embodying of God's Word to us and, as such, he is the Truth. Ultimately truth, like beauty and holiness, are perfections of God and, consequently, truth cannot be reduced as mere verbal and propositional correspondence; truth ultimately is personal since ultimately truth is identical to God himself; grace and truth, therefore, 'happen' in Jesus Christ; grace and truth are narrated in this story.[22] The prayer here, then, is not simply that the church might be made holy through its hearing of words, all be they truthful words; the prayer more profoundly is that the church might be made holy through its relatedness to Christ and participation in him. Within this prayer the church's sanctification is linked to the sanctification of Christ which, in context must refer to his passion and resurrection (the tradition has consistently affirmed the sanctifying power mediated through the gospel sacraments as deriving from Christ's sacrifice). The holiness of the church, then, is an outcome of participation in Christ and, in the context of this Gospel, that participation is sacramentally mediated. And here we arrive at the reiterated heart of this prayer:

> I have given them the glory that you gave me, that they may be one as we are one: I in them and you in me. May they be brought to complete unity to let the world know that you sent me and have loved them even as you have loved me.[23] (Jn 17.22-23).

In his discussion of the church as 'the Image of the Trinity', specifically in response to the Free Church ecclesiology expressed in the writings of John Smyth (the seventeenth-century General Baptist), Miroslav Volf founds a definition of the church chiefly on a reading of the text of Matthew 18.20 ('...for where two or three are gathered in my name, I am there among them'[24]).[25] To this degree Volf is reiterating a Free Church tendency to oppose sacramentally mediated notions of Christ's presence (as represented in Volf's preceding discussion of the work of Joseph Ratzinger and John Zizioulas) with an affirmation of an unmediated and

---

[22] ἡ χάρις καὶ ἀλήθεια διὰ Ἰησοῦ Χριστοῦ ἐγένετο (Jn 1.17).

[23] κἀγὼ τὴν δόξαν ἣν δέδωκάς μοι δέδωκα αὐτοῖς, ἵνα ὦσιν ἓν καθὼς ἡμεῖς ἕν· ἐγὼ ἐν αὐτοῖς καὶ σὺ ἐν ἐμοί, ἵνα ὦσιν τετελειωμένοι εἰς ἕν, ἵνα γινώσκῃ ὁ κόσμος ὅτι σύ με ἀπέστειλας καὶ ἠγάπησας αὐτοὺς καθὼς ἐμὲ ἠγάπησας.

[24] οὗ γάρ εἰσιν δύο ἢ τρεῖς συνηγμένοι εἰς τὸ ἐμὸν ὄνομα, ἐκεῖ εἰμι ἐν μέσῳ αὐτῶν.

[25] Volf, *After Our Likeness*, p. 135.

'direct presence' of Christ to the church through the Spirit, albeit in Volf's case a presence made actual through the 'concrete relations' of Christians with other Christians; a presence conditional not just on the 'performance of objective activities' but more fundamentally consequent upon the 'subjective conditions' of 'genuine faith and obedience to God's commandments'.[26]

My purpose here is not to comment on the rather individualized notion of faith assumed here (though later corrected), nor on the common but delusory disjunction between the objective and the subjective, nor on the insinuation that Catholic and Orthodox traditions are any less concerned for 'genuine faith and obedience'. My purpose rather is to question Volf's subsequent focus on 'assembly' as the means of Christ's presence to and through the church, and thereby as defining of the church.[27] Though Volf affirms the sacraments of baptism and the Lord's supper as belonging to 'the *esse* of the church', albeit as means of the confession of faith, these sacraments of indwelling feature surprisingly little in Volf's account of the church's gathering;[28] and though Volf refers more than once to the text of this high priestly prayer and its overtly participatory expression of the church's unity[29]—a participatory unity that Volf never denies—the emphasis is overwhelmingly on a unity of assembly, a participation in Christ identified in our participation in one another and this primarily expressed other than sacramentally. Volf responds to Schleiermacher's distinction between Catholic and Protestant notions of Christian communion—the Catholic rendering relation to Christ as dependent on the church and the Protestant rendering relation to the church as dependent on relation to Christ[30]—by identifying the trinitarian and pneumatological nature of Christian personhood and the consequent 'Ecclesiality of salvation', but the discussion here focuses on the nature of faith and not at all on sacramental mediation.[31]

In this focus on 'assembly', especially as this is read from the text of Matthew 18.20 (which serves almost as a mantra in some Free Church circles, often with little reference to its immediate context and focus, and with less reference still to the text of Matthew 16.18, the only other occurrence of the word ἐκκλεσία in the Synoptic Gospels), Volf is an able and accurate representative of a Free Church tradition and an imaginative interpreter of the work of Smyth. But I greatly doubt that this ultimately non-sacramental defining of the church will ever prove ecumenically persuasive, and, in response to this prayer of Jesus, it is a defining of the church that is seriously and foundationally defective. Jesus prays, not that we might be one with each other as a means of being one with him; he prays rather that we might be one with him as a means of being one with each other: that we are one

---

[26] Volf, *After Our Likeness*, pp. 134-35.
[27] Volf, *After Our Likeness*, pp. 137-45.
[28] Volf, *After Our Likeness*, pp. 152-54.
[29] See especially Volf, *After Our Likeness*, p. 128.
[30] Volf, *After Our Likeness*, p. 159. See Friedrich Schleiermacher, *The Christian Faith* (eds. H.R. Mackintosh and J.S. Stewart; Edinburgh: T&T Clark, 1928), §24 (pp. 103-108).
[31] Volf, *After Our Likeness*, pp. 159-89.

as the Father and the Son are one is an outcome of our participation in the Son and his participation in us, just as his oneness with the Father issues from his participation in the Father and the Father's participation in him. And, more especially in response to Volf, in the context of this Fourth Gospel this language of participation and indwelling is profoundly sacramental. John includes no standard account of the institution of the eucharist and no explicit command to baptize yet the language and symbolism of baptism and eucharist pervades the witness of this most intensely sacramental of the Gospels. We participate in Christ and correspondingly are indwelt by Christ through the mediating agency of the Spirit and this mediated communion is itself mediated through the water of baptism and through the bread and wine of holy communion: to be born from above is to be born of water and of the Spirit (Jn 3.5);[32] to dwell in Christ and to be indwelt by Christ is to eat his flesh and to drink his blood (Jn 6.56).[33]

This inversion of the dynamic of oneness is ubiquitous in Free Church life, and probably beyond. Fellowship (κοινωνία) for many Baptists implies a cup of coffee and a biscuit after morning worship or a Saturday evening 'social' rather than any sense of a sacramental participation in Christ. Exhortations to community have little to do with communion. Baptism may necessarily imply faith but faith rarely necessarily implies baptism. Free Church understandings (or rather misunderstandings) of fellowship—which is only another way of saying Free Church ecclesiologies—therefore tend towards the voluntaristic and the non-sacramental. In extreme form such accounts are both explicitly memorialist and implicitly Pelagian: they are memorialist in their understanding of baptism and communion, and they are Pelagian in their understanding of voluntarism. A memorialist understanding of holy communion, deriving chiefly from Ulrich Zwingli, finds classic baptistic expression in the writings and practice of Balthasar Hubmaier, an Anabaptist of the sixteenth century working in Waldshut, for whom the elements of the supper were but tokens of one absent and the focus of the supper was the covenant relationship between the gathered members of the church rather than the crucified and risen Christ and our sacramental participation in him. Here it is the mutual bond and act of love uniting Christian believers that is the sign and means of God's presence and action within the world.[34] And this memorialist understanding of the supper itself generates Pelagianism since a primarily human notion of covenant, responding to an explicit divine absence, is a moralistic rather than gracious dynamic, an outcome of human commitments rather than of divine indwelling.

---

[32] ἀπεκρίθς Ἰησοῦς, Ἀμὴν ἀμὴν λέγω σοι, ἐαν μή τις γεννηθῇ ἐξ ὕδατος καὶ πνεύματος, οὐ δύναται εἰσελθεῖν εἰς τὴν βασιλείαν τοῦ θεοῦ... μὴ θαυμάσῃς ὅτι εἶπόν σοι, Δεῖ ὑμᾶς γεννηθῆναι ἄνωθεν.

[33] ὁ τρώγων μου τὴν σάρκα καὶ πίνων μου τὸ αἷμα ἐν ἐμοὶ μένει κἀγὼ ἐν αὐτῷ.

[34] Balthasar Hubmaier, *Balthasar Hubmaier: Theologian of Anabaptism* (trans. and ed., H.W. Pipkin and J.H. Yoder; Scottdale, PA/Waterloo, ON: Herald Press, 1989), pp. 11, 24-26; cf. J.D. Rempel, *The Lord's Supper in Anabaptism: A Study in the Christology of Balthasar Hubmaier, Pilgram Marpeck and Dirk Philips* (Scottdale, PA/Waterloo, ON: Herald Press, 1993).

Though Hubmaier would be unknown to most contemporary British Baptists his memorialist and voluntarist account of Christian communion is commonplace and Miroslav Volf seems to attribute such to John Smyth, perhaps assuming that, as a 'General' Baptist sojourning in Holland and anticipating Jacob Arminius' response to Calvinist predestinarianism, Smyth might prove closer to continental Anabaptism than later 'Particular' Baptists. But this apparent assumption would be hard to sustain: though a division developed between John Smyth and Thomas Helwys with respect to relations with Dutch Mennonites,[35] Smyth's origins are in English Puritanism and his account of the Lord's supper clearly affirms Calvin's notion of Christ's real though spiritually mediated presence.[36] Despite its inclusion in his 'works', Smyth's authorship of the *Defence of de Reis's Confession* has been questioned, though his agreement with its sentiments can be assumed and his authorship can be defended.[37] Here with graphic clarity our oneness with each other is an outcome of our oneness with Christ mediated in the supper; it is through the sacrament that we are one with Christ and with each other:

> ...it places before his eyes the feeding and nourishment of the new creation through the spiritual flesh which is indeed food. And this is changed into the essence of the new creation in order that from it the faithful may be made genuine brothers of Christ though the *koinonian* of the same spiritual flesh and the consanguinity of the same spiritual blood; for those two, that is, Christ and the church, are of one flesh through this great sacrament of this spiritual union...[38]

At this point Volf but poorly represents Smyth: there is a remarkable absence of reference to the eucharist in the latter part of his work and the notion of covenant here, as with Hubmaier, is voluntaristic; our covenantal unity with each other is a means of Christ's mediated presence rather than *vice versa*. Paul Fiddes has argued that the notion of covenant is of the essence of a Baptist understanding of ecclesiology but he is careful to defend this notion of covenant from the mere voluntarism that inevitably degenerates into Pelagianism: that covenant which unites us in the church is God's initiative; we participate in one another as an outcome of

---

[35] See, for instance, B.R. White, *The English Baptists of the Seventeenth Century* (A History of the English Baptists, 1; London: The Baptist Historical Society, 1983), pp. 24-27.

[36] John Smyth, 'A Short Confession' (1610), Article 32, in William L. Lumpkin, *Baptist Confessions of Faith* (Valley Forge, PA: Judson Press, rev. edn, 1969), pp. 102-113, p. 110.

[37] James Robert Coggins, *John Smyth's Congregation: English Separatism, Mennonite Influence, and the Elect Nation* (Studies in Anabaptist and Mennonite History, 32; Scottdale, PA: Herald Press, 1991), pp. 89-94.

[38] John Smyth, *Defense of de Ries's Confession*, Article 34, in Coggins, *John Smyth's Congregation*, pp. 172-94, pp. 192-93.

our participation in Christ, and this participation is sacramentally mediated.[39] In holy baptism we are joined to Christ and thereby joined to his body, the church, and in holy communion that participation is reiterated, celebrated, and renewed. The life of the church is its sacramentally mediated participation in its Lord. While, at the level of contemporary consciousness, it may be a commitment to voluntarism—and that in a radically individualistic and Enlightenment sense—that is distinctive of Free Church self-definition, that which more authentically is and was foundationally distinctive for Free Church understandings of church is an affirmation of the integrity of the local congregation, a rejection of hierarchical accounts of the church and its ministry, together with a corresponding commitment to that separatism that arises from dissent. Free Churches are 'free' in relation to hierarchical structures and the pretensions of state dominance rather than necessarily 'free' in relation to liturgical ordering and sacramental practice. There have always been sacramentally defined expressions of Free Church ecclesiology and, supplementary to Volf's account, Smyth is a notable representation of such. For Smyth, then, as for the catholic tradition, the unity of the church, expressed in its gathering, is grounded sacramentally.

Nor is this displacing of a sacramentally mediated unity an exclusively Free Church tendency. The ordering of the 'Peace' within eucharistic liturgy itself is suggestive of a unity between believers that precedes our participation in Christ and is the condition of that participation. This ordering can, of course, be defended—it is appropriate that we affirm our peace with one another and our forgiveness of one another as we come to share in bread and wine—but it nonetheless detracts from the recognition that our mutual unity derives from our sacramentally mediated participation. And this detraction is inevitably compounded by the form this 'Peace' increasingly assumes—the celebration of an all too human and unmediated unity. Is there not a case as good or better for celebrating the 'Peace' at the conclusion of the communion and prior to the dismissal as a recognition that our communion with one another is an outcome of our communion with Christ? Moreover, this celebration of the 'Peace' by greeting our immediate neighbours similarly distracts from the catholicity which is the true form of the church's unity. Through that participation in Christ mediated through holy communion we participate in and with the whole church in every time and in every place, with the church in heaven as much as the church on earth, with the universal church as much as the local church. The Free Churches, in response to the text of Matthew 18.20, rightly affirm the integrity (rather than the simple independence or autonomy) of the local. But this distinct integrity of the local, in reflection of the perichoretic oneness of the Holy Trinity, is an outcome of its sacramentally mediated participation in the catholic and universal. The church in every place and in every time is one by virtue of its

---

[39] See, especially, chapter 2 in Paul S. Fiddes, *Tracks and Traces: Baptist Identity in Church and Theology* (Studies in Baptist History and Thought, 13; Carlisle: Paternoster Press, 2003), pp. 21-47.

participation in its one Lord, its one faith, its one baptism, and (following the logic of the text of Ephesians 4) the mediated connectedness of its ministers.

This unity and catholicity of the church, then, as sacramentally mediated, remains a 'being-given' rather than a simple 'given', a prayer in response to a promise rather than a presumption, a mystery of faith rather than an institution capable of hierarchical organization, an outcome of indwelling rather than an outcome of social interaction. The church is mystery inasmuch as it is sacramentally defined and constituted.

And as this sacramentally defined mystery, the church is itself the sacrament of Christ's presence and sanctifying grace within the world. The apostolicity of the church may indeed have something to do with its catholicity, the connectedness of its faith and its ministry in every place and in every time, but principally the apostolicity of the church is surely a matter of its 'being-sent-ness', its being sent into the world as the Son was sent into the world. This 'being-sent-ness' is as much of the essence of the church as is its sacramentally mediated holiness, oneness, and catholicity. And this 'being-sent-ness' is as much a matter of mystery, as much a sacramentally mediated 'being-givenness', as is its sacramentally mediated holiness, oneness, and catholicity. The all too common language of 'doing mission' is distorting in two respects: it suggests that mission is a matter of the church's action rather than the church's being and, as such, it suggests that mission is something of which the church is capable rather than something in which the church remains utterly dependent. Grammatically the church is mission; it is sent into the world; mission, in this sense, is something done to the church rather than something the church itself does. As a people who are one, holy, and catholic through their sacramental participation in Christ, the church is apostolic; it is sent into the world; it is located here; its mission is continuous with its identity. And since its identity is sacramentally derived, is a matter of mystery, the church remains wholly impotent in itself for the fulfilment of its 'being-sent-ness'; it can no more make Christ present to the world than it can manipulate Christ's presence and sanctifying power in holy baptism or holy communion; here, as there, it can only hope in prayer for the fulfilment of promised presence and transforming grace.

I want not to be misunderstood at this point: so much that the contemporary church does with respect to mission is appropriate and laudable—appropriate, that is, providing that the church recalls its own impotence and mediated identity here; providing that the church never comes to presume that it can, by its own efforts and commitments, cause Christ to be present to the world in sanctifying grace. Jobseeker clubs, support groups, counselling centres, shelter schemes, may all be forms of identification and service through which the Spirit may make Christ present, through the church, to the world; but this can only ever be a matter of prayer and hope; never a matter of presumption. And should such wholly appropriate activities ever become the focus of the church's attention and self-understanding they at once, for all their worthiness, are rendered inappropriate. As integral to its sacramental identity, the church's mission is an outcome of its sacramental indwelling; the church is an instrumental means of the presence of Christ to the world as a consequence of its own sacramental indwelling—and in both cases, with respect to Christ's presence to the church and with respect to Christ's presence through the church, this can only be a matter of promise and prayer, a hoped for 'being-givenness' rather than a presumed givenness. To conclude then: the church is the sacramental presence of Christ in the world by virtue of its own sacramental life and worship and, in both respects, the sacramental is the outcome of gracious mediation, a dynamic rather than a static, a 'being-givenness' rather than a 'givenness'.

This high priestly prayer of Christ witnessed in John 17, with all its ecclesiological richness and eschatological assurance, is immediately succeeded in the narrative of the Gospel by Jesus' betrayal and arrest and the disciples' desertion: a scene of confident hopefulness gives way to a scene of futility, failure, and despair; Peter's bravado gives way to Peter's denial; a high-priestly petition gives way to the darkness of the cross and the ultimate hiddenness of God's glory. Even in this most triumphant of the Gospels there is no place for unrealistic triumphalism; even the narratives of the resurrection include Mary's slowness to recognize the risen one and Thomas' understandable doubt. To define the church sacramentally in its oneness, holiness, catholicity, and apostolicity is precisely to resist idealism, to acknowledge failure and frailty, and to rest in mystery. The church is the church not on the basis of the merits of the material elements that are its members, nor on the basis of the antiquity and efficacy of its hierarchical structures (structures that so often only obscure the church's true sacramental identity), nor, in Free Church terms, on the basis of the assembly and social interaction of its diverse members (a dynamic of assembly that so often exposes disunity and dysfunction). The church is the church 'in the nature of sacrament', on the basis of promise, in response to prayer. The presence of Christ to and through the church can only ever be a matter of mystery, of gracious mediation, of humble expectation. Christ sends us into the world as he was first sent into the world, and he prays that he may be present in us as we are present in him, as he is present to the Father, as the Father is present to him. It is in its sacramental life and worship that the church echoes this prayer of Christ and attests its true identity—and only in such a manner is the church truly the church.

CHAPTER 5

Re-Thinking a Sacramental View of Baptism and the Lord's Supper for the Post-Christendom Baptist Church

Michael F. Bird

In the evangelical Baptist tradition there is an excessive suspicion of anything that smacks of tradition, sacramentalism, creed, and ceremony. Such attitudes are expressed most vividly in Baptist attitudes towards baptism and the Lord's supper which are most usually defined as 'ordinances' rather than 'sacraments'.[1] The Baptist discomfort with sacraments could derive from an aversion to the language and concept of sacrament itself or else stem from a concern that a sacramental theology is a form of quasi-Catholicism.[2] On the one hand, I resonate with the Baptist ambivalence towards sacraments since in the sphere of *Religionsgeschichte* ('religious history') there is a specific word for rituals that convey salvific benefits independent of the recipient's disposition where the ritual is said to be effective *ex opere operato*. That word is of course 'magic'. If by sacrament one means an event or ritual that imparts salvific benefits and blessings independent of the recipient's faith, then I shall have to roll my eyes and shake my finger. On the other hand 'ordinance' can be itself problematic if it is taken to denote a *mere* symbol that is nothing more than an act of obedience and public confession of faith and *not a means of grace*. The

---

[1] See the 1689 London Baptist Confession which in article 28 states that 'Baptism and the Lord's Supper are ordinances of positive and sovereign institution; appointed by the Lord Jesus, the only Law-giver, to be continued in his Church to the end of the world'. See W.L. Lumpkin, *Baptist Confessions of Faith* (Valley Forge, PA: Judson Press, rev. edn, 1969), p. 290.

[2] David F. Wright, *What has Infant Baptism done to Baptism? An Enquiry at the End of Christendom* [Milton Keynes: Paternoster, 2005], pp. 87-88, writes, 'A certain anti-sacramentalism, or at least disinterest in the sacraments, has characterized too much evangelicalism, often as a reaction against an intolerably high sacramental theology, of the kind associated in the Anglican tradition with the Tractarians' Oxford Movement or with Anglo-Catholicism in general.' For examples of Baptist anti-sacramentalism, see Anthony R. Cross, 'The Myth of English Baptist Anti-Sacramentalism', in Philip E. Thompson and Anthony R. Cross (eds), *Recycling the Past or Researching History?: Studies in Baptist Historiography and Myths* (Studies in Baptist history and Thought, 11; Milton Keynes: Paternoster, 2005), pp. 128-32.

'ordinance' perspective fails to answer the question as to why these practices were ordained by the Lord in the first place.[3]

We should keep in mind, however, that 'ordinance' and 'magic' are not the only two liturgical shows playing in town. I sense that Baptists (by that I mean modern Baptists for the most part) have been somewhat rash in dispensing with of any concept of 'sacrament' for their understanding of baptism and the Lord's supper. In doing so they have not only by-passed a rich and sweet stream of Christian tradition for understanding baptism and the Lord's supper, but they have also misrepresented the biblical materials which are not nearly so anti-ritual or anti-sacramental as many Baptists might suppose. In light of that, what I aim to do in this study is to argue that a *biblical sacramentalism* can enrich the witness and body life of our churches and help us to proclaim with effective symbols the gospel of God's Son in our post-Christian, post-modern, pluralistic, and neo-pagan world. My underlying premise is that there is but one sacrament, Jesus Christ himself, who is Holy God and Holy Man, and it is through the proclamation of the gospel that we receive this sacrament that saves our souls that are sickened unto death by sin. Accordingly, baptism and the Lord's supper are sacramental only in so far as they provide a participation in Jesus Christ. What sacralizes the waters and the bread and wine is not the priest or pastor but the one in whom we are baptized and the one in whose name we eat and drink.

What is more, I am cognizant of the fact that much theology of the sacraments in Baptist circles takes places in the halls of Baptist universities, colleges and seminaries and never really filters down to the Baptist people in the pews. For this reason I think it worthwhile to heed the plea of Paul Beasley-Murray who complains of '[T]he enormous gulf between the thinking reflected by those Baptists who write scholarly articles and the practice of baptism in the average Baptist church. If Christian scholarship is to be the servant of the church, then scholars must find ways of mediating their thinking which are intelligible to the church as a whole'.[4] With that in mind I intend to keep one eye on the subject of how my thoughts on a renewed approach to baptism and the Lord's supper will actually translate into practice in Baptist churches.

Baptism: Consummating our Conversion

Considering that it is precisely their view of baptism that so distinguishes Baptists from other Protestant churches, it is fiercely ironic that Baptists attribute such little significance to the act of baptism itself. When it comes to baptism it seems to me

---

[3] Stanley J. Grenz, 'Baptism and the Lord's Supper as Community Acts: Towards a Sacramental Understanding of the Ordinances', in Anthony R. Cross and Philip E. Thompson (eds), *Baptist Sacramentalism* (Studies in Baptist History and Thought, 5; Carlisle: Paternoster Press, 2003), p. 89.

[4] Paul Beasley-Murray, 'Review: *Dimensions of Baptism: Biblical and Theological Studies*, edited by Stanley E. Porter and Anthony R. Cross', *Evangelical Quarterly* 78.2 (April, 2006), p. 173.

that the majority of Baptists are primarily concerned with the proper orientation of the recipient (a convert of responsible age) and the proper mode of baptism (full immersion), rather than being concerned with what baptism actually does or what it actually means. The Baptist view of baptism seems to be defined in the *via negativa* or understood by virtue of what baptism does not do, i.e., it does not confer salvation. The non-saving nature of baptism is the anchor point for a modern Baptist view of baptism. In many Baptist churches one hears various statements about baptism to the effect that 'it is an outward expression of an inward experience' and that it involves 'nailing one's colours to the mast' and other similar theological aphorisms. The problem is that, in the words of David F. Wright, 'There is not a single text which prima facie ascribes to baptism only a symbolic or representational or significatory function.'[5] Even the great Baptist New Testament scholar George R. Beasley-Murray stated, '[T]he idea that baptism is a purely symbolic rite must be pronounced not alone unsatisfactory but out of harmony with the New Testament itself.'[6] I am not denying that baptism is in a certain sense symbolic, nor am I attributing to baptism a determinative salvific function; rather, I am advocating that baptism is more than a symbol. In what follows I shall not give an exhaustive survey of baptismal passages but draw attention to those texts that imply a more-than-symbolical baptismal rite.

A lot of attention is given to baptism and the reception of the Spirit in the Acts of the Apostles and whether or not baptism confers the Spirit or signifies baptismal regeneration.[7] The fact of the matter is that there are approximately twenty-four conversions in Acts and no two of them are the same. In Acts 2.37-38 baptism is clearly linked with the forgiveness of sins and the gift of the Holy Spirit. In Acts 8.12-17 receipt of the Spirit is a post-baptismal event for the Samaritans. For Cornelius and the Gentiles the coming of the Holy Spirit occurs prior to baptism in Acts 10.44-48. The reasons for these differences are due to the unique redemptive-historical circumstances surrounding the birth and expansion of the church: the Jews needed to experience the Spirit in a rite that incorporated them into Jesus and the church, the Samaritans needed to learn that salvation is from 'the Jews' (cf. Jn 4.22), and the apostles needed to see first hand that salvation is also for Samaritans and Gentiles (cf. Acts 1.8). This is based on the sovereignty of God and the freedom of the Spirit to regenerate, illuminate, convict, and baptize with the Spirit when and where it is appropriate in the divine economy. Although this may wreak havoc with our attempts at constructing an *ordo salutis* (order of salvation), the fact of the matter is that the scriptures are more concerned with showing the unfolding development of God's plan of salvation than with creating a neat little package where regeneration, faith, and baptism all have their prearranged logical and chronological position. What

---

[5] Wright, *What has Infant Baptism?*, p. 91.

[6] George R. Beasley-Murray, *Baptism in the New Testament* (London: Macmillan, 1962), p. 262.

[7] For a survey of the key texts, see Beasley-Murray, *Baptism*, pp. 93-125; Stanley E. Porter, 'Baptism in Acts: The Sacramental Dimensions', in Cross and Thompson (eds), *Baptist Sacramentalism*, pp. 117-28.

is common to all accounts in Acts, however, is that baptism is an integral part of the conversion-initiation process.

In the 'great commission' of Matthew 28.19-20, the command to make disciples is probably defined in terms of the surrounding participles that include 'going' (πορευθέντες), 'baptizing' (βαπτίζοντες), and 'teaching' (διδάσκοντες).[8] There are no disciples without baptism and no baptism without would-be disciples. The invocation at baptism is stated here in triune terms, 'in the name of the Father and of the Son and of the Holy Spirit'. The meaning of which is that the candidate *formally* submits to the authority of God and is *finally* incorporated into the life of God and his church.[9]

There is a great deal in 1 Corinthians on baptism. It seems that partisan factions developed around key figures who administered baptism (1 Cor. 1.12-17). Paul remarks that Israel was 'baptized into Moses' (1 Cor. 10.2) signifying their incorporation into Moses' redemptive act in the Red Sea. Paul appeals for unity in Corinth by claiming that they have all been 'baptized by one Spirit into one body' (1 Cor. 12.13). The peculiar practice of conducting vicarious baptisms on behalf of the dead (1 Cor. 15.29), as if the act were salvifically efficacious, is countered by Paul's thought in 1 Cor. 10.1-4 that baptism does not guarantee salvation. In 1 Cor. 6.11, Paul associates baptism with the salvation and transformation of believers. In 1 Corinthians baptism entails incorporation into the community of believers, it symbolizes their transference into the sphere of Christ's lordship, and it points to the reception and empowerment of the Spirit.[10] It is on 1 Corinthians 6.11 that I wish to concentrate. In 1 Corinthians 6.1-8 Paul deals with the issue of lawsuits among the Corinthian church and then catalogues a list of vices that prevent entrance into the kingdom (1 Cor. 6.9-10). After his vice list (adulterers, male prostitutes, drunkards, etc.), Paul adds in v. 11 'and this is what some of you were', which is then set in contrast to the rest of the verse, 'but you were washed, but you were sanctified, but you were justified in the name of the Lord Jesus Christ and in the Spirit of our God'. Paul sharply contrasts[11] the former pagan lifestyle and the current carnal conduct of the Corinthians with the saving power of God that has been experienced by them. Their behaviour is singularly inappropriate and unfitting for those whose identity is now bound up with Christ (cf. 1 Cor. 6.15-18) since they

---

[8] It is disputed how the participles (going, baptizing, and teaching) relate to the main verb 'make disciples' (μαθητεύσατε): (a) make disciples by going, baptizing and teaching, or (b) go and make disciples by baptizing and teaching. It seems that 'going' (πορευθέντες) is coordinate with 'make disciples' (μαθητεύσατε) instead of subordinate (i.e. 'Therefore, as you are going, make disciples...'), nonetheless, 'going' is still implied as the presupposition to baptizing and teaching and the means by which the ἔθνη ('Gentiles') are reached.

[9] John P. Meier, *Matthew* (New Testament Message; Wilmington, DE: Michael Glazier, 1980), p. 372.

[10] Victor Paul Furnish, *The Theology of the First Letter to the Corinthians* (New Testament Theology; Cambridge: Cambridge University Press, 1999), pp. 92-93.

[11] Hence the repeated use of the strong adversative ἀλλά ('but').

have been cleansed of their sins ('washed'), set apart for holiness ('sanctified'), and God's verdict against them has been transformed into God's verdict for them ('justified'). What creates this reality is three things. (1) Faith is implied on two fronts. First, the verb ἀπολούομαι is in the middle voice and may be reflexive, i.e., 'I wash myself', and refer to the conscious act of an adult believer who decides to be baptized. Second, Paul mentions justification and for Paul this is always by faith (e.g., Gal. 2.15–3.28; Rom. 3.20–5.1; 9.30–10.15). (2) Baptism is signified by the reference to 'the name of the Lord Jesus Christ' which was a technical term used in baptism (Acts 2.38; 10.48; 22.16; probably equivalent to 'baptized into Christ' in Rom. 6.3 and Gal. 3.27).[12] But the phrase refers to more than baptism and also suggests that the whole work of God in the Corinthians depends on Jesus Christ and their relation to him.[13] (3) The 'Spirit of our God' makes a further reference to the pneumatic power that cleansed, sanctified, and justified the Corinthians. The mention of 'Spirit' might relate to the gift of the Spirit in conjunction with baptism (whether before, at, or after baptism is not stated) and the sanctifying work of the Spirit in the life of the believer (Rom. 7.6; 8.1-14; Gal. 5.22-25; Eph. 4.30-31; 2 Thess. 2.13; 2 Tim. 1.7). Barrett contends that in 1 Corinthians 6.11, Paul is referring to the moral effects of conversion sealed in baptism and Furnish similarly emphasizes that baptism does not mediate God's saving power or initiate one's acceptance of the gospel.[14] While this may be true, it can obscure the reality that for Paul, faith, baptism and the work of the Spirit are all intrinsically part of the one saving event whereby a person is transferred from the old age to the new age. Baptism is no mere seal and is properly related to the saving and transforming work of God.

A final text that I wish to overview is 1 Peter 3.20-22:

> [Those] who disobeyed long ago when God waited patiently in the days of Noah while the ark was being built. In it only a few people, eight souls in all, were saved through water, and this water symbolizes baptism that now saves you also—not the removal of dirt from the flesh but the pledge of a good conscience toward God, through the resurrection of Jesus Christ, who has gone into heaven and is at God's right hand—with angels, authorities and powers in submission to him.

The unit contained in 1 Peter 3.19-22, including the reference to Jesus preaching to the 'spirits in prison', is among the most disputed portions of 1 Peter. The flow of thought is that Peter is referring to the flood of Genesis 6–8 as corresponding to or prefiguring Christian baptism (ἀντίτυπος). But what is the link between 'then' (ποτέ) and 'now' (νῦν) in vv. 20-21? It is possible that both waters are salvific so

---

[12] In 1 Cor. 1.12-17 Paul lampoons the idea of being 'baptized into the name of Paul' and in 1 Cor. 10.2 he refers to the Israelites as being 'baptized into Moses'. This confirms the link of baptism and a named patron/saviour.

[13] C.K. Barrett, *The First Epistle to the Corinthians* (Black's New Testament Commentaries; London: A&C Black, 2nd edn, 1971), pp. 142-43.

[14] Barrett, *First Epistle to the Corinthians*, p. 142; Furnish, *First Letter to the Corinthians*, pp. 93-94.

that baptism saves in the same way as the waters carried the ark of Noah and his family.¹⁵ But that is unlikely since the waters brought judgment and death, not salvation. Thus the water of Noah is contrasted rather than correlated with the water of baptism, although both lead to the same effect: salvation. The link is probably in the theme of judgment since the flood waters brought God's judgment and Christians are saved by being baptized into Christ's death (cf. Rom. 6.3). Christ's death being the moment when he bore our sins, underwent God's wrath, and was punished vicariously on the believer's behalf (cf. 1 Pet. 2.24; 3.18). This implies that salvation comes only through judgment.

More difficult to interpret is the following phrase detailing how baptism saves, 'not the removal of dirt from the flesh but the pledge of a good conscience toward God'. Some commentators think that the 'removal of dirt from the flesh' refers to a spiritual cleansing of putting off the evil impulses (cf. 1 Pet. 2.1; Col. 3.8-9; Eph. 4.22). This would have Peter saying that baptism does not effect an inward cleansing.¹⁶ A more likely connection is a contrast between 'mere' water and the reality that stands behind the waters of baptism. Peter is saying that baptism is more than having a bath and is more than wiping off the dirt from one's flesh. This is hardly 'banal'¹⁷ but sets the contrast in terms of substance and effect rather than an interiorizing of the idea of cleansing and then negating it. But how does baptism save? The way that baptism saves, in contrast to a mere bath, is explicated as a 'pledge/appeal to God out of a good conscience' and 'through the resurrection of Jesus Christ'. Baptism is not salvific of itself but it points to something beyond the waters, viz., one's 'pledge', 'appeal', or 'resolution' to God out of a good conscience. In other words, baptism saves because it marks the responsive act towards God to yield to him in loyalty and obedience. That makes good sense since 1 Peter has much to say about conversion (1.18-25; 2.3, 9-10, 24-25). Baptism is the candidate's response to questions of whether he or she has committed themself wholly to God.¹⁸ Furthermore, the human response to God is contingent upon the objective grounds of salvation which are spelled out in terms of Jesus Christ's resurrection (cf. 1 Pet. 1.3). The power of baptism is the resurrection of Christ.¹⁹ Thus, baptism is not a ritual that imparts salvation, but it is no mere 'bath' either. Baptism pictorializes our salvation by symbolizing in the water the judgment we

---

¹⁵ That would involve taking the relative pronoun ὅ ('which') of v. 21 as relating back to ὕδατος ('water'). While grammatically possible, the contrast is more of agency since Noah and the eight were saved διά ('through') the waters as believers are saved 'through' (διά) the resurrection of Jesus Christ.

¹⁶ Cf., e.g., J. Ramsay Michaels, *1 Peter* (WBC, 49; Waco, TX: Word, 1988), pp. 216-17.

¹⁷ Michaels, *1 Peter*, p. 216.

¹⁸ Peter H. Davids, *The First Epistle of Peter* (New International Commenatry on the New Testament; Grand Rapids, MI: Eerdmans, 1990), p. 145; Beasley-Murray, *Baptism*, p. 261.

¹⁹ Beasley-Murray, *Baptism*, p. 261.

have been plunged into, it announces our pledge to God in our choice to enter the waters, and our rising from the water speaks of union with Christ in his resurrection.

In sum, in so far as baptism is an act of faith, a means of incorporation into the church, a symbolic enactment of our dying and rising with Christ, and the consummation of our conversion, baptism can be said to be an effective symbol of salvation and has a sanctifying effect upon the believer—it is a sacred act.

Communion: Eating Means Believing and Belonging

I contend that the usual Baptist expression of the Lord's supper consists of ministers acting as if they are dispensing a sacrament and yet are at pains to stress that they are doing nothing that has any sacral benefits. In other words, the Lord's supper has all the form and regalia of a full-blown pre-Reformation sacramental service but without actually attaching to itself any sacral significance. While Baptists might believe in the 'real absence of Christ' from the elements they still continue their communion service as if they were handing out tiny pieces of Christ's flesh and drops of his blood. The Baptist practice of communion looks a lot like a bunch of hurried deacons dispensing edible post-it notes to remind Christians that Christ died for them, but without ever putting us in deeper communion with Christ or with each other. We have what looks like a sacramental service but with no sacrament on offer. What is wrong with this scenario?

For 2,000 years one of the most visible emblems of historical Christianity is that believers have ordinarily met together to share a meal celebrating the death and resurrection of Jesus Christ, varyingly called the breaking of bread, communion, the Lord's table, Lord's supper, an *agape* feast, eucharist or mass. But to be blunt in most Baptist churches where I see the Lord's supper enacted it seems to be little more than an intermission prior to the sermon. It is tragic that one of the most powerful and poignant symbols of the gospel is often performed in a manner so austere and orchestrated but without capturing the magnificence of the moment whereby the body of Christ comes together to remember the passion and glory of Jesus Christ. One should not come away from communion with feelings of melancholy after hearing a short five-minute 'guilt-trip' sermonette and receiving an economy size piece of bread (that doesn't taste anything like bread) and an overly sweet drop of grape juice (that invokes all manner of face expressions once swallowed). Once this necessary digression in the service is over, one is able to return to the more regular components of Sunday worship, namely, singing and sermon.

I believe that the way we do communion in contemporary Baptist churches appears to be a hangover from the days of pre-Reformation sacramental theology that never really caught up to the Reformation. I cannot imagine anyone in the earliest church performing communion proximate to the way that it is often done in many Baptist churches. Robert Jewett states this with even greater clarity:

The purely symbolic meal of modern Christianity, restricted to a bit of bread and a sip of wine or juice, is tacitly presupposed for the early church, an assumption so preposterous that it is never articulated or acknowledged.[20]

When the early Christians met together they shared a meal, not just a crumb of bread and a drop of juice accompanied by a habitual recitation of 1 Corinthians 11.23-29. The New Testament knows of no distinction between a communal *agape* (love-feast) and the *eucharist* (sacramental/memorial meal).[21] Communion should be a meal, but why? There are several reasons.

First, food tells a story. A birthday party includes the strange ritual (or at least strange to outsiders) of setting a cake on fire with candles to commemorate the birth anniversary of someone who is a year older. A wedding cake with two figurines on top and the accompanying festivities celebrates the union of man and woman together in life-long partnership. The Jewish Passover told the story of the exodus, God's great act of redemption from Egypt, remembering what God had done for them and looking forward to what God would do again in a new exodus. The various feasts like Booths or Pentecost celebrated God's continuing provisions and blessings for the people. In fact, in the Old Testament the future salvation of Israel could be imagined as a great banquet hosted by the Patriarchs to which even the nations are invited (e.g., Isa. 25.6; cf. Ezek. 39.17-28; Joel 2.24-28). Jesus used this same image in Matthew 8.11 (cf. Lk. 13.28-29), 'I tell you, many will come from east and west and will eat with Abraham and Isaac and Jacob in the kingdom of heaven.' The patriarchal banquet was symbolic for God's great act of vindication which God's people would experience in the future. John the Seer picks up this same imagery when he refers to the 'wedding supper of the Lamb' (Rev. 19.1-10) that awaits the faithful and the martyrs who enter the world to come. Thus, when Jesus instituted his own meal at the Last Supper he was telling a story about God, God's kingdom, God's people and God's Messiah. The long awaited act of redemption, the much hoped for new exodus, and the anticipated new covenant would be fulfilled in his death and resurrection. The Jesus-meal tells a story that we are invited to listen to and even participate in. It is the story of God's people, the redeemed and the renewed children of Abraham, who come together to encourage one another in following Christ and to pursue the task of heralding the gospel of Jesus Christ. As Tom Wright puts it, 'The question for us must be: how can we, today, get in on this story? How can we understand this remarkable gift of God and use it properly? How can we make the best of it?'[22]

Second, meals indicate boundaries and create identity.[23] If all of your friends are invited to a party and you are not invited, you cannot help but feel a little rejected.

---

[20] Robert Jewett, 'Tenement Churches and Pauline Love Feasts', *Quarterly Review* 14 (1994), p. 44.

[21] Richard B. Hays, *First Corinthians* (Louisville, KY: John Knox, 1997), p. 193.

[22] Tom Wright, *The Meal Jesus Gave Us: Understanding Holy Communion* (Louisville, KY: Westminster/John Knox, 2002), p. 34.

[23] Cf. Grenz, 'Community Acts', pp. 84-89.

Invitations to share food, to come to a party, and attend certain festivities indicate one's membership within a certain social circle. In the Jewish world, Passover was only for those who had been circumcised and were members of Israel. The Pharisees formed dining fellowships where they could eat with other Jews who observed identical purity scruples and shared their vision for the renewal of Israel through a strict regime of purity observance on a scale normally reserved only for priests.[24] The Pharisees perhaps shared the view of the later rabbi's whereby if Israel would keep two Sabbaths then the Messiah would come. To hasten the day, Israel must keep herself pure and insulated from 'sinners', that is Gentiles and Jews who do not obey the commandments properly. The Qumranites had their own distinctive community meals that, in their mind, operated to demarcate them from Gentiles and other Jews, and defined themselves as the true keepers of the covenant.[25] Then along comes Jesus proclaiming the kingdom of God, carrying out a ministry of exorcisms and healing and dining openly with sinners (Lk. 7.31-35/Mt. 11.16-19; Mk 2.15-17; 14.3; Lk. 15.2; 19.1-10). Jesus shows no fear of impurity or contamination by associating with such people and he operates with a perspective whereby holiness rather than impurity is a contagion.[26] Resultantly Jesus is called 'a glutton and a drunkard, a friend of tax collectors and sinners' (Lk. 7.34). The parables of Luke 15 (lost sheep, lost coin, lost son) are told as a parabolic defence of Jesus' habit of accepting and eating with sinners (e.g., Lk. 15.1-2). Table-fellowship with Jesus is an expression of the outrageous depths of the grace of God. The only requirement to sit at Jesus' table is faith in him as God's prophetic envoy. In fact, there is to be a great reversal and those who recline with Jesus will enter the kingdom while those who think themselves assured of a place in the world to come will find themselves on the outside (e.g., Mt. 8.11-12/Lk. 13.28-29; Lk. 14.16-24). Jesus was, to the disgust of opponents, flouting and redefining the boundaries of covenant identity. As I have argued elsewhere,

> The subversive element of Jesus' praxis is that he is celebrating the messianic banquet in advance and celebrating it with the wrong people. Jesus' action in 'reclining' with sinners was much like serving the figurative *hors d'oeuvres* of the messianic feast and foreshadowing exactly who would be vindicated in the renewed Israel that he was creating around himself. This coheres with the statement found in Matthew: 'Truly I tell you, the tax collectors and the prostitutes are going into the kingdom of God ahead of you' (Mt. 21.31). Jesus conceived of his banquet partners as entrants into the future kingdom.[27]

---

[24] *Jub.* 22.16; Mk 7.1-5; *m.Hag.* 2.5-3.3.
[25] 1QS 5.13; 6.13-23; CD 10.10-13; 12.16-18; 4QMMT B; 4Q274; 4Q394 frags. 3-7; see about the Essenes in general Josephus, *War* 2.129-33, 138-39, 143.
[26] Cf. Craig Blomberg, *Contagious Holiness: Jesus' Meals with Sinners* (New Studies in Biblical Theology; Downers Grove, IL: IVP, 2005).
[27] Michael F. Bird, *Jesus and the Origins of the Gentile Mission* (Library of New Testament Studies, 331; London: T&T Clark, 2006), p. 105.

This is why the biggest debates in the early church were not about the ordination of women, were not about worship music, were not about the rapture, but were about food and fellowship. A cursory reading of Acts 15, 1 Corinthians 8–10, Galatians 2 and Romans 14–15 shows that food was the catalyst for various disputes and divisions; in a nutshell, what type of food and who can eat the food? The issue of food in the early church was related to the question of whether or not Gentiles have to become Jews in order to become a Christian (circumcision) and do they have to live like Jews in order to remain in fellowship with Jewish Christians (dietary laws)? This is why Paul reacts with such rancor against Peter in Galatians 2.11-14. Whereas Peter previously ate openly with Gentiles, when 'certain men from James arrived' he withdrew. The withdrawal meant that Gentiles were no longer regarded as equal participants and would have to judaize (i.e., convert to Judaism or at least follow certain Jewish customs) if they were to be equal membership in Christian fellowship. Paul's response in Galatians 2.15-21 is not a tirade against legalism, but constitutes a robust case that justification by faith entails fellowship by faith for Jews and Gentiles. Those whom God has justified, both Jew and Gentile, belong at the one fellowship table.[28]

To summarize so far, the Jesus-meal or communion tells a story, namely, that God's saving purposes have been revealed in the faithfulness, death, and resurrection of Jesus Christ. Additionally, this meal identifies the people of God and it proclaims quite visibly their κοινωνία or partnership with one another and it is a partnership of equals. Eating together as a body reminds us that we are the body of Christ and that Christ's own body was broken for us and his blood was shed for us. This meal binds us together in intimate fellowship and affirms that what unites us is ultimately stronger than anything that might separate us. This is not something that I find readily apparent in the crumb of bread and drop of juice served up in communion in most Baptist churches. In fact, I think this kind of theology is wholly lacking precisely because we conduct communion in this microscopic form as if the minister was imparting grace to us through the crumb of bread and drop of juice. Instead, a communal meal that is marinated in scripture, sautéed in worship, and garnished with the imagery of Christ (artistic, iconic, poetic, liturgical and even cinematic) is more likely to remind us of what God has done, what God is doing, and what God will do in his time.

But there's more to think about. What does communion actually achieve and what makes it sacred? The answer I think is apparent in 1 Corinthians 10–11 and John 6. In 1 Corinthians 10, Paul is using the exodus and wilderness narratives from the Pentateuch in order to warn the Corinthians of the serious offence posed by idolatry. In support of this point he appeals to the practice of the Lord's supper in 1 Corinthians 10.15-22.

---

[28] See further Michael F. Bird, *The Saving Righteousness of God: Studies in Paul, Justification and the New Perspective* (Paternoster Biblical Monographs; Milton Keynes: Paternoster, 2007).

I speak as to sensible people; judge for yourselves what I say. The cup of blessing that we bless, is it not a *participation* in the blood of Christ? The bread that we break, is it not a *participation* in the body of Christ? Because there is one bread, we who are many are one body, for we all share of the one bread. Consider the people of Israel; are not those who eat the sacrifices *partners* in the altar? What do I imply then? That food sacrificed to idols is anything, or that an idol is anything? No, I imply that what pagans sacrifice, they sacrifice to demons and not to God. I do not want you to be *partners* with demons. You cannot drink the cup of the Lord and the cup of demons. You cannot partake of the table of the Lord and the table of demons. Or are we provoking the Lord to jealousy? Are we stronger than he?

We must preface our remarks here by noting that Paul's immediate point is a warning against idolatry rather than offering a theology of the Lord's supper. Paul makes a comparison between three different meals: the Lord's supper (vv. 16-17), Jewish meals in association with the Jerusalem cultus (v. 18), and meals connected to pagan worship (vv. 19-21). Paul's point is that each meal creates a type of relation between the participant and the deity being honoured. This relationship is described in terms of κοινωνία/κοινωνός, which can be translated as 'fellowship', 'partnership', 'sharing' or even 'participation'.[29] Paul's adoption of the word is not a direct importation from secular usage in the sense of a society of brothers (e.g., Aristotle, *Ethica Eududemia* 7, 10), but something which refers strictly to a relationship of faith to Christ and Christians (1 Cor. 1.9; 2 Cor. 13.14; Gal. 2.9; Phil. 1.5; Philem. 6) and it results in a generous sharing of spiritual and physical blessings.[30] Those who offer sacrifices in the temple of Yahweh in Jerusalem also partake of them and have fellowship with Yahweh (see Dt. 14.22-26). Although idols are religious non-entities, to partake of a pagan meal in a pagan temple is to have fellowship with the deity worshipped who is in reality a demon. That is why pagan festive meals are to be strenuously avoided. On the Lord's supper, the participation in the blood and body of Christ is not achieved by some mysterious ingestion of the elements as if the bread and cup was the 'Lord', but rather the meal brings the participant into fellowship with Christ. This fellowship is a celebration of their life in Christ based on the arrival of the new covenant and their possession of the Spirit of Christ.[31] The corollary of this point is, according to Richard Hays, that 'all members of the community are brought together into covenant relation with Christ through eating the one bread, they become in effect one body; the eucharistic celebration creates not only κοινωνία with Christ but also unity within the community'.[32] The Lord's supper puts believers into fellowship with Christ and

---

[29] Anthony C. Thiselton, *The First Epistle to the Corinthians* (New International Greek Testament Commentary; Grand Rapids, MI: Eerdmans, 2000), p. 50, translates the word in 1 Cor. 10.14-22 as 'communal participation'.

[30] J. Schattenmann, 'κοινωνία', in Colin Brown (ed.), *New International Dictionary of New Testament Theology* (3 vols; Exeter: Paternoster Press, 1975), I, p. 639.

[31] Gordon D. Fee, *The First Epistle to the Corinthians* (New International Commentary on the New Testament; Grand Rapids, MI: Eerdmans, 1987), p. 467.

[32] Hays, *First Corinthians*, p. 167.

fellowship with one another and this latter aspect is symbolized most aptly by the fact that there is one loaf as there is one body and one Lord (cf. 1 Cor. 8.6). The theological or vertical dimension of sharing in Christ creates the horizontal or social dimension of ecclesial unity.[33] Hence, communion is sacramental in so far as it constitutes an act of fellowship with Jesus Christ and an act of fellowship among the body of Christ. This dual fellowship with Christ and with other believers is what makes communion sacred and what sets it apart from other meals. The sacrament in the Lord's supper is not in the elements, but it is the presence of Christ as the bond between the community. While the meal creates Christian fellowship its basis remains the death and resurrection of Jesus, and the celebration of his presence is what places believers in fellowship with one another. As believers share in a common meal they celebrate their fellowship with a common Lord and are thus united in fellowship as the eschatological community of the new covenant.

This brings us most naturally to 1 Corinthians 11.23-25:

> For I received from the Lord what I also passed on to you: The Lord Jesus, on the night he was betrayed, took bread, and when he had given thanks, he broke it and said, 'This is my body, which is for you; do this in remembrance of me.' In the same way, after supper he took the cup, saying, 'This cup is the new covenant in my blood; do this, whenever you drink it, in remembrance of me.' For whenever you eat this bread and drink this cup, you proclaim the Lord's death until he comes.

Following the section on propriety and modesty in worship (1 Cor. 11.2-16), Paul next rebukes the Corinthians for their abuse of the Lord's supper (1 Cor. 11.17-34). The abuses in question seem to relate to: (1) the fermenting of divisions; (2) carousing and drunken revelry; and (3) discrimination against poorer members of the church. These gatherings (συνέρχομαι) serve to divide rather than unite God's people and they foster divisions according to social and economic distinctions which are contrary to Paul's message (cf. 1 Cor. 12.13; Gal. 3.28; Col. 3.11).[34]

Paul's response in vv. 23-26 is to highlight that the meal is rooted in the tradition which he received and passed on to them (cf. 1 Cor. 15.3), he repeats the words of institution (that are in accordance with the Lucan version of the Last Supper), and states that the meal proclaims the Lord's death until he comes. Then in vv. 27-29 Paul warns against eating 'in an unworthy manner' and eating 'judgment' upon oneself. These warnings show that the Corinthians' actual practice of communion does not match the intent for which it was instituted.[35]

Several pertinent points emerge from his section. (1) There is nothing to support the idea that the elements themselves are the body and blood of Christ. The sinning against the body and blood (v. 27) and the failure to recognize the body of Christ (v.

---

[33] Thiselton, *First Epistle to the Corinthians*, p. 751.

[34] For a compelling social reconstruction behind Paul's remarks, see Bruce Winter, 'The Lord's Supper at Corinth: An Alternative Reconstruction', *Reformed Theological Review* 37 (1978), pp. 73-82.

[35] Fee, *First Corinthians*, p. 556; Thiselton, *First Corinthians*, p. 850.

29) is not due to a failure to recognize what the elements actually are, but a failure to recognize why the elements were given in the first place, a failure to remember what they are meant to symbolize, and a failure to observe the praxis which they are supposed to generate. One can add here that the meal assumes that Jesus' body was absent from the gathering since the meal was given as a signpost of Jesus' death in-between the resurrection and the *parousia* and was designed to proclaim Jesus' death 'until he comes', that is, in lieu of his bodily return. (2) The meal itself is a kerygmatic act. The proclamation of the Lord's death is not an additional proclamation given during the meal,[36] as much as it is the proclamation created by the elements of bread (= 'body' given 'for you') and wine (= 'blood' which instituted the new covenant with a sacrifice) in conjunction with an oral proclamation (cf. 1 Cor. 1.18-25). (3) The disruption to the community negates its capacity to embody the *cruciformed* and *anastasized* ideals to which the gospel calls them to live out.

A third passage I wish to look at is part of the 'eucharistic' discourse in John 6. To begin with, John is frequently touted as the most sacramental of the four Gospels. Many commentators detect allusions to the eucharist in John 6, baptism in John 3, and mystical union with Christ in John 15. My own perspective is that John is decidedly the most *unsacramental* book of the entire New Testament. There is no example of Jesus baptizing and there is no institution of the Lord's supper. For John, if there is any sacrament to speak of, if there is anything that gives us access to God, then it is exclusively Jesus the Word. C.K. Barrett writes, 'The incarnation was itself sacramental in that it visibly represented truth and at the same time conveyed that which it represented.'[37] According to John the proper way to approach God is not through sacrament but through faith in Jesus the Christ. The Fourth Gospel is dominated by the call to believe, the urgent need for faith, and necessity of trusting in Jesus (see, e.g., Jn 20.31). I submit that in John 6, even amidst all the so-called eucharistic echoes, that faith is still the theme that dominates. We read in Jn 6.51-58,

> 'I am the living bread that came down from heaven. If anyone eats of this bread, he will live forever. This bread is my flesh, which I will give for the life of the world.' Then the Jews began to argue sharply among themselves, 'How can this man give us his flesh to eat?' Jesus said to them, 'I tell you the truth, unless you eat the flesh of the Son of Man and drink his blood, you have no life in you. Whoever eats my flesh and drinks my blood has eternal life, and I will raise him up at the last day. For my flesh is real food and my blood is real drink. Whoever eats my flesh and drinks my blood remains in me, and I in him. Just as the living Father sent me and I live because of the Father, so the one who feeds on me will live because of me. This is the bread that came down from heaven. Your forefathers ate manna and died, but he who feeds on this bread will live forever.'

---

[36] Contra Fee, *First Corinthians*, p. 557.
[37] C.K. Barrett, *The Gospel According to St. John* (London: SPCK, 2nd edn, 1978), p. 82.

The speech is preceded by the Johannine sign of the feeding of the multitudes (6.1-15) and the nature miracle of Jesus walking on the water amidst the storm (6.16-21). The crowds then go looking for Jesus (6.22-25) and Jesus responds that their quest to find him is based on the fact that they think he is a moveable-feast (6.26). The subsequent discourse in 6.27-59 focuses on Jesus as the 'bread from heaven' and his unique role as the vivifying agent of God who imparts heavenly life to those who believe in him.

In vv. 51-58, the climax of the discourse, Jesus identifies himself as a type of heavenly manna that provides life through faith. While many commentators contend that salvation is based on two prior acts, eating and believing, this is mistaken as David Gibson comments: 'this section *binds together as identical both the thing to be eaten and the person to be believed* so that it does not speak of believing *and* eating. It depicts believing as metaphorical eating because the subject of belief is being described metaphorically'.[38] In v. 51, the flesh that Jesus gives 'for the life of the world' is not the eucharist, but his crucified flesh. Thus, 6.51 (and other passages like 3.13-15, 10.11-16, 12.24, 15.13) show that John most definitely has a theology of atonement.

John underscores the fact that Jesus gives his 'flesh' in order for us to have life and life is received by believing; that is what it means to eat Jesus' flesh and to drink Jesus' blood. Yet we must not dismiss the fact that the references to 'bread' and 'blood' would quite naturally remind John's readers of the eucharist. While John may not want his Christian readers to think that eating the eucharist is a substitute for believing, neither is he saying that the eucharist has nothing to do with believing. If one regards participation in the Lord's supper as an expression of faith then one can reasonably regard the Lord's supper as an act of feasting on Christ which becomes a metaphorical way of believing that he is the Son sent by the Father to give us life.

In sum, when the church meets to share a meal in Jesus' name their eating and drinking has several functions and effects: (1) professing their belief in Jesus Christ as the crucified and risen Lord who will return to put the world right; (2) embodying the memory of Jesus' life and death and displaying emblems of the gospel; (3) setting their own identities within the storied life of the church who is a key agent in the redemptive saga; (4) participating in the life of Christ; (5) creating solidarity with one another as joint members of the new covenant community; and (6) committing themselves to the mission of Jesus Christ. What makes communion sacramental is that it is a faith-act whereby one *believes* in the Lord Jesus Christ and one *belongs* to the body of Christ.

Conclusion

Christendom is finished and Europe, North America, and the former British colonies are now bastions of secularism and pluralism. Thus, creating churches that function

---

[38] David Gibson, 'Eating is Believing? On Midrash and the Mixing of Metaphors in John 6', *Themelios* 27 (2002), p. 10 (italics original).

as chaplains for Christendom where the nominally Christian masses arise Sunday morning and come to church so that we might convert them, baptize them, and let them participate in the Lord's supper are gone.

What do we do then? I suggest that we are to conceive of the church as a missional and displaced community that does not really fit into contemporary society rather than comprising the religious wing of modernity. Instead of inviting nominal Christians into a deeper faith, we should see ourselves as modelling an alternative way of being human before the world and heralding the good news that God was in Christ reconciling the world to himself. The church must become a menace to our pluralistic society and threaten to undermine the philosophical premises that the *pax postmoderna* is built on. The scandalous message and perplexing praxis of Christians should invoke umbrage and curiosity. Why don't you abort foetuses? Why don't you approve of gay marriages? Why do you believe that only your religion is true? The answer is not a programme, not four spiritual laws, and not seeker sensitive services; rather, the answer is a *story* and a *community*. Let me tell you how the story *really* goes: God, Adam, fall, Abraham, Israel, exile, Christ, church, and consummation. Let me show you what renewed and redeemed humanity *really* looks like: justified and Spirit-led new creations, abounding in love for one another, where there is neither Jew nor Gentile, male nor female, slave nor free, but all one in Christ Jesus. And what tools do we have that *tells the story* and *displays the community*: baptism and eucharist. That is where the postmodern pagans may come and hear, see, taste, and experience the goodness of God in word, symbol and presence among his people. That will require re-thinking the theology and actual practice of baptism and communion.

Accordingly, baptism is no mere ordinance as it marks the decisive moment of transference from the world to Christ, from darkness to light, from condemnation to righteousness and holiness. It is an effective symbol that seals our conversion and marks our empowerment with the Spirit to be obedient slaves of Jesus Christ. The public confession creates a new social reality and personal identity as one formally enters the body of Christ and counts oneself as crucified to the world and alive to God. What is sacral about baptism is that it is the place where one puts off the old way of life and the old identity so that the candidate is no longer a Jew, Gentile, British, American, Australian, Black, Hispanic, Asian, but a Christian. Identity can never again be defined exclusively in terms of race, class, gender, or nationality. After baptism the 'I' can only be used if there is a horizontal line running through it turning the 'I' into a † [cross]: I am only known as one who has been crucified with Christ (see Gal. 2.20). The Lord's supper is more than an ordinance but is sacramental because it puts us in fellowship with Christ and with the body of Christ. It might be more proper to regard the meal as an *effective symbol* since it actually creates something, viz., a relationship between the believer and Christ and secures a bond of fellowship between believers themselves. The meal tells a sacred story and creates a sacred community.

We must move away from the view that baptism and the Lord's supper are ordinances that provide only the blessing of obedience and are merely human responses to divine acts. They are sacraments *in* Christ and emblems *of* the gospel. They are divine–human acts since the Holy Spirit facilitates our participation in the reality of salvation which is symbolized by the elements and it results in real fellowship with Christ and real membership in a holy community. Baptism and the Lord's supper are a means of grace in so far as they are events where we experience God's presence and Christian fellowship in a way that we do nowhere else. The church, in the business of grace, needs to make sure that its theology and praxis more readily promote the grace of God by proclaiming the gospel in word and in effective symbols. The result should hopefully be a church that is filled with the life of the Spirit, nurtured on the gospel, and also prepared to set forth a testimony to the world about God's story and God's people.

CHAPTER 6

Ambiguous Genitives, Pauline Baptism and Roman *Insulae*: Resources from Romans to Support *Pushing the Boundaries of Unity*[1]

Sean F. Winter

I arrived as a new student at Bristol Baptist College in the autumn of 1986. Very soon into the new academic year we were invited as a student body to read, reflect upon and respond to the recently published World Council of Churches' report, *Baptism, Eucharist and Ministry*.[2] I can remember neither the content nor the conclusion of our conversations, only that for me the process formed an initial exposure to ecumenical dialogue that continues to shape my commitment to the ecumenical journey. What I do remember is that, later that year, the student body watched a television documentary celebrating the tercentenary of the college and offering an overview of the Baptist movement. One of our college tutors was interviewed on the programme and was asked why Baptists reject the practice of infant baptism found within almost every other mainstream Christian denomination. The answer came quickly: 'one might say it is because Baptists have read the New Testament'. The quip elicited a raucous cheer from the student body, for despite our engagement in ecumenical dialogue we knew, as all Baptists know deep down, that the main reason why Baptists of past and present generations do not recognize the validity of paedobaptism is relatively simple: the clear witness of scripture forbids us from doing so.

I have often heard the same argument made since. Although many Baptists in the United Kingdom are committed to the ecumenical journey, to our ecumenical

---

[1] An earlier version of this essay was delivered as a paper to the 'Baptists Doing Theology in Context' Consultation at Luther King House, Manchester in August 2006. I am grateful to those who contributed to the discussion on that occasion, especially to the Rev. Professor Paul Fiddes.

[2] *Baptism, Eucharist and Ministry* (Faith and Order Paper, 111; Geneva: World Council of Churches, 1982). The Principal of Bristol Baptist College at that time, the Rev. Dr Morris West had played a significant role in the drafting of *BEM*. See Keith Clements, 'The Larger Context: Morris West, Servant of World Ecumenism', in J.H.Y. Briggs and Faith Bowers (eds), *Baptists Together: Papers Published in Memory of W.M.S. West, JP, MA, DTheol, Hon LLD 1922–1999* (Didcot: Baptist Historical Society, 2000), pp. 19-29.

partners and to ecumenical dialogue, when push comes to shove they cannot recognize or affirm the validity of infant baptism because they believe that they possess no biblical warrant to support such an affirmation.[3] I confess, however, that I grow increasingly uneasy about such appeals. The claim that scripture speaks unambiguously on this matter leads to the implicit conclusion (or is perhaps based on the unstated assumption) that those who practice infant baptism have really not understood the plain witness of scripture. For me this is problematic methodologically, in so far as it fails to give sufficient weight to the significance of interpretive diversity within ecumenical dialogue.[4] However, I also think that such claims fail to do justice to the complexity of the biblical texts themselves, not least the writings of Paul whose understanding of the gospel and of the relation between baptism and faith has shaped subsequent reflection so significantly. Furthermore, biblical scholarship moves on, and generates new ways of seeing old texts, such that old certainties become less clear and new understanding is made possible.

In what follows I hope to show that Paul's letter to the churches in Rome might offer Baptists biblical resources to support a reconsideration of their attitudes to the practice of infant baptism. I argue that these exegetical resources lend weight to the appeal for Baptists to recognize some validity in infant baptism. Typically the case for such recognition is made on the basis of our contextual location (we now live in an 'ecumenical paradigm'); the need for appropriate pastoral welcome of those who are our brothers and sisters in Christ; or historical recovery of neglected aspects of our own Baptist history and tradition.[5] For the case to be convincing to Baptists, it

---

[3] For the general point, see *Believing and Being Baptized: Baptism, So-called Rebaptism and Children in the Church: A Discussion Document by the Doctrine and Worship Committee of the Baptist Union of Great Britain* (Didcot: The Baptist Union of Great Britain, 1996), pp. 13-16. The most recent example of an explicit appeal to scripture occurred during the meetings of the Baptist Union of Great Britain Council in November 2006. In a debate about the Baptist–Church of England report *Pushing at the Boundaries of Unity: Anglicans and Baptists in Conversation* (London: Church House, 2005), the Council declined to 'welcome' the report, but chose instead to 'receive' it. The argument that led the majority to vote this way was the simple point that, while as committed ecumenical participants we would *like* to welcome such a report, the witness of scripture prevents us from doing so. The present author was Moderator of the Council debate on that occasion.

[4] I explore some of the issues surrounding interpretive diversity in Sean F. Winter, *More Light and Truth?: Biblical Interpretation in Covenantal Perspective* (The Whitley Lecture 2007; Oxford: Whitley Publications, 2007). On the question of method in ecumenical dialogue see G.R. Evans, *Method in Ecumenical Theology* (Cambridge: Cambridge University Press, 1996); and Peter Bouteneff and Dagmar Heller (eds) *Interpreting Together: Essays in Hermeneutics* (Faith and Order Paper, 189; Geneva: World Council of Churches Publications, 2001).

[5] For the first two strategies see *Believing and Being Baptized*, p. 13: 'Today...there is a growing realization that we need to be more sensitive to the way other Christians feel about [re-baptism] and to the hurt that can unwittingly be caused by Baptist practice. Such awareness belongs to living and working in relationship with others.' The latter

will also need to show how it does justice to neglected aspects of those scriptural texts that have traditionally formed the basis for central Baptist convictions.[6]

I intend to explore three main issues that arise out of the study of Romans. The first concerns the nature of Paul's gospel and the relation between divine action and human response as these come to expression in the key phrases and structural arrangement of the letter's opening chapters. The second looks in more detail at Romans 6, a text that is unavoidable with regard to this issue, but that, when set within its context, perhaps says more about baptism than many Baptists have been prepared to admit. The final focus is on the possible contextual situation of Romans as this comes to light in chapters 14–15: how might Paul's teaching to a church divided on ethnic lines, relate to the contemporary church in its theological divisions?

All three topics are, of course, complex and deserving of separate treatment, not least as a way of doing justice to the scholarly literature on Romans and Paul's theology. Here, I engage with the literature to the extent that it clarifies the exegetical issues and thus brings into view the possibility of Baptists reading scripture differently in relation to the issue of infant baptism.

Ambiguous Genitives: The Pivot of Paul's Gospel

It is commonly assumed that the argument of Romans begins with an identification and description of the human condition. In Romans 1.18–3.19, Paul attempts to demonstrate that Jew and Gentile alike are under the power of sin, and that in the case of the Jew, the covenantal gifts of election and Torah provide no escape. This way of reading these opening verses (as an articulation of a basic anthropological 'problem') leads to the inevitable reading of what follows, not least the crucial Romans 3.21-26, as Paul's disclosure of the soteriological 'solution' to that

---

argument from history can be found in Paul S. Fiddes, *Tracks and Traces: Baptist Identity in Church and Theology* (Studies in Baptist History and Thought, 13; Carlisle: Paternoster Press, 2003), pp. 175-85, relating to the issue of open communion among early Baptists.

[6] In following this exegetical line of enquiry, I am developing the insights offered in *Pushing at the Boundaries*, pp. 36-38. There the focus is on the meaning of the phrase 'one baptism'/ἐν βάπτισμα in Ephesians 4.5. Suggesting that Baptists should refuse the all too easy assumption that 'one baptism' equates to 'common baptism' the report identifies the phrase with the 'one baptism' of Jesus himself in his life, death and resurrection (Mk 10.38-39). This christological reading (which does justice to the structural parallel between Eph. 4.5 and 5.26) leads to three conclusions. First, baptism is 'as unrepeatable as the drama of salvation'. Secondly, in baptism the initiative is taken by God. Thirdly, baptism is to be understood as a relational act (between God in Christ and the believer) and thus a communal act (the believer's response of faith is a faith shared by the 'body' into which the believer is baptized). For Baptists, it is crucial to note that the chapter argues that believers' baptism gives fuller expression to these implications of the phrase 'one baptism' than the baptism of infants. We shall return to this point below.

problem. This solution, however, needs to be appropriated by human beings under the power of sin, and so Paul's emphasis is, finally and fundamentally, on the need for the human response of faith. Salvation or justification comes through such faith—the faith of the believer in Jesus Christ—and not through works (whether Paul's phrase be understood incorrectly as human works in general, or correctly as obedience to Torah as the key mark of covenantal identity).

This understanding of the central idea of Paul's gospel, as we encounter it in Romans (and earlier in Galatians), is often summarized, and now often dismissed, with a single epithet: 'Lutheran'. Whether or not such a summary does justice to the complexity of Luther's thought, it is now clear to many New Testament scholars that such a reading of Romans fails to do justice to the original intention and context of Paul's thought.[7] Scholars who espouse the so-called 'New Perspective on Paul' offer a welcome corrective to earlier misconstruals of the nature of Judaism and Jewish covenantal theology, and provide an important reminder that Paul's teaching about justification by faith alone was forged in a specific set of contextual circumstances.[8]

What is interesting about the New Perspective, however, is that for many of its proponents, it leaves intact the idea that Paul's gospel offers a soteriology in which justification (now re-interpreted as membership of the covenant community as well as eschatological acquittal) is secured through the human response of faith. While not underestimating the fact that the gospel is the manifestation of God's faithfulness in the death and resurrection of Jesus the Messiah, nonetheless the key, the pivot on which the gospel moves, is faith, understood as something that human beings do in response to what God has done in Christ.

So here, in the interpretation of Romans old and new, we encounter the whole question of the interplay between grace and faith: what God has done and is doing, and what human beings do to receive/appropriate what God has done (the human 'yes' in response to God's 'yes'). Many scholars within the old and new perspectives, while recognizing that Paul is concerned with both aspects, read Paul's gospel as innovative precisely at the point that he insists on a certain kind of human response as that which brings justification: they must believe rather than rely on their status as God's covenant people or their law-observance. For many Baptists, it is, I suggest, precisely this understanding of Paul's gospel that enables them to understand baptism as the testimony to, and outward manifestation of what James

---

[7] For a helpful summary of the constituent elements of the 'Lutheran' interpretation of Paul, see Francis Watson, *Paul, Judaism and the Gentiles: Beyond the New Perspective* (Grand Rapids, MI: Eerdmans, rev. and expanded edn, 2007), pp. 28-40. For the idea that Lutheran heritage may in fact distort or neglect aspects of Luther's own thought, see Carl Braaten and Robert Jenson (eds), *Union With Christ: The New Finnish Interpretation of Luther* (Grand Rapids, MI: Eerdmans, 1998).

[8] For a seminal collection of essays exploring these ideas, see James D.G. Dunn, *The New Perspective on Paul* (Grand Rapids, MI: Eerdmans, rev. edn, 2008).

Dunn calls 'a relation of utter dependence, of unconditional trust'.[9] Believers' baptism is true baptism because human belief is crucial.

Before modifying this reading of Paul's gospel, I want to introduce an important caveat. Nothing that follows is meant to suggest that Paul has no room in his gospel for human belief. It is crucial for him, and thus for us in our understanding of the nature of baptism. But I do want to suggest that in the interplay between divine grace and human faith, Paul's gospel at crucial points lays greater emphasis on the former aspect than the conventional interpretation allows. In particular, I suggest that two ambiguous genitival phrases in Romans should be read as subjective genitives, thus providing us with a reading of Paul that insists that what God reveals in the gospel is not just that human beings are made righteous through faith (the revelation of what human beings must now do to be saved); rather the gospel reveals what God has done. In short, the pivot of Paul's gospel is the claim that God's saving power is revealed in the faithful obedience of Jesus Christ. We can briefly outline the arguments in favour of reading Paul's language in this way, and then survey the main texts.

The Righteousness of God/ἡ δικαιοσύνη θεοῦ

The alternative possible renderings of the ambiguous genitive phrase 'righteousness of God' were well described in an appendix to E.P. Sanders' influential *Paul and Palestinian Judaism*:

> Is *dikaiosynê theou* to be understood as an objective genitive, i.e. the righteousness given to man by God and which counts before God? Or are we to interpret the construction as a subjective genitive, referring to God's own righteousness.[10]

In broad terms, Luther, and much of Protestant Christianity after him, took the phrase as an objective genitive. Paul's gospel consists in the revelation that human righteousness is a gift from God appropriated through faith, so Romans 1.16-17. This interpretation is clearly consistent with an understanding of the gospel that places the human condition at its centre.

However, since Ernst Käsemann's programmatic essay, based on a lecture given in Oxford in 1961, it is clear to many New Testament scholars that the phrase in its original context refers to God's own righteousness, understood as his saving power

---

[9] James D.G. Dunn, *The Theology of Paul the Apostle* (Edinburgh: T&T Clark, 1998), p. 379.

[10] Manfred T. Brauch, 'Perspectives on "God's Righteousness" in Recent German Discussion', appendix in E.P. Sanders, *Paul and Palestinian Judaism: A Comparison of Patterns of Religion* (London: SCM Press, 1977), p. 524.

to establish the covenant, and deliver Israel.[11] The phrase describes what God does as God. It is

> God's sovereignty over the world revealing itself eschatologically in Jesus...the rightful power with which God makes his cause to triumph in the world which has fallen away from him and which yet, as creation, is his inviolable possession.[12]

Others have gone on to show in more detail how the Old Testament and other Second Temple Jewish sources support this interpretation.[13] For our purposes it is important to note that the focus on God's action does not exclude all reference to human status; righteousness language is inherently relational and God's saving power is directed towards creation, inviting, even demanding, appropriate transformation and response. Yet, it is God's righteousness which effects this transformation: to see this is to see the central focus of Paul's gospel.

The Faith(fullness) of Christ/ πίστις Χριστοῦ

The phrase πίστις Χριστοῦ is currently at the centre of a major debate within Pauline studies. While many scholars continue to assert that it is an objective genitive referring to human faith in Jesus Christ, a significant number are convinced that Paul's language (and by implication his gospel) gives a central role to Christ's own faithfulness understood primarily in terms of his obedience to death.[14] Briefly put, the arguments in favour of such an interpretation are: (a) that this is the natural reading of the phrase in the light of Romans 4.16 which speaks of the πίστις Ἀβραάμ, that is, Abraham's own faith; (b) the meaning of πίστις in the ancient world clearly incorporates the notion of 'faithfulness' understood as loyalty, trust and obedience;[15] (c) when Paul uses the phrase it is immediately followed by a verbal

---

[11] Ernst Käsemann, '"The Righteousness of God" in Paul', in Ernst Käsemann, *New Testament Questions of Today* (London: SCM Press, 1969), pp. 168-82.

[12] Käsemann, '"The Righteousness of God"', p. 180.

[13] See, for example, the helpful overview in N.T. Wright, 'The Letter to the Romans: Introduction, Commentary, and Reflections', in *New Interpreters Bible: Volume X* (Nashville, TN: Abingdon Press, 2002), pp. 398-405.

[14] The seminal work is that of Richard Hays, *The Faith of Jesus Christ: The Narrative Substructure of Galatians 3:1–4:11* (Grand Rapids, MI: Eerdmans, 2nd edn, 2002). The issues were helpfully clarified at presentations made by Hays and James Dunn at the 1991 meetings of the Society for Biblical Literature: see E. Elizabeth Johnson, David M. Hay (eds), *Pauline Theology*: Volume 4. *Looking Back Pressing On* (Society for Biblical Literature Symposium Series, 4; Atlanta, GA: Scholars Press, 1997), pp. 35-92, for the essays. An up to date bibliography on the topic is kept online by Mike Bird and Preston Sprinkle at http://web.infoave.net/~jwest/pxbib.pdf. Two major contributions to the debate are still awaiting publication, from Douglas Campbell (subjective genitive) and Barry Matlock (objective genitive).

[15] See especially Douglas A. Campbell, *The Quest for Paul's Gospel: A Suggested Strategy* (London: T&T Clark, 2005), pp. 178-207.

form that unambiguously refers to human belief. If πίστις Χριστοῦ is an objective genitive, then this renders Paul's language tautologous and introduces redundancy into the argument; (d) reading πίστις Χριστοῦ in this way connects it more closely with the meaning attributed above to the righteousness of God. While it is probably true that the subjective genitive reading remains a minority position within New Testament scholarship, I am convinced that it offers a more credible account of the central focus of Paul's gospel, not least as that gospel comes to expression in the argument of Romans.

The Key Texts: Romans 1.16-17; 3.21-26

In the light of the revised interpretations of these two key phrases, we can now attend briefly to their deployment at two strategic points in the argument of Romans. In Romans 1.16-17, often understood to be a programmatic summary of the central theological claims of the letter, we read these words,

> For I am not ashamed of the gospel; it is the power of God for salvation to everyone who has faith, to the Jew first and also to the Greek. For in it the righteousness of God (δικαιοσύνη θεοῦ) is revealed through faith for faith; as it is written, 'The one who is righteous will live by faith.' (NRSV)

The use of the phrase δικαιοσύνη θεοῦ in 1.17 denotes the central idea in Paul's summary of the gospel. That central idea does not focus on the question of how human beings can be made right with God, but on the question of how God's justice and covenant faithfulness are revealed in the world. While this central affirmation is clearly surrounded by references to the need for belief in response to divine action (the power of God for salvation is 'to everyone who believes'/παντὶ τῷ πιστεύοντι) it is divine action that has priority in Paul's articulation and, we must assume, ongoing proclamation of the gospel. While there is no explicit reference to Christ here within this summary, 1.3-4 has already made it clear that the gospel concerns God's Son, Jesus Christ our Lord. Furthermore, some have argued that the the references to 'faith' in 1.17 may in fact be oblique references to Christ's own faithfulness. The debated ἐκ πίστεως εἰς πίστιν might mean that God's righteousness is revealed 'from Christ's own faithfulness' and be directed towards 'human faith'.[16] Likewise, the closing scriptural citation from Habakkuk 2.4 may well be interpreted as having a christological reference.[17] From both a grammatical

---

[16] The preposition ἐκ is used regularly within the key πίστις Χριστοῦ texts: see Romans 3.26; Galatians 2.16; 3.22. The key observation is that the preposition suggests in 1.17 that πίστις is the means by which God's righteousness (as defined earlier) is made manifest in the world; it secures God's revelatory activity. The idea that it is human faith that plays this role theologically is problematic from every angle. It is much more satisfactory to read the phrase in the light of Paul's apocalyptic christology.

[17] See Richard B. Hays, *The Conversion of the Imagination: Paul as an Interpreter of Israel's Scripture* (Grand Rapids, MI: Eerdmans, 2005), pp. 119-142; and now Desta

and theological point of view, the focus of these verses is clearly on God's saving action (described as 'power' and 'righteousness') which is revealed in Christ's own 'faithfulness'. The reference to the necessary human response to God's action is an inevitable and appropriate development of these major themes in Paul's theology, but it does not constitute the central or controlling idea.

Turning to Romans 3.21-26 we find the same theological dynamics at work. There we read,

> But now, apart from law, the righteousness of God (δικαιοσύνη θεοῦ) has been disclosed, and is attested by the law and the prophets, the righteousness of God through the faithfulness of Jesus Christ (διὰ πίστεως Ἰησοῦ Χριστοῦ) for all who believe. For there is no distinction, since all have sinned and fall short of the glory of God; they are now justified by his grace as a gift, through the redemption that is in Christ Jesus, whom God put forward as a sacrifice of atonement by his blood, effective through faith. He did this to show his righteousness (τῆς δικαιοσύνης αὐτοῦ), because in his divine forbearance he had passed over the sins previously committed; it was to prove at the present time that he himself is righteous (εἰς τὸ εἶναι αὐτὸν δίκαιον) and that he justifies the one who has the faith of Jesus (τὸν ἐκ πίστεως Ἰησοῦ).[18]

Of course, the exegesis of this passage is fraught with difficulties. However, on the assumption that the subjective genitive reading of both key phrases is correct, the focus of Paul's argument here is relatively clear. God's saving righteousness is disclosed through Jesus Christ's faithful obedience, with a view to human trust in Christ's death as the manifestation of divine grace (Rom. 3.22). Human justification is established through the 'redemption that is in Christ Jesus' (Rom. 3.24). His sacrificial death is the demonstration of God's righteousness (Rom. 3.25) and God rectifies the one who shares Jesus' faith (Rom. 3.26). When read in this way, Romans 3.21-26, functions less as the soteriological 'solution' to the anthropological 'problem' that is Paul's primary concern in Romans 1.18–3.20, and more as a restatement of the central claims of Paul's apostolic proclamation.

This way of reading these crucial texts helps us to establish a fairly straightforward, but essential theological point; one that we now see has good exegetical foundations in the language and argument of Romans itself. *God's saving activity as revealed in the faithful trust and obedience of Jesus Christ makes possible the human response of faithful trust and obedience.* The gospel (and thus by implication gospel sacraments) concerns God's gracious intervention in creation through Jesus Christ for the purposes of redemption. For our purposes the

---

Heliso, *Pistis and the Righteous One: A Study of Romans 1:17 against the Background of Scripture and Second Temple Jewish Literature* (Wissenschaftliche Untersuchungen zum Neuen Testament, 2.235; Tübingen: Mohr Siebeck, 2007).

[18] I have amended the NRSV translation in the light of my reading of the phrases under discussion. While the rendering 'the one who has the faith of Jesus' is not elegant, one should probably interpret it to mean something like 'the one whose status rests on the faithful death of Jesus', so Wright, 'Letter to the Romans', p. 474.

implications of this way of reading Paul is not the simplistic observation that Paul places the emphasis on divine grace rather than human faith. This is not a case of either/or. But if the weight of Paul's gospel tilts, as it should and as even Luther knew, towards the prevenience and priority of God's gracious, salvific activity revealed in the faithful obedience of Christ then it should be possible to recognize that a baptism, in which the prevenience of grace is present but the human response of faith is less than fully present, might nonetheless be a valid, gospel, baptism. John Webster has stated that, ultimately, Christian faith is 'primarily an account of divine action' and 'only secondarily an account of the believing subject'.[19] Paul, I suspect, would have agreed and the key statements of his gospel in Romans are evidence of that agreement. It follows that, far from preventing us from attributing validity to infant baptism, a more nuanced appraisal of the nature of Paul's gospel actually provides us with a warrant for so doing.

Pauline Baptism

With a wider understanding of the nature of Paul's gospel in place, we turn our attention to the narrower issue of Paul's understanding of baptism in Romans 6. Those who deny any validity to infant baptism feel constrained to do so by scripture not just because of a misreading of Romans 1–3, but also by failing to grasp the full import of Romans 6.1-11.

In fact the two issues are related. If we read Romans 1–3 as an account of the human 'problem' and God's 'solution' then we must assume that subsequent chapters of Romans address some of the 'spin off' issues that follow on from that account. Therefore, in Romans 4, Paul selects Abraham's story as a nice Old Testament proof-text in support of the central claim of Romans 1–3: justification comes through faith and not works.[20] In Romans 5–8 Paul turns his attention to issues of sanctification. On this reading, the focus on baptism in 6.1-11 concerns the outworking of a salvation that is already fully inaugurated in the justification that comes through human faith. In short, and to use language all too commonly found on the lips of Baptists, baptism is the sign of a salvation already attained. There is every evidence, however, that such language when used to describe the role and significance of baptism, fails to do justice to the place of Romans 6 within the argument of Romans, and the nature of the language that Paul uses in these verses.

Romans 6.1-11 in Context

We have seen that traditional readings of Romans tend to understand Paul's central argument as the claim that justification comes through the human response of faith, rather than through works of the law. If this is the case then Paul has made his point

---

[19] John Webster, 'Faith', in Alister E. McGrath (ed.), *The Blackwell Encyclopedia of Modern Christian Thought* (Oxford: Blackwell, 1993), p. 210.

[20] A reading of Romans 4 which rests, among other things, on a mistranslation of 4.1. For the better interpretation see Hays, *Conversion of the Imagination*, pp. 61-84.

by the end of chapter 3 and everything that follows has the character of a set of semi-detached addenda to the main idea. If, however, Paul's central argument relates to the nature of God's saving action in Christ, then Romans 5–8 constitute the fullest exposition of that argument, only now with a view to describing how human beings are able to participate in it, or more accurately participate 'in Christ'. Two observations follow in relation to Paul's teaching about baptism in Romans 6. First, baptism is not something that takes place after salvation has been received, instead it is the means by which that salvation is appropriated by the believer. Secondly, we should take particular notice of the ways in which the argument in Romans 6 picks up the key ideas of Romans 5.

That preceding chapter strikes two notes that are key for our understanding. First, salvation is not, for Paul, a complete, one-off event but a process that embraces the past, present and future life of the believer. In 5.1-2 Paul, in language that alludes back to 3.21-26, indicates that past justification enables present peace and grace and secures the hope of future incorporation into God.[21] The same dynamic appears in 5.8-11. Secondly, in chapter 5 Paul moves to discuss salvation in participatory terms through his use of the Adam–Christ comparison in 5.12-21.

These two notes are played again in 6.1-11. When Paul appeals to the Roman Christians' experience of baptism (note the ἢ ἀγνοεῖτε of 6.3), he understands that baptism to be related not just to justification by faith in the past, but also the present and future dimensions of salvation. Paul's language confirms this. In baptism we *were* baptized into his death. This event leads to a transformation of behaviour such that we 'walk in newness of life'. Furthermore, our sharing in Christ's death through baptism is intimately connected to the promise of future resurrection. All of this is expressed in language that is best described as 'participatory'. Baptism is *into* the Messiah and his death (εἰς Χριστὸν Ἰησοῦν, εἰς τὸν θάνατον αὐτοῦ) and the ensuing explanation of that phrase contains a number of compound words suggesting the past, present and future identification of the baptized with Christ.[22]

The force of this language, and the clear parallels with chapter 5, strongly suggest that, for Paul, baptism is not simply an outward sign of past justification, but is the very means by which the believer participates in Christ's death and resurrection and thus passes over from the dominion of sin/death/the law/Adam to the dominion of Christ. Baptism is here understood, first and foremost, as the sacramental means of the believer's incorporation into Christ's death and resurrection, and not simply as the outward symbol of an inward and pre-existent faith.

---

[21] Of course the interpretation of Romans 5.1-2 is also a complex affair, not least in the light of textual variations. I prefer to read the indicative ἔχομεν over the hortatory subjunctive ἔχωμεν, not least because it seems to me that the past/present aspects of 5.1 are then reflected and reiterated in the use of the alliterative perfect tenses in 5.2 ἐσχήκαμεν…ἐστήκαμεν.

[22] See σύμφυτος (v. 5); συσταυρόω (v. 6); συζάω (v. 8).

Sacramental Realism

I have been arguing that, once we see that Romans is ultimately about the gospel of God's saving action in Christ, it naturally follows that Paul understands baptism to be the point at which God's action meets with human response: God does something in baptism, even as, in the act of entering the water, the believer is responding to what God has done, is doing and will do in their own life. Romans 6.3-5 are verses that are replete with the language of sacramental realism. As George Beasley-Murray notes, being baptized 'into Christ Jesus' (εἰς Χριστὸν Ἰησοῦν) is not mere shorthand for being baptized in Christ's name. It is that which enables the believer to become 'in Christ Jesus' (ἐν Χριστῷ Ἰησοῦ).[23] The experience that is described is portrayed as a real experience. Although Paul's language exhibits metaphorical characteristics (physical death and burial are not at issue) the language has, as Stanley K. Fowler notes 'much more than a pictorial significance for baptism'.[24] John E. Colwell expresses it well:

> Here again, the sacramental realism of biblical language can only be avoided through extreme special pleading: in this text...Paul is arguing from this realistic understanding of baptism rather than towards it; he is arguing on the assumption that his readers will already acknowledge the realistic and narratival significance of baptism.[25]

The location of these verses within the argument of Romans, combined with the sacramental force of Paul's language, combine to make a strong case for the notion that Pauline baptism is the means by which the believer is incorporated into Christ. In this sense it is sacramental: God's appointed means of mediating God's saving presence and action. To recognize this is, for many Baptists, to acknowledge that an over-emphasis on the absolute necessity of prior human faith is to make far too little of baptism itself. It also opens a way to affirming that in infant baptism, despite the absence of the explicit, prior faith of the child, God is at work.

Roman *Insulae*

In the discussion so far I have tried to suggest that Paul's letter to the Christians at Rome offers theological resources that, when taken seriously, might prompt Baptists to consider: (a) whether they might indeed allow for some kind of validity in infant

---

[23] G.R. Beasley-Murray, *Baptism in the New Testament* (London: Macmillan, 1962), p. 128. The connection between the two ideas is most clearly made in Galatians 3.26-28.

[24] Stanley K. Fowler, *More Than a Symbol: The British Baptist Recovery of Baptismal Sacramentalism* (Studies in Baptist History and Thought, 2; Carlisle: Paternoster Press, 2002), p. 161. As Fowler suggests, there is a deep irony in the fact that Baptists have insisted that Paul's language requires a form of baptism in which immersion should be literal/real, but where the spiritual experience is only symbolic.

[25] John E. Colwell, *Promise and Presence: An Exploration of Sacramental Theology* (Milton Keynes: Paternoster, 2005), p. 121.

baptism, in so far as it functions as a witness to the central claims of the gospel and as a sacramental action through which God's saving presence is mediated; and (b) whether Baptist ritual and practice gives sufficient weight to the theological and sacramental dimensions of baptism. Lest I be misunderstood, I am *not* arguing that Baptists should adopt the practice of infant baptism. Given the fact that baptismal practices will therefore continue to differ, we are left with the question of how we ought to treat those who differ from us on these issues.

Resources for thinking this through can also be found in Romans, specifically through attention to the possible contextual reasons for the letter's composition. Paul Fiddes has repeatedly reminded us that for some of our Baptist forebears there was a biblical imperative in relation to those from a paedobaptist tradition: namely that one should 'welcome one another just as Christ has welcomed you' (Rom. 15.7) and that those who espouse believers' baptism should be prepared to withhold judgement on those who baptize infants because 'it is before his own lord that he will be judged' (Rom. 14.4, 10-12).[26] Attention to the socio-cultural dynamics of Paul's teaching in these verses, might help us to sharpen the challenge.

Ecclesial Conflict in the Insulae *of Rome*

In a recent monograph, Philip Esler offers a convincing interpretation of the situation that lay behind Romans 14–15.[27] Paul is clearly addressing an ethnically mixed community, in which conflict over food laws has arisen. Although it is notoriously difficult to determine the identity of the 'weak' and the 'strong' (Rom. 15.1), it seems likely that the conflict developed along ethnic and possibly socio-economic lines, leading to a breakdown in relationships between different Roman house churches. Paul acknowledges the differences in theology and practice, but offers teaching which encourages genuine, reciprocal encounter with those from whom you differ. Three brief observations support this idea.

First, the Roman Christians most likely met in domestic settings, perhaps in houses, but much more probably in high-rise, overcrowded tenement apartments known as *insulae*. This social context provides the most plausible explanation for hostility and enmity between different Christian groups in the city.[28] The references to domestic servants (οἰκέται) in 14.4 and use of terms relating to the well being of the household (οἰκοδομή) in 14.19 and 15.2 confirm the suggestion.[29]

This explains, secondly, why Paul uses the verb προσλαμβάνω in 14.1 and 15.7. In context it clearly means 'take one another into your dwellings'. For Robert

---

[26] Fiddes, *Tracks and Traces*, pp. 175-85.
[27] Philip F. Esler, *Conflict and Identity in Romans: The Social Setting of Paul's Letter* (Minneapolis, MN: Fortress Press, 2003), pp. 339-56.
[28] Esler, *Conflict and Identity*, pp. 107-108.
[29] Paul's greetings in Romans 16 also betray the essentially domestic context for early Christian communities in Rome at this time. See the classic study of Peter Lampe, *From Paul to Valentinus: Christians at Rome in the First Two Centuries* (trans. Michael Steinhauser; ed. Marshall D. Johnson; Minneapolis, MN: Fortress Press, 2003).

Jewett it here 'carries the technical sense of reception into the fellowship of the congregation, that is, to the common meal'.[30] For our purposes it is enough to remind ourselves that the image is not of mutual respect from a distance, but of radical hospitality and mutuality.

Thirdly, Paul's fundamental instruction is framed in two ways. Negatively, the command is to refrain from despising and judgement (Rom. 14.3-4, 10-12). Positively, the command is to mutual welcome. The latter imperative occurs twice, and it is interesting to note that, while in 15.7 it is reciprocal, in 14.1 Paul places special emphasis on the responsibility of those who understand the implications of God's saving action in Christ, to welcome those who have not yet grasped those implications fully. He does not say it in those words, but the fact that Paul himself quite clearly identifies himself with the 'strong' suggests that, when push came to shove, he would side with them in any theological dispute over the place of food-laws in the Christian community.

The implications for our discussion should be clear. Differences in baptismal practice should be no barrier to genuine ecumenical welcome. For such mutual hospitality to be genuine, we are required to leave our own 'homes' and cross the threshold of the other. Such encounters might mean that there are things that we will desist from doing, in order not to put a stumbling block in the path of our brothers and sisters, so as not to injure them (Rom. 14.13-15). Baptists might want to consider whether their practice of offering so-called 're-baptism' to a person who has already been baptized in infancy, is still appropriate, no matter how 'strongly', they feel about it.

The Root That Supports Us (Romans 11.18)

One further observation is in order. It is clear from Paul's language in Romans 14–15, and indeed from his words at several other places in the letter, that he is especially concerned with the Gentile-Christian believers in Rome.[31] By way of addressing the problem of Gentile boasting, Paul, in Romans 9–11, mounts a sustained argument in support of the claim that those whose place in salvation history is essentially derivative, and thus secondary, have no legitimate reason to disturb the unity of the church through arrogance or boasting. Paul's rhetoric is

---

[30] Robert Jewett, *Romans* (Hermeneia; Minneapolis, MN: Fortress Press, 2007), p. 835; see also Esler, *Conflict and Identity*, pp. 346-47.

[31] This is to enter a scholarly minefield. Suffice it to say that I am largely persuaded by the 'Gentile audience' theory, which accounts for the content of the letter by suggesting that Paul's real rhetorical target are the Gentile-majority house churches whose arrogance and boasting over Jewish-majority house churches is perceived by Paul as a threat to the unity of the church and as an undermining of the covenant faithfulness of Israel's God. See especially, Neil Elliott, *The Rhetoric of Romans: Argumentative Constraint and Strategy and Paul's Dialogue with Judaism (Journal for the Study of the New Testament* Supplement Series, 45; Sheffield: Sheffield Academic, 1990); and most recently A. Andrew Das, *Solving the Romans Debate* (Minneapolis, MN: Fortress Press, 2007).

aimed at those whose behaviour betrays attitudes of independence and superiority when the deeper reality is that they have been grafted into the foundational covenant community of Israel. Despite the fact that his Gentile audience has correctly understood certain implications of his gospel, Paul insists that they must recognize that God's judgment awaits them if they sacrifice the unity of the Roman church for the sake of their justified convictions. I leave it to the reader to tease out the implications that such a warning might have for descendants of the Baptist offshoot of a Separatist twig of a Protestant bough of a western branch of the tree that is the church catholic.

Conclusion: Pushing the Boundaries of Unity

In this essay I have argued that, as well as making too little of baptism itself, Baptists are often in danger of making too little of scriptural teaching about baptism; the two points are clearly related. I have chosen to explore Romans, not least because that letter has traditionally shaped our understanding of the gospel in general and baptism in particular, and I have argued that Paul's letter, when read as a sustained articulation of the gospel of God's saving action in Jesus Christ, offers scriptural resources that might help us in ongoing reflection and ecumenical conversation.

There are those who will respond to my argument by asking why, if I am right, I remain a Baptist. The answer to that question is, in relation to the issue of baptism, simply that I am still of the opinion that believers' baptism sacramentally embodies the interplay between divine grace and human faith in its fullest form. My own view is that infant baptism, while still baptism in so far as both elements are present, possesses a derived validity.[32]

Others will want to question my interpretation of Romans, arguing (correctly) that I have taken sides in debates that are notoriously complex and difficult. I make no apologies for this. If we acknowledge, as I think we should, that biblical texts do not have a single, fixed, correct, stable 'meaning' and if we allow for the inevitable diversity, provisionality and instability that results from the interpretive process, then it seems to me that we are required to ask questions about the ends of our interpretive decisions. In an ecumenical age, should we not seek to interpret scripture *in the direction of unity*?[33]

The report of recent conversations between the Church of England and British Baptists, *Pushing the Boundaries of Unity*, helpfully ends the section on baptism by

---

[32] See *Believing and Being Baptized*, p. 14, for a description of this position. Note too the conclusions in David F. Wright's important 2003 Didsbury Lectures, *What has Infant Baptism done to Baptism?: An Enquiry at the End of Christendom* (Milton Keynes: Paternoster, 2005), p. 9, to the effect even for paedobaptist churches there should be recognition that 'answering-for-oneself baptism is in an appropriate sense the norm'.

[33] I aim to explore this way of conceiving of ecumenical hermeneutics in a forthcoming book.

posing several questions to both Anglican and Baptist churches. Three are pertinent to this study:[34]

> Could the member churches of the Baptist Union of Great Britain reflect on the nature of Christian initiation as a process, and consider whether they might recognize a place for the baptism of infants within the whole journey which marks the beginning of the Christian life?

I have argued that there is biblical warrant for offering just such a recognition because both believers' and infant baptism bear witness to two fundamental claims made about the gospel in Romans: that the gospel is primarily about what God has done in Christ, and that baptism is a place where God promises to act. Moreover, the language in the report of 'journeys of initiation' does justice to Paul's location of baptism within the ongoing process of salvation. Baptism is not the event that symbolizes a salvation already achieved. It is the act that belongs to the initial stages of the process of ever-greater participation in Christ.

> Will member churches of the Baptist Union of Great Britain which practise open membership resolve that, where they agree to a request for a second baptism, it should only be after careful pastoral counselling of enquirers?

If we take Paul's teaching in Romans 14–15 seriously, it seems to me that this is the least we can do. I am of the view that scripture pushes us further, and invites us to desist from agreeing to such a request, in view of the damage that re-baptism has done to the unity of the church.

> Can the Church of England and Baptist churches determine that neither differences in baptismal practice nor the situation of second baptisms should prevent them from seeing in each other the presence of the one true Church of Jesus Christ?

In so far as different baptismal practices bear witness to the gospel, and in recognition that our distinct ecclesial identities are actually the product of a shared history, I think there is ample New Testament support for such a process of mutual recognition.

In conclusion, Baptists are right to state that their understanding of baptism is the result of a desire to take the witness of the New Testament seriously. Interpretation should never be set in stone, however, and new or different interpretations are not necessarily the threat to identity that some fear them to be. In returning to a central text like Romans we discover resources for the re-visioning of Baptist understanding of baptism. Such resources may not provide us with all the answers that we seek, but they may enable us to be more open to the dialogue that we need.

---

[34] *Pushing the Boundaries*, pp. 73-74, questions 1, 2 and 10 respectively. Note should also be made here of the report *Conversations Around the World 2000–2005: The Report of the International Conversations between the Anglican Communion and the Baptist World Alliance* (London: Anglican Communion Office, 2005).

CHAPTER 7

A Feast for All? Reflecting on Open Communion for the Contemporary Church

Anthony Clarke

An Invitation to Whom?

It is the first Sunday of the month and the congregation has gathered for worship. Central to their gathering, both physically and spiritually, is the Lord's table, and after appropriate opportunities to offer God praise and thanksgiving and to hear God's word read and expounded the minister indicates that they are approaching the moment when bread and wine will be shared. She reminds the congregation that it is Christ's table and that it is open for all those who love the Lord Jesus and wish to follow him.

Such a scene would be typical of many Baptist churches around the country. There may, of course, be a variety of responses to the choice of hymns and songs, but the basic pattern may elicit little discussion, at least among Baptists in the congregation, for this would be a standard pattern. But there is in this sketched outline much of historical and theological significance, principally in connection with who is invited and welcome to share in the elements. Again the common position among contemporary British Baptist churches would be to welcome all those who believe—in Jesus Christ as Lord and Saviour—without any reference to baptism. This is not true of all churches and is certainly not true historically.

In the early days of Baptist congregations the accepted understanding was that the Lord's supper was open only to those who had been baptized as believers. Benjamin Cox, for example, in an appendix to The Particular Baptist *London Confession* of 1644, published two years later, makes such a position clear,[1] although we should

---

[1] Benjamin Cox, *An Appendix to a Confession of Faith or a More Full Declaration of the Faith and Judgement of Baptized Beleevers* (London, 1646), Chapter XX, available at http://www.reformedreader.org/ccc/appendix.htm: 'Though a beleever's right to the use the Lord's Supper doe immediately flow from Jesus Christ, apprehended and received by faith; yet in as much as all things ought to be done not onely decently but also in order…accordingly the Apostles first baptised disciples and then admitted them to the use of the Super, we therefore doe not admit any to the use of the Supper, nor communicate with any in the use of this ordinance, but disciples baptised, lest we should have fellowship with them in their doing contrary to order.'

note that the *Second London Confession* (1677, revised 1689) does not add any such an explicit connection between baptism and communion. There were exceptions within the Baptist community in the seventeenth century, such as John Bunyan, who adamantly insisted that Christ, not baptism, was the door of the sheepfold and so Christ's table must be open to all Christians, regardless of baptism,[2] although such occasions were rare. But a century later, the debate between 'open' and 'closed' became a dominant issue among the Particular Baptists.

The argument in favour of open communion won out, later to be strengthened by the rise of the ecumenical movement and today this is the norm for churches within the Baptist Union of Great Britain, even though some retain a closed membership.[3] But these past controversies are more than just historically interesting because they also explore issues within a theology of communion that are relevant for our practice today. Of particular interest will be the nature of the relationship between baptism and communion, a significant factor in the issues outlined above, and then the nature of the Lord's supper as a sacrament.

While it is impossible to establish an official Baptist theology of the Lord's supper, some recent publications reflect what might be recognised as normal among British Baptists. So Keith Jones, in the *Baptist Basics* series, writes, 'we believe communion is for the believer, and normally follows baptism as a believer'.[4] While recognizing that attending a well-conducted communion service can be an occasion to see and hear the good news of Jesus, Jones also believes there is strength in the argument that encourages only those who are baptized and active believers to be present at the Lord's supper. '[I]t is not usual', he writes, 'for children to be present and certainly unusual for them to receive bread and wine'.[5] So a typical Baptist understanding of the Lord's supper connects it strongly with baptism—although in an ecumenical context baptism as a believer is not required—and also with active faith. So the table is fenced with the words we use for invitation that circumscribe who may attend. Being ecumenically sensitive, yet retaining a stress on faith, Jones

---

[2] John Bunyan, *Difference in judgement about water baptism being no bar to communion* (1673) 'The Church of Christ hath no warrant to keep out of communion the Christian that is discovered to be a visible saint in the world, the Christian that walketh according to his own light with Christ', quoted in Roger Hayden, *English Baptist History and Heritage* (Didcot: Baptist Union of Great Britain, 1990), p. 103.

[3] This would not be true of all Baptist groupings. See Nathan Finn, 'Baptism as a Prerequisite to the Lord's Supper' (Centre for Theological Research White Paper 9; Southwestern Baptist Theological Seminar, Fort Worth, Texas, 2006, www.BaptistTheology.org) for a robust defence of closed communion among Southern Baptists.

[4] Keith G. Jones, *The Lord's Supper* (Baptist Basics, 4; Didcot: Baptist Union of Great Britain, n.d. [1993]), p. 6 (this is a leaflet and pagination corresponds to the relevant leaf)

[5] Jones, 'The Lord's Supper', p. 6.

suggests 'inviting those who love our Lord Jesus Christ and desire to be his true disciples to share in the meal'.[6]

The aim of this paper is to offer an alternative understanding of the relationship between baptism and communion, based on an alternative reading of the key biblical texts and an exploration of some of the wider theological issues, looking to find creative ways to make the Lord's supper open to all as an experience of grace. But first let us reflect more carefully on recent trends within our churches.

Liturgical Practice

Without a substantial piece of empirical research it is impossible to make a fully accurate assessment of current liturgical practice, but an examination of worship material produced within the Baptist Union, which might be considered to both shape and be shaped by contemporary trends, does suggest that our communion practice has tentatively developed. Taking, for example, the *Manual for Free Church Ministers* compiled by G.P. Gould and J.H. Shakespeare at the beginning of the twentieth century, we find no words of invitation as such, simply some suggested scripture readings, although there is a note that communion tickets should be collected with the offering, perhaps indicating that participation is already fixed.[7] A very similar content is repeated in the *Minister's Manual* compiled by M.E. Aubrey in 1927, although without the reference to communion tickets![8]

In D. Tait Patterson's manual, *The Call to Worship*, first published in 1930, we find a much more comprehensive service for communion, including material still familiar from current use. After suitable scripture sentences, a further section is introduced with the phrase 'Then the Minister may use this exhortation'. It begins,

> Ye that do truly and earnestly repent of your sins, and are in love and charity with your neighbours, and intend to lead a new life, following the commandments of God, and walking from henceforth in His holy ways: draw near with faith and take this holy sacrament to you comfort.

> Come to this sacred Table, not because you must but because you may; come not to testify that you are righteous, but that you sincerely love our Lord Jesus Christ, and desire to be his true disciples: come, not because you are strong, but because you are weak; not because you have any claim on heaven's rewards, but because in your

---

[6] Jones, 'The Lord's Supper', p. 4.

[7] G.P. Gould and J.H. Shakespeare, *A Manual for Free Church Ministers* (London: The Kingsgate Press, n.d. [1905]), p. 57.

[8] M.E. Aubrey, *A Minister's Manual* (London: The Kingsgate Press, 1927), pp. 34-41. Published three years later, Frederic C. Spurr's *Come, Let us Worship: A Book of Common Worship for Use in Free Churches* (London: The Kingsgate Press, 1930), also has no words of invitation, but notes the appropriate moment for non-communicants to leave if they desire, p. 120.

frailty and sin you stand in constant need of heaven's mercy and help: come not to express an opinion, but to seek a presence and pray for a Spirit.[9]

Some thirty years later, *Orders and Prayers for Church Worship*, compiled in 1960 by Ernest A. Payne and Stephen F. Winward, draws significantly on Tait Patterson. This book also contains one main order for the Lord's supper (though as in Tait Patterson there is a second short order which does not include a distinct invitation), although it is moved to the beginning of the book after 'vestry prayers'. Payne and Winward simply take the material from Tait Patterson, omitting the sentence 'come not to express an opinion, but to seek a presence and pray for a Spirit', and arrange it as three alternative options which can be used to invite the people to the Lord's supper. The first two begin:

> Ye that do truly and earnestly repent of your sins, and are in love and charity with your neighbours, and are resolved to lead a new life, following the commandments of God...[10]

or

> Come to this sacred Table, not because you must but because you may; come not to testify that you are righteous, but that you sincerely love our Lord Jesus Christ, and desire to be his true disciples...[11]

Both of these make it very clear how the table is to be 'fenced'. The third invitation does not specify who is invited in the same way as the first two statements, but is rather an encouragement to 'lift up your minds and hearts', although it clearly has the same participants in mind as it concludes,

> ...consecrate your lives afresh to the Christian obedience and service, and pray for strength to do and bear the holy will of God.[12]

Much of this material was repeated in the 1980 publication *Praise God*. Here there is one order for 'Sunday Worship' which includes the Lord's supper, and the first two options in the earlier *Orders and Prayers* are re-combined into one invitation followed by various suggestions of appropriate scripture readings.[13] Then, in 1991 the Baptist Union produced a new guidebook for worship leaders entitled *Patterns and Prayers for*

---

[9] D. Tait Patterson, *The Call to Worship: A Book of Services for the Help and Guidance of those who Minister in the House of God* (London: The Carey Press, rev. edn 1938), p. 159.

[10] Ernest A. Payne and Stephen F. Winward, *Orders and Prayers for Church Worship* (London: Baptist Union of Great Britain and Ireland, 1960), p. 14.

[11] Payne and Winward, *Orders and Prayers*, p. 14.

[12] Payne and Winward, *Orders and Prayers*, p. 15.

[13] Alec Gilmore, Edward Smalley and Michael Walker, *Praise God: A Collection of Resource Material for Christian Worship* (London: Baptist Union of Great Britain and Ireland, 1980), p. 124.

Christian Worship. Here the Lord's super becomes a distinct section again, with three different patterns offered, together with some introductory comments in which the matter of appropriate participants is touched upon.

> There is a need for clear words of invitation. This is important as a reminder that the Table is the Lord's and the invitation is his. Our sharing in this meal is sheer grace and does not rest on our goodness or attainments.[14]

But recognizing the contemporary context in which churches have brought together word and sacrament in one service, rather than celebrating the Lord's supper as a separate service, the compilers go on to note that this

> may have led to a situation where some people remain at the service without being able to enter into its meaning wholeheartedly. It is pastorally wise, therefore, to precede the Supper with some statement as to its meaning and how to respond.[15]

Altogether there are six different invitations offered for use, including all the material from the two previous publications, although the language has been slightly changed to make it more contemporary. One of the original three invitations from *Orders and Prayers*, beginning 'Come to this table, not because you must, but because you may…', is included twice both in its original language and also slightly altered to lay greater stress on the availability of grace rather than the demands made of the participant. Thus it omits the lines '…that you sincerely love our Lord Jesus Christ and desire to be his true disciples…', adding instead, 'Come, because you love the Lord a little and would like to love him more.'[16]

Two of the other alternatives offered stress the theological aspects of the supper as a way of reminding those who are participating of the nature of the meal, but without explicitly suggesting who should and could participate, although one ends with the collective:

> Therefore, we need to come in faith, conscious of our weakness, seeking to renounce our sin, humbly putting our trust in Christ, and seeking his grace.[17]

Finally, there is an invitation that takes full account of possible diversity within the congregation:

> The Table of the Lord is spread. It is for those who will come and see in broken bread and poured out wine symbols of his life shed for us on the cross and raised again on the third day. The Risen Christ is present among his people and it is here that we meet with him. It is for those who know him a little and long to know him

---

[14] *Patterns and Prayers for Christian Worship* (Oxford: Oxford University Press, 1991), p. 67.
[15] *Patterns and Prayers*, p. 67.
[16] *Patterns and Prayers*, p. 81.
[17] *Patterns and Prayers*, p. 76.

more. We invite all who are seeking him and all who are weary of their sin and doubt to come and share in the feast. If you do not feel able to take a full part, you are welcome to remain among us without receiving the bread and wine.[18]

This invitation ends by presuming inclusion but giving those within the congregation permission to opt out of sharing in bread and wine if they prefer. The table is still 'fenced' with words, but the language is much gentler and more inclusive. The exact extent of this inclusivity depends on whether the invitations herein contained—and there are four, 'It is for those... It is for those... We invite all...and all...'—are intended to be heard collectively, each of the four statements describing the same group of people, or as alternatives. If we take this latter interpretation the supper is for those who know Christ a little, but it is also for those who are seeking him (but have not yet found him, at least in any full degree) and also for those who are weary of their sin and doubt (but perhaps have not yet found forgiveness and faith).

Although there is no suggestion that *The Call to Worship* and *Orders and Prayers* intend to convey anything other than the grace of God encountered in bread and wine, by comparison with later books the language used is much stronger and the requirements of participants more extensive, that they sincerely love the Lord Jesus Christ and earnestly repent of their sins. At the same time, the 'new' invitations in *Patterns and Prayers* lay a greater stress on our continual human frailty and seem intended to be more inclusive. The Lord's supper is for those who love the Lord a little, or who are seeking to renounce their sin, who know Christ a little and or who are seeking him and are weary of their doubt. The intention of these additional invitations certainly seems to aim at including those on the fringes of the church, those who feel they have faith, but are also full of doubts and uncertainties and somehow feel they are not 'good enough' to belong to the church. If this last invitation is read as offering alternative categories for admittance at the supper, then it stretches even further into the fringes of the church, welcoming those still seeking Christ.

In the most recent such publication, *Gathering For Worship*, there are seven different patterns for the Lord's supper, returned to their place in *Orders and Prayers* at the beginning of the book. Some are designed for more general use and others for a specific context, for example, at a covenant service. Each pattern has its own invitation, but together they introduce wholesale change, for much of the previous material has been replaced, with the exception of the gentler version of 'Come to this table...come, because you love the Lord a little...', which is retained in two of the orders.[19]

The tendency to stress both grace for human weakness and inclusivity, which we noted in *Patterns and Prayers*, continues in this resource, although other emphases

---

[18] *Patterns and Prayers*, p. 76.

[19] Christopher J. Ellis and Myra Blyth (eds), *Gathering for Worship: Patterns and Prayers for the Community of Disciples* (Norwich: Canterbury Press, 2005), pp. 14 and 22.

are included. This trend is captured in the pattern focusing on making a covenant, which concludes,

> So we come to this table, you and I,
> companions on the journey.
> Some of us fresh and eager,
> others weary, in need of nourishment.
> All of us conscious of our failings.
>
> ...
>
> Come now, don't hesitate,
> the feast is ready
> and the Lord himself invites you.[20]

On the other hand, the pattern emphasizing hungering for justice uses words from an Iona liturgy, that the table is 'for those who love him and want to love him more'.[21] And the final pattern, designed to be used in a home as part of a table fellowship, actually includes a reference to baptism in the invitation:

> We are invited to come together around this table as those who belong to the household of Christ, brothers and sisters who in our baptized lives live out the death and resurrection of Jesus. The family of the reborn and reconciled, who inhabit a universe of grace.[22]

Gathering for Worship also includes an invitation that is all-embracing, with no restrictive clauses appealing to those who love, know or seek, and seems to deliberately emphasize that here is a table for all.

> Here is the table of the Lord
> we are gathered to his supper,
> a foretaste of things eternal.
>
> Come, when you are fearful, to be made new in love.
> Come, when you are doubtful, to be made strong in faith.
> Come, when you are regretful, and be made whole.
> Come, old and young,
> there is room for all.[23]

---

[20] Ellis and Blyth (eds), *Gathering for Worship*, p. 36.
[21] Ellis and Blyth (eds), *Gathering for Worship*, p. 31.
[22] Ellis and Blyth (eds), *Gathering for Worship*, p. 43.
[23] Ellis and Blyth (eds), *Gathering for Worship*, p. 18.

Although there has not been significant debate on this issue, as in previous centuries, there has certainly been change. Whereas we would have expected language to have changed with subsequent publications, at least to ensure it communicates in a contemporary context, it also seems to change due to a mission imperative. It seems to be assumed in minister's manuals from the beginning of the twentieth century that participants at communion were to a significant degree already settled. By 1960 the issue of correct participation has given rise to words of invitation, and in *Orders and Prayers* these seem designed to 'fence' the table correctly and ensure that only those who are sincere believing Christians partake. On the other hand, the language of the most recent publications suggest a desire to be much more inclusive, positively to reach out and draw people in that they may find grace. This seems to have happened in both an implicit and explicit way.

Desiring to be seen as welcoming and friendly congregations, and with an approach to mission that has encouraged visitors to attend on Sundays, an invitation to communion may describe those for whom the supper is intended, but participation is then a matter of personal choice. Surely the normal practice would be to offer bread and wine to all, including visitors, and allow them to make that choice, even if they have little understanding of what is happening? Although a church's theological understanding may confine the table to sincere and believing Christians, the mission imperative is eager not to exclude. The boundaries of the table become implicitly, but perhaps deliberately, blurred. On the other hand, increasingly local churches are beginning to wrestle with the place of children in the church and particularly their involvement around the table. Various different and creative alternatives have been tried and there is explicit and deliberate reflection on the nature of the invitation. Both the implicit and explicit changes demand further biblical and theological reflection.

Biblical Reflections

There are three distinct clusters of passages that we will briefly consider: those that relate Jesus' practice of table fellowship; those that contain Jesus' teaching relating to the great banquet; but first, those passage that deal more directly with the Lord's supper.

The Last Supper

Central to the church's reflections on the meaning and nature of the Lord's supper has been the biblical accounts of the Last Supper. This immediately raises a number of issues regarding the nature of the Last Supper and especially its link to the Jewish Passover, but this firm connection between Lord's supper and Last Supper has privileged those biblical passages that describe the night before Jesus died. And within these passages themselves, Paul's teaching to the church at Corinth has been decisively dominant. There a number of reasons for this. It is the earliest such description, probably predating the earliest extant Gospel account by perhaps a dozen years or so,[24] becoming an integral part of the eucharistic liturgy. It is also the account that offers the most sustained theological reflection on the meaning and practice of sharing bread and wine in the light of this final meal Jesus shared with his disciples. We will have cause later to suggest that this privileging of the Last Supper accounts needs to be balanced by giving greater attention to other aspects of the Gospel narratives, but we also need to reflect further on the place of 1 Corinthians within the theological tradition, and the way it has shaped our practices.

One significant aspect of the theological reflection that Paul offers to the Corinthians is the attitude with which the Corinthians should approach their eucharistic celebrations. Framing the particular verses that describe what is commonly called the 'institution of the Lord's Supper' (11.23-26) are Paul's revelation of his knowledge of abuses that have happened among the Corinthians (vv. 17-22) and his exhortation to some inner spiritual reflection (vv. 27-33). Interpreting the former will require some reconstruction of the socio-historical context in which the Corinthian church met, and interpreting the latter will require discussion of some contested Greek phrases. What is clear, however, is that many of the phrases and verses of this whole passage have developed a tradition largely shaped by later ecclesiastical contexts. This is true, in particular, of v. 27 in which Paul warns that the bread and wine should not be consumed in an 'unworthy' or 'unfitting' manner (ἀναξίως) lest this lead to some 'guilt' or 'accountability' (ἔνοχος) in connection with the Lord's body and blood. The dominant traditional interpretation has been that with such words, and those which follow about self-examination, Paul has clearly fenced the table. The argument runs: those who are unworthy to eat and drink are those who do not and cannot examine themselves and who cannot and do not recognize the body of the Lord. This certainly includes those who are not committed believers, and since Paul indicates that the consequences of such unworthy participating is judgement, even including sickness and death, it is imperative for all concerned that the church safeguard the table for true and sincere believers. However, further consideration may suggest that this owes more to the tradition than to Paul's intentions.

The social context of the Corinthian church is clearly one of divisions, as is significantly reinforced here (v. 18), but also appears throughout chapters 1–4. Although there is some uncertainty as to the exact situation, it is generally agreed that the divisions portrayed here are between the wealthy few and the much poorer many.[25] If the meeting of the church is being hosted in the house of one of the wealthy patrons, as seems most likely both because of the force of the class system and the practicalities of space, and includes some kind of wider meal or agape, as Paul's comments on eating and drinking suggest, then it is most likely that the small number of similarly wealthy patrons would have eaten in the dining room while the others stood in the hall way. Such a scenario would have been entirely the

---

[24] This assumes that 1 Corinthians was written in around 54 CE and Mark in the second half of the seventh decade of the Common Era.

[25] For a general introduction to the social context of Corinth, see James D.G. Dunn, *1 Corinthians* (T&T Clark Study Guides; London: T&T Clark, 2003).

social norm. It may be that the wealthy few started their dinner early, spared the rigours of work, so that they were already well fed and well wined when the others arrived later. The force of Paul's instruction in v. 33 (ἐκδέχεσθε) would be to wait for the others and eat together. Or it may be that the story Paul has heard is that the elite eat and drink sumptuously, while the host provides only meagre fare for the others. Again this would reflect the normal patterns of Greco-Roman life, but in this case Paul's call is rather to welcome each other, so challenging the cultural norms.[26] Whichever the exact intended meaning of ἐκδέχεσθε (welcome or wait for), it is clear that Paul is responding to a particular and specific local situation and this in itself should make us cautious in applying the apostle's words to other contexts without careful interpretation.

But when we make such an investigation, it may actually lead us to a quite different conclusion to the fenced position outlined above. Paul's censure of the Corinthian church is because they have made a mockery of the Lord's supper, explicitly contradicting and undermining its very purpose.[27] We might describe this as an example of selfishness, in which the good news of the gospel is under cut by existing cultural practices. The strength of Paul's appeal arises because in this not uncommon attitude the very essence of the gospel is at stake. This is firstly because the message of Jesus is subordinated to cultural practice, but also and most significantly because, for Paul, the Lord's supper is a most profound proclamation of the meaning and significance of the Lord's death. It is imperative that this message is rightly proclaimed and so the supper rightly celebrated. But instead, in the assessment of P. Lampe, *'the love of the other, the outsider, and the "weak", which characterised the death of Christ, was thrust aside'*.[28]

Lampe's interpretation offer us both an interpretation of the central significance of Jesus' life and death as 'love for the other' and a fundamental critique of church life at Corinth—the failure of this essential gospel principle. This highlights the rhetorical force of Paul's description of this meal as κυριακὸν (v. 20).[29] The contrast Paul makes between κυριακὸν and ἴδιον (in v. 21) is clear and forceful. Paul must have in mind here the powerful elite who eat a supper that is their own (ἴδιον), both in the sense that there is no sharing and fellowship, but also because it is characterized by their own values, instead of a supper that is truly the Lord's (κυριακὸν) characterized

---

[26] See Ben Witherington, III, *Conflict, Community and Corinth* (Grand Rapids, MI: Eerdmans/ Carlisle: Paternoster, 1995), p. 248.

[27] See Anthony C. Thiselton, *The First Epistle to the Corinthians* (New International Greek Testament Commentary; Grand Rapids, MI: Eerdmans/Carlisle: Paternoster Press, 2000), p. 850.

[28] Thiselton, *First Epistle to the Corinthians*, p. 850, italics original, summarizing P. Lampe, 'Das Korinthische Herrenmahl im Schnittpunkt hellenistisch-römischer Mahlpraxis und paulinischer Theologia Crucis (1 Kor 11:17-34)', *Zeitschrift für die neutestamentliche Wissenschaft* 82 (1991), pp. 183-213.

[29] There is some uncertainty whether 'κυριάκον' is in any sense a technical or semi-technical term for communion and, as we make clear later, its force may be rhetorical.

by his values. What Paul expects, therefore, is gospel behaviour at the Lord's supper, and this is behaviour in which love for the other is paramount.

This then offers us a very different approach to interpret vv. 27-34. Behaviour that is unfitting or unworthy holds on tight to the physical food present, revealing an underlying selfishness of the heart. This, then, is the context for a necessary self-examination, which rather than a general reflection on our thoughts and words and deeds asks us to consider whether we approach the table with open arms or closed hearts. This suggests that an interpretation of the difficult phrase in 11.29, 'recognizing the body' (μὴ διακρίνων τὸ σῶμα), must include, indeed centre upon, some understanding of the congregation as the body of Christ.[30] We also need to note the rhetorical nature of v. 28, and that while it is addressed to all, 'let anyone examine him or herself', it is rhetorically aimed at the few wealthy members of the congregation.

From all that we have said, it is quite clear that the specific context of Paul's comments is the behaviour amongst themselves of the Corinthian congregation, and does not envisage the situation of outsiders who are not yet believers in Christ. Paul's concern is for internal cohesion, as it is throughout the letter, rather than the maintenance of boundaries.[31] But the exegesis and interpretation we have offered suggests that the underlying theme is that of gracious hospitality, and two conclusions seem justifiable. First, Paul's exhortation to self-examination and his corresponding comments about participating unworthily and expecting judgement are not in an attempt to fence the table, for all those whom Paul addresses expect and are accustomed to be present. They are strong words about how those who habitually share, and perhaps oversee, the Lord's table behave. Likewise, then, we should not fence our tables based on an interpretation of these verses. Secondly, Paul commends an attitude of heart that reflects the generous and self-giving death of Jesus and suggests that, above all, our eucharistic practice should reflect these same qualities.

Although this is the central passage in 1 Corinthians concerning the Lord's supper, Paul has also touched upon it earlier in chapter 10. Here Paul speaks of these same relationships within the church at Corinth as bound within the sharing of one loaf. What is clear from the passage, as has been forcefully set out by John Colwell, is that Paul's eucharistic language is used as an example to respond to an ethical dilemma, and 'it is the assumption underlying this passage, rather than its underlying argument, that is so startling'.[32] In appealing to the Corinthians not to be involved in pagan sacrifices, Paul likens participating in such practices to Christian believers breaking bread. Both involve a real sense of participation. It would seem, therefore, that sharing in the bread and wine is a significant moment of

---

[30] See, e.g., Thiselton, *First Epistle to the Corinthians*, pp. 891-94, for a discussion of the issues.

[31] See Wayne A. Meeks, *The First Urban Christians: The Social World of the Apostle Paul* (New Haven, CT: Yale University Press, 2003), pp. 97-103, for a discussion of purity and boundaries.

[32] John E. Colwell, *Promise and Presence: An Exploration of Sacramental Theology* (Milton Keynes: Paternoster, 2005), p. 155.

participating in Christ, and Colwell proceeds to argue, beginning with this passage, for a strongly sacramental understanding of the Lord's supper. The significance of this passage for seeking an understanding of communion is increased by its being the one occasion that offers some direct link to baptism.

The wider theological context of this passage is clearly that of covenant,[33] striking in itself given all we have so far suggested about this particular congregation. Paul begins chapter 10 with a comparison between the Corinthian Christians and those who left Egypt with Moses. All of the latter were baptized into the fellowship of Moses and ate the supernatural food and drank the supernatural drink. But some of these, in fact most of these, acted in ways that displeased God. On the one hand, Paul uses the Old Testament example as a warning to inculcate covenant faithfulness in the Corinthians. This is his stated aim and this is what the text attempts to do. On the other hand, the passage actually undercuts the direct link between covenant and ethical purity. In vv. 1-10 there is a clear contrast between the repeated 'all' (vv. 1-4) who were included in the covenant, and 'some' who displeased God (vv. 6-10). It was those who were baptized and who ate and drank that turned away. There seems to be a clear resonance with the situation Paul faces.

It is this covenant thought which then provides the background for Paul's eucharistic image. Sharing in the physical elements, which is to share in the body and blood of Christ, is to participate in the covenant. Thiselton sets out the case for understanding the two significant words in these verses, 'κοινωνία' (fellowship/ participation) and μετέχειν (share) with a fundamental vertical dimension and then a subsequent horizontal one.[34] This passage then seems to suggest that sharing in the Lord's supper is more than a sign of a covenant already made, it is a remaking of the covenant itself. Here there is a real participation in Christ, in which the many who are disparate and divided have a unity within this covenant. This is further emphasized if ὅτι in 10.17 is given a strong causal translation, that is *'because* there is one bread'. Clearly the unity Paul envisages does not derive from one actual loaf of bread in mechanistic sense, but neither can bread simply be read as 'Christ'. Rather Paul suggests that it is in the act of sharing in bread (and wine), which is a real participation in Christ, that the many become one. The force of this verse may then be that the many, who share in one bread, are *made* one body. The Lord's supper is a significant covenant-making event in its own right.

Earlier on in chapter 10, in the example of the Israelites, the events of the cloud, the sea, the food and the drink are all significant within this covenant motif. What is unclear is any intended distinction that Paul intends between them. The movement in Paul's thought seems clearly from Christian baptism towards the Old Testament story—the experience of cloud and sea seems to warrant this description—in which, as has been pointed out by those more inclined to paedobaptism, the emphasis is on

---

[33] See, e.g., the section 'Exclusive Loyalty to God: Covenantal Allegiance in Sharing the Lord's Supper (10:14-22)' in Thiselton, *First Epistle to the Corinthians*, pp. 750-79.

[34] Thiselton, *First Epistle to the Corinthians*, pp. 761-64.

God's act of grace.[35] While baptism and communion are both covenant events, this chapter offers no precise connection.

In a latter passage, 1 Corinthians 12.13, Paul brings together again themes of baptism and the body, in a way that seems to suggest baptism is the event that initiates the covenant. But interpretation of this passage is also contested. Although attempts to read eucharistic significance in the reference to 'drink' in the second half of the verse are generally discounted, the intended reference to baptism is uncertain. Clearly Paul has in mind the physical event of water baptism, but it may or may not be a direct reference to this event. Verse 13 could refer to the occasions when the Corinthians were baptized in water, in which case 'ἐν' is intended instrumentally — in the act of water baptism they were baptized into the body by the Spirit. Alternatively, baptism could be used more metaphorically to refer to that moment or process in which they were all, and this is the stress, transformed through the Spirit, in which case 'ἐν' could be in a locative sense — they were baptized in the Spirit. The significance for us is whether this impacts on the relationship between baptism and communion. Noting that, as in chapter 10, Paul is using this image to stress their unity, rather than argue for particular sacramental practice, it would be unwise to draw too rigid a conclusion.

It would seem most likely that within the particular context, the church at Corinth was comprised of those who were first baptized and then shared in communion and this would seem to be the likely pattern in the Pauline churches.[36] Paul then addresses them on this particular basis, assuming this social reality rather than arguing for it. The judgement we must make is to the extent that Paul's comments are based on a reality that Paul would defend from principle, and to what extent the nature of the church community was shaped by its cultural circumstances.

There is a strong feeling in the Pauline corpus of a distinction between those inside and outside the church, witnessed here in 1 Corinthians 5.12-13 and 14.33. Such separation from the world is a firm part of Paul's inherited tradition, taken to its extreme at Qumran, but there are clear signs that Paul does not see such separation as absolute. In discussing the eating of meat, the issue only arises because some of the Christians, probably the wealthy, would be invited to share in meals with non-Christian friends and acquaintances. Nevertheless, as a persecuted, marginal group a strong sense of belonging and boundaries was necessary, and this shapes Paul's context. We have suggested that in 1 Corinthians Paul is not arguing for the maintenance of clear boundaries between those who were included and excluded, but is concerned for the internal relationships of those who were part of the church. In such a social context where there is a very clear distinction between those 'in' and 'out' baptism will be the boundary marker and communion will always follow.

Later we will consider Gospel passages that might influence our understanding of the Lord's supper and we will notice some different perspectives. We may also find

---

[35] See, e.g., Oscar Cullman, *Baptism in the New Testament* (Studies in Biblical Theology, 1; London: SCM Press, 1950), p. 45.

[36] Meeks, *First Urban Christians*, p. 102.

some tension between the social context of Jesus' ministry with its more open boundaries and that of Paul with its more closed Christian communities, which in itself will shape the practice of these two sacraments and their relationship together. Our task will be to reinterpret Paul's teaching for our contemporary context in which there is a greater possibility and desire to have more open boundaries. In our discussions above, we have argued Paul does not address either the issue of right boundaries or the proper relationship between baptism and the Lord's supper, working instead within that particular context. But we have highlighted two central features that seem to be part of an underlying understanding of the Lord's supper: first that it proclaims the gracious hospitality of Jesus for the other, and secondly that communion is a covenant-making or remaking event. Bringing together these two underlying insights, the Lord's supper does not necessarily need to be based on one body already existing within fixed boundaries, but in gracious hospitality re-forms one body in the process. This seems to leave open the possibility that individuals can enter the covenant, and a covenant that is based on divine grace, at the Lord's supper for the first time

If, finally, we look further afield and draw on the other accounts of the Last Supper to shape our understanding of communion we must note how the Synoptic Gospels all frame the sharing of bread and wine in some way with the betrayal and denial of Jesus. This seems to do more than set it in a historical context, although these are all crucial events of the last days of Jesus' life, but provide a departure for theological reflection. Jesus quite deliberately shares this Last Supper at which he encourages his friends to continue to celebrate his transforming presence in bread and wine with those he knows will betray and deny him; they are included to the last. Such framing of the meal was clearly an early part of the church's tradition, for Paul also recalls that theses events happened not simply on the night before he died, but on the night when he was betrayed (1 Cor. 11.23). The context is, of course, of those who were his friends and disciples and had followed him from the beginning. It is these who have let him down. It is interesting how Luke frames the meal, not only with the thoughts and actions of Judas and Peter, but also with the dispute about greatness that engulfs the whole group (Lk. 22.1-38). Once again these passages which recall the Last Supper do not address the issue of the inclusion of those beyond the group of disciples, but it lays some further foundations about the nature of the meal that may cut across those Baptist understandings of communion that stress the purity of the table. The Last Supper, and so we may suggest the Lord's supper, is indeed a celebration of grace in the midst of human brokenness.

Table Fellowship

Whereas it is the Last Supper that has particularly shaped the church's understanding of the Lord's supper, a second cluster of passages that command attention are those concerned with shared meals. Two particular kinds of story can be identified. First, there are those accounts of Jesus at table with others, either as host or guest, which are normally used by the Gospel writers to draw attention to the company that Jesus kept. Secondly, there are those accounts which also centre around table fellowship, but in which some have seen eucharistic elements that either prefigure or echo the meal at the Last Supper.

The first group of narratives might include the dinner at Levi's, or Matthew's, house, an evening with Simon the Pharisee, a Sabbath meal with another Pharisee, Zacchaeus, the wedding at Cana and the Samaritan woman at the well. In some the context clearly involved those on the fringes of society, who act as the host. So Jesus responds to an invitation from Levi, invites himself to Zacchaeus' house and requests water from the Samaritan woman. In a clear and noted distinction from the expected behaviour of society at the time, Jesus refuses to construct fences around his table fellowship. In the two occasions that Luke, and Luke alone, records Jesus accepting invitations from a Pharisee, the point drawn out in the Gospel explicitly contrasts the attitude of Jesus with that of his host. In Luke 7.36-50 Simon is presented as someone who stands aloof from Jesus, despite the normal customs of hospitality, and pointedly separate from the woman who enters his house, who herself performs the duties of the host. Jesus, on the other had, in an acted and spoken parable, welcomes and willingly receives all the woman has to offer and in return speaks words of grace. In Luke 14.1-14, after a further invitation and further disruption, controversy is initiated by healing on the Sabbath. But rather than explore this contentious issue the dialogue quickly moves on to the customs of table fellowship, first in respect of the honoured seats and then in respect of the invitation list.

There are no direct eucharistic elements in these stories or even inferences, but they convey an important aspect of Jesus' ministry and offer significant insight into Jesus' attitude to sharing food and drink. We see in Jesus someone who, rather than erecting fences, deliberately dismantles those erected by religious tradition. Furthermore, they also suggest an important link to Paul's discussion in 1 Corinthians 11, since we have suggested that Paul's fundamental exhortation is for the Christians at Corinth to show a real love for the other which is revealed and proclaimed in Jesus' death. The proclamation of the Lord's death, so central to the bread and wine, is a death for the other, the marginalized, as exemplified in Jesus' own table fellowship. Bringing together such passages suggests that a radical invitation in our own celebration of communion might best proclaim the life and death of Jesus.

The second group of narratives centre upon the feeding of the 5,000 and 4,000, the post-resurrection meal with the two disciples at Emmaus (Luke 24.13-35), and the post-resurrection breakfast on the beach (John 21.1-14), although some would want to extend such a list.[37] Discussions about the feeding miracles in the Synoptic Gospels are divided in regard to any possible eucharistic significance of the meal. Whereas the actions of Jesus in taking, blessing, breaking and sharing the bread

---

[37] John Henson, e.g., would list a number of other passages where bread, wine, water and fish are involved, including the wedding at Cana and the woman at the well. See John Henson, *Other Communions of Jesus* (Cardiff: John Henson, 1994).

reflect the same actions at the Last Supper, they are also the familiar and everyday action of any meal. The question is whether or not the Gospel writers intended us to make that kind of connection. Although Jesus' actions were certainly commonplace, in the Gospel accounts the repeated pattern of language in the feeding stories and the Last Supper suggest that such an intention is certainly possible.

The Johannine account of the feeding of the 5,000 has also received opposing interpretations, but there are certainly those who see unmistakable eucharistic undertones to the whole passage in John 6. So John Colwell writes,

> Though John's Gospel contains no explicit account of the institution of the Lord's Supper, the narrative of Jesus' sermon at Capernaum, following the feeding of the 5000, is astonishing in its paschal imagery and—at least in the thinking of some commentators—fulfils the same function...[38]

Now, if this line of interpretation is correct, then it is not just the imagery that is astonishing. If John 6 fulfils the function of the institution of the Lord's supper, then the context of the crowd is very different to that of the upper room. John's eucharistic reflections, though much more implicit, suggest that the invitation to the table is open and welcoming. The bread is offered to all on the basis of sheer grace.

The Great Banquet

The third cluster of readings are those Gospel passages which refer in some way to a future messianic banquet. In both Matthew and Luke there is a longer parable that focuses on a banquet (Matthew 22.1-14/Luke 14.15-24) and also a shorter saying (Matthew 8.11-12/Luke 13.28-9). There is some uncertainty as to both the relationship between these different passages, and the very similar parable in the Gospel of Thomas, saying 64, and also to their proper interpretation, given the different Gospel settings in which they have been placed, though clearly all four are drawing on a wider and long established tradition. George Beasley-Murray concludes that it was a common Jewish symbol to portray the kingdom of God as a banquet, and so this would be assumed by the hearers.[39] There is evidence from within the Qumran community that meals were infused with such an eschatological symbolism, and in the Old Testament this is expressed most clearly in Isaiah 25.6-9:

> On this mountain the Lord Almighty will prepare a feast of rich food for all peoples, a banquet of aged wine—the best of meats and finest of wines. On this mountain he will destroy the shroud that enfolds all peoples, the sheet that covers all nations; he will swallow up death for ever.

---

[38] Colwell, *Promise and Presence*, p. 157.
[39] George Beasley-Murray, *Jesus and the Kingdom of God* (Grand Rapids, MI: Eerdmans/Exeter: Paternoster, 1978), p. 120.

In interpreting the parables it is often commented that Luke's version is the simpler and has the greater claim to originality (and is most similar to the version in the Gospel of Thomas), whereas in Matthew there are greater signs of editing.[40] In both Matthew and Luke the parable deals with issues of judgment and grace, although with seemingly a greater emphasis on judgement in Matthew and grace in Luke. However, and especially pertinent to our theme, the parable in both versions deals with the issue of who is in and who is out, although as will be made clear, the interpretation is not that simple.

If we turn to Luke's setting, Kenneth E. Bailey, in his book *Through Peasant Eyes*, helpfully describes the way that both the saying and parable function within this section of the Gospel text.[41] From this it is clear that the parable is working at two different levels, at least! The setting of the parable is one of the meals in the house of a prominent Pharisee, mentioned above, where they are described (14.15) as reclining to eat. These indications suggest that the setting itself was some kind of banquet or celebratory meal in the home of a wealthy individual who has bought into the Greco-Roman dining customs and social status. The parable then clearly reflects the setting—in Scott's description, it has real verisimilitude, for the parable as a story rings true[42]—and it follows on from Jesus' previous comments about choosing the lowest places at the meal, clearly a response to the jockeying for position that he has just witnessed.

The parable itself is in response to the declaration that the man is indeed blessed who eats at the feast in the kingdom of God. Whereas the parable does indeed have echoes of this great banquet, at this first level Jesus' response to the outburst is to bring his fellow diners, whom we can assume were all of this elevated social status, back to reality. What matters is not some pious longing for the future banquet but radically different social behaviour in the present. In the parable, the host responds to the social snub of rejection, the excuses for which are all lame to the point of insulting, not by seeking vengeance within the rules of the social system, but by breaking apart the whole social system and inviting those who could not come. It was because this social gap was so great that they had to be compelled to come in, for the poor could not imagine such an invitation. This then at one level is a parable about table fellowship and the company we keep in the here and now. It reflects Jesus' own practice and in narrative terms prepares the way for the muttered comment in 15.2, which introduces the parables of the lost sheep, coin and son, that 'This man welcomes sinners and eats with them.'

But the parable also clearly works at another level, exemplified in the pious outburst about the messianic banquet. Such an understanding is already in the frame, but this comment highlights the fact that the parable will address this issue as well. Bailey's detailed discussion shows how the earlier saying that those from east and

---

[40] See, e.g., Bernard Brandon Scott, *Hear then the Parables: A Commentary on the Parables of Jesus* (Minneapolis, MN: Fortress Press, 1990), pp. 162-63.

[41] Kenneth E. Bailey, *Through Peasant Eyes: More Lucan Parables their Culture and Style* (Grand Rapids, MI: Eerdmans, 1989).

[42] Scott, *Hear then the Parables*, p. 162.

west and north and south will take their place at the feast of the kingdom of God prepares the way for the parable. He suggests that the verses at the end of Luke 13 form a chiastic structure beginning with the gathering of the feast and ending with the gathering of the mother hen, and so focuses attention on the verses in between which discuss the death of Jesus and include the two enigmatic references to the third day. Having clearly linked the eschatological feast to the death and resurrection of Jesus, Luke proceeds with the Sabbath meal and the parable. At this level the parable is about those welcomed into the messianic banquet and contains this mingling of judgement and grace, although with the stress on the latter. But that might still leave us with the sense that the poor are invited as something of an afterthought when the rich had declined the invitation. This is partly and, perhaps, fundamentally explained by the two levels on which the parable works—it is firstly about table fellowship. But Bailey also suggests it is also partly explained by understanding the second command of the host to send his servant 'outside' the city as a symbolic reference to the Gentiles, noting the way that in the parable the command is given but not yet acted upon.[43]

Whereas the passage from Isaiah 25 clearly stresses that all will be welcomed to the feast and the veil will be destroyed, other Old Testament passages suggest a more ambiguous role for the Gentile nations, and this was reflected in later writings. So the Targum on Isaiah 25 rewrites the welcome for all by introducing plagues that will affect the Gentiles;[44] *1 Enoch* 62.1-16 suggests the Gentiles will be killed and the righteous eat with the son of man; and the messianic *Rule of the Community* (1QS 2.1-22) at Qumran not only excludes the Gentiles from the feast but also imperfect and blemished Jews. Bailey suggests that this passage deliberately reiterates the gracious invitation of Isaiah 25 and echoes the concern for the Gentiles found elsewhere in Luke's Gospel.

So at both levels, the parable offers an image and a challenge of grace—the graciousness of God who invites all to the messianic banquet and the call to such gracious living in the here and now. The parable also combines these two levels of the here and now and the future feast, but not in a simplistic way, rather in such a way that the messianic banquet shapes the way we live and act in the present, that the grace implicit in such an invitation might be the mark of our own table fellowship in the here and now.

Bailey concludes,

> Those who ate and drank with Jesus during his earthly ministry were engaged in a proleptic celebration of the messianic banquet at the end times. This parable offers a least in part a theological rational for that celebration. Is not the communion service an extension of this same celebration?[45]

---

[43] Bailey, *Through Peasant Eyes*, p. 101.
[44] See Bailey, *Through Peasant Eyes*, p. 90.
[45] Bailey, *Through Peasant Eyes*, p. 112.

It is clear from these clusters of passages that when we have thought about communion we have been right to focus on issues of inclusion and exclusion. The parable of the banquet in Luke addresses this issue in such a way that combines present dining patterns with the future feast. Jesus exemplified an attitude to exclusion and inclusion in his own table fellowship, and the various passages that describe the Lord's supper all contain these issues. But it seems to me clear from these passages that in our churches we have not focused on exclusion and inclusion in the right way. I do not, therefore, want to come straight away to a simple, even naïve, conclusion that Jesus welcomed all we around his table and therefore so should. But I do want to argue for an unfenced table based both on the above passages and also further reflections on the nature of communion. And it is to these more theological issues we must now turn.

Theological Themes

The Nature of Communion as a Sacrament

The minister has spoken words of invitation and the gathered community have confessed their sins and heard words of forgiveness. She then takes the loaf of bread, offers a prayer of thanksgiving, breaks it and offers it to be shared amongst the congregation. Explaining what is happening here has been the subject of much interest in recent Baptist writings. Whereas for some time, and perhaps still amongst many within our churches, the understanding of communion tends towards memorialism, there has been something of a revival of a more sacramental approach. Typical of this, and in a way that pushes Baptist thinking into new areas, is John Colwell's excellent and previously mentioned study, *Promise and Presence: An Exploration of Sacramental Theology*.

Now how we understand communion to 'function' could implicitly affect our approach to exclusion and inclusion. For example, it would seem that the greater stress we place on the part of human faith which remembers Jesus' death the greater the necessity to fence the table, at least in theory. There is no meaning to those who are not in a position to remember and draw on the importance of the cross through their own faith, although this understanding can reduce the significance of communion, so that in practice churches are much less concerned to actively restrict participation. On the other hand, the more we might stress communion as a means of grace, the greater the possibility there is for communion to be a space in which faith is found rather than only reaffirmed. The resurgence of a greater sacramental understanding may offer a yet unexplored opportunity for reflecting on a greater openness at the table.

John Colwell develops a sacramental understanding of the Lord's supper through which we participate in Christ, drawing, significantly, on the way the Passover is a participation in the Exodus. In attempting to tease out the sacramental nature of the meal, Colwell uses various descriptions, including that of indwelling the story:

by means of this sacrament we are brought to indwell the gospel story: the story becomes present to us; it is not merely heard, it is indwelt... As we indwell the story so we are indwelt through the story and so we are changed; this story becomes our story, the defining truth of our lives.[46]

As hinted earlier, the link between Passover and Lord's supper is significant, for the former was a celebration among a gathered community, but with open edges that allows space for others. Colwell suggests that both were participatory sacrificial meals.[47] Whereas this sets Passover and Lord's supper apart from other meals it does so in way that is not exclusive. If to participate in the Lord's supper, and Passover, is to indwell the story, then much of Jesus' ministry could be described in the same way. Those who participated in table fellowship with Jesus were indwelling the story, the story of God's unbounded grace. Such meals can, therefore, be properly described as sacramental, if not sacraments, for the free grace of God is mediated through created reality. Jesus' table fellowship is, therefore, much more than a vivid challenge to contemporary customs—I will eat with those people whom you will not—but participatory meals in which those who ate indwelt the story and experienced God's grace.

Drawing on this sacramental perspective might then help us to do two things. First, it offers a way to understand the connections, the similarities within the differences, between the Last Supper and other meals Jesus shares in the Gospels. In all of them the story is indwelt and all act as a means of grace. Secondly, it suggests a theological underpinning of a truly open table. Among the community of God's people the story of the gospel is retold and indwelt; it is a story of the unbounded grace of God that reaches its climax in the cross; it the story told and indwelt by the people of God among whom the crucified and risen Christ is present. But it is a story in which there is always space for others to come and experience grace and find the story.

This means that the story and the table are entrusted to the church, but not that the story and table are restricted to the church. In this sense it seems to me that Paul Beasley-Murray strikes the wrong note when he concludes that an unfenced table is not in the spirit of the New Testament: 'The Lords' Supper', he writes, 'is for the Lord's people and the Lord's people by definition will be those who have publicly committed themselves to the Lord and his people.'[48] Surely it would be better to say that the Lord's supper is celebrated by the Lord's people—it would clearly make no sense if the Lord's supper were to be celebrated outside the church community—but within which there is always space, space to experience God's grace and grow into the story.

This would bring us, amongst other things, to the delicate question of children and communion. When is it appropriate for children within the church, not only to

---

[46] Colwell, *Promise and Presence*, p. 158.
[47] Colwell, *Promise and Presence*, p. 156.
[48] Paul Beasley-Murray, *Faith and Festivity: A Guide for Today's Worship Leaders* (Eastbourne: MARC, 1991), p. 63.

be present at communion, or even to be offered a carefully thought through alternative, but to fully participate? One argument suggests that if participation is based on faith, and the invitation is to those 'who love the Lord', then children need to be given the opportunity to participate on the basis of the faith that they have. This would suggest that it would not be appropriate for all children to participate, but for those who express and show a clear faith. This would either require someone within the church community, a parent, minister or other leader, to talk with the children and be a gentle process of vetting, or for space to be given for children to opt in the same way as adult visitors. Nigel Wright suggests both practices, recognizing that communion is one way in which people are drawn among the people of God into the deeper life of the body, while suggesting that issues of correctness, though important, are secondary to matters of open and gracious acceptance. He proposes that children above the age of accountability might receive communion, if they wish to, from those who serve, while others might be served by their parents, with all those not partaking of bread and wine receiving a blessing.

An opposing argument, as for example expressed by Paul Beasley-Murray, is that normally communion should be reserved for those baptized in a Baptist context or those in good standing with their local church: 'The Lord's Supper is for those who have committed their lives to Christ. Inevitably baptism (or in other traditions confirmation) is presupposed.'[49]

But there is an alternative, suggested by our argument above. Participation around the table can be a way into the story and the grace of God, rather than be dependent on prior commitment. This is line with the ministry of Jesus, his own table fellowship, an understanding of the Lord's supper that draws on its Passover roots, and also has the benefit of a certain simplicity, although not a pragmatic one. Nor does it devalue communion or make it somehow less significant, although it does challenge some of our previous understandings and practices, but is based on strong biblical and theological principles, particularly the ministry of Jesus and the sacramental nature of communion. There will be practical questions concerning how a local church handles communion which is both a way into the story as well as a recommitment to it, particularly as afar as children are concerned. There will also be certain more emotional arguments to be considered. I myself am someone for whom my first occasion participating around the table, although a few weeks before my baptism, is a clear and vivid memory. There will always be a suggestion that perhaps people should wait, so they too can have such a memory. But theologically, the church can celebrate the Lord's supper in such a way that they indwell the story and invite others to join the story for themselves. It can be a way of shaping the emerging faith of our children.

This is not the conclusion that John Colwell reaches—which is a passionate argument for eucharistic unity among the denominations. He can conceive of no

---

[49] Paul Beasley-Murray, *Faith and Festivity*, p. 64. This approach raises some interesting practical issues about those baptized as infants but not confirmed and those from a Salvation Army background.

'basis sufficient to exclude any baptised person or persons from participating here and from the grace that is offered here'.[50] This suggests a very clear relationship between baptism and communion, in which the once for all event precedes the repeatable. But a suggestion in his earlier chapter on baptism might lead us, without this definitive link, to a more inclusive view of communion. Colwell regards baptism 'not so much a first step on the pathway of discipleship and obedience, as it is the means through which we are set on that pathway'.[51] This argument is partly drawn from Calvin's argument that baptism (and he means paedobaptism) as a sign of God's promise is a means to faith since it is a means of grace. So Colwell continues,

> We do not become disciples in detachment from the Church and the means of grace that constitute its sacramental life; rather we are shaped in the habits and virtues of discipleship precisely through our participation in the Church and its sacramental life.[52]

The Relationship between Communion and Baptism

Earlier we began to reflect on the connection between baptism and communion in which the first is normally thought of as the sacrament of initiation and the second of continuation. Moltmann expresses this well when he writes that 'just as baptism is the eschatological sign of starting out...so the table of the Lord is the eschatological sign of being on the way'.[53] In many ways it makes perfect sense, with the once for all act of baptism coming first. This is particularly true in a Christendom setting, when all would have been baptized as infants. But there is a certain circularity to the argument here. Communion is for those who are clearly part of the covenant community and so should follow baptism which is the public initiation into this community. Then again, the baptism of infants necessarily precedes communion, so communion is, therefore, for the baptized community. We must return again to any necessary connection between baptism and communion and the significance of this connection in the current mission context.

In the Acts of the Apostles, 3,000 are added to the church on the day of Pentecost. Assuming that the baptisms happened that same day, and it certainly seems that there was no preparation phase but baptism followed repentance, the pattern here is that baptism marks entry into the believing community which is nourished by breaking bread. By the second century, some very firm boundaries had been put in

---

[50] Colwell, *Promise and Presence*, p. 178.
[51] Colwell, *Promise and Presence*, p. 131.
[52] Colwell, *Promise and Presence*, p. 132.
[53] Jürgen Moltmann, *The Church in the Power of the Spirit* (London: SCM Press, 1977), p. 243.

place, and non-believers were barred from Christian assemblies.[54] This was in part, at least, a clear response to the continued threat of persecution. There had also established by this time a lengthy period of catechumenate, in which both baptism and admittance to the Lord's table came after much teaching and preparation. In between we have suggested that the Pauline churches were shaped quite significantly by their social context that created a significant distinction between the church and the rest of society, necessary for these new groups to form and function, but a distinction that was certainly not absolute. It was this context that shaped the experience of the Lord's supper as secondary to baptism, which was to become fixed in church tradition.

Nigel Wright suggests that 'practically speaking open communion reverses the likely order of sacraments, since worshippers are more likely to encounter a communion than a baptism', although he includes the caveat that such changes have happened without the longer term consequences necessarily having been assessed.[55] One of the consequences would be to create a certain flexibility within the relationship between baptism and communion which itself would impact the way that baptism and communion function. For some, whose conversion is sudden and immediate, baptism will precede communion, which will be a celebration of new found faith. For others, whose conversion is a longer journey within the company of the gathered community, the Lord's supper may provide occasions of movement on the journey to baptism. Drawing on an earlier suggestion from 1 Corinthians 10, we might describe both events as covenantal, but recognizing a range of understandings of covenant language.

Baptism is a clear boundary marker in which both faith in Christ is declared and an individual is incorporated into membership of the covenant community. Communion, on the other hand, may be a covenantal occasion in that the promises of the covenant are proclaimed and celebrated and the invitation to find God's grace is offered. The church will then be both a baptized and eucharistic community. It will be a baptized community for this will be the boundary marker that marks the decisive entry of disciples into the covenant community. It will be a eucharistic community, because the table will be at the heart of the church's experience of God, but not because communion will act as a boundary marker in the same way as baptism. Rather the table will be a place of grace for all those 'on the way', which can include those on the way to baptism and those on the way of their Christian journeys post-baptism. In this way the two sacraments can function in complementary ways, baptism declaring the membership of the church and communion proclaiming its openness to the world.

---

[54] Alan Kreider, *The Change of Conversion and the Origin of Christendom* (Harrisburg, PA: Trinity Press International, 1999), p. 14.

[55] Nigel G. Wright, *Free Church, Free State: The Positive Baptist Vision* (Milton Keynes: Paternoster, 2005), p. 155.

Communion and Salvation

This leads on to one final reflection, which is the connection between communion and our understanding of salvation. Jürgen Moltmann comments that 'in the Lord's Supper Christ's redeeming future is anticipated'.[56] But what is the nature of this redeeming future? And, more particularly, does our decision for an open or closed table both reflect and influence our understanding of this future? A closed table is a sign of the covenant community as it will be in the eschaton, a provisional manifestation of the messianic banquet. But does it also suggest that as the closed table excludes now so some will be excluded from the final banquet, and if so who will be excluded? An open table is a table that is becoming, that looks to the great feast but has a sense of provisionality. Does it suggest that at the end there might be a sense of incompleteness, because the banquet is spread, the places are laid and the invitations are given, but some will have chosen not to be there?

As crucial as it is to pursue biblical investigations into the practice of the early church and theological reflections on the nature of sacraments, the celebration of the Lord's supper that declares the great work of God in Christ is also linked to our very understanding of the gospel itself. This is exemplified in the Episcopal Church of the United States of America. As part of the worldwide Anglican communion it practices the discipline of baptism as the one requirement before participation in the eucharist, but one of a number of its recent controversies has been the practice of open communion by some of its churches in which those not baptized are welcomed to participate. In considering this practice, Philip Turner, one of its own ministers, specifically connects this to an underlying understanding of the gospel he perceives throughout ECUSA.[57] This he describes as a gospel of acceptance not of redemption, in which God has already included everyone, and so the working theology of ECUSA is one in which there is no place for challenge.

But this need not be the case. The meals of Jesus were often marked both by radical inclusion but also by radical challenge — the story of Zacchaeus being perhaps the most striking. Although an open table can be a place of radical inclusion it, too, can also be a place of challenge that becomes a point on the journey towards fuller discipleship. The story of redemption is remembered and celebrated and the invitation is for all to come and indwell this story for themselves, that the story might indwell them. As in the case of Zacchaeus, radical inclusion can lead not simply to acceptance but to a radical conversion.

This leads us to back to where we began, with the liturgy of the Lord's supper. Not only might we change the invitation we use, to make it clear that here is time and a space when the grace of God can be found by all, we might also reflect on the order within the supper. Traditionally a prayer of confession, and maybe an assurance of forgiveness, will continue after the invitation and precede the sharing of bread and

---

[56] Moltmann, *Church in the Power of the Spirit*, p. 243.

[57] Philip Turner, 'ECUSA'S God: A Descriptive Comment on the "Working Theology" of the Episcopal Church USA', at http:www.anglicancommunioninstitute.org/articles/ECUSA_God.htm, accessed 23 August 2006.

wine—the influence of 1 Corinthians 11.28—and the need for self-examination. But there is also an argument for confession after the sharing of bread and wine, for while we were still sinners Christ died for us. The offer of bread and wine is, then, the radical offer of unmerited grace, which draws out of us a new repentance and conversion and to which we respond with confession.

Conclusion

We began by reflecting on liturgies for the Lord's supper produced within the British Baptist family and noticed a gradual change in tone and language that suggested a more inclusive attitude. It would appear that in practice in our churches' edges have been deliberately blurred to make our congregations more welcoming, but without addressing the underlying theology of communion. In this paper I have attempted to suggest some biblical and theological reasons why such blurring of the edges is not only acceptable, but is to be encouraged. Interpreting the Pauline passages both within their specific context and building a theology of the Lord's supper from the ministry and teaching of Jesus, as well as 1 Corinthians, I have proposed an understanding of communion that is an offer of grace through which all may be invited to find and indwell the story of God's salvation.

It is John Wesley who is famously linked to the phrase 'a converting ordinance',[58] although it must be admitted that the situation of his time in which virtually all were baptized members of the Church of England, but not fully converted, is very different from our post-Christendom age. But in our particular mission context a truly open table might be an important part of the church's future mission, and so we may find the Lord's supper to be a converting ordinance in an even deeper way.

---

[58] John Wesley, *The Works of John Wesley* (ed. T. Jackson; 14 vols; London, 1831), I, p. 262: 'But experience shows the gross falsehood of the assertion that the Lord's Supper is not a converting ordinance. For many now present now know, the very beginning of your conversion to God...was wrought at the Lord's Supper', cited by Horton Davies, *Worship and Theology in England:* Volume 2. *From Watts and Wesley to Martineau, 1690–1900* (Grand Rapids, MI: Eerdmans, 1996), p. 208 n. 69.

CHAPTER 8

Penance

Paul Sheppy

Introduction

What is the Baptist doctrine of the sacrament of penance? The question is, of course, absurd. It assumes that there is a common Baptist doctrine about anything in particular, whereas it is proverbial that where two Baptists meet there are three opinions. It assumes that Baptists have a common understanding about what a sacrament might be (although an extremely careful and coherent analysis and argument was made by Clark Pinnock in *Baptist Sacramentalism*, it would not convince all Baptists).[1] Finally, it assumes that if Baptists could agree about the nature and number of the sacraments they would include penance as one of that group.

If Baptists have historically demonstrated a common attitude to penance, it may be thought to have been one of extreme disapprobation and opposition.[2] It offends

---

[1] Clark H. Pinnock, 'The Physical Side of Being Spiritual: God's Sacramental Presence', in A.R. Cross and P.E. Thompson (eds), *Baptist Sacramentalism* (Studies in Baptist History and Thought, 5; Milton Keynes: Paternoster, 2003), pp. 8-20.

[2] This opposition arises primarily from the historical context of the Reformation as a protest against Roman Catholic practice. It may be worth noting that among the liturgical reforms following Vatican II, there was a working group dedicated to tackling penance (reconciliation). Its terms were established by the relevant text in *Sacrosanctum Concilium* (72): 'The rites and formularies for the sacrament of penance are to be revised so that they more clearly express both the nature and effect of the sacrament.' See, *Documents on the Liturgy, 1963–1979: Conciliar Papal and Curial Texts* (Collegeville, MN: The Liturgical Press, 1982), p. 17.

Annibale Bugnini, *The Reform of the Liturgy 1948–1975* (Collegeville, MN: The Liturgical Press, 1990), p. 665, records that at the first meeting of the group it established a number of points to be kept in mind:

> Sin is by its nature both an offense [*sic*] against God and a wound inflicted on the Church.
> Sacramental reconciliation is reconciliation with both God and the Church.
> The entire Christian community works together for the conversion of sinners.

Few Baptists, one imagines, would have any difficulty with the first and third of these propositions. The continuing difficulty resides in how reconciliation with God and one another is effected and expressed.

against the doctrine of the priesthood of all believers (or at least the individualistic exposition of that teaching) and it is contrasted to its disadvantage with penitence and repentance. The latter may be designated 'godly', whereas penance clearly belongs to the despised activities of priestcraft.

Why, then, am I drawn to attempt an essay on 'the sacrament of penance'? Those who know me well will put it down to my wilfulness; others, who know me better, may attribute my interest to the influence of my devout Anglo-Catholic mother. However, while both views may contain elements of truth about me, neither finally delivers an adequate answer. At least in part, my determination to think about this matter arises from a central difficulty for Christian psychology: how do I know that I am forgiven? The saving bath of baptism cleanses me from a guilty conscience before God (cf. 1 Pet. 3.21), and it is the event in which I die to sin (Rom. 6.1-11). The Christian, who has died to sin, cannot live in sin or practise sin (1 Jn 3.6). This is what I read; yet my life still bears the marks of daily sin. How can I quieten my conscience? And, more importantly, how can I amend my life?

It is to these questions that the sacrament of penance addresses itself. Small wonder, then, that I question whether we have not thrown out the baby and bathwater in one outraged Reformation revolt against the kind of abuse that resulted in the selling of indulgences.

Sacrament

Before directly answering these questions, however, I want to address the question of what is meant by a sacrament. In the volume of essays previously referred to, there were several references to the idea of a sacrament as the outward and visible sign of an inward and spiritual grace. However, there was no real consideration of the other thing that those whom we might call sacramental in their expression of Christian worship, teaching and practice want to say about a sacrament. For such Christians a sacrament is indeed the outward sign of the inward grace; but there is more: it effects what it signifies. Twelfth-century Scholasticism makes clear this indissoluble link of sign and cause.[3] We will need later to address the question of causality, which can

---

Bugnini was successively Secretary of the Commission for General Liturgical Restoration (1948–1960), Secretary of the Pontifical Preparatory Commission on the Liturgy (1960–62), Peritus [Expert] of the Conciliar Commission on the Liturgy (1962–64), Secretary of the Consilium for the Implementation of the Constitution on the Liturgy (1964–69), and Secretary of the Congregation for Divine Worship (1969–75). There was no one in the Roman Catholic Church who knew more of the details of the reform than Bugnini. Indeed, he effectively managed the enterprise. *The Reform of the Liturgy* (along with the International Commission on English in the Liturgy's *Documents on the Liturgy 1963–1979: Conciliar, Papal and Curial Texts* [Collegeville, MN: The Liturgical Press, 1982]) is primary evidence of how the liturgy and rites of the Roman Catholic Church developed following Vatican II.

[3] The *Summa Sententiarum* (ca. 1140) puts the matter thus: 'Sacramentum est visibilis forma invisibilis gratiae in eo collatae, quam scilicet confert ipsum sacramentum. Non est

lend itself to a quasi-magical view of the sacraments. For the moment, we note that it is in many definitions assumed; there is more to the sacraments than the issue of signification.

J.L. Austin and others have taught us to recognize some forms of speech as being performative.[4] Where the argumentation of the Schoolmen may prove problematic to some, Austin and his interlocutors have demonstrated that speech-events may be both causative and symbolic. And if speech-events may have this bipolar quality, it is at least worth wondering why other action-events may not share this duality.

Among the examples best known of performative utterance are the promissory words in the marriage rite and the kinds of formulae that open or close formal meetings, or that name ships, or that accompany the cutting of ribbons when buildings and bridges are opened. The speech-act accomplishes something sensibly and coherently real. A moment ago you were not married; now you are. The bridge was closed to traffic; now it is open for use. The congress had not begun; now it is in session.

When a sacrament is described as effecting what it signifies, we are being asked to understand that the symbolic act is symbolic of something real and that the declaration 'Your sins are forgiven you' has what we might call 'a cash value'. Many Baptists may, on reflection, be able to accept the idea that baptism is an outward and visible sign of an inward and spiritual grace. I suspect, however, that fewer would be happy to understand baptism as effecting what it signifies: that is, the making of a Christian. Whatever 1 Peter 3.21 may say ('And baptism...now saves you'), few Baptists will want to read those words other than 'symbolically'—which is precisely to beg the question: What does the symbol symbolize? If there is no direct link between the symbol and a something other that it symbolizes, then there is no symbol. An empty symbol is, indeed, no symbol at all.

Whether we like it or not, we ought not to imagine that to describe a sacrament as 'an outward and visible sign...' is, of itself, adequate for Christians whose native theological air is sacramental. Without the additional notion of the sign's efficacy, there is little being said. However, as John Colwell reminds us, this can become a misleading way of speaking, since the effective and efficient agent of grace is God; the sacrament is the instrumental means by which that grace is mediated.[5]

---

solummodo sacrae rei signum, sed etiam efficacia... Sacramentum non solum significat, sed etiam confert illud cuius est signum vel significatio' ('The sacrament is the visible form of the invisible grace contained in it, which the sacrament itself confers. Not only is it the sign of the holy thing, but also its efficacy... The sacrament not only signifies but also confers that of which it is the sign or significance') in J.-P. Migne (ed.), *Patrologiae Cursus Completus: Series Latina* (Paris: Garnier, 1844–64), 176, p. 117.

[4] J.L. Austin, *Philosophical Papers* (Oxford: Clarendon, 1961).

[5] John E. Colwell, *Promise and Presence: An Exploration of Sacramental Theology* (Carlisle: Paternoster, 2005), pp. 7-9. Colwell notes that both Aquinas and Calvin hold this distinction—the latter in conscious approval of Aquinas' position on this point. Colwell again urges the distinction between the 'who' and the 'what' of sacramental

Strictly speaking, therefore, we should say that God effects through the sacrament what it signifies. What is important to recall is that grace is an expression of God's freedom to be God. Grace may not be manipulated or 'magicked'; God's covenantal relationship with the creation is mediated through the creation in acts of new creation. God's grace is known in the outward and visible sign as through it God effects the new creation to which the sign points.

From such a perspective, the ministers of the sacrament (baptizers, eucharistic presidents, confessors) are themselves instruments through which God effects grace. The priest, or minister of the sacrament, is not therefore a shaman who possesses grace for distribution upon request; it is God who is at work through the sacrament and its ministers. With such an understanding, the possibility of priestcraft is removed.

Sin

Certainly, no one in the various movements of the Reformation wanted to do away with a doctrine of sin or to underestimate its seriousness. Our alienation and estrangement from God, our rebellion and defiance against God, our refusal to be dependent upon God and our consequent inability to live in the freedom of the children of God by which we grow into the image of Christ were all self-evident to those who, for a variety of reasons, wished either to see themselves in a reformed Catholic Church or to separate themselves from a degenerate institution which no longer manifested what the dissidents saw as the marks of true Christian practice as evidenced in the New Testament and the early apostolic period.

The appeal to an earlier 'pure' church is beset with problems. Anything more than a cursory reading of the New Testament will reveal that the earliest Christian communities were not as free from sin as abstract doctrine argued they should have been. Incest, gluttony and drunkenness at the table, and a divisive spirit of pride among the members marred the church in Corinth—to cite but one example, and this a church that St Paul describes as being possessed of every spiritual gift (1 Corinthians 1.7). Moreover, the notion that there is a golden age lying in the past which we should seek to recapture runs contrary to the New Testament's forward look where the goal lies before us rather than behind us. Yet again, the idea that there are those who are 'spiritually pure' who constitute 'the true church' leads to a gnostic view. Its adherents are, of course, always themselves the 'spiritual' who find salvation, while others are the 'carnal', doomed to eternal damnation. In such a view, there is a serious danger of not taking sin seriously in oneself; what is condemned in others may be excused in the elect.

Whatever the other reasons for that confluence of streams we call the Reformation, those caught up in this visionary spring-cleaning/radical departure shared a concern in common with all Christendom. They differed in how they

---

efficacy ('agency' and 'instrumentality') at the conclusion of his chapter entitled 'Sacramentality and the Doctrine of Creation' on pp. 60-61.

understood baptism's curative effect in relation to sin, yet all agreed that the continuing experience of sin constituted a problem both in the life of the individual Christian and in the communion and community of the church.

Church Discipline

Although Baptists throughout their history have been suspicious of auricular confession and priestly absolution, they have nonetheless maintained (in varying forms and degrees of rigour) a penitential practice.[6] However, in order to uncover it, we must look through library catalogues and bibliographies not for 'penance' or 'confession' or 'penitential rites' but for 'church discipline'. Under such a heading all sorts of records spring to light.

From their earliest communities and congregations Baptists produced codes of church discipline. Two of these will serve to provide examples from seventeenth-century England and eighteenth-century America.[7]

T. Dowley, writing about the early English practice (which he describes as 'intended to achieve holiness of life and character in the members of the church'[8]), notes a distinction between preventive and corrective discipline. The first was aimed at maintaining the individual and corporate spiritual health of the membership; for this purpose members might be asked to sign a covenant that embodied a set of rules. These, together with visitation and meetings for prayer and fasting, provided a means of pastoral discipline and supervision that we may call preventive.

Where this failed, corrective measures were a subsequent and frequent recourse. For example, the 1656 meeting of the General Assembly of General Baptists records the following.

> 10. It is agreed that when any sepreate (*sic*) or not seppreate (*sic*) if they be convicted of Sin from the Church and departe from the faith of Christ that they should be (by two fitt messengers appointed & sent from the Church) declared against as incommunicable in things p'taining to the worshipe of God and also not to be eaten with in common eating and this be and this to be (*sic*) looked upon as the first admonition Matt. 18:12. I Cor. 5:9, 10, 11. Tit. 3:11, 12. II Thess 3:6, 14, 15. I King. 13:8, 9. Pro. 29:1.Psal. 50:17, 68:21.

---

[6] As indicated below, in its more rigorous forms penitential discipline was frequently public (where private admonition failed). Such public rigour is not currently fashionable in contemporary British congregations. Nonetheless, private admonition is not abandoned and in most services of worship there will be general confessional material—sometimes accompanied by a general declaration of God's faithfulness to forgive the penitent.

[7] T. Dowley, 'Baptists and Discipline in the 17th Century', *Baptist Quarterly* 24.4 (October, 1971), pp. 157-66; and J.L. Garrett, *Baptist Church Discipline* (2nd edition). (Paris, AR: The Baptist Standard Bearer, 2nd edn, 2004).

[8] Dowley, 'Baptists and Discipline', p. 158

11. Moreover, that thos thus under admonition should be again after the exerciseing of patience toward them according to the natour of the offence decleared against by Agreement of the Church they Remaing obstinate and this to be looked upon as the second admonition yet not forbiding persons to admonish as they shall occasionally meete wt. them. Tit. 3:1. II Thess. 3:15.

12. Moreover it is agreed that such after their first & second admonition should be Rejacted. that is to say such as kick against the counsel of God given by the Church going on in the error of their ways should not be looked upon as Brethren nor any ways belonging to the body so as the Church hath any more to do to looke after them, being such as are subverted and sineth being condemed of themselves. Titt. 3:10, 11. I Cor. 6:16, 22. Heb. 10:26, 27, 28, 29. Heb. 6:4, 5, 6, 7, 8. Jude 12.

13. It is agreed that those three distinct proceedings be declared to the offenders with all solemnity gravely & wisely at times set apart for this purpose after perticuler & plain discovery of their errors.

14. It is agreed that in case of necessity as betwixt man & wife members may eat common food with P'sons that are incommunicable in other things. Matt. 12:1 to 8. Joh. 7:22, 23.[9]

The Baptist Church at Loughwood, beginning its meetings in 1653 and more evidently Calvinist in theology, was similarly exercised a year later, noting:

That Bro. Phillipp and Bro. Jno. Demigge havinge neglected to assemble with the church on the first day and that tyme meett with those persons which hold the doctrines of freewill, fallinge from grace and generall redemption; and doe upon examination profess themselves to be of that judgement, and beinge warned to come to the church that soe their scruples touchinge these doctrines might be removed. But doe neglect the same and refuse to heare the church therein. It is ordered that Bro. Jno. Davy and Bro. James Hitt doe sometyme this weeke warne them to doe their duty in cominge to the church the next first day in order to their satisfaction.[10]

In 1658, one brave woman explained herself to the church meeting (though it seems to little avail):

Bro. Gryland and Bro. Martin then informed the church of the disorderly walkinge of sister Hossiter of Honiton. Carelesse attendinge the meetings at that place; and her manifestinge an inclination to the delusions of the Quakers. The said brethren informed the church also that she hath been dealt with severall tymes by particular

---

[9] See Dowley, 'Baptists and Discipline', pp. 158-59. Taken from Church Book of Speldhurst and Penbury (kept in the British Museum among its Additional Manuscripts Number 36709, p. 30).

[10] J.B. Whiteley, 'Church Discipline in the Loughwood Records', *Baptist Quarterly* 31.6 (April, 1986), p. 288. The record is dated 25 February 1654.

members and joyntly by the whole people in that place on those things and as yett they see noe amendment in her.

Sister Hossiter for herself.

That she did question whether she did sitt under the ministry of the gospel at the meetinge of the members at Honiton. And havinge severall scriptures laid before her (as 2 Kings 7 the case of the lepers for one) she was then minded to goe to the Quakers meetinge and did accordingly goe to their meeting and was taken sick at that tyme; and have since been convinced of their error and hath nott gone to those meetings any more. She seemeth also to be satisfied to sitt downe in her place in the church; yet seemeth of an unstable spiritt as to the ordinances of it. Some endeavours were then used to convince her of it. On the whole the church agreed to admonish her to more close walkinge for future which done accordingly.[11]

Unfortunately, despite this meeting on 29 October 1658, less than two months later (16 December) she was back with the Quakers. The Baptist meeting then decided 'in regard of her persistinge in her unsoundnesse and disorder above mentioned she be withdrawne from which was accordingly done this day'.[12]

Withdrawal was a common recourse in case of persistent breach of discipline, but it could be reversed. Sister Sprague 'havinge offered satisfaction by repentance before the church is received into full communion againe'.[13] In the case of full excommunication, it appears that the matter was irreversible

Purity of doctrine was a major consideration among the early Baptists. Richard Copp was excommunicated because of his adherence to doctrines of freewill, falling from grace and general redemption:

he still stiffly persisting therein and indeavouring to cause divisions in the church and to draw away others after him, was by the church in the name of Christ—delivered up to Satan, and was judged fitt to be no further communicated with than a heathen or publican...[14]

However, public behaviour was also a matter for church discipline: drunkenness in the street, lying, slander, pregnancy when unmarried and the like were all occasions for record in the minute book of the church at Loughwood, whose disciplinary zeal persisted at least into the nineteenth century. In 1834 a new set of rules was approved which concluded with a robust defence of the practice:

Laws are absolutely necessary to the well being of earthly kingdoms... How much more necessary to the peace of the Christian church is discipline.[15]

---

[11] Whiteley, 'Church Discipline', p. 289.
[12] Whiteley, 'Church Discipline', p. 289.
[13] Whiteley, 'Church Discipline', p. 290. Record dated 14 December 1655.
[14] Whiteley, 'Church Discipline', p. 290. Record dated 24 August 1654.
[15] Cited by Whiteley, 'Church Discipline', p. 293.

In eighteenth-century America, there was a similar concern among Baptists for church discipline. In 1773, the Baptist Association in Charleston, South Carolina, adopted a 'Summary of Church Discipline', which they published in the following year. It dealt in turn with 'a True and Orderly Gospel Church', 'Church Officers', 'Receiving Persons to Church Membership', 'the Duties Incumbent on Church Members', 'Church Censures' and 'the Association of Churches'. By far the longest section related to censure.

In the introduction to this section, the writers argue that reward and punishment are the means by which law gains its force. In the case of church law, God may punish directly,[16] or by means 'which Christ, by his Word, authorizes his church to inflict upon its rebellious and unworthy members'.[17]

Three levels of punishment are listed in increasing order of severity.[18] First, rebuke or admonition points out the error, appeals to the conscience, counsels and encourages repentance, and prays for the sinner's reclamation. It is reserved for failures of care and attention to the life of the fellowship. Secondly, suspension includes removal from office, from the Lord's table and from judging and voting at the church meeting. Aggravating breaches of fellowship merit this level of censure, as do espousing heretical principles, gossip and slander, laziness in the duties of daily life and gross crime (the last of these, however, only where accompanied by 'some tokens of repentance'). Thirdly, excommunication 'is a disfranchising from all the immunities of a fellow-citizen with the saints' and involves delivering an offender 'unto Satan for the destruction of the flesh'. It is reserved for 'notorious and atrocious crimes'—some of which are listed: all sins against the letter of the ten commandments; those that call for severe corporal punishment from human laws (provided that such laws are not contrary to the laws of God); those that are scandalous in their nature and which expose the church to contempt.

> No man has a right of himself to perform this censure; it is a punishment inflicted by many (2 Cor. 2:6). But this great censure is to be executed by the elders (ministers) of churches, with the consent of the members of them; for they have a right to do this, previous to their having elders, and when they have none, as to receive members, so to expel them. The power of it originally lies in the church; the authority of executing it lies in the elders with the consent and by the order of the church, as the directions to the churches concerning this matter testify.

Reading the body of material from which the above extracts are drawn, it may be that the reader inclines to John Milton's opinion that 'New Presbyter is but old Priest writ large'.[19]

---

[16] Nothing is said about God rewarding the faithful and obedient, only of punishment 'to be inflicted on the rebellious'.

[17] Garrett, *Baptist Church Discipline*, p. 49.

[18] Garrett, *Baptist Church Discipline*, pp. 49-53.

[19] J. Milton, *On the New Forcers of Conscience under the Long Parliament*. See, e.g., *Milton: Complete Shorter Poems* (ed. John Carey; London and New York: Longman, 1971), pp. 293-96.

What I hope to have demonstrated in this brief historical excursus is that, whatever early Baptists may have thought about auricular confession and the sacrament of penance—and it is pretty clear that they rejected it—they were still faced with the problem of how to deal with the believer who sins.

A harsher view might be that the power of the priest was at least exercised in private; the power of the congregation was extremely public. In the preface to the second edition of his work, Garrett notes an increasing body of Baptist writing since he first wrote on the topic of church discipline. Commentators have varied in the rigour they espouse, though most advocate some degree of discipline. Garrett observes the gradual diminution of church discipline among Southern Baptists and suggests one possible cause as being a rejection of 'the legalistic and punitive character of the earlier practice of corrective discipline'.[20] What becomes clear is that, while many of the more recent advocates have urged the purpose of church discipline as being restorative rather than punitive, none appears to think of its mode as being sacramental. Yet, as Dowley notes, the purpose of church discipline was the endeavour to maintain the holiness of the congregation (individually and corporately), citing the *Berkshire Association Records* which comment about those who have been disciplined that 'Diligent indevor be used according to the Scriptures for thaire recovery'.[21] At Spilshill General Baptist Church in Kent, it is recorded that elders were to ask searching questions of an offender and that the pastor was to add a grave exhortation before the offender could be received back into fellowship.[22] At the White's Alley church those received back into fellowship stood up before the breaking of bread; an elder read out their names and declared the church's satisfaction with their repentance and restoration.[23] Some congregations were extremely rigorous. At the Mill Yard Seventh Day Baptist church there are several instances or offenders asking to be received back into fellowship, but being refused as having failed to meet the congregation's requirements.[24] The process of sifting and searching which preceded restoration to the table fellowship of the church is very similar to the practice of the confessional in the sacrament of penance.

---

[20] Garrett, *Baptist Church Discipline*, p. iv, citing Stephen M, Haines, 'Church Discipline as Practiced by Representative Southern Baptist Churches, 1880–1939' (PhD diss. Southwestern Baptist Seminary, undated).

[21] Dowley, 'Baptists and Discipline', p. 160. Berkshire Association Records, 1652–1708, transcript 1905, p. 8, kept at the time Dowley was writing in the Library of Baptist Church House.

[22] Dowley, 'Baptists and Discipline', p. 160, citing Christopher Blackwood, 1606–68, sometime Rector of Staplehurst, Elder of Spilshill General Baptist Church, Kent.

[23] Dowley, 'Baptists and Discipline', p. 160, citing the White's Alley Church Book, p. 26.

[24] Dowley, 'Baptists and Discipline', pp. 160-61, citing the Speldhurst and Penbury Church Book, p. 14.

Forgiveness

Within the dissenting traditions of the Reformation churches, confession of sin has undeniably found a regular place in public worship—whether formally or informally structured. The experiential reality of post-baptismal sin requires confession of that sin as the prelude to seeking the forgiveness of God and renewal (or continuing conversion) in the journey to the fullness of the measure of Christ. The difficulty with the public liturgical expression of confession is that it has rarely been conceived of as other than a general confession made by the congregation together. What such general confession fails directly and specifically to do is to afford the individual the occasion to address specific sins, to make proper restitution to those who have been wronged, and to find appropriate direction for an amendment of life.

To ask for forgiveness and to know that forgiveness may well be two different things. Equally, to seek renewal and to know renewal in oneself may not be the same. The pastoral questions to be answered are, 'How do I know that I am forgiven?' and 'How may I find grace to grow in obedience to the way of Jesus Christ?'

Penance opposes the tendency we have to excuse and justify ourselves. It begins by bringing us into contact with another who witnesses our confession and who inhibits swift and easy forgiveness by requiring us to put the past right (insofar as we can) and to adopt a regime of living for the future which will keep us from falling again into the same sin. Only then will we hear the promise (in the name of God, Father, Son and Holy Spirit) of forgiveness.[25]

When we make our confession in private by our bedsides, there is no one to check that we are not cheating. If we confess to ourselves (as it were), we may find that we forgive ourselves too quickly: a practice that leads to cheap grace. When the younger son returns to his father (Lk. 15.11-32), his confession is not just of sin 'against

---

[25] Bugnini, *Reform of the Liturgy*, p. 672 n. 23, records that during the discussions relating to penance, the Vatican Secretariat of State made the following comment: 'The Our Father does not seem to be a prayer sufficiently suited to expressing sorrow and the determination not to sin again, which the sacrament of reconciliation requires. What is needed is an act more directly expressive of "contrition" and "determination" and more directly related to the *metanoia*, or change of heart, proper to this sacrament.'

When, in 1974, the *Ordo Paenitentiae* was published, the authentic renewal which the sacrament expresses was to be found in the following elements: the primary requirement of an interior disposition to conversion, trusting in the grace and mercy of God; an ecclesial dimension which reminded individual penitents of their need to make and find reconciliation with their brothers and sisters as well as with God; the use of scripture and its task in enlightening the conscience and urging conversion; a real confession of sins in which particular sin is addressed beyond a general and abstract acknowledgement of sinfulness; a reminder that reconciliation is a gift of God beyond moral and psychological release in which the gift of the Spirit is renewed in us; the role for restoration in the acts of penance; the need to move from confession to thanksgiving and praise for the mercy of God—this last very appropriately expressed in a subsequent celebration of the eucharist.

heaven' but 'before you'. Jesus' comment about the ease of saying 'Your sins are forgiven' (cf. Mk 2.5-11) hints at some of the difficulty relating to dispensing forgiveness when the offender has not confessed to the injured party. The Pharisees assert that only God can forgive sins. If we confine sin to being an offence against God only, then the Pharisees are right. If, however, we also understand sin as an offence in the realm of human relations, then a quick 'Sorry, God' is not enough; we must, like the younger son, make our confession to the human 'you'.

Moreover, I suspect that we do not find forgiveness when we do not acknowledge the full force of our sinfulness and our sinning in the lives of others. Forgiving oneself is not real forgiveness; the guilt remains along with the feeling and sense of guilt. In part, our reluctance to confess to another may result from our abhorrence of having to rehearse and relive the offence we have given.

Penance and Eucharist

Reference was made earlier to the question of post-baptismal sin; the problem was sharpened by the relationship between such sinning and consequent attendance at the table and participation in the communion of bread and wine. The ancient invitation 'Holy things for holy people' expresses a clear link between the bread and wine as signs of the body and blood of Christ and those who will receive them as signs of God's holy people in the world. How can the sinner be holy?[26] The succinct answer from within the first-century church was, 'If we confess our sins, he who is faithful and just will forgive us our sins and cleanse us from all unrighteousness' (1 Jn 1.9). Confession was the indispensable condition for forgiveness and cleansing.

It now becomes immediately obvious why there arose a practice of confession with an accompanying assurance of divine forgiveness and cleansing. Without it, how could one attend that most primary expression of communion with and participation in Christ, the eucharist?

John Colwell argues that private confession can lead to 'legalism, selectivity and artificiality', adding

> A general confession is comprehensive by its very nature but it need not thereby be insincere or cursory. Rather, by identifying the essence of sin—that we have not done that which we ought to have done—a general confession identifies that which can too easily be overlooked within private confession and yet which lies at the root of all that there is confessed.

It might equally be argued that general confession fails to address anything specific and that the 'lazy penitent' thus escapes a close examination of conscience. The 'cheap grace' argument always works where a worst-case scenario is predicated.

---

[26] One is reminded of the riddle 'If salt loses its saltiness, how can you restore it?' (Mt 5.13; Mk 9.50; Lk 14.34). The later rabbinic riposte, 'With the afterbirth of a mule', simply underlines the apparent impossibility of the enterprise.

Colwell is not advocating general confession at the expense of private confession. He avoids an either-or choice and takes care to suggest that, used alongside general confession, private spiritual direction provides a mediated means of grace in cleansing us from the stains of daily pilgrimage. If he is right (and I think he is), it might be useful to consider why private confession (or its equivalent) has fallen into comparative disuse in so many situations—even those where it was previously widely practised.

The link between penance and participation in the eucharistic meal may suggest an important factor in the decline in attendance at the penitential sacrament in churches where its practice has been the traditional norm. Simply put, the issue is (it seems to me) one of frequency.[27]

The liturgical reforms of the twentieth century included the exhortation to all the faithful to receive the eucharistic elements at every Sunday celebration they attended. In traditions where there had always been a weekly (or even daily) celebration of the eucharist, there had not been any accompanying expectation that those attending would all present themselves for communion—or even that the majority would. In many other traditions the liturgy of the table was celebrated comparatively infrequently; monthly, quarterly and even annual celebrations were not unknown. Such celebrations were often linked to the great feasts of the church and in such circumstances (at Christmas or Easter, for example) there was a greater presumption of communion by those present.

Hearing several hundred confessions once or twice a year represents quite a different commitment of time and energy from hearing hundreds each week. The increased onus on the priest in the new circumstances of frequent communion was matched by a corresponding additional burden on the penitent. Unless one is highly scrupulous or systematically wicked week by week, attending auricular confession every Saturday prior to the Sunday mass becomes unsustainable. It appears to have been the case that wherever there has been an increasing emphasis on weekly communion, there has been a drop in the number of regular penitents.

Where infrequent communion was or is the norm, penance and its equivalents are easier to enforce or administer. In the Church of Scotland, the practice used to be for quarterly communion. The elders visited the members and examined them as to their fitness for receiving the elements. A token was then handed over (or withheld) which admitted the person to the table and the gifts. It is difficult to imagine that this kind of pastoral oversight and discipline is possible where weekly communion is assumed.

---

[27] The matter is exacerbated by the smaller number of priests. In the big urban parishes, there used to be several clergy living in community in the presbytery. The priest in the parish next door to my congregation 'only' gets about 900 at mass on a Sunday—and he is on his own. How might he cope with regular weekly confession from all his communicants? Assuming no more than ten minutes with each person, he would need 150 hours each week. Even with only 10% coming once a fortnight, a full working day each week would be given over to nothing other than the confessional.

Whatever we think of the examples of churchly discipline to which I have referred and the implied workload if all communicants confessed every week before they received communion, the underlying pastoral issue remains. How do we address the fact of post-baptismal sin, and how do we establish true amendment of life and quietness of conscience in our own lives and those of our people? It seems to me that the practices of both general and private confession have much to commend them. I recognize that in saying this I shall meet a considerable amount of resistance, so I will start with what I consider to be the easier case and then move to the more difficult. The grounds in each instance arise from considerations of pastoral theology.

General Confession

General confession is the corporate acknowledgement by the congregation of its sin. It is the recognition that we stand on holy ground.[28] Wonderful as are the words of Cranmer (and it ought to be possible for Baptists to use them still), they are not the only form of general confession available to us. Many of our contemporary Baptist congregations use extempore forms of general confession with varying degrees of liturgical elegance and pastoral effect.

Too often, the forms of confession that we use seem designed more to convict people of sin than to assure them of forgiveness. We ought not to forget the pastoral importance of telling those who truly repent that they are forgiven. Simply to tell God that we are sinful and to bemoan our wicked state may have an opposite effect from that intended. If the doctor tells us only that we are sick before we leave the consulting room, we are unlikely to feel that the visit has been a healing experience. Indeed, we may feel the worse for it. What we hope for, beyond diagnosis, is cure.

Confession, therefore, has always to be accompanied by the word of forgiveness, if we want it to have sacramental force. That does not necessarily mean that we offer cheap grace. In June 2004, my wife and I worshipped with the Community of the Holy Transfiguration (a monastic community of Baptist foundation) in Geelong.[29] After the gathering rite, we moved to a general confession before the liturgy of the word. The pronouncement of absolution brought me up short, and I have never since been able to shake off its wording.

If you forgive the sins of any, they are forgiven.

So far, so good. What followed brought the shock:

---

[28] In much of the world and among most world religions it is the practice of worshippers to remove their shoes before entering the place of worship. The admonition to Moses (Ex. 3.5) is an echo (some might say a pre-echo) of this apprehension of the contrast between the sinner and the transcendent holy. I could sometimes wish that worshippers in our Baptist chapels would remove their shoes and abstain from idle chatter in the sanctuary. We are not good at practising the sense of the holy.

[29] Geelong is an Australian stone's throw from Melbourne, Victoria.

If you do not, what will you do with them?

Suddenly, my complacent liturgical *savoir-faire* was overturned like no apple cart you have ever seen. If I do not forgive the sins of others, what will I do with them? Can I be a sin-bearer? Or will I force others to live imprisoned in their past, when I want my future free?

Such a general confession rocks us to (and beyond) our foundations. Absolution by the declaration of God's free grace purchased by the blood of Christ, yes; but not by cheap grace grounded in self-excuse and justification.

General confession is important and should be carefully prepared. A series of sentences 'just wanting' to tell God this and that is really not good enough. Confession begins by recognizing who God is; we confess first and foremost the greatness of God. The wall looks upright and true until the plumb line reveals its inadequacy (cf. Amos 7.7-8). How might confession look if we were to confess our sins by reference to the nature and character of God?

In 1997, I prepared a doxological confession for use by British Christians on the Sunday 1,000 days before the new millennium.[30] It included a sung congregational response (*Kyrie eleison*), which gave the prayer the feel of a litany, and it was drafted to be specific enough to avoid any suggestion of its being vague. It would have been immensely strengthened by the Geelong absolution!

Eternal God,
your love is from everlasting to everlasting.
Through your Son Jesus,
you call us to love you,
to love our neighbour,
to love our enemy.

Kyrie eleison.
or
Lord, have mercy.

Eternal God,
your word is truth,
it stands as ageless as the hills.
You call us
to speak and live the truth.

Kyrie eleison.

---

[30] The version reproduced is amended at one or two places but remains substantially the same. I used a Taizé setting of the Kyrie in the original, but printed the alternative response 'Lord, have mercy' for those who disapprove of non-English words in the liturgy—apart, of course, from Amen, Hallelujah, Alleluia, Hosanna and the like! The text was used on the radio broadcast of morning worship for the Sunday in question.

Eternal God,
where your Spirit is
there is freedom.
You call us to live as your sons and daughters,
freed from all slavery,
delivered from all tyranny.

Kyrie eleison.

Eternal God,
your kingdom is justice and peace,
you call us to be its citizens,
men and women of hope,
and generous integrity.

Kyrie eleison.

Eternal God,
you made us in your image,
you make us anew in the image
of your Son, Jesus Christ.

Kyrie eleison.

Eternal God,
in Jesus you show us
that to be holy
is to sit with the outcast,
to embrace the unclean,
to welcome the unloved,
to love with heart and mind and all our strength.
You call us to be holy
as you are holy.

Kyrie eleison.

By rooting confession in the dominical commands, we at once declare the righteousness of God and our own sinfulness. There are many ways of articulating prayers of general confession. Our prayer may be extempore, but we should never lead others without our own careful and private preparation.

Private Penance

I have attempted to show that the practice of church discipline is not in itself alien to Baptist understandings of being in membership with God's holy people. In early days, discipline appears to have been practised within the public forum of the church meeting. In more recent and more tender times, pastoral discipline has inclined less to the public correction of sinners. Where defection has occurred, churches may have written to the lapsed severing communion, but it has always been undertaken with a heavy heart.[31] Sometimes, that sensitivity has allowed the offender to assume a liberty that has become license. Such a state of affairs is unsatisfactory—not least because it leads to the charge of preaching one thing and practising another.

The horror of priestcraft persists; and it is frequently opposed by an individualistic preaching of the doctrine of the priesthood of all believers. It frequently expressed in such terms as, 'I believe in the priesthood of all believers. I need no human intermediary between me and God.' It seems to me that there is a confusion in this line of argument between two different matters.

The New Testament argues our right of direct access to God from the high priesthood of Jesus—whose priesthood is 'after the order of Melchizedek' (see, e.g., Heb 4.14-16). The New Testament doctrine of the priesthood of all believers seems more to be drawn from Old Testament traditions about the levitical priesthood whose task was to offer sacrifices to God and to bless and anoint those who presented themselves. In other words, the role of the Old Testament priest was to offer the world to God and to offer God to the world. Direct access was not possible, precisely because only the priest could approach God in the *cultus*. The priesthood of all believers inducts us (individually and corporately) into the priestly task of bringing the world to God and God to the world. Direct access destroys the levitical system—a fact demonstrated by the tearing of the Temple curtain as Jesus dies on the cross (See Mt. 27.51; Mk 15.38; Lk. 23.45). Whether we can move directly between these two priestly pictures is at least questionable. Access to God in prayer is mediated by the high priesthood of Christ—by his sacrifice we find forgiveness; but our priesthood is not for private benefit—it is for the world outside the church.

Pastorally, I believe that we have a task in mutual submission to minister Christ to one another. In part, that pastoral care involves admonition, reproof and correction. I do not believe that we can 'priest' ourselves. Crudely expressed this means that the sort of activity which says, 'Lord Jesus, I am sorry I did X; please forgive me. Amen', and then assumes that I am forgiven is little short of manipulative and self-exculpating. That will not do. We need to speak to another (where possible, the one we have sinned against) and hear their word of forgiveness.

---

[31] I do not, by the way, wish to suggest that in earlier days the banning of members from the table was accomplished without sorrow. Of course, there may have been instances (almost certainly there were) of self-righteousness among those who made the judgement. But just as we and they felt sorrow, so we are just as prone to self-justification as any in the past.

The Geelong words of absolution stand: 'If you forgive the sins of any, they are forgiven. If you do not, what will you do with them?'

If we cannot directly address the one we have offended, then we still need to confess—and not in such a way that avoids an amendment of life. Aquinas spoke of three elements in penance: contrition, confession and satisfaction.[32] We may want to use words like 'remorse', 'restoration' and 'return'. When we speak of confession, we look for more than words; we hope for an amendment of life, which puts right what has gone wrong. As far as in us lies, we need to make amends—otherwise the suspicion remains that we are more sorry about having been caught than about what we have done. To submit ourselves to the direction and counsel of another is to open ourselves to know from outside the generous grace of God.

For many of my Baptist brothers and sisters, to espouse the notion that there may be those appointed to listen to confession and to pronounce absolution is a step too far. I understand; I have in the past shared their suspicions. In my own case, I have come to terms with the possibility for a variety of reasons—some personal and experiential, others more theoretical.

My mother was an Anglo-Catholic and her own penitential practice made an indelible impression on me. Many of my clerical friends are Catholic (in the sense of being those who make and hear confession), and my discussions with them have taught me that they view their priestly role in confession as being more about careful pastoral listening than ever it is about the powerful dispensation of some ghostly substance called 'grace'. I am not convinced that we help one another to grow into the fullness of the measure of the stature of Christ when we leave each other to get on with it as best we can. We need consistent direction beyond the weekly sermon. We need counsel that supervises our amendment of life—what the New Testament calls *metanoia* (μετάνοια): a change and renewal of will and mindset resulting in Christ-shaped activity and identity.

Our suspicion about this task being remitted to a priestly caste is understandable—though, as I have tried to suggest, it is based on a doctrinal confusion or, at best, an over-simplification of something extremely complex. However, it is fuelled by another suspicion which relates to ordination. It makes no sense to me to imagine that the ministry of the ordained nullifies the ministry of all the faithful. At the same time, the ordained are set aside within the household of faith to exercise a ministry of word, sacrament and pastoral care. All believers share in the proclamation of the word. All share in the celebration of the table. All share in the mutual care and discipline of the body. Yet we still set aside some to undertake these tasks in particular ways for and on behalf of all without disenfranchising any. In such a context, the correction of the sinner and the promise of forgiveness to such a one who is truly penitent may be the occasion for us to consider whether in denying the sacrament of penance we have not also denied to ourselves a means of grace, poured out by God and mediated to us in the words, 'God

---

[32] Thomas Aquinas, *Summa Theologica*, III.90.2

forgives you'. And these words, so uttered, I take to be performative (as Austin describes such speech): effecting what they signify.

CHAPTER 9

Can a Baptist Believe in Sacred Space?
Some Theological Reflections

Graham J. Watts

> For the blood of Thy martyrs and saints
> Shall enrich the earth, shall create holy places.
> For wherever a saint has dwelt,
> Wherever a martyr has given his blood for the blood of Christ,
> There is holy ground.[1]

By tradition, Baptists and other groupings which may loosely be termed 'evangelical Protestant' will be ambivalent, if not unsympathetic to the concept of sacred space. Our ecclesiology tends to favour such models as the people of God and the body of Christ. While fine architecture may impress us, we are not inclined to express ourselves in the language of holy place.

There are understandable reasons for this, not least our generally received patterns of reading the Bible. Even a cursory reading of scripture suggests that while the Old Testament emphasizes the sacredness of certain places, this seems to be radically transformed in the New Testament. In the Jewish tradition, Israel is the centre of God's dealings with the world; the promised land, Jerusalem, the Temple and the Holy of Holies are symbolically and experientially crucial in the covenant relationship between God and his people. Yet, the New Testament seems much more reticent with regard to such associations with specific locations. It can be argued that, in the New Testament, the concept of the sacred is redefined; the holy place now finds analogues in such contrasts as clean/unclean. Indeed, the destruction of the Temple seems to signify this shift of emphasis from holy place to holy people. The realm of the sacred is no longer localized primarily in terms of place, but in relation to people.[2]

---

[1] T.S. Eliot, 'Murder in the Cathedral', *The Complete Poems of T.S. Eliot* (London: Faber, 1969), p. 281.

[2] For a lengthy review of this, see David J.A. Clines, *On the Way to the Postmodern: Old Testament Essays 1967–1998* (*Journal for the Study of the Old Testament* Supplement Series, 292; Sheffield: Sheffield Academic Press, 1998), II, pp. 542-54.

Theologically, at least within the post-liberal, Protestant tradition, the concept of sacred space has received little attention. It is usually regarded as the preserve of religious studies where the focus tends towards general religious experience of the holy. In religious phenomenology, the works of Mircea Eliade and Rudolf Otto are perhaps the most prominent. For existentialist Eliade, the sacred is experienced in 'hierophonies', which are general experiences of the transcendent.[3] Otto is better known for his exploration of 'the numinous' as a non-rational, extra-sensory experience of that which is beyond.[4] While not a distinctively Christian approach, both seek to articulate the human experience of the transcendent whether that arises within a specifically religious context or not. When the idea of holy place is mentioned in modern theological writing it is largely in negative ways; Barth's approach would probably find support from many. Commenting on the conversation between Jesus and the Samaritan woman in John 4, focusing on the nature of true worship, he states that the abolition of a special place of worship does not mean that the presence of God in the world is ubiquitous and undifferentiated. This is the error of liberalism; rather 'the opposite of Jerusalem, Gerazim...Rome and Wittenburg is Jesus'.[5]

So it was not surprising that, when I mentioned my intention to write on this issue, certain colleagues in the academic world expressed surprise and were sceptical that anything that was truly theological could be said. 'It is not a theme that is specifically Christian; it's for the religious studies specialists; I don't think it's possible to think of a place as holy', were typical comments.

Given such scepticism, why pursue this topic at all? Does this reflect a desire for theological obscurantism or perversity? Simply, it seems that the idea of sacred space is one that is gaining currency in contemporary Christianity. Although some colleagues in academic circles are sceptical, many local church leaders are more open. 'Of course some places are places of prayer and seem more holy', is one response from a youth leader. There are other trends too. The popularity of pilgrimage has increased, especially among fellow Baptists, partly related to the resurgence of Celtic spirituality and new forms of monasticism which highlight places of historical significance. Iona, Lindisfarne—the 'Holy Island'—all testify to renewed interest in places of prayer and retreat. As part of my own recent sabbatical studies I spent some time on retreat at the Northumbria Community where, in seeking to create some form of contemporary monasticism, there is an overwhelming belief in the presence of God in the special place. At the time of writing there has been a wave of popular media unrest at the news that the maker of a violent computer game used Manchester Cathedral as the setting. There is a sense that a sacred place of prayer has been desecrated. Within our post-Christian culture there seems to be a desire to protect

---

[3] M. Eliade, *The Sacred and the Profane: The Nature of Religion* (trans. Willard R. Trask; New York, NY: Harper Torchbooks, 1961).

[4] R. Otto, *The Idea of the Holy* (Oxford: Oxford University Press, 1923).

[5] Karl Barth, *Church Dogmatics II/1: The Doctrine of God (Part 1)* (Edinburgh: T&T Clark, 1956), p. 479.

some semblance of 'the holy' in ancient places of worship—even if most no longer attend.

The developing impetus behind new forms of church—'fresh expressions' and all things emerging are increasingly high priorities in many mainstream denominations, in an attempt to engage with the changing winds of postmodern culture. Part of the emergent language makes much of sacred space, described by Moynagh as a place set apart for prayer, somewhere that 'feels special' and has a 'spiritual ambience'.[6] Even within the latest Baptist handbook of prayers and liturgies one can find reference to a holiness of place; 'walk softly as you come here for this is holy ground. God dwells in this place.'[7] So it seems that many streams of contemporary Christian culture are flowing together with a growing belief that God is present in particular ways in certain places. As Eugene Peterson expresses it in his most recent work, the holy God unveils his presence in often unexpected ways which break forth into our awareness: 'the Bush blazes, the heavens open, the temple rocks, the stump puts forth a green shoot. Holy, Holy, Holy.'[8]

Yet, does any of this require a strictly Christian, theological reconsideration of the idea of sacred space? That is the question addressed here, and the tentative nature of the enquiry and the proposals suggested are very much of the exploratory kind, as might have been suggested by the ubiquitous theological title 'towards...'. I have resisted the temptation to use such a phrase, partly due to my own lack of conviction that this will move us towards very much by way of a theology of holy place. However, we may find that the journey will lead to other related, but more significant theological questions. If so, the journey will prove worthwhile.

Mapping the Landscape

What do we mean by the term 'sacred space'? A general understanding would be one which relates human spiritual experience, some form of encounter with the divine, to a sense of place and history. It is a place which has gained some sort of significance, either because of historical events, or because of communal and collective human encounter with God. This may be a place of Christian worship and prayer, or a place where some important event has taken place in the past, which leads to that place becoming a focus for Christian pilgrimage. It has been customary for us to play down any suggestion which emphasizes the place of such events as carrying sacred significance in and of themselves. The purpose of this rather tentative and exploratory paper is to enquire as to possibility of a theological approach which might facilitate a more fruitful understanding of place within the divine–human encounter. Can there be a sacramentality of place?

---

[6] Michael Moynagh, *emerging church.into* (Oxford: Monarch Books, 2004), p. 166.

[7] Christopher J. Ellis and Myra Blyth, *Gathering for Worship: Patterns and Prayers for the Community of Disciples* (Norwich: Canterbury Press, 2005), p. 298.

[8] Eugene Peterson, *The Jesus Way: A Conversation in Following Jesus* (Grand Rapids, MI: Eerdmans, 2007), p. 147.

The Reformed tradition has always sought to link any concept of sacramental efficacy with the word of promise, so denying that there is anything in the natural elements of water, bread and wine that is materially sacramental. That is an important and profound principle. Yet even Calvin did not wish entirely to exclude the idea that a Christian doctrine of the sacraments could be based on the wider activity of God within creation.[9] In the mid-twentieth century the concept of a sacramental universe gained some popularity, partly by those seeking to draw upon this aspect of Calvin's thought. William Temple's Gifford Lectures explored the theme, and just a few years later D.M. Baillie drew upon this in his *Theology of the Sacraments*.[10] This was not an attempt to construct some form of natural theology, but rather to recognize and give theological expression to the biblical affirmation that 'the earth is the Lord's and everything in it' (Ps. 24.1) So, 'because nature is God's and He is its creator, it lends itself to his use, and He can make its natural elements to speak sacramentally to us'.[11] God, by his word, can use natural objects to address us, and we, by faith, can receive something of the grace and faithfulness of God. It is in the speech of God and our reception of that word that the natural object can be understood to be sacramental. Of course, care is needed here. This is no attempt to deify nature or collapse God's transcendence into divine immanence. For Baillie, this is simply one way of understanding the relationship between God and his creation that grounds and deepens a particular understanding of the sacraments of baptism and eucharist. Yet, there are dangers in using the language of sacramentality in such a broad sense. If so many things are potentially sacramental, then the very meaning of the word is threatened; equally, to see creation as a potential vehicle of God's self-revelation is hardly a novel idea.[12]

A more recent attempt to explore the idea of God's presence within creation, written out of the American experience of the emerging church, is offered by Jon Pahl.[13] He starts with a clear, though hardly original, critique of Augustine. Pahl argues the, for Augustine, importance of place is subsumed under the concept of time. This priority of time over space tends to emphasize God's transcendence and leads to a model of God's immanence as one of interruption. Although this is somewhat simplistic, the point is followed through by reference to the work of Sallie McFague, to whom much of the analysis offered is hugely indebted.[14] In

---

[9] J. Calvin, *Institutes of the Christian Religion* (trans. F.L. Battles; Grand Rapids, MI: Eerdmans, 1995), 4.14.18.

[10] William Temple, *Nature, God and Man* (London: Macmillan, 1951); D.M. Baillie, *The Theology of the Sacraments* (London: Faber, 1957).

[11] Baillie, *Theology of the Sacraments*, p. 46.

[12] For further discussion on these points, see John Christopherson, 'Christian Community as Sacrament', in *Word and World* 20.4 (2000), pp. 400-409. See www.luthersem.edu/word&world/Archives/20-4Congregation/20-4_Christopherson.pdf.

[13] Jon Pahl, *Shopping Malls and other Sacred Space* (Grand Rapids: MI, Brazos Press, 2003).

[14] Sallie McFague, *The Body of God: An Ecological Theology* (Minneapolis, MN: Fortress Press, 1993).

seeking to describe the nature of God's immanence, McFague employs the metaphor of the world as the body of God. This is required, according to McFague, to counter the prevailing western theological heritage, which over-emphasizes God's transcendence. What is demanded, in the light of the incarnation, is a model of God which helps us to understand the world as the place of our meeting with God.

This approach has some potentially serious flaws, not least a tendency to minimize the uniqueness of Christ, so that the incarnation becomes just one of many manifestations of the presence of God in the world. Given these influences we should be wary of Pahl's proposition. Yet, he rightly reminds us that modern science has taught us that time and space are intimately interwoven. He insists that we seek a theology of place which is not based solely on the idea of God's interruption of space—the model that gives priority to time over space—but rather one which is secured through our participation in communal activity in the presence of the God who is already there, in the midst. In other words, the significance of a place is not simply that which we construct. Places shape people; to what extent does a certain place invite you deeper into the presence of God? Does this place enable you to live life more fully? Yet, is this actually the case? Do places shape people, and, if so, to what extent has this anything to do with God?

A more sustained account of sacred space, written from an Anglican perspective, is found in a recent work by John Inge.[15] He examines the distinction between space and place. Philosophically, space looks to the absolute, the infinite, whereas place identifies a specific location within time and space. He agrees with Pahl that within the western tradition, time has come to have priority over space. As a consequence, Reformed theology has tended to play down the idea of place; place is subordinate to practice. A place is 'holy' when holy people use it for worship. Inge questions whether this is faithful to the Bible. The Old Testament narrative is centred around the concept of land—a particular place that is tied to the promises of God. Here land is a 'storied place'; it carries memories and hopes for the future, based on the covenant promises of God. Inge formulates a three-way relationship between God, people and place which defines the Old Testament narrative in such a way that it is not possible to leave any one of the three out of the account. This relational network links the creator God with the God of the covenant. Place is not privileged over people, neither people over place.

So what of the New Testament? Inge argues that the significance of place continues but has to be interpreted in the context of Jesus and his ministry. Theologically, the incarnation continues the biblical emphasis on place and leads Inge to assert that 'places are the seat of relations or the place of meeting and activity in the interaction between God and the world'.[16] This leads Inge to construct a sacramental theology of place. In a carefully worded exposition, he covers possible misunderstandings and seeks to avoid the theological red herrings of pantheism and dualism. If the whole of creation points equally, without differentiation, to God—if

---

[15] John Inge, *A Christian Theology of Place* (Aldershot: Ashgate, 2003).
[16] Inge, *A Christian Theology of Place*, p. 52.

the whole of creation is sacramental—this removes the significance and ultimate meaning of the incarnation and atonement. The coming of Christ cannot be a matter of confirming the world as it is; it is about redeeming the world and inaugurating a new creation. Equally, if everything is understood to be a sign, then nothing is; if the whole of creation is sacramental, this obscures the fact that sacraments are dependant upon the word of God. A better approach is to see the world as the place of potential sacramental encounter. The place of encounter is specific and part of the event.

So, are some places more holy than others? Here Inge returns to his triangular relationship between God, people and place. Sacramentality is based on action and relationship and not on the material nature of the place of encounter. 'The world in itself is not sacramental, because sacramentality is an event that involves action by God and a response by unique human beings.'[17] Yet, and this is the crucial point, the place of encounter is intrinsic to it and once an encounter has happened it will remain associated with that place. Now, especially when that encounter is a collective experience, the place itself can retain a sense of identity which lasts through time. For example, a place of worship which has witnessed baptisms, weddings, prayer and has been repeatedly a place of encounter, is forever linked to those events. For Inge, the idea of holy place is not just psychological or phenomenological, but theological. God has been in this place. He goes on to say that such sacramental encounters help to root believers in the faith and the very locatedness of those encounters points to the final redemption of all places in Christ.

So, does this work as a piece of theology? The first observation would be that this might offer a foundation for a theology of church buildings as holy places. With Inge's emphasis on the collective encounter over a period of time, the application to emerging churches in pubs and cafes, while not impossible, seems less secure. Secondly, there are some important points made during the course of the book. It is certainly true to state that if all the world is already holy, then the need for the atonement is lost. If all the world is a sacrament, the end result is that we have no sacraments. It is equally important to retain the central importance of divine action, the uttering of the word of promise which finds a response in faith, in any definition of the sacramental.

Yet, some troubling questions arise. Given the significance of land and place in the Old Testament, is the appeal to the incarnation a sufficient or satisfactory articulation of the same concept in the New Testament? Jesus was born in a certain place which relates to Old Testament prophecy; the location of his death and the city of Jerusalem are clearly of significance. The Gospel narratives place due emphasis on the location of certain events in the life of Jesus. Yet, in other ways, is it not the case that the teaching and ministry of Jesus indicates that the signs and symbols of the old covenant are being re-defined in and through himself? The sign of the new covenant is not a location, but an act of remembrance and communal response. Further, surely the very fact of the incarnation requires a specific location. In

---

[17] Inge, *A Christian Theology of Place*, p. 81.

assuming human flesh, the Word of God has taken on the limitations of human existence, which includes space, time and location. This leads to a further, more general point. To maintain the significance of place in relation to a divine–human encounter may not, in the end, say very much more than the fact that by our very humanity we are located beings. Every encounter of significance that I have will, rather obviously, require me to be somewhere. At the time, the place will be significant, and over time I may gain some sentimental attachment to the place, but is that expressing a truly theological concept? How many arguments over church architecture and changing the furnishings have a foundation in theology rather than human sentimentality? So, whatever the sophistication of Inge's argument, there remains a question. Is this anything more than a detailed statement of the obvious? Or is there an alternative approach that takes the incarnation seriously, but travels by a different route? We will examine that question in due course.

Emerging Church and the 'Transformation of Secular Space'

Our plotting of the landscape must now turn to the understanding of holy place which resonates throughout much emerging church literature. How do these writers understand the idea of holiness? Is there a theological agenda which is driving their understanding, or is this a case of resorting to mysticism or emotionalism?

Two writers will illustrate the concern to find God in the everyday world, to understand a place as holy on the basis of a particular understanding of the relationship between God and the world. Both are from the United States, but on this point there is broad agreement between writers on both sides of the Atlantic. Rob Bell, an American pastor, has come to prominence partly through a series of DVDs which explore contemporary themes from a Christian angle. In his writing he typically moves from contemporary story telling to biblical narrative while inserting a piece of popular theological reflection. In his book *Velvet Elvis*, he relates the story of two friends wanting to be married, but not in a church and with 'no Jesus or God or the Bible or religion…'[18] Instead they prefer to get married in a thick forest. When asked why, they reply that here they feel like something holds this beautiful country together. The discussion turns to the idea of this 'binding force', and the possibility of naming it God. Bell then links this with an exposition of Old Testament teaching on the presence of God in creation, focusing on Joseph's dream. It is only retrospectively that Joseph understands God was in that place, but he had not realized it. It is not God who suddenly determines to be present at any time or place; God is always present, but we fail to recognize that presence. The place is holy, even though we do not always sense the presence of God: 'for the ancient Jew, the world was soaked in the presence of God'.[19]

---

[18] Rob Bell, *Velvet Elvis* (Grand Rapids, MI: Zonderrvan, 2005), p. 76.
[19] Bell, *Velvet Elvis*, p. 78.

The second writer who takes a similar approach is Brian McLaren.[20] Written in narrative form and set in the context of the events of 11 September 2001, he relates the story of his alter-ego, Neo, and his relationship with a researcher, Kerry, who is terminally ill. Out for a boating trip and picnic one day, the conversation turns to spiritual issues. Kerry has no church background and claims to have little doctrinal understanding, but she has learned about Jesus and has come to a point of decision to follow him. McLaren writes quite movingly of her baptism there and then in the river and the experience that came over the gathered party. 'I'll never forget what it felt like, standing there in the breeze and in the sunshine and in the water and in the company of three people, who seemed at once so holy and so human and so wonderful.' As they return from their trip he again speaks of the conversation being filled with 'something special... I guess the best word for it is *holy*.'[21]

At one level many will want to respond sympathetically to such an account. Who has not stood before a glorious landscape, admiring the panorama and felt some sense of awe—an experience of the transcendent? Yet how can we understand this theologically in such a way that does not simply dissolve into the mystical? One of three core practices and priorities of emerging churches identified by Eddie Gibbs and Ryan Bolyer is described as the 'transformation of secular space', finding God in the everyday, mundane realities of life. Mission is not about the church taking God to the world; it is finding where God is already active and then drawing alongside. 'For emerging churches there are no longer any bad places, bad people or bad times. All can be made holy. All can be given to God in worship.'[22] This encounter with God in the world tends to be understood as both symbolic and sacramental; the immanence of God within the created world is central in the thought of many emerging church leaders. It seems that this is the primary theological model which defines the idea of holy place. But is that the only model? Is it the most appropriate?

Before looking more closely at some of the theological issues, it is worth noting that some of the emerging church leaders have come from backgrounds in charismatic renewal, and in some ways will have been influenced by certain charismatic/pentecostal writers. Of relevance to the current discussion is the work of C. Peter Wagner, partly known for his work in the church growth movement and his collaboration at Fuller Seminary with John Wimber. In the 1990s he developed a form of demonology, territorial spirits, which grew to be influential in a number of circles.[23] This was part of a wider theology of the kingdom which sees mission and evangelism as 'taking the ground' for the Lord. According to Wagner, there are differing levels of demonic activity; some spirits dominate in certain places, holding power and influence over both particular geographical locations. This is referred to as

---

[20] This illustration is drawn from Brian McLaren, *The Story We Find Ourselves In* (San Francisco, CA: Jossey-Bass, 2003).

[21] McLaren, *The Story We Find Ourselves In*, pp. 112-13.

[22] Eddie Gibbs and Ryan Bolyer, *Emerging Churches: Creating Christian Communities in Postmodern Cultures* (London: SPCK, 2006), p. 67.

[23] See C. Peter Wagner, *Breaking the Strongholds in Your City* (Ventura, CA: Regal, 1993); also *Territorial Spirits* (Chichester: Sovereign World, 1991).

strategic level spiritual warfare and has found a popular audience in the novels of Frank Peretti.[24] A full account of this is beyond the confines of a short paper; it is sufficient to note that this has been criticized on a number of counts, not least a questionable biblical foundation.[25] While not diminishing the reality of spiritual warfare, which I'm sure many ministers of the gospel will be all too aware of, this attempt to locate the presence of evil in certain places finds a counterpoint in the desire to make places holy. The appeal of this should not be underestimated and plays upon a common human experience. We do have feelings about certain places; the role of the exorcist in the Anglican Church is a busy one and it is not confined to people but can involve the sanctifying of places or buildings. Yet, our theology struggles, not with the reality of the spiritual battle, but with the theology of place implied by the notion of territorial spirits. And it is the same sort of problem we encounter when trying to speak theologically about holy places.

Theological Considerations

Three systematic issues need to be explored if we are to root such discussions in more theologically secure ground. The relationship between God's transcendence and immanence is a recurring theme in the debate, though often not clearly delineated. A related concern is the recovery, or recasting of a Christian theology of experience. More fundamental still, we require a clear Christian theology of creation, the detail of which will be far beyond this paper, but one essential element may assist in clarifying both the strengths and weaknesses of the renewed quest for the holy presence of God within the world.

Biblically, the theology of place is not quite as clear cut as is sometimes suggested. In the Old Testament there is a clear relationship between land and covenant, Temple and sacrifice, the promise and the place of fulfilment. Yet this is balanced by narratives of landlessness and exile. The God of Abraham, Isaac and Jacob is the same God gathering his people in the promised land as he is in Babylon. Old Testament theology is worked out in dialogue with both experiences and while certain places are holy to the Lord, it is equally the case that the people of God are to seek and serve the same God while in exile. In the New Testament, a similar dialogue occurs, but in a different form. Jesus of Nazareth set his face towards Jerusalem, prayed in Gethsemane; the risen Lord was seen on the road to Emmaus. Yet the Son of Man has no place to lay his head, prophesies the destruction of the Temple and tells the woman of Samaria that God will not be worshipped on a particular mountain. The kingdom of God is not located in a particular place; it is the active presence of God.[26]

---

[24] Frank Peretti, *This Present Darkness* (Wheaton, IL: Crossway, 2003).

[25] E.g., see C. Lowe, *Territorial Spirits and World Evangelisation* (Dublin: Mentor, 2001).

[26] For a further exploration of these issues, see Susan White, 'The Theology of Sacred Space', in David Brown and Ann Loades (eds), *The Sense of the Sacramental* (London: SPCK, 1995), pp. 31-43.

This dialogue between place and no-place is also typical of much Celtic writing. There is a double emphasis here on the idea of sacred space and pilgrimage; God is understood to be present in particular places through history, encountering his people in the place of prayer. Yet God also calls the pilgrim to the margin—the boundary. God is with his people and yet also beyond. This dialogue is usually expressed in some form of trinitarian language. Christ is within yet without, beside yet above, in the midst yet beyond. In different ways, this is seeking to express the relationship between God's transcendence and immanence.[27]

The doctrine of the Trinity remains the truly distinctive way to express the relationship between transcendence and immanence. Some have already attempted to express this in relation to a doctrine of the church. Kerry Dearborn argues that any recovery of a truly sacramental, evangelical ecclesiology must be rooted and shaped by a fully trinitarian theology.[28] Such a model will encourage community and be focused outwardly in mission, expecting to meet God in the world and in the other. With regard to the idea of sacred place, a fully trinitarian approach will also guard us against any tendency to slip into neo-pagan or pre-Christian concepts. Just so will we be able to affirm that this encounter in this place is to do with the God of Jesus Christ and not the god of the religions or the deity of the philosophers.

The key question remains; can we formulate a trinitarian theology of holy place, and, if so, how does that relate to a theology of encounter? To make the rather obvious points first, the world is God's creation and he can and does indwell that creation by the Spirit. Through the Spirit creation takes form, life is given and creation is carried forward towards the final consummation. The Spirit also particularizes the universal work of Christ, so that we are invited and called into the divine life of God in such a way that we are not divinized, but participate in the life of God and his mission in the world. That enables us to affirm that creation always carries within it the potential for sacramental encounter. Yet, if we are to retain the meaning of the word sacrament, this has to remain tied to God's word of promise in Christ which arouses faith. In such an encounter, the presence of God is always mediated, signified, whether by the rainbow to Noah or in bread and wine. That might mean that an overwhelming encounter with the Spirit of God takes place in a church building or on the street; in a pub or a hospital beside a dying man or woman. This is holy ground; we encounter the God who is other than us, a holiness that is alien to us, a presence that fixes our limited, located existence in space and time within the grander, universal, transcendent, eschatological reality of God. The place is significant; but cannot be divorced from the living presence of God in that moment of encounter. Places can only be holy in relation to the revelatory event that happens there; it is holy to the extent that the content of the revelation is Christ. To then assert that the place in and of itself retains some form of sacredness risks

---

[27] For a fuller description of this, see Thomas O'Loughlin, *Journeys on the Edges: The Celtic Tradition* (London: Darton, Longman and Todd, 2000).

[28] Kerry Dearborn, 'Recovering a Trinitarian and Sacramental Ecclesiology', in John Stackhouse (ed.), *Evangelical Ecclesiology: Reality or Illusion?* (Grand Rapids, MI: Baker Academic, 2003), pp. 39-73.

divorcing the event from its historical particularity and limits the Spirit, who is in himself, the freedom of God.

The second area which demands consideration is the Christian theology of experience. Modern theology after Barth has tended to be somewhat sceptical of experience, fearing a return to the pitfalls of Protestant liberalism. With the impact of charismatic renewal, that ground has shifted somewhat, but there remains a certain wariness among systematic theologians. Yet the mystical and experiential is increasingly popular among Christians who have reacted against cerebral, over-intellectual versions of evangelical Christianity. In the popular view, the mystical experience is valued often because it is thought that is gives unmediated, direct access to God, usually through senses other than the conscious mind. David Brown correctly points out that this understanding is erroneous.[29] From a Christian perspective, all experiences of God are mediated, whether that is by scripture, religious art and music, architecture or iconography.

If we accept that creation is a potential vehicle for some form of mediated encounter with God, and if we take the necessary precaution of affirming that the content of the encounter is the true word of God, then surely we need some way of expressing a theology of experience. Brown asserts that experiences of the divine were once considered commonplace, and much social research would suggest that such experiences are still very common in our increasingly spiritually open culture. Yet, Brown contends, theology has skewed our understanding of such experiences; following Barth such encounters tend to be seen as 'all or nothing' affairs. One consequence is that Christian experience is removed from the everyday and seen as something out of the ordinary. Indeed, this would find a resonance with some of the critiques of traditional church offered by emerging church writers. For Brown, we have to find a way of taking these commonplace experiences seriously so that 'religion is recognised as part of people's ordinary way of interacting with their environment, not something that can only be justified by appeal to the exceptional'.[30] Such experiences may need interpretation, which in turn will doubtless mean engagement with the Christian community at some point, but let us not play down the reality of the raw experience. God is free and his ways are beyond us, but that does not mean we abdicate our responsibility to think theologically. Neither do we stop seeking the presence of the holy God in his creation.

This brings us to the key theological question. What sort of theology of creation can best facilitate a conception of God's presence in the world that might enable us to speak responsibly about such things? Although such a theology is ultimately beyond the confines of a short paper, some preliminary comments are necessary. As has been previously suggested, we need a trinitarian theology of creation which holds together the biblical truths that creation is 'in Christ' and 'for Christ', while

---

[29] David Brown, 'Experience Skewed', in Kevin Vanhoozer and Martin Warner (eds), *Transcending Boundaries in Philosophy and Theology* (Aldershot: Ashgate, 2007), pp. 159-75.

[30] Brown, *Experience Skewed*, p. 175.

affirming the creative and particular act of the Spirit.[31] Such a theology will avoid certain avenues of compromise. Christian theology has usually wanted to steer away from the twin errors of pantheism, which dissolves God into the world, and deism, which posits a creator who has absented himself from any on-going involvement with the world. In some modern theology, particularly associated with Moltmann, a third way has become popular. This is referred to as panentheism, in which creation is viewed as time and space within the being of God.[32] While this has some attraction, it has also been criticized on the grounds that this risks compromising the distinctness and separateness of creation from God. Creation has its own being which is contingent upon God, but it is separate from him.

Colin Gunton offers a way forward in suggesting that the Son is the principle of distinction between God and the world. 'As the particular and free presence of God in the world Jesus Christ is the basis of a doctrine of omnipresence.'[33] The Son is the presence of God in the world in a way that is distinct from the Father; for God to create 'in the Son' expresses the form of mediation by which God creates a world that is separate from himself yet related to him. It enables us to conceive of creation as both related to and within God (as in panentheism) and yet distinct from God. Now, a doctrine of omnipresence which follows this pattern requires the mediation of the Holy Spirit, through whom the Son became incarnate. The Spirit particularizes the universal work of Christ in such a way that omnipresence cannot be understood as a homogenous, universal presence of God in all things. Rather, through the Spirit God perfects and completes the work of creation; through the Spirit God upholds and drives forward the world towards the final consummation and the world is held in relation with God, while remaining distinct from God.

Now, this model enables us to critique much emerging church language about the presence of God in the world. A trinitarian theology of creation does not permit us to talk of omnipresence as undifferentiated presence, as if the world were some sort of container for God. Yet the emergent emphasis on the incarnation, though not worked through in a nuanced way, is certainly an instinctive move in the right direction. Similarly, Inge's emphasis on incarnation points in the right direction, but does not explore the implications in a fully trinitarian way. The incarnation defines the manner of God's relationship to the world in a particular space and time. As Gunton points out, the centrality of the incarnation is often missed in theologies of creation. Yet, it is key if we are to understand creation as separate from, yet ordered by God. Creation is determined yet not deterministic; there is a real openness to the future which is enabled by the action of the Holy Spirit. The Spirit enables things to become what they were intended to be, and defines the presence and experience of God as truly Christian. All such encounters between God and humanity are thus particular expressions of the relationship between God and the world which was

---

[31] For a detailed exposition of this, see Colin E. Gunton, *The Triune Creator* (Edinburgh: Edinburgh University Press, 1998), especially pp. 134-45.

[32] See, e.g., Jürgen Moltmann, *God in Creation* (San Francisco, CA: Harper and Row, 1985).

[33] Gunton, *Triune Creator*, p. 143.

uniquely expressed in the incarnation. Only thus can we conceive of a genuinely Christian theology of nature; just so can we properly express a trinitarian doctrine of omnipresence.

Setting the Parameters—Speaking Responsibly about Divine Presence

As indicated at the start, whether we can construct a theology of sacred space has really become a secondary issue. If anything of theological interest can be expressed it will rest on the way in which we understand other, more important theological issues that are being driven by contemporary church writers who are using the language of holy place. These coalesce around the themes of transcendence and immanence, Christian experience and, crucially, a trinitarian doctrine of creation. In the light of the previous discussion, some provisional comments are offered, more by way of an invitation to further debate than conclusion.

The fact that mission is asking theology the question is healthy. The desire to build relationships with those outside the church, to remove the unhelpful accretions of cultural tradition which have accumulated in church life over the years, is a true and positive expression of our response to the Great Commission. If our ecclesiology is stretched in the process, those who are involved in the work on the ground are unlikely to shed a tear. For those concerned for right theology it is a reminder that the best doctrinal reflection takes place contextually. The necessary dialogue between systematic theology and missionary praxis, though sometimes engaged in with a degree of suspicion, will bear fruit for both theology and mission. Each voice needs to hear the other, and this is particularly true of those working in the emerging church. There is a great deal of creative work taking place and whenever there is a pioneering spirit there will be the inevitable theological questions. It is not an adequate response to ignore these. Recent church history teaches us that the pioneering spirit left unchecked can degenerate into the maverick; the Christian faith can too easily be led down the dangerous paths of neo-paganism.[34]

The doctrine of the Trinity provides us with the truly Christian framework within which we can engage with ideas of transcendence, immanence and omnipresence. Equally, it is a lack of trinitarian thought that compromises much popular level writing, especially in the emerging church. In particular, a trinitarian theology of creation will enable us to construct a doctrine of omnipresence and help us to speak intelligently about the way in which God relates to the world. As argued above, this will avoid the pitfalls of pantheism, deism and will ask questions of the popular alternative—panentheism. Rather, it will affirm that creation is contingent upon God while retaining a distinct identity from God. This is seen most clearly in the incarnation, where Christ takes human flesh, becomes that which is other than the

---

[34] E.g., the case of the infamous nine-o-clock service in Sheffield in the early 1990s. It is interesting that the church which gave birth to that now operates a strong degree of accountability in leadership.

Father yet united with him in the Spirit. Just so, the creative and providential action of God is through the Son and in the Spirit. This requires us to construct a doctrine of omnipresence which does not posit the divine presence in all things without distinction. This is one of the dangers of much emerging church literature.

Yet, the emergent emphasis on incarnation is instinctively correct. Since this is determinative and descriptive of the manner of God's presence with us, then seeking to engage with the presence of the living God within his world, beyond the confines of the local church, must be part of truly biblical mission. As is often claimed in the popular literature, God is already there. But this cannot be understood as a presence that is unmediated or uniform. Ultimately, it is hard to dissociate any of this from some sort of theology of encounter and consequently our own locatedness in space and time. It is impossible to dissociate ourselves from our own experience—our participation in the reality of which we seek to speak. It thus remains difficult to see any way in which a place can retain a sense of holiness beyond the God–human encounter.

So, can a Baptist believe in sacred space? Given that Baptists don't always have all the right answers, let us cast the question more widely. Is a Christian theology of sacred space a possibility? A cautious affirmation can be made, provided we express that in a way that is shaped by a trinitarian understanding of the manner of God's presence in the world. That will be shaped by our view of the incarnation and will consequently inform a theological understanding of our locatedness in space and time. It will also require a clear and precise doctrine of the Spirit, which remains an underplayed and elusive goal in much western theology. The result will be a theology of participation and encounter, rather than a phenomenology of religious experience. As for those who remain sceptical about such an endeavour, why should we let the religious studies specialists have all the fun?

CHAPTER 10

Baptismal Regeneration: Rehabilitating a Lost Dimension of New Testament Baptism

Anthony R. Cross

I

Anyone familiar with the history of Baptist baptismal theology and practice will be instantly aware that the juxtaposition of the two words that comprise the title of this paper will already have elicited strong feelings both to this chapter and its author. Yet separately Baptists have no difficulty with either term—though in regard to the former Baptists have often been criticized, and rightly so, for asserting what baptism is not rather than positively what it is,[1] and in regard to the latter the term is not used that frequently anyway.

That this subject is more than just an esoteric 'theological' exercise is evident in a recent official guideline and its accompanying unofficial position paper from the International Mission Board (IMB) of the Southern Baptist Convention (SBC) on the criteria to be used in assessing prospective missionaries.[2] These were approved by the IMB's trustees at their meeting in Huntsville, Alabama, 14-17 November 2005. The approved policy states that missionary candidates eliminate themselves from consideration as an IMB missionary if they practise 'tongues or a "private prayer language" as an ongoing part of his or her conviction or practice' and that 'future

---

[1] E.g., see the observation of the Presbyterian J.M. Ross, 'The Theology of Baptism in Baptist History', *Baptist Quarterly* 15.3 (July, 1953), p. 100, 'the doctrine of baptism does not occupy a central place in Baptist theology... When Baptists do write of baptism, they have been more concerned to prove the impropriety of the sprinkling of infants than to define what happens at the immersion of believers.' However, three years after Ross made this observation, Neville Clark produced the first of what became a steady stream of works exploring the theology of baptism/initiation, a stream that has grown particularly in the last decade or so. On Clark and others, see the following discussion and A.R. Cross, *Baptism and the Baptists: Theology and Practice in Twentieth-Century Britain* (Studies in Baptist History and Thought, 3; Carlisle: Paternoster Press, 2000), pp. 194-243, 320-34 and 341-48.

[2] 'Guideline on baptism' (15 November 2005), <http://www.imb.org/core/story.asp?storyID=3837&LanguageID=1709>, accessed 9 March 2006, and 'Position Paper Concerning the IMB Guideline on Baptism' (6 March 2006), <http://www.imb.org/core/story.asp?storyID=3840&LanguageID=1709>, accessed 9 March 2006.

missionary candidates *must* have been baptized in a church that: practices believer's baptism by immersion alone; *does not view baptism as sacramental or regenerative*, adding that they must also hold to the doctrine of the security of the believer.[3]

The guideline cites the 2000 version of the *Baptist Faith and Message*,[4] and then stipulates that the missionary candidate is to be examined on their 'individual' understanding of baptism, followed by that of the local church from which they come. After stating that believer's baptism is by immersion and that 'Baptism by immersion *follows* salvation',[5] the guideline states that 'Baptism is symbolic, picturing the experience of the believer's death to sin and resurrection to a new life in Christ', adding 'Baptism *does not* regenerate.'[6]

Baptism is recognized as 'a church ordinance' and the guideline reiterates the point that 'Baptism must take place in a church that practices believer's baptism by immersion alone, [and] *does not view baptism as sacramental or regenerative*'.[7] In the fourth century, the Donatists, mirrored by the Anabaptists in the sixteenth century,[8] adopted a theology and practice of baptism which made the legitimacy of baptism dependent on the worthiness of the minister and the genuineness of the church, and thus required re-baptism when these were irregular. The guideline is a modern expression of this position:

> A candidate who has not been baptized in a Southern Baptist church or in a church which meets the standards listed above is expected to request baptism in his/her

---

[3] 'IMB trustee chairman Hatley sends "open letters" to Southern Baptist pastors, laity explaining decisions', <http://www.imb.org/core/story.asp?storyID=3841&LanguageID =1709>, accessed 9 March 2006, italics added. The two letters were posted as 'Letters from the board of trustees chairman Tom Hatley', <http://www.imb.org/core/story.asp? storyID=3847&LanguageID=1709>, accessed 9 March 2006, italics added. At the time of writing, it is unclear whether or how the guidelines will be implemented.

[4] *Baptist Faith and Message* (2000), Article VII: 'Christian baptism is the immersion of a believer in water in the name of the Father, the Son, and the Holy Spirit. It is an act of obedience symbolizing the believer's faith in a crucified, buried, and risen Savior; the believer's death to sin; the burial of the old life; and the resurrection to walk in the newness of life in Christ Jesus. It is a testimony to his faith in the final resurrection of the dead. Being a church ordinance, it is a prerequisite to the privileges of church membership and to the Lord's Supper.'

[5] 'Guideline on baptism', 1.a, italics added. However, see discussion below on baptism as part of the process of becoming a Christian.

[6] 'Guideline on baptism', 1.b, italics added.

[7] 'Guideline on baptism', 2.a, italics added.

[8] See D.F. Wright's discussions of these in 'Donatist Theologoumena in Augustine? Baptism, Reviviscence of Sins, and Unworthy Ministers', and 'The Donatists in the Sixteenth Century', in D.F. Wright, *Infant Baptism in Historical Perspective: Collected Stuides* (Studies in Christian History and Thought; Milton Keynes: Paternoster, 2007), pp. 105-15 and 212-25 respectively.

Southern Baptist church as a testimony of identification with the system of belief held by Southern Baptist churches.[9]

This adoption of re-baptism has serious ramifications with reference not just to those from paedobaptist traditions but also from other credobaptist traditions—other Baptists, Churches/Disciples of Christ and many of the new churches, for example—for it identifies the only 'legitimate' form of baptism to be that set out by the IMB, and by extension the SBC. But there are other matters which directly relate to our present subject.

The opening paragraph of the 'Position Paper' boldly states that the 'guideline on baptism...represents the historic Baptist understanding and, more importantly, the Scriptural teaching regarding this primary of the two church ordinances'. 'Four key parameters' are then set out which are claimed to be 'derived from Scripture and consistent with historic Baptist ecclesiology' and inform and shape the IMB policy:

> **First,** that **the only biblical mode for baptism is immersion. Second,** that **the only proper candidate for immersion is a regenerate believer in Jesus Christ. Third,** that **the act is purely symbolic and distinct from salvation itself** and has no saving merit. **Fourth,** that **baptism is a church ordinance** and therefore the only proper administrator of it is a local New Testament church that holds to a proper view of salvation. (Emphasis original.)

It should be noted that while in its discussion of its first two points the 'Position Paper' speaks of 'Baptists', its third and fourth points speak only of 'Southern Baptists'. These are *not* the same, and the claim that the 'Southern Baptist' (or any other stream of the Baptist tradition) position represents 'the historic Baptist' position does not stand up to careful scrutiny. The 'Baptist' position on any subject is not the same in all expressions of Baptist life and thought, nor is it the same throughout the four centuries of its existence,[10] and the claim to speak for all Baptists, or to be the genuine voice of Baptists, is not something that can be claimed by any one stream of the Baptist tradition.[11] As the most 'evangelical' of the

---

[9] 'Guideline on baptism', 2.b.

[10] For examples of this, including discussion of baptism, see the collection of essays in P.E. Thompson and A.R. Cross (eds), *Recycling the Past or Researching History?: Studies in Baptist Historiography and Myths* (Studies in Baptist History and Thought, 11; Milton Keynes: Paternoster, 2005).

[11] The diversity of the Baptist tradition in the United States is well-illustrated in the title of the recent historical survey edited by W.G. Jonas, Jr, *The Baptist River: Essays on Many Tributaries of a Diverse Tradition* (Macon, GA: Mercer University Press, 2006); and on a global scale by H.L. McBeth, *The Baptist Heritage: Four Centuries of Baptist Witness* (Nashville, TN: Broadman Press, 1987); and I.M. Randall, T. Pilli and A.R. Cross (eds), *Baptist Identities: International Studies from the Seventeenth to the Twentieth Centuries* (Studies in Baptist History and Thought, 19; Milton Keynes: Paternoster, 2006).

mainstream denominations, Baptists share much with Evangelicalism, and this extends to the fact that it has not remained static, but developed and changed in response to the cultural ethos in which it has found itself, whether that be, for example, Enlightenment Rationalism, Romanticism or cultural modernism.[12]

Both the IMB guideline and position paper claim to locate their position in scripture and Baptist history, and it is around these two foci, plus the third of the tradition of historic Christian doctrine, that this study is structured.[13] Justification for the third focus needs to be established, and this is easy to do, and is linked to the appeal to the 'historic Baptist understanding' of baptism (and the Lord's supper). Baptist theology has never taken place in isolation from the wider Christian faith. The earliest Baptists saw themselves as members of the catholic church of Christ. The 1679 General Baptists' *Orthodox Creed*, article XXIX, stated, 'There is one holy catholick church, consisting of, or made up of the whole number of the elect, *that have been, are, or shall be gathered*, in one body under Christ...',[14] while the *Second London Confession* of 1677, the second edition of which (1688/89) is regarded by many Baptists as foundational,[15] opened its articles on the church, 'The Catholick or universal Church, which...may be called invisible, consists of the whole number of the Elect, *that have been, are, or shall be gathered into one*, under Christ the head thereof...'[16] Both confessions locate the main Baptist traditions within the wider

---

[12] See D.W. Bebbington, *Evangelicalism in Modern Britain: A History from the 1730s to the 1980s* (London: Unwin Hyman, 1989); and D.J. Tidball, *Who are the Evangelicals? Tracing the Roots of Today's Movements* (London: Marshall Pickering, 1994), pp. 36-37, 38-40, 53, 221-20. It is worth noting that Tidball, a Baptist and an Evagelical, asserts that '*no* evangelical would say that regeneration is conveyed through baptism' (p. 131, italics added). As will be shown, this is simply the restatement of an unsupportable assertion.

[13] In their discussion of readers' interpretation of scripture (what they head 'Legitimate Reader-Response Interpretation'), W.W. Klein, C.L. Blomberg and R.L. Hubbard, Jr, *Introduction to Biblical Interpretation* (Dallas, TX: Word Publishing, 1993), p. 193, contend that 'Biblical texts must be understood within the context and confines of the believing community in which each interpreter resides, though, admittedly, these interpretations will differ among communities.' This 'believing community' is neither just the historic Baptist community or the Evangelical tradition but historic Christianity which spans two thousand years of theology and practice. Neither theology nor interpretation (if these can be separated) should—and I believe cannot—take place in supposed isolation from the broader (and full) Christian tradition.

[14] *An Orthodox Creed*... (1679), article XXIX, in W.L. Lumpkin, *Baptist Confessions of Faith* (Valley Forge, PA: Judson Press, rev. edn, 1969), p. 318, italics added.

[15] See the study on the British Baptist churches influenced by the *Second London Confession*, J.M. Renihan, *Edification and Beauty: The Practical Ecclesiology of the English Particular Baptists, 1675–1705* (Studies in Baptist History and Thought, 17; Milton Keynes: Paternoster, 2008).

[16] *Confession of Faith... [Second London Confession]*, chapter XXVI, in Lumpkin, *Baptist Confessions*, p. 285, italics added. It will be significant later to note that the *Second London Confession* (as well as the *Orthodox Creed*) was deeply influenced, and in

Christian church. It is also worth noting that the first Baptists (the General Baptists) were influenced by the Arminian tradition, while the Particular Baptists were Calvinists—and both Arminius and Calvin were paedobaptists and sacramentalists![17] Recently, an increasing number of Baptist[18] scholars have been doing theology explicitly in interactive and critical dialogue with the historic Christian tradition, and this is taking place within a broader movement within Evangelicalism.[19]

---

no small measure shaped by, the *Westminster Confession of Faith* (1647, hereafter *WCF*). See McBeth, *Baptist Heritage*, pp. 70-71, who describes them as 'to some extent' modeled on the *WCF*, while P.E. Thompson, 'Towards Baptist Ecclesiology in Pneumatological Perspective' (PhD dissertation, Emory University, 1995), p. 44, describes the *Second London Confession* as 'a slightly modified version' of the *WCF*. (This is forthcoming as *The Freedom of God: Towards Baptist Theology in Pneumatological Perspective* [Studies in Baptist History and Thought, 20; Milton Keynes: Paternoster, 2009].)

[17] On their paedobaptism, see Jacobus Arminius' *Private Disputation* LXII, in J. Nichols and W. Nichols, *The Works of Arminius* (ed. C. Bangs; Grand Rapids, MI: Baker Book House, 1991 [1825, 1828 and 1875]), II, pp. 439-440, cited by F.S. Clarke, *The Ground of Election: Jacobus Arminius' Doctrine of the Work and Person of Christ* (Studies in Christian History and Thought; Milton Keynes: Paternoster, 2006), p. 120; and J. Calvin, *Institutes of the Christian Religion* (1559), 4.16. On their sacramentalism, see Clarke, *Ground of Election*, pp. 119-21; Calvin, *Institutes* 4.14. It is worth noting that Arminianism's evangelical credentials have recently been reasserted by R.E. Olson, *Arminian Theology: Myths and Realities* (Downers Grove, IL: IVP Academic, 2006).

[18] For detailed discussion of these 'Catholic Baptists' and an outline of their work, see S.R. Harmon, *Towards Baptist Catholicity: Essays on Tradition and the Baptist Vision* (Studies in Baptist History and Thought, 27; Milton Keynes: Paternoster, 2006), ch. 1 '"Catholic Baptists" and the New Horizon of Tradition in Baptist Theology', pp. 1-21, but also the whole of this book.

[19] See, e.g., J.E. Colwell, *Promise and Presence: An Exploration of Sacramental Theology* (Milton Keynes: Paternoster, 2005), and *The Rhythm of Doctrine: A Liturgical Sketch of Christian Faith and Faithfulness* (Milton Keynes: Paternoster, 2007); P.S. Fiddes, *Tracks and Traces: Baptist Identity in Church and Theology* (Studies in Baptist History and Thought, 13; Carlisle: Paternoster Press, 2003); S.J. Grenz, *Theology for the Community of God* (Carlisle: Paternoster Press, 1994); J.W. McClendon, Jr, *Systematic Theology* (3 vols; Nashville, TN: Abingdon Press, 1988–2000); S.R. Holmes, *Listening to the Past: The Place of Tradition in Theology* (Carlisle: Paternoster Press, 2002), and *Tradition and Renewal in Baptist Life* (The Whitley Lecture 2003; Oxford: Whitley Publications, 2003); R.E. Webber, *Ancient-Future Faith: Rethinking Evangelicalism for a Postmodern World* (Grand Rapids, MI: Baker Books, 1999), and *Ancient-Future Time: Forming Spirituality through the Christian Year* (Grand Rapids, MI: Baker Books, 2004); R.E. Webber and P.C. Kenyon, 'A Call to an Ancient Evangelical Future' (Chicago, IL: Northern Seminary, 2006); D.H. Williams, *Retrieving the Tradition and Renewing Evangelicalism: A Primer for Suspicious Protestants* (Grand Rapids, MI: Eerdmans, 1999), and *Evangelicals and Tradition: The Formative Influences of the Early Church* (Deep Church; Milton Keynes: Paternoster, 2005); and D.H. Williams (ed.), *The Free Church and the Early Church: Bridging the Historical and Theological Divide* (Grand Rapids, MI: Eerdmans, 2002).

The aim of this paper, then, is to rehabilitate an evangelical understanding of baptismal regeneration for Baptists in the belief that this will help us towards a fuller appreciation and application of baptism as it is found in the New Testament. We will begin this by examining our own Baptist tradition, then Christian thought working through the centuries, focusing on the patristic and Reformations periods, and finally the New Testament. This procedure of working backwards has been adopted because, while what Christians of previous centuries have thought is often informative, it is what scripture teaches that is most important for Baptists and Evangelicals alike.

II

That an understanding of baptismal regeneration is not inimical (though it has by no means been widespread) to Baptist thought can be seen in its acceptance by some key Baptist pastor-theologians down the centuries.[20]

Thomas Grantham (1634–93) described baptism as 'the sacrament of initiation', and that 'being the Sacrament or washing of Regeneration, [it] belongs to those who are born from above'.[21] Philip E. Thompson rightly notes that while Grantham could distinguish these two dimensions he could not separate them.[22]

Similarly, the one time General Baptist turned Particular Baptist, Benjamin Keach (1640–1704), recognized the link between regeneration and baptism. With Titus 3.5 explicitly in mind, Keach argued that baptism 'is a lively Sign or Symbol—Hence 'tis called *the washing of Regeneration*... Baptism is frequently called the *Laver of Regeneration*, it being a Sign or Figure of it to the Person Baptized.'[23] He later clarified his position by mention of the necessity of faith, citing with approval the Presbyterian Puritan Stephen Charnock, that

---

[20] In Cross, *Baptism and the Baptists*, p. 28 (see more fully pp. 28-29, 114 and *passim*), I made the statement that 'Baptists have always staunchly opposed this doctrine [baptismal regeneration]' (citing the representative example of A.C. Underwood, 'Baptism and Regeneration', *Baptist Times* 1 March 1928, p. 144). While at the time I had in mind the *ex opere operato* understanding of baptismal regeneration, this statement cannot stand in the absolute way it was made, for, as this paper shows, there have always been some Baptists who have maintained a biblical understanding of baptismal regeneration.

[21] T. Grantham, *The Loyal Baptist: or An Apology for the Baptized Believers* (London, 1684), see *The Second Part of the Apology for the Baptized Believers*, p. 15.

[22] P.E. Thompson, 'A New Question in Baptist History: Seeking a Catholic Spirit Among Early Baptists', *Pro Ecclesia* 8.1 (Winter, 1999), p. 67. See Grantham's comments in *Christianismus Primitivus: or, The Ancient Christian Religion* (London, 1678), II/2.ii.4, where, following Calvin, he asserted that baptism involves first mortification and vivification. Cf. Calvin, *Institutes*, 4.15.5.

[23] B. Keach, *Gold Refin'd; or, Baptism in its Primitive Purity* (London, 1689), p. 83, italics original.

Baptism is a means of conveying this Grace, when the Spirit is pleased to operate with it; but it doth not work a physical Cause upon the Soul as a Purge doth upon the Humours of the Body: for 'tis the sacrament of Regeneration, as the Lord's-Supper is of Nourishment. As a Man cannot be said to be nourished without Faith, so he cannot be said to be a new Creature without Faith...[24]

In his *Jachin & Boaz*,[25] the evangelistically-minded Yorkshire Particular Baptist William Mitchill (modern spelling, Mitchel[l], 1662–1705) stated of baptism that it is a New Testament ordinance of dominical origin, administered to those who profess repentance towards God, and faith in and obedience to Christ. It is a sign of the baptized's fellowship with Christ in his death, burial and resurrection, of being ingrafted into Christ, of remission of sins, and that they will live and walk in newness of life.[26] However, he concluded his brief article on baptism acknowledging that '...Grace and Salvation are not so inseparably annexed unto it, as that no Person can be regenerated and saved without it, or that all are undoubtedly regenerated and saved who are Baptized'.[27] Here is clear recognition that it is possible to be regenerated and saved without baptism, but equally that not everyone baptized will be regenerated and saved—the key in both scenarios is clearly the presence or absence of saving faith.[28] As he said of saving faith earlier, 'So the Grace of Faith, whereby the Elect are enabled to believe, to the saving of their Souls, is the gracious Work of the Spirit of Christ in their Hearts, and is ordinarily wrought by the Ministry of the Word, by which also, and by the Administration of the Sacraments, Prayer, and other

---

[24] Keach, *Gold Refin'd*, pp. 128-29.

[25] W. Mitchill, *Jachin & Boaz: or, an Epitome of the Doctrine and Discipline Instituted by Christ in the Churches of the New Testament...* (London, 1707), transcribed by W.E. Blomfield, 'William Mitchill's "Jachin & Boaz" 1707', *Transactions of the Baptist Historical Society* 3 (1912–13), pp. 65-88, 154-75 (page references are to the transcribed version, while pagination in parenthesis is to the original). On Mitchell, see W.E. Blomfield, 'The Baptist Churches of Yorkshire in the 17th and 18th centuries', in C.E. Shipley (ed.), *The Baptists of Yorkshire: Being the Centenary Memorial Volume of the Yorkshire Baptist Association* (Bradford and London: Wm. Byles and Sons/London: Kingsgate Press, 1912), pp. 73-86, and *passim* throughout the volume.

[26] Mitchill, *Jachin & Boaz*, 'XXXI of Baptism', p. 160 (p. 28).

[27] Mitchill, *Jachin & Boaz*, 'XXXI of Baptism', p. 161 (p. 29).

[28] That God is not limited to his working through the sacraments, or any other means he has chosen/ordained, is what P.E. Thompson emphasizes in his discussion of 'The Freedom of God', see his 'Toward Baptist Ecclesiology in Pneumatological Perspective', *passim*, 'People of the Free God: The Passion of Seventeenth-Century Baptists', *American Baptist Quarterly* 15.3 (September, 1996), pp. 223-41, and 'Practicing the Freedom of God: Formation in Early Baptist Life', in D.M. Hammond (ed.), *Theology and Lived Christianity* (The Annual Publication of the College Theology Society, 45; Mystic, CT: Twenty-Third Publications, 2000), pp. 119-38. Colwell, *Promise and Presence*, p. 124: 'the sacraments are not God's prison. He has promised to act by his Spirit through these ordained means but he is not entrapped by such means, he remains free to act elsewhere and through other means (though he has not promised to do so).' Cf. also pp. 120 and 124-25.

Means, it is increased and strengthened.'[29] Mitchill understood the two sacraments of baptism and the Lord's supper to be 'holy Signs of the Covenant of Grace' representing Christ 'and his Benefits' and he could do this because he believed that

> There is in every Sacrament a spiritual Relation, or a Sacramental Union between the Sign, and the thing signified: Whence it comes to pass that the Names and Effects of the one is ascribed to the other: The Grace which is exhibited in or by the Sacraments rightly used, is not conferred by any power in them, neither doth the Efficacy of a Sacrament depend upon the Piety or Intention of him that doth administer it, but upon the Work of the Spirit, and the Word of Institution, which contains, together with a Precept authorizing the use thereof, a Promise of benefit to the worthy Receivers.[30]

Stanley K. Fowler notes that this understanding of the sacraments is essentially an abridged form of the *WCF* (ch. 27) and is evidence of the abiding influence of Calvin's sacramentalism.[31]

The former evangelical Anglican Baptist Wriothesley Noel (1798–1873) believed that 'Baptism can not be the baptism of regeneration except with respect to those who are previously regenerate; and as Christian baptism is the baptism of regeneration...regenerate believers alone ought to be baptized.'[32] Noel, too, was careful to emphasize the essential presence of faith. Commenting on Acts 2.38, he noted that Peter's hearers 'were not to expect the remission of their sins through baptism without previous repentance, nor through repentance without baptism, but through repentance and baptism'. Later, 'Since, then, baptism is thus necessary to remission of sins, and is so closely connected with it as no mere acts of obedience ever are, baptism must be a profession of faith, and none but believers ought to be baptized.'[33] He developed this line of thought on the basis of Titus 3.5:

> baptism is the washing of regeneration, or the washing which is the manifestation and completion of regeneration.

---

[29] Mitchill, *Jachin & Boaz*, 'XVII of Saving Faith', p. 82 (p. 13).

[30] Mitchill, *Jachin & Boaz*, 'XXX of the Sacraments', pp. 159-60 (p. 27).

[31] S.K. Fowler, *More Than a Symbol: The British Baptist Recovery of Baptismal Sacramentalism* (Studies in Baptist History and Thought, 2; Carlisle: Paternoster Press, 2002), p. 31. D.F. Wright, 'Baptism at the Westminster Assembly', in Wright, *Infant Baptism in Historical Perspective*, pp. 244-45, shows how 'The Westminster divines viewed baptism as the instrument and occasion of regeneration by the Spirit, of remission of sins, of ingrafting into Christ', see *WCF* 27–28 on 'Of the Sacraments' and 'Of Baptism' respectively, esp. 28.1 and 28.5. Wright notes the *WCF*'s qualifications of this, but these do not alter the fact of regeneration's presence in the confession.

[32] B.W. Noel, *Essay on Christian Baptism* (London: James Nisbet, 1849), p. 113. On Noel, see D.W. Bebbington, 'The Life of Baptist Noel: Its Setting and Significance', *Baptist Quarterly* 24.8 (October, 1972), pp. 389-411. On Noel as a prominent Anglican Evangelical, see N.A.D. Scotland, *Evangelical Anglicans in a Revolutionary Age 1789–1901* (Carlisle: Paternoster Press, 2004), *passim*.

[33] Noel, *Essay on Christian Baptism*, pp. 98 and 99 respectively.

> By these two things, the washing and the renewing, the spiritual renovation and the baptism which manifests it, God saves his people.[34]

This position Fowler attributes, as with Mitchill previously, to Noel's Calvinistic sacramentalism.[35]

For Neville Clark, later Principal of the South Wales Baptist College, Cardiff (1985–91), 'the inseparability of divine action and human response must never be denied' in the theology of baptism.[36] Later he expands on this, explicating the roles of the Holy Spirit and faith in baptism:

> Divine action through the Holy Spirit remains the controlling, all-decisive, factor [in insertion into the body of Christ]; but at baptism the question of the response of faith emerges. This faith is not a human act, some autonomous, human element in the transaction of redemption, separable from the divine gift and summons. It is the creation of the Spirit of God and, as such, it belongs not to some artificially distinguished, conscious level of human personality but to the whole of man called to the wholeness of redemption.[37]

According to Clark, baptism is a sacrament 'of the cross and resurrection, or rather the whole Christ in His work from Bethlehem to the ascension and beyond' and this forms the basis of his statement that 'Baptism effects regeneration and new birth because and only because it sets us at Golgotha and the empty tomb.'[38] On the foundation of Romans 6.3-5 and Galatians 3.27, Clark elsewhere states that 'the New Testament is...clear that the point at which redemption becomes effective for us is at baptism'.[39] He then proceeds to state boldly, 'Baptism *and new birth* are inseparably bound together, for the gift of the Holy Spirit involves a radical change at the centre of man's being. The divine promises attached to the sacraments are not empty promises; what God says, "goes".'[40]

In his *magnum opus*, R.E.O. White, first a tutor (1951–54 and 66–68) then Principal (1968–79) of the Scottish Baptist College, and a prominent British

---

[34] Noel, *Essay on Christian Baptism*, p. 111. Later Noel referred to baptism as 'the sign, manifestation, and completion of regeneration', and declared that 'true baptism' secures pardon, secures the gift of the Spirit, is generally necessary to salvation, and thus 'True baptism saves', p. 117.

[35] Fowler, *More Than a Symbol*, p. 75

[36] N. Clark, 'The Theology of Baptism', in A. Gilmore (ed.), *Christian Baptism: A Fresh Attempt to Understand the Rite in Terms of Scripture, History, and Theology* (London: Lutterworth Press, 1959), pp. 311-12.

[37] Clark, 'The Theology of Baptism', p. 323.

[38] Clark, 'The Theology of Baptism', pp. 312-13.

[39] N. Clark, *An Approach to the Theology of the Sacraments* (Studies in Biblical Theology, 17; London: SCM Press, 1956), p. 81.

[40] Clark, *Approach to the Theology of the Sacraments*, p. 82, italics added.

evangelical scholar,[41] comments that the bath of Titus 3.5 'is doubly characterized' as both 'of regeneration', which he immediately notes is 'the passing to a new status', and 'of renewal', which is 'the moral change which brings about this transaction', and that 'both are ascribed to the Holy Spirit'.[42] This brief acknowledgement of a form baptismal regeneration comes within White's discussion of Titus 3.5 along with 1 Corinthians 6.11 and Ephesians 5.25-26, which together are set within Paul's interpretation of baptism with the death and resurrection metaphor of salvation. That none of this is separated from faith is shown when he continues, 'The teaching of all three passages is the same', for baptism is 'a lustration, a real ethical purification' and it is 'always…accompanied by acceptance of the word and constitutes the believer's response to the life-giving Spirit'.[43]

Stephen Winward, a leading evangelical Baptist in the mid-twentieth century,[44] drew a clear distinction between the different connotations of faith in the New Testament, rejecting Paedobaptist claims that vicarious faith can suffice for a person's salvation. 'Hearing with faith, the "Yes" of the whole personality to the interpreted fact of Jesus Christ, trusting him and entrusting oneself to him, can never be a vicarious act.' He immediately adds, 'Baptism is the encounter between the Lord and man, the place where the enacted word of God meets the enacted human response.' With reference to 1 Corinthians 12.13 and Galatians 3.27 he continued, 'Through baptism, the sacrament of the word, the spirit [sic] is active, incorporating the believer into Christ, into the body.' Then, on the basis of Titus 3.5, 'Through the kerygma he regenerates and reveals, moving the sinner to repentance and faith. In baptism the work of regeneration is consummated in the remission of sins, in the gift of the Holy Spirit.' The notion that a person becomes a Christian solely by their own personal decision Winward rejects, stating that it is only 'by the work of the Spirit and the word' (2 Thess. 2.13) which moves them to repentance and faith, which is confessed and consummated in their baptism, and through which they are united with Christ in his body. 'The New Testament pattern of baptism is perverted',

---

[41] See G.W. Martin, 'Biographical Sketch: Revd R.E.O. White, BD, MA', in S.E. Porter and A.R. Cross (eds), *Baptism, the New Testament and the Church: Historical and Contemporary Studies in Honour of R.E.O. White* (*Journal for the Study of the New Testament Supplement Series*, 171; Sheffield: Sheffield Academic Press, 1999), pp. 18-32.

[42] R.E.O. White, *The Biblical Doctrine of Initiation* (London: Hodder and Stoughton, 1960), p. 202. In his discussion of Jn 3.5, White, p. 255, speaks of 'this experience of regeneration in baptism', adding that 'The conditions of repentance ("water") and faith are sufficiently clear in the whole discourse [Jn 3] to show that "there is nothing magical in the connection of the new birth with the sacrament…"', quoting J. Denney, 'Holy Spirit', in J. Hastings (ed.), *A Dictionary of Christ and the Gospels* (2 vols; Edinburgh: T&T Clark, 1906–08), I, p. 732.

[43] White, *Biblical Doctrine of Initiation*, pp. 202-203. Cf. his *Invitation to Baptism: A Manual for Inquirers* (London: Baptist Union of Great Britain and Ireland, 1962), p. 64.

[44] On whom, see I.M. Randall, *The English Baptists of the Twentieth Century* (A History of the English Baptists, 4; Didcot: The Baptist Historical Society, 2005), *passim*.

he continues, 'if the rite is severed from hearing the word with faith, from the activity of the Holy Spirit...'[45]

That recognition of a form of baptismal regeneration is not an exclusively British Baptist phenomenon is seen in its advocacy by Johannes Schneider, at the time of writing Professor of New Testament Studies in Berlin University, who from Titus 3.5 noted that 'The close connection of baptism and the outpouring of the Spirit also finds expression in John iii, 5, where it is said that water and Spirit together bring about regeneration.'[46]

None of the above figures can be dismissed as un-Baptist or un-influential in the history of Baptist thought, and their acceptance of a form of baptismal regeneration—even if not always much developed and certainly not the same for the different authors—is enough to rebut the claim of the IMB's 'Position Paper' that the *unequivocal* rejection of any form of baptismal regeneration 'represents the historic Baptist understanding'. Another important factor is that such a view of baptismal regeneration was not an innovation, rather it occupies a significant place in the church's soteriology, pneumatology and sacramental theology down through the ages. To this we must briefly turn.

III

In the post-apostolic, ante-Nicene period we find the theology of baptismal regeneration at the beginning of the third century, though paedobaptism had clearly arisen before this.[47] In his *First Apology* 61 (c.148), Justin Martyr refers to the Christian's consecration of themself to God 'when we were regenerated through Christ'. Here there is no notion of an *ex opere operato* view of regeneration or baptism for he continues,

> Those who are *convinced* and *believe* what we say and teach is the truth, and pledge themselves to be able to live accordingly, are taught in prayer and fasting to ask God to forgive their past sins... Then we lead them to a place where there is water, and they are regenerated in the same manner in which we ourselves were regenerated.

---

[45] S.F. Winward, 'The Church in the New Testament', in A. Gilmore (ed.), *The Pattern of the Church: A Baptist View* (London: Lutterworth Press, 1963), pp. 68-69.

[46] J. Schneider, *Baptism and Church in the New Testament* (trans. E.A. Payne; London: Carey Kingsgate Press, 1957), p. 26. See also p. 28, and cf. p. 37. I am grateful to the Rev. Dr John E. Morgan-Wynne, former Principal of Bristol Baptist College and minister of Ilkley Baptist Church, for drawing my attention back to Schneider's work on this. For another German Baptist maintaining this view, see Wiard Popkes, 'Rebirth in the New Testament', *Journal of European Baptist Studies* 6.1 (September, 2005), pp. 5-10.

[47] See Tertullian's *On Baptism* 18. Scholars are divided on how long before this infant baptism appeared, though there is no reference to infant baptism in the Apostolic Fathers, c.A.D. 90–170, see D.F. Wright, 'The Apostolic Fathers and Infant Baptism: Any Advance on the Obscurity of the New Testament?', in Wright, *Infant Baptism in Historical Perspective*, pp. 44-54.

In the name of God, the Father and Lord of all, and of our Savior, Jesus Christ, and of the Holy Spirit, they then receive the washing with water.

Justin then quotes John 3.3.[48] Theophilus of Antioch, c.180, speaks of the reception of 'repentance and remission of sins, through the water and laver of regeneration,—as many as come to the truth and are born again, and receive blessing from God.'[49] In his *Demonstration of the Apostolic Preaching*, Irenaeus, who died c.202, states that Gentiles received the cleansing of their souls and bodies by the baptism of water and the Holy Spirit (*Dem.* 41), the latter being given by God in the former (*Dem.* 42). Then, using the language of new birth, which theologically is the meaning of 'regeneration', he writes,

> we have received baptism for the remission of sins, in the name of God the Father, and in the name of Jesus Christ, the Son of God, who was incarnate and died and rose again, and in the Holy Spirit of God. And that this baptism is the seal of eternal life, and *is the new birth* unto God... (*Dem.* 3)

Later he makes this explicit:

> the baptism of our regeneration proceeds through these three points: God the Father bestowing on us regeneration through His Son by the Holy Spirit. For as many as carry [in them] the Spirit of God are led to the Word, that is to the Son; and the Son brings them to the Father; and the Father causes them to possess incorruption. (*Dem.* 7)[50]

Around the time when infant baptism probably began to appear (tentatively between the end of the period of the Apostolic Fathers, c.170, and the time Tertullian wrote *On Baptism* in the early years of the third century), Clement of Alexandria (c.160–215) wrote his *Paidagogus/The Instructor*. Following a passage in which he speaks of Christians as 'children' (*Paed.* 1.5), he refers to believers' baptism as 'our regeneration' when 'we attained that perfection after which we aspired. For we were illuminated, which is to know God.' He then states that 'Being baptized, we are illuminated; illuminated, we become sons; being made sons, we are made perfect; being made perfect, we are made immortal.'[51] Later he brings together

---

[48] Justin Martyr, *First Apology* 61, in T.M. Finn, *Early Christian Baptism and the Catechumenate: Italy, North Africa, and Egypt* (Message of the Fathers of the Church, 6; Collegeville, MN: Liturgical Press, 1992), pp. 38-39 (italics added).

[49] Theophilus of Antioch, *Theophilus to Autolycus*, book 2 ch. 16, in A. Roberts and J. Donaldson (eds), *The Ante-Nicene Fathers. Volume 2: Fathers of the Second Century* (rev. A.C. Coxe; Edinburgh: T&T Clark, 1994), p. 101.

[50] Quotations from J.A. Robinson's translation in I.M. MacKenzie, *Irenaeus's Demonstration of the Apostolic Preaching: A Theological Commentary and Translation* (Aldershot: Ashgate, 2002), pp. 2 and 13 respectively, italics added.

[51] Clement of Alexandria, *The Instructor*, book 1 ch. 6, in Roberts and Donaldson (eds), *The Ante-Nicene Fathers*, II, p. 215.

faith, baptism and the Holy Spirit: 'For instruction leads to faith, and faith with baptism is trained by the Holy Spirit. For that faith is the one universal salvation of humanity...', and shortly after refers to Galatians 3.27-28 and 1 Corinthians 12.13.

After the unequivocal appearance of infant baptism the connection between baptism, the believer's faith and regeneration continued. In the *Apostolic Tradition*, for many years mistakenly attributed to Hippolytus and regarded as a single, third-century text,[52] the bishop lays his hands on the newly baptized and prays, 'Lord God, you have made them worthy to receive remission of sins through the laver of regeneration of the holy Spirit...'[53] The newly baptized were those who had been through a three-year catechumenate (*Ap.Trad.* 17), who throughout the conferral of baptism are interrogated and express their faith with 'I believe' (*Ap.Trad.* 21).[54] In a letter written before 250, Cyprian is more explicit. The stain of original sin is washed away 'by the help of the water of new birth', and this 'second birth...restored me to a new man' by 'the agency of the Spirit'.[55] In another letter, written in 253, Cyprian makes explicit the connection between baptism and faith when he explains that it is 'by baptism the Holy Spirit is received' (*Ep.* 62.8) and that 'the water of life eternal' is to 'be given to *believers* in baptism' (*Ep.* 62.9).[56]

In the post-Nicene period we continue to find the same pattern we have found previously. For instance, Theodore of Mopsuestia states that 'We are united to Christ and made symbolically to partake in His risen life by the spiritual regeneration of Baptism, wherein we receive His quickening Spirit.'[57] In his second *Baptismal Homily*, Theodore writes, 'For it is with faith in what is to take place

---

[52] On this, see P.F. Bradshaw, M.E. Johnson and L.E. Philipps, *The Apostolic Tradition* (Hermeneia; Minneapolis, MN: Augsburg Fortress, 2002), pp. 1-13. They date the material in this composite work between the mid-second to mid-fourth centuries.

[53] *Apostolic Tradition* 21, in G.J. Cuming, *Hippolytus: A Text for Students* (Grove Liturgical Study, 8; Cambridge: Grove Books, 2nd edn, 1987), p. 20. G.W.H. Lampe, *The Seal of the Spirit: A Study in the Doctrine of Baptism and Confirmation in the New Testament and the Fathers* (London: Longmans, Green, 1951), pp. 136-37, adds 1 Cor. 12.13 and Jn 3.5 to the clear reference to Tit. 3.5 as the biblical basis for this prayer.

[54] According to the *Apostolic Tradition* 20, anyone who 'is not good or not pure' was rejected as a candidate for baptism 'because he has not heard the word with faith', Cuming, *Hippolytus*, p. 17.

[55] Cyprian, *Epistle 1: To Donatus* 4, in A. Roberts and J. Donaldson (eds), *The Ante-Nicene Fathers. Volume 5: Fathers of the Third Century* (Edinburgh: T&T Clark, 1995), p. 276.

[56] Cyprian, *Epistle 62: To Caecilius, on the Sacrament of the Cup of the Lord*, sections 8 and 9 respectively, in Roberts and Donaldson (eds), *The Ante-Nicene Fathers*, V, p. 360, italics added

[57] Theodore of Mopsuestia, commentaries on Rom. 13.14 and Gal. 2.13-14, quoted by H.B. Swete, *The Holy Spirit in the Ancient Church: A Study of Christian Teaching in the Age of the Fathers* (London: Macmillan, 1912), p. 261. For Theodore, baptism is the sacrament and normal means of regeneration, but the gift of the Spirit is not so tied to it that it cannot be forfeited by the unworthy, see his commentaries on 1 Tim. 3.2 and Rom. 6.17, cited by Swete, *Holy Spirit in the Ancient Church*, p. 262.

that you came forward to receive the holy gift of baptism; you mean to be reborn, to die with Christ and rise again with him, in order that this second birth may replace your first and obtain for you a share in heaven.'[58] Elsewhere he states, 'You are born in water because you were formed originally from earth and water',[59] and, a short while later, he speaks of the 'need to undergo...renewal by baptism' and that 'we have been formed afresh by baptism and received the grace of the Holy Spirit'.[60] In his pre-baptismal catechesis, Cyril of Jerusalem says, 'Great indeed is the Baptism which is offered to you. It is a ransom to captives; the remission of offences; the death of sin; the regeneration of the soul; the garment of light; the holy seal indissoluble;...the gift of adoption.'[61]

But the pattern we have seen of the work of the Spirit and the faith of the believer expressed in water-baptism[62] changed largely due to the theology of Augustine. It was he who argued that 'regeneration...is the work exclusively of the Spirit', but he did so in the course of his advocacy of the view that was to dominate baptismal theology for over a thousand years and which supports the theology and practice of paedobaptism, that 'the regenerating Spirit is possessed in common both by the parents...and by the infant that is presented [for baptism] and is born again'. While the former possession is acceptable to Baptists, the latter is not. However, after quoting John 3.5, he proceeded: 'By the water, therefore, which holds forth the sacrament of grace in its outward form, and by the Spirit who bestows the benefit of grace in its inward power..., the man deriving his first birth originally from Adam alone, is regenerated in Christ alone.'[63]

---

[58] Theodore of Mopsuestia, *Baptismal Homily II*, section 14, in E. Yarnold, *The Awe-Inspiring Rites of Initiation: The Origins of the R.C.I.A.* (Edinburgh: T&T Clark), p. 176.

[59] Theodore of Mopsuestia, *Baptismal Homily III*, section 11, in Yarnold, *The Awe-Inspiring Rites of Initiation*, p. 187.

[60] Theodore of Mopsuestia, *Baptismal Homily III*, section 13, in Yarnold, *The Awe-Inspiring Rites of Initiation*, p. 188.

[61] Cyril of Jerusalem, *The Procatechesis* 16, in F.L. Cross (ed.), *St Cyril of Jerusalem's Lectures on the Sacraments: The Procatechesis and the Five Mystagogical Catecheses* (Texts for Students, 51; London: SPCK, 1966), p. 50. In his notes on Cyril's lectures, Cross, p. xxv, reminds us that the actual baptism itself included a solemn profession of faith in the Trinity before the actual baptism.

[62] Swete, *Holy Spirit in the Ancient Church*, p. 395, summarized the work of the Spirit in the sacraments, 'Of the reality and greatness of the Spirit's work in Christian Baptism the ancient Church entertained no doubt. The Lord had joined together water and the Spirit in the mystery of the New Birth, and no Christian in the early centuries dared to put them asunder... [T]here was no disposition to regard the baptismal rite as magical. The water of Baptism was seen to be but the outward and visible sign, and the spiritual efficacy of the Sacrament to be due to the Holy Spirit whose action it symbolized.'

[63] Augustine, *Letter* 98, section 2, in P. Schaff (ed.), *The Nicene and Post-Nicene Fathers. First Series*, Volume 1: *The Confessions and Letters of St. Augustin* (Edinburgh: T&T Clark, 1994), p. 407.

Of particular significance for Baptists is the presence of baptismal regeneration in John Calvin's thought.[64] For him,[65] the sacrament of baptism 'is the initiatory sign by which we are admitted to the fellowship of the Church, that being ingrafted into Christ we may be accounted children of God' (*Inst.* 4.15.1), and its purpose is to contribute to the believer's faith in God and be a confession to others (*Inst.* 4.15.1). Its contribution to the former is threefold, the second of which is that it 'shows our mortification in Christ and new life in him' (citing Rom. 6.3-4 in support). Calvin here is not simply exhorting believers to imitate Christ but that 'Christ by baptism has made us partakers of his death, ingrafting us into it', so that 'those who receive baptism with true faith truly feel the efficacy of Christ's death in the mortification of their flesh, and the efficacy of his resurrection in the quickening of the Spirit'. After reference to Colossians 2.12,[66] he quotes Titus 3.5 then states, 'We are promised, first, the free pardon of sins and imputation of righteousness; and, secondly, the grace of the Holy Spirit, to form us again to *newness of life*' (*Inst.* 4.15.5, italics added).[67]

---

[64] The jump from Augustine to Calvin is not to imply the absence of theories of baptismal regeneration in the intervening thousand years, but is simply a matter of practicality. (However, e.g., see Thomas Aquinas, *Summa Theologiæ* volume 57, 3a.69.10, in James J. Cunningham, *St Thomas Aquinas: Summa Theologiæ* [Cambridge: Cambridge University Press, 2006 (1975)], p. 153, 'baptism is spiritual rebirth [regeneration]', cf. 3a.66.9, p. 41. In *ST* 3a.69,4 p. 133, citing Tit. 3.5-6, he says, 'Therefore the grace of the Holy Spirit and abundance of virtues are given in baptism.' Aquinas argues for the necessity of baptism for salvation, and that while it can be lacking in reality it cannot be lacking in desire, as when someone dies before receiving baptism, *ST* 3a.68.2, pp. 85-86. But while faith is necessary, it is the faith of the church that suffices, thereby providing the theology which supports the practice of infant baptism, see, e.g., *ST* 3a.69.8, p. 145. For a general discussion of baptism and regeneration in the Middle Ages, see B. Leeming, *Principles of Sacramental Theology* [London: Longmans, 2nd edn, 1960], pp. 252, 262, 325, 625 and 627.) Focusing on Calvin is also not to suggest its absence in the theology of other magisterial reformers. For baptismal regeneration in Luther, see, e.g., J.D. Trigg, *Baptism in the Theology of Martin Luther* (Leiden: E.J. Brill, 2001), pp. 75-81, and *passim*.

[65] All citations from Calvin's *Institutes* are taken from J. Calvin, *Institutes of the Christian Religion* (trans. H. Beveridge; 2 vols; London: James Clarke, 1949). For a summary and critical interaction with Calvin's theology of baptism from a Baptist perspective, see A.R. Cross, 'Baptism in the Theology of John Calvin and Karl Barth', in N.B. MacDonald and C. Trueman (eds), *Calvin, Barth, and the Reformed Tradition* (Paternoster Theological Monographs; Milton Keynes: Paternoster, 2008), pp. 57-87.

[66] In his discussion of circumcision and infant baptism, Calvin admits there are differences between the the two but dismisses them as insubstantial, because behind both signs lie 'the promise of the paternal favour of God, of forgiveness of sins, and eternal life. And the thing figured is one and the same—viz. Regeneration' (*Inst.* 4.16.4).

[67] Cf. *Inst.* 3.3–7 on baptism as the external means which effects repentance and regeneration. Also on Tit. 3.5, see Calvin's comments in *The Second Epistle of Paul The Apostle to the Corinthians and the Epistles to Timothy, Titus and Philemon* (ed. D.W. Torrance and T.F. Torrance; trans. T.A. Smail; Calvin's Commentaries; Carlisle: The

All this rests, though, on the doctrine of predestination, for no-one is 'granted the spirit of regeneration, except those whom God elects',[68] and, like Augustine before him, Calvin applies this to Christians and their children, and, because both of them are elect, they are, therefore, already regenerated by God,[69] a position that enables him to say of elect children who die in infancy that they have 'received the sign of regeneration' (*Inst.* 4.16.21).

Calvin's theology of baptismal regeneration is of great significance for Baptists because, historically, the largest of the Baptist traditions, the Particular Baptists, are Calvinists. In so saying, there is a great deal in chapters 14 and 15 of book 4 of the *Institutes* with which Baptists can agree, though this is not the case with chapter 16's defence of infant baptism.[70] However, insofar as the majority of Baptists have adopted an anti-sacramental,[71] as well as an anti-baptismal regeneration, theology of baptism they have departed from their Calvinist roots. Instead, they have adopted a more Zwinglian, merely symbolic baptismal theology. It is this understanding of baptism that has dominated Baptist thought, despite the fact that it was Zwingli who 'did what nobody had yet done: he severed baptism from faith'[72] and, in so doing, 'baptism was severed from faith and regeneration'.[73] It is this Zwinglianism, coupled

---

Paternoster Press, 1996), pp. 381-83. On the work of the Holy Spirit in this, see *The Catechism of the Church of Geneva that is a Plan for Instructing Children in the Doctrine of Christ* (French 1536, Latin 1538), in J.K.S. Reid (ed.), *Calvin: Theological Treatises* (Library of Christian Classics, 22; London: SCM Press, 1954), p. 102: 'He [the Holy Spirit] regenerates us, and makes of us new creatures (Tit. 3:5). Hence whatever gifts are offered us in Christ, we receive them by virtue of the Spirit.'

[68] J. Calvin, *Articles concerning Predestination* (n.d.), in Reid (ed.), *Calvin: Theological Treatises*, p. 179.

[69] Cf. *Inst.* 4.16.17. For his more detailed argument, see *Inst.* 4.16.17-21; also *Catechism of the Church of Geneva*, pp. 133-35; and *Second Defence of the Pious and Orthodox Faith concerning the Sacraments, in Answer to the Calumnies of Joachim Westphal* (1556), in H. Beveridge (trans.), *Treatises on the Sacraments: Catechism of the Church of Geneva, Forms of Prayer, and Confessions of Faith* (Foreword by J.R. Beeke; Fearn, Ross-shire: Christian Heritage, 2002 [1849]), pp. 336-40.

[70] For a critical examination of Calvin's argument for infant baptism in *Inst.* 16, and especially the inconsistencies and tensions that result between this chapter and the earlier, biblical chapters 14 and 15, particularly, though not solely, through the criticisms leveled against him by Karl Barth, see Cross, 'Baptism in the Theology of Calvin and Barth', pp. 73-79 and 86-87.

[71] On this, see Fowler, *More Than a Symbol*; and A.R. Cross, 'The Myth of English Baptist Anti-Sacramentalism', in Thompson and Cross (eds), *Recycling the Past or Researching History*, pp. 128-62.

[72] J.H. Rainbow, '"Confessor Baptism": The Baptismal Doctrine of the Early Anabaptists', in T.R. Schreiner and S.D. Wright (eds), *Believer's Baptism: Sign of the New Covenant in Christ* (Nashville, TN: B&H Academic, 2006), p. 197. See the whole of his discussion of Zwingli's baptismal theology, pp. 196-200.

[73] T.A. Schreiner and S.D. Wright, 'Introduction', in Schreiner and Wright (eds), *Believer's Baptism*, p. 8. Cf. M.F. Bird, *The Saving Righteousness of God: Studies on Paul, Justification and the New Perspective* (Paternoster Biblical Monographs; Milton

with Baptists' antipathy towards the mechanical *ex opere operato* view of baptism, that has led them to eschew a biblical understanding of baptismal regeneration.

The question that remains, and which is of especial concern to Baptists and Evangelicals, is whether this doctrine can be found in the New Testament. We have already noted a small selection of Baptist writers over four centuries who believed it can, but a little more time needs to be spent exploring this.

IV

The reason why baptismal regeneration has featured in the writings of the church's theologians and in its initiatory rites is because it is present in the New Testament. While early Baptists—and a small number of Baptists since, though this number has increased during the twentieth century, as we have seen—recognized this, the majority of Baptists have rejected the connection, in large measure due to their emphasis on a form of justification *sola fide* that has not seen baptism as faith-baptism,[74] and, more importantly, because of the development of the *ex opere operato* views of baptism that owe so much to Augustine and his doctrines of infant baptism and original sin.[75] Here, David F. Wright's comment is entirely pertinent: 'modern evangelical unease with the efficacy of baptism is not fully intelligible without taking cognizance of what "the long reign of infant baptism" has done to it.'[76]

That baptismal regeneration is to be found within the New Testament has been demonstrated by George Beasley-Murray, former Principal of Spurgeon's College, London, and Professor of New Testament at both the International Baptist Theological Seminary in Rüschlikon, Zurich, and The Southern Baptist Theological Seminary in Louisville, Kentucky.[77] Beasley-Murray's argument for baptismal

---

Keynes: Paternoster, 2006), p. 61, who notes that one of the ways in which 'the Protestant view of justification...for the most part...represented a theological *novum*' was in that it made a distinction 'between justification (a divine declaration of righteousness) and sanctification or regeneration (inner transforming work of the Spirit)', italics original. Cf. also p. 103 on justification and regeneration.

[74] The argument that New Testament baptism is faith-baptism is outlined below and in n. 83.

[75] D.F. Wright, *What has Infant Baptism done to Baptism?: An Enquiry at the End of Christendom* (Didsbury Lectures 2003; Milton Keynes: Paternoster Press, 2005), p. 94.

[76] Wright, *What has Infant Baptism done to Baptism?*, p. 100.

[77] See P. Beasley-Murray, *Fearless for Truth: A Personal Portrait of the Life of George Beasley-Murray* (Carlisle: Paternoster Press, 2002). On baptism, see pp. 120-28. Given that the subject of this chapter is to reclaim baptismal regeneration for Baptist theology, only B/baptist scholars have been cited in this section. While I have no delusion that the contentious nature of the subject is going to be resolved here, my intention is to make a viable case and, in so doing, further the study of baptism within our tradition. On the use of 'B/baptist', see McClendon's three-volume *Systematic Theology, passim*, where lower case 'baptist' refers to the wide range of groups holding common convictions which are

regeneration is a biblical-theological one, and, in making it, he was not unaware of Baptist mistrust of this language, observing that 'baptismal regeneration' is frequently understood in attachment to the *ex opere operato* view of baptism. In contrast, however, he showed that the New Testament writers 'think of baptism in terms of grace and faith—always grace, always faith'. He then noted that for

> Paul baptism witnesses to a rising from the dead (Rom. 6.1ff, Col. 2.12), the reception of the Spirit (1 Cor. 12.13), life in Christ (Gal. 3.27), which involves the believer in participation in the new creation (2 Cor. 5.17); the believer puts on the 'new man' (Col. 3.9ff), which is the new nature bestowed through union with the Second Adam, thus again signifying the life of the new creation. *What is all this but 'regeneration' under different images?* It is the reality without the word. The reality and the word come together in Tit. 3.5ff.[78]

In a key and highly controversial essay on baptism in Paul's letters, Beasley-Murray conjectured that Titus 3.5-7 could be part of a baptismal hymn or liturgy (as is suggested by verse 8's reference to it being a 'faithful saying'), and therefore antedated the writing of the Pastorals. The term 'regeneration' has an eschatological significance in its only other New Testament occurrence, Matthew 19.28, and so here probably signifies 'the life of the new world'. This is the idea found in 2 Corinthians 5.17 ('if anyone is in Christ, there is a new creation' [NIV]), an observation which, when coupled with the eschatological elements of these verses (grace, justification, outpouring of the Spirit, inheritance of eternal life), 'strengthens the view that it is present in this saying also'. He continued:

> Its central conception is that in baptism the corresponding event occurs in the life of the individual as happened to the church at Pentecost: the Spirit is 'poured out' through the risen Christ—an idea in direct line with the earliest interpretation of baptism, Acts 2:33, 38. Certainly the saying implies a realistic rather than symbolic understanding of baptism, but that applies to most of the Pauline utterances on baptism.[79]

That Beasley-Murray is not an isolated Baptist New Testament scholar in this regard has already been shown but is reinforced in the work of two contemporary Southern Baptist scholars, Robert H. Stein, Senior Professor of New Testament

---

generally baptist and the upper case Baptist only used with reference to denominations and local churches. Similarly, see Rainbow, '"Confessor Baptism"', p. 203 n. 39.

[78] G.R. Beasley-Murray, *Baptism in the New Testament* (Exeter: The Paternoster Press, 1972 [1962]), p. 278, italics added.

[79] G.R. Beasley-Murray, 'Baptism in the Epistles of Paul', in Gilmore (ed.), *Christian Baptism*, pp. 143-44. For his detailed interpretation of the 'washing of regeneration' as baptism, see his *Baptism in the New Testament*, pp. 209-16 and *passim*. On Beasley-Murray's baptismal theology as a whole, see A.R. Cross, 'Faith-Baptism: The Key to an Evangelical Baptismal Sacramentalism', *Journal of European Baptist Studies* 4.3 (May, 2004), pp. 5-21.

Interpretation, and Tom Schreiner, James Buchanan Harrison Professor New Testament Interpretation and Associate Dean for the Scripture and Interpretation Division, both at The Southern Baptist Theological Seminary.

Stein argues similarly to Beasley-Murray that passages such as Acts 22.16, Ephesians 5.26, Titus 3.5, Hebrews 10.22 and 1 Corinthians 6.11 'when taken at face value, all suggest that the experience of regeneration by the Holy Spirit takes place at conversion when people repent, believe, confess Christ, and are baptized'.[80] Tom Schreiner recognizes that not all scholars accept that the washing in Titus 3.5 refers to baptism. However, he shows that the nouns 'regeneration' and 'renewal' modify the term 'washing', and both 'point to the same reality: the new life granted to believers upon conversion'. This reflects the initiatory character of baptism in Paul's thought[81] in which it 'designates the boundary between the old life and the new'. But this is not to separate it from the work of the Holy Spirit, who 'is the genitive of source for both "regeneration" and "renewal."' He continues,

> Both regeneration and renewal represent a work of the Spirit, so that he is the one who grants new life to believers. The new life of believers is fittingly described in terms of washing, which recalls baptism where sins are washed away. Baptism in Titus, then, is closely associated with the work of the Spirit, as it is in 1 Cor. 12:13. Here the regenerating and renewing work of the Spirit is central. Verse 7 shows that baptism is also linked with justification ('being justified by his grace'), so that we have further evidence that baptism is associated with the decisive saving work of God that occurred at conversion.[82]

The Paedobaptist argument that this text (and implicitly others) can support the practice of infant baptism, and, for that matter, any notion that baptism is effective other than through being faith-baptism[83] (not a term Schreiner uses), is, Schreiner

---

[80] R.H. Stein's 'Baptism in Luke-Acts', in Schreiner and Wright (eds), *Believer's Baptism*, p. 46 n. 25. Cf. also his 'Baptism and Becoming a Christian in the New Testament', *The Southern Baptist Journal of Theology* 2.1 (Spring, 1998), pp. 6-17.

[81] See the whole of his discussion, T.R. Schreiner, 'Baptism in the Epistles', in Schreiner and Wright (eds), *Believer's Baptism*, pp. 67-96.

[82] Schreiner, 'Baptism in the Epistles', pp. 85-86. See also Fowler, *More Than a Symbol*, pp. 184-85 and *passim* on Tit. 3.5.

[83] That New Testament baptism is to be interpreted as faith-baptism can be demonstrated by recognizing that the benefits attributed to faith are also attributed to baptism: forgiveness, cf. Rom. 4.5-7 and 1 Jn 1.9 with Acts 2.38 and 22.16; justification, Rom. 3–5 and Gal. 2–3 with 1 Cor. 6.11; union with Christ, Eph. 3.17 with Gal. 3.27; being crucified with Christ, Gal. 2.20 with Rom. 6.2-11; participation in Christ's death and resurrection, Rom. 8.12-13 with Rom. 6.2-11 and Col. 2.12; sonship, Jn 1.12 with Gal. 3.26-27; the gift of the Spirit, Gal. 3.2-5 and 14 with Acts 2.38 and 1 Cor. 12.13; initiation into the church, Acts 5.14 and Gal. 3.6-7 with Gal. 3.27 and 1 Cor. 12.13; regeneration and life, Jn 3.3, 14-16 and 20.31 with Jn 3.5 and Tit. 3.5; the kingdom and eternal life, Mk 10.15 and Jn 3.14-16 with 1 Cor. 6.9-11; salvation, Rom. 1.16 and Jn 3.16 with 1 Pet. 3.21. This is possible when baptism is recognized as an example of synecdoche in passages such as, e.g., Acts 2.38, 1 Cor. 12.13, Eph. 4.5 and 1

declares, somewhat understatedly, 'unlikely' because 'Baptism is closely associated here with the work of the Spirit in regenerating and renewing sinners so that they have new life', a view which could only be used for infant baptism if an *ex opere operato* view of baptism was adopted. 'Such a view, however', he writes, 'is quite unlikely since justification is also mentioned in v. 7, and both baptism and justification occur at the inception of the Christian life. Indeed, Paul invariably links justification with believing (see Rom 3:22; 5:1; Gal 2:16).'[84]

The other two key passages that are relevant to rehabilitating baptismal regeneration within Baptist theology are John 3.5 and 1 Peter 3.21, and to these we must briefly turn, looking at them through the work of other Baptist scholars.

Donald Guthrie, lecturer in New Testament at what was then London Bible College (1949–82; now London School of Theology), recognized that the 'new birth' discussed by Jesus in John 3, and especially vv. 3 and 5, is 'a vital factor in the initiation process' and identifies it with 'regeneration', which also figures explicitly in Titus 3.5 and 1 Peter 3.21.[85] Guthrie rightly recognized that 'the whole

---

Pet. 3.21, that is, an indispensable part of conversion that can be used for the whole process of becoming a Christian. So Cross, 'Spirit- and Water-Baptism in 1 Corinthians 12.13', in S.E. Porter and A.R. Cross (eds), *Dimensions of Baptism: Biblical and Theological Studies* (*Journal for the Study of the New Testament Supplement Series*, 234; Sheffield: Sheffield Academic Press, 2002), pp. 138-42, and 'The Evangelical Sacrament: *Baptisma Semper Reformandum*', *Evangelical Quarterly* 80.3 (July, 2008), pp. 201-16; and Stein, 'Baptism in Luke-Acts', pp. 51-52; Schreiner, 'Baptism in the Epistles', p. 75 n. 23.

[84] Schreiner, 'Baptism in the Epistles', p. 86. The significance of these comments by Stein and Schreiner, but also by Beasley-Murray who taught at The Southern Baptist Theological Seminary between 1973–80, is seen when it is noted that *Believer's Baptism* is a volume of essays from leading Southern Baptist scholars and is published by a Southern Baptist publisher. Elsewhere, however, Schreiner separates regeneration from conversion in a similar way that Calvin does on the basis of election, i.e., the elect are already regenerate before their conversion and baptism. See his 'Does regeneration necessarily precede conversion?', <http://www.9marks.org/CC/article/0,,PTID314526|CHID598016|CIID1731702,00.html>, accessed 18 July 2007, to which he gives an affirmative answer. However, I believe that recognition that becoming a Christian is a process makes unnecessary attempts to try and fathom the mysterious workings of God and the order in which such elements occur. See Cross, 'The Evangelical Sacrament', p. 206, and '"One Baptism" (Ephesians 4.5): A Challenge to the Church', in Porter and Cross (eds), *Baptism, the New Testament and the Church*, pp. 173-78; and Stein, 'Baptism and Becoming a Christian in the New Testament'.

[85] D. Guthrie, *New Testament Theology* (Leicester: Inter-Varsity Press, 1981), pp. 585-87 (Guthrie also adds Js 1.18). For his discussion of Tit. 3.5, see *The Pastoral Epistles* (Tyndale New Testament Commentaries; Leicester: Inter-Varsity Press, rev. edn, 1990), pp. 216-18, where he thinks it not improbable that it formed part of a baptismal hymn, links 'washing' with the teaching not only of Jn 3.5 but also Eph. 5.26 and the new creation of 2 Cor. 5.17, and ties 'renewal by the Holy Spirit' to 1 Cor. 6.11, which he accepts as having a baptismal reference. It is important to note that he emphasizes that the reference to 'washing' is not unrelated to faith, and while 'washing' is not the

conception of regeneration is expressed in terms which assume the action of God' and is, therefore, 'an act of grace',[86] and that a 'person is regenerate only through the action of the Spirit'[87] — and, we must add, that faith is clearly presupposed in John 3 given the climax of the passage in v. 16's 'whoever believes...' While Guthrie rejected the arguments made for a reference to water-baptism in John 3.5, he nevertheless left it open as a possibility,[88] one that is all the more plausible given his later statement that 'for Paul, as for the other early Christians, conversion and baptism were regarded as one event'.[89] Further, it must not be lost sight of the fact that the New Testament offers a range of metaphors for salvation that includes new birth/regeneration, but also propitiation, reconciliation, adoption, vivification and justification,[90] and each of these shows how someone becomes a Christian, and none of them are mutually exclusive. While the argument that John 3.3 and 5 include reference to baptism will continue to be hotly debated, acceptance[91] that it does is significantly reinforced by the observation that John 3.5 was the favourite baptismal text in the second century.[92]

J. Ramsey Michaels, an American Baptist, notes that 1 Peter 3.21's 'simple statement that "baptism saves" raises for many (especially Protestants) the specter of "baptismal regeneration," i.e., a view that identifies the new birth with water

---

means of the washing away of sin it is a symbol of it. On Guthrie's Baptist commitment, see Cross, *Baptism and the Baptists*, pp. 445-46 n. 282.

[86] Guthrie, *New Testament Theology*, p. 610.

[87] Guthrie, *New Testament Theology*, p. 553, see also pp. 527, 665.

[88] Guthrie, *New Testament Theology*, pp. 728-29. This is in accord with the way Guthrie, *The Pastoral Epistles*, p. 218, closes his discussion of Tit. 3.5: 'It should be noted that "washing" in this context is a symbol but not the means of the washing away of sin.'

[89] Guthrie, *New Testament Theology*, p. 756.

[90] E.g., P.A. Rainbow, Lecturer in New Testament at the North American Baptist Seminary (now Sioux Falls Seminary), South Dakota, *The Way of Salvation: The Role of Christian Obedience in Justification* (Milton Keynes: Paternoster Press, 2005), p. 97, see also pp. 6-7, 23-24, and cf. pp. 233-34.

[91] E.g., Beasley-Murray, *Baptism in the New Testament*, pp. 226-32, *Gospel of Life: Theology in the Fourth Gospel* (Peabody, MA: Hendrickson, 1991), pp. 65-67 and *passim*, and *John* (Word Biblical Commentary, 36; Nashville, TN: Thomas Nelson, 2nd edn, 1999), pp. 47-49, 55; White, *Biblical Doctrine of Initiation*, pp. 251-57; J.R. Michaels, *John* (New International Biblical Commentary; Peabody, MA: Hendrickson, 1989 [1984]), pp. 55-57, and his 'Baptism and Conversion in John: A Particular Baptist Reading', in Porter and Cross (eds), *Baptism, the New Testament and the Church*, pp. 141, 144; J.E. Morgan-Wynne, 'References to Baptism in the Fourth Gospel', in Porter and Cross (eds), *Baptism, the New Testament and the Church*, pp. 121-26; and Fowler, *More Than a Symbol*, pp. 162-63 and *passim*. It is worth noting that interpreted this way, Jn 3.5 theologically coheres with Acts 2.38. On the inseparability of Spirit- and water-baptism, see A.R. Cross, 'Spirit- and Water-Baptism in 1 Corinthians 12.13', pp. 120-48.

[92] See E. Ferguson, 'Inscriptions and the Origin of Infant Baptism', *Journal of Theological Studies* 30 (1979), p. 45 (and n. 1 listing those fathers who used it as such).

baptism', and observes that Peter's reference to water baptism recalls the new birth of 1.3 and that both 'are said to take place "through the raising of Jesus Christ."' The new birth is 'unmistakably an act of God' (cf. 1.3) whereas baptism, whether an 'appeal' or a 'pledge', 'is just as unmistakably a human act directed toward God' (3.21).[93] He then explicates how this can be:

> A statement such as 'baptism saves' is a provisional, not an absolute statement—yet no more provisional than the statement 'faith saves.' In the final analysis, neither baptism nor faith 'saves'; only God saves, and as such human acts as faith and baptism are simply ways of approaching God to receive salvation... Faith 'saves' in that it cleanses the heart and conscience from sin, and so prepares a person to turn to God. Baptism is the actual turning; it is the 'appeal to God out of a good conscience,' and in that sense, according to Peter, 'baptism saves.' If 'faith' (or repentance, or the voluntary cleansing of the conscience) corresponds to Christ's death (i.e., the removal of sins, cf. 2:24; 4:1), baptism corresponds to his resurrection (v 21b; contrast Paul). One is the inside of the conversion experience; the other is the outside. One is the negative; the other is the positive. Neither is optional for Peter, and neither is sufficient by itself; together they define what it means to be a Christian, both in one's heart and in a hostile society.[94]

---

[93] J.R. Michaels, *1 Peter* (Word Biblical Commentary, 49; Waco, TX: Word Books, 1988), p. 221.

[94] Michaels, *1 Peter*, pp. 221-22. See his detailed exegetical study of 3.21 on pp. 213-18, and on the whole of 3.18-22, pp. 194-222. See also his *1 Peter* (Word Biblical Themes; Dallas, TX: Word Publishing, 1989), pp. 20-26, and *passim*. O.S. Brooks, Professor of New Testament Studies at Golden Gate Baptist Theological Seminary, San Francisco, California, *The Drama of Decision: Baptism in the New Testament* (Peabody, MA: Hendrickson, 1987), does not make the same point explicitly, though pretty well all the elements of baptismal regeneration (as we are discussing it) are present in his discussion. See, e.g., pp. 156-57: 'Being fully aware of the source of salvation, the one who is the object of faith, the demands to obedience, the challenge of the model for conduct, a convert comes to the moment when he or she is consciously aware that these are the things appropriate to a right relation to God. This is the moment when he or she is baptized, for baptism is "a declaration of an appropriate awareness toward God." That is the convert's salvation!' On p. 146: 'Baptism, as the declaration of an appropriate relation to God in the resurrection of Jesus Christ, *saves*! The content of baptism in 3:21 is the theme in 1:3-12. That which constitutes salvation is openly declared in baptism.' Earlier, p. 144, Brooks links 1 Pet. 1.3-12 (most likely a baptismal hymn which he ties in with the teaching of Tit. 3.5-7, 1 Jn 3.1-9 and Col. 3.1-4) and the theme of new birth with Jn 3.3, and then with the concept of being born again/regeneration in Mt 19.28, see also p. 159 n. 22. See the whole of his discussion of 1 Pet. 3.21 on pp. 139-59. Other Baptists who accept a regenerative view of baptism in 1 Pet. 3.21 include Stein, 'Baptism and Becoming a Christian', p. 11: 'If those reading this passage had experienced a repentance-faith-confession-regeneration-baptism conversion and all these dimensions took place at the same time, this passage is quite understandable'; Cynthia Long Westfall, a member of the Canadian Baptist Convention of Ontario and Quebec and Assistant Professor of New Testament at McMaster Divinity College, Hamilton, Ontario,

It is easy for misunderstanding to arise during the discussion of such an emotive issue for Baptists as baptismal regeneration. It has happened before. In 1959, when a group of young Baptist ministers explored *Christian Baptism* from the biblical, historical and theological perspectives, controversy erupted and lasted for several years, often generating more heat than light.[95] In defence of the biblical sacramentalism adopted by many of the authors, George Beasley-Murray, one of the contributors, went to great pains to emphasize that the teaching they were presenting

> relates to *baptism in the apostolic Church*, not to baptism in the average modern Baptist church. Where baptism is sundered from conversion on the one hand, and from entry into the Church on the other, this language cannot be applied to it; such a baptism is a reduced baptism.

Those who objected to the volume, he argued, were guilty of transferring the theology of apostolic baptism to that practised and known among the majority of contemporary Baptists (both in 1959 and still today, it should be added). They had, therefore, misunderstood Beasley-Murray and his colleagues whose

> concern...[was] to put before Baptists the picture of ideal baptism, as it is portrayed in the apostolic writings, in the hope that we may strive to recover it or get somewhere near it. To insist on keeping our impoverished version of baptism would be a tragedy among a people who pride themselves on being the people of the New Testament.[96]

V

The foregoing has made no pretence at comprehensiveness, nor even to have begun to unpack the complexities and nuances of the theologies of the various writers so briefly mentioned. Nor is it to suggest that this is the only way these passages

---

Canada, 'The Relationship between the Resurrection, the Proclamation to the Spirits in Prison and Baptismal Regeneration: 1 Peter 3.19-22', in S.E. Porter, M.A. Hayes and D. Tombs (eds), *Resurrection* (*Journal for the Study of the New Testament Supplement Series*, 186/Roehampton Institute London Papers, 5; Sheffield: Sheffield Academic Press, 1999), pp. 106-35, especially pp. 112-13, 114, 116 and 120; and Fowler, *More Than a Symbol*, pp. 163-64, 191-92, and *passim*.

[95] The most detailed study of this controversy is S.K. Fowler, 'Is "Baptist Sacramentalism" an Oxymoron?: Reactions in Britain to *Christian Baptism* (1959)', in A.R. Cross and P.E. Thompson (eds), *Baptist Sacramentalism* (Studies in Baptist History and Thought, 5; Milton Keynes: Paternoster, 2003), pp. 129-50. See also Fowler, *More Than a Symbol*, pp. 113-33; and Cross, *Baptism and the Baptists*, pp. 96-98, 228-43 and *passim*. It is worth noting that all the contributors to *Christian Baptism* later became leading Baptists both in the UK and internationally, see Cross, *Baptism and the Baptists*, p. 197 n. 55.

[96] G.R. Beasley-Murray, 'Baptism Controversy. "The Spirit is There—Declares Dr. G.R. Beasley-Murray', *Baptist Times* 10 December 1959, p. 8, italics his.

(chiefly, but certainly not exclusively, Tit. 3.5; Jn 3.5; 1 Pet. 3.21) can be interpreted. Rather, I have argued that such an interpretation is both legitimate and viable,[97] and is not alien to Baptist thought, either in the twenty-first or any of the preceding four centuries.[98] I have set out to illustrate that the doctrine of baptismal regeneration has its basis in the New Testament and has been maintained down the centuries emphasizing the complementary roles of both the Spirit and faith as the divine and human side of becoming a Christian. While baptismal regeneration has become a mainstay of the theology and practice of infant baptism, and has come to be regarded by many as having efficacy *ex opere operato*, this is not the only way that it can be interpreted. Just because many forms of the doctrine are unacceptable to all Baptists does not mean that we should discard baptismal regeneration altogether, particularly as we find it in the New Testament.

What this chapter is not arguing is that the writers surveyed were right in every aspect of their exegesis and theology of these biblical texts, simply that a biblical and evangelical understanding of baptismal regeneration is *not* inimical to being a Baptist and an Evangelical. What they also bear witness to is a significant and almost totally ignored strand of baptismal theology that reaches back through the *Westminster Confession*, Calvin, the Fathers to the New Testament, and, therefore, is not alien to a genuinely biblical-based theology of baptism and its integral place in becoming a Christian. If separated from the gracious work of God by his Spirit and faith in Christ, baptismal regeneration is, of course, to be rejected, but when understood as the believer's faithful, subjective response to the gracious, objective call of God in the gospel of Christ and the working of the Holy Spirit, then it is something we need to re-discover in our quest to be more biblical in our theology and practice of baptism.

---

[97] For the development of these and related arguments, see Fowler, *More Than a Symbol*, chs 3 and 4, pp. 156-247, which analyze respectively the biblical and theological foundations and formulations of a sacramental interpretation of baptism, of which baptismal regeneration is a part; Colwell, *Promise and Presence*, pp. 109-34; Cross, 'The Evangelical Sacrament', and *Recovering the Evangelical Sacrament: Baptisma Semper Reformandum* (Milton Keynes: Paternoster, forthcoming 2010-11)

[98] It does not matter that the place of 'baptismal regeneration' occupies different places within the soteriologies of the Baptists we have so briefly examined; what is important is that these Baptists have recognized the biblical-theological connection between baptism and regeneration in the New Testament and sought to apply it, with varying degrees of success, to their own understanding of what it is to become a Christian. Equally it does not matter that these Baptists constitute a small minority, for when has discerning the mind of Christ rested on the majority vote? If this was the essential criterion, then our Baptist forebears would never have become Baptists, but remained Separatists, Puritans, Anglicans or even Roman Catholics. What matters for Baptists, as for other Evangelicals, is whether a theology is in accord with the word of God, and the fact that other Christians (Baptists among them—even the majority of Baptists) do not interpret New Testament baptism in this way does not mean that those who do are not authentically Baptist, or, for that matter, not called and equipped by God for mission service.

This brief survey, then, disproves the absolute claim of the IMB's 'Position Paper' that *it* represents 'the Scriptural teaching regarding this primary of the two church ordinances'. And while it reflects a widespread interpretation of New Testament baptism, the 'Position Paper' represents only one possible evangelical interpretation, and those who interpret it differently should not be stigmatized in any way or discounted from sharing in the commission of Christ to make disciples of all nations by baptizing and teaching them to obey all his commands (Mt. 28.19). In actual fact, rather than preserving the New Testament doctrine and practice of baptism, the guideline's and position paper's rejection of a regenerative view of baptism witnesses to the majority of Baptists' departure from the New Testament doctrine and practice of baptism. It is true that believer's baptism, when separated from conversion, is antithetical to a doctrine of baptismal regeneration, but New Testament baptism *is* conversion-baptism/faith-baptism, and when baptism is seen as an integral part, not just of the message of the gospel we proclaim (Acts 2.38, 41),[99] but of the process of becoming a Christian, then a doctrine of baptismal regeneration/rebirth/new life is inevitable. As Tom Schreiner puts it, 'The issue of baptismal regeneration [understood in the *ex opere operato* sense] arose in later church history when baptism was separated from faith, though those who promoted baptismal regeneration rightly saw that baptism was irretrievably tied to initiation into the people of God in the [New Testament].'[100] What is needful, then, is not the rejection of a regenerative understanding of baptism, but the reform of Baptist baptismal theology and practice along more rigorously biblical lines.

It is important to note that the rehabilitation of baptismal regeneration in Baptist theology rests upon the reform of Baptist baptismal theology and practice in its entirety, as called for, for example, by George Beasley-Murray nearly fifty years ago:

> For too long we have regarded it as our vocation to demonstrate *who* are the proper recipients of baptism, but have been unable to supply a coherent account from the Scriptures of *what* that baptism is that must be administered to the right persons. Anyone acquainted with our churches knows that there exist in them traditions as stereotyped as can be found in any other churches, and we are dangerously near to mistaking our own popular traditions for the Word of God as are the rest. We Baptists pride ourselves on being churches of the New Testament. It behooves us to take our own medicine—to cast aside our pride, *search afresh the Scriptures*, submit ourselves to their teaching, and be prepared for *reform according to the Word*.[101]

In this, Beasley-Murray is by no means alone. Timothy George, Dean of Beeson Divinity School of Samford University, Birmingham, Alabama, states,

---

[99] Rarely does baptism figure in the message of the gospel proclaimed by Baptists, but is something brought up later, after conversion. See Cross, 'The Evangelical Sacrament', pp. 214-15 n. 73.

[100] Schreiner, 'Baptism in the Epistles', p. 92.

[101] G.R. Beasley-Murray, 'Baptism in the New Testament', *Foundations* 3.1 (January, 1960), p. 30, italics added.

> The recovery of a robust doctrine of believers' baptism can serve as an antidote to the theological minimalism and atomistic individualism that prevail in many credobaptist churches in our culture. Baptism is not only the solemn profession of a redeemed sinner, our 'appeal to God for a clear conscience,' as the New Testament puts it (I Pet. 3:21); it is also a sacred and serious act of incorporation into the visible community of faith. Such an understanding of baptism *calls for the reform of our baptismal practice* at several critical points.[102]

Similarly, Jonathan Rainbow calls for 'baptists to recover a full-bodied doctrine of baptism instead of the minimalistic view that is often heard in baptist circles today',[103] while Tom Schreiner notes that this reformation of theology and practice is an on-going process, for 'Baptists...need to continually reform their practice according to the word of God'.[104]

At present Baptist baptismal theology is that of believer's baptism, that is, the baptism of those who have *already* come to faith. Since their 'becoming a Christian' has already taken place—which is what regeneration refers to, as do the synonymous images of rebirth/being born again—at some earlier time (sometimes a few months, years or even decades previously) baptismal regeneration is understandably to be rejected because baptism is not part of the process of conversion. However, if Baptists reform their theology and practice to the conversion-baptism of the New Testament, in which faith-baptism is an integral part of both the gospel we preach and the process of becoming a Christian, then, *and only then*, will it be possible to reclaim baptismal regeneration as part of our theology of conversion, our soteriology.

---

[102] T. George, 'The Reformed Doctrine of Believers' Baptism', *Interpretation* 47.3 (July, 1993), p. 251 (italics added).

[103] Rainbow, '"Confessor Baptism"', p. 205.

[104] Schreiner, 'Baptism in the Epistles', p. 95 n. 67.

CHAPTER 11

The Lord's Supper and the Spirituality of C.H. Spurgeon

Peter J. Morden

Introduction

On 9 October 1880 the *Boy's Own Paper* published silhouettes of those it considered to be the greatest 'celebrities' of late-Victorian England. Unsurprisingly, the collection included the two most notable Prime Ministers of the age, William Gladstone and Benjamin Disraeli, as well as the poet-laureate Alfred (Lord) Tennyson and the essayist Thomas Carlyle. Also pictured, in the centre of the nine silhouettes, was the Baptist pastor Charles Haddon Spurgeon (1834–92).[1] The bracketing of Spurgeon and, say, Gladstone can seem strange to modern commentators but, as Patricia Kruppa observes, 'many Victorians would have found it appropriate'.[2] As David Bebbington states, Spurgeon was by far 'the most popular preacher of the day' in an era where religion bulked large in the life of the nation.[3] As such he was a 'personality of national standing'.[4] Principally because of the circulation of his printed sermons, Spurgeon's reputation and influence also crossed the Atlantic. As early as 1858, when Spurgeon was only twenty-four, the *North American Review* was reporting that Americans returning from a trip to England were invariably asked two questions, namely: 'Did you see the Queen?' and 'Did you hear Spurgeon?'[5] Charles Spurgeon was a figure of international importance in the nineteenth century.

This essay seeks to examine aspects of the spirituality of this remarkable evangelical Baptist, and to do so with reference to his theology and practice of the 'sacrament' of the Lord's supper. Spurgeon preferred to use the term 'ordinance'

---

[1] *Boy's Own Paper*, 9 October 1880, in C.H. Spurgeon, *Autobiography: Compiled from his Diary, Letters, and Records by his Wife and his Private Secretary* (4 vols; London: Passmore and Alabaster, 1899), IV, p. 185. The other silhouettes were of the Marquis of Hartington, John Ruskin, the Duke of Argyle and John Bright.

[2] P.S. Kruppa, *Charles Haddon Spurgeon: A Preacher's Progress* (New York: Garland Publishing, 1982), p. 1.

[3] D.W. Bebbington, *Evangelicalism in Modern Britain: A history from the 1730s to the 1980s* (London: Unwin Hymen, 1989), p. 145.

[4] D.W. Bebbington, *The Dominance of Evangelicalism: The Age of Spurgeon and Moody* (Leicester: IVP, 2005), p. 57.

[5] As cited by Kruppa, *Spurgeon*, p. 250.

when describing the supper but, as Tim Grass and Ian Randall point out in the first *Baptist Sacramentalism* volume, Spurgeon was 'happy to employ the common definition of a sacrament—"an outward and visible sign of an inward and spiritual grace"—to explain what he meant by ordinance.' They go on to say that, in Spurgeon's thinking, both baptism and the Lord's supper were 'associated with God's gracious activity'.[6] With regards to baptism, this statement does, I think, need to be qualified.[7] But, as far as the Lord's supper is concerned, there is ample evidence to support it. Grass and Randall conclude their survey by stating, 'The sacraments were central to the spirituality of C.H. Spurgeon.'[8] This essay seeks to build on their groundbreaking work by investigating in detail the relationship between one of those sacraments, the Lord's supper, and Spurgeon's spirituality.

Understanding Spirituality

Definitions of 'spirituality' are legion, even if the focus is restricted to specifically Christian spirituality, and some explanation of what is intended by its use here is necessary. Some of the different understandings of spirituality on offer today are so broad as to encompass almost all of human experience and hardly help to establish conceptual limits for the term. But other approaches that focus exclusively on prayer and the spiritual exercises are too narrow, certainly for the purposes of this essay.[9] Helpfully, as Linda Wilson notes, there is a growing trend to define spirituality as consisting of 'more than just devotion'. For Wilson, as well as other writers,

---

[6] T. Grass and I.M. Randall, 'C.H. Spurgeon on the Sacraments', in A.R. Cross and P.E. Thompson (eds), *Baptist Sacramentalism* (Studies in Baptist History and Thought, 5; Paternoster Press: Carlisle, 2003), p. 55.

[7] Spurgeon did not believe baptism conferred 'any grace upon the person who is baptized'. See C.H. Spurgeon, 'Fencing the Table', *New Park Street Pulpit* (hereafter *NPSP*)/*Metropolitan Tabernacle Pulpit* (hereafter *MTP*) (London: Passmore and Alabaster, 1856–1917), *MTP*, 50, sermon number 2865, on 1 Corinthians 11.28, delivered 2 January 1876, p. 13. Rather, baptism was seen as a human response to grace previously received, although this did not mean the rite was unimportant to him. Overall, Grass and Randall, 'Spurgeon on the Sacraments', pp. 56-67, make it clear that Spurgeon's view of baptism was not as 'sacramental' as his approach to the Lord's supper. For more on Spurgeon and baptism, see S.K. Fowler, *More Than a Symbol: The British Baptist Recovery of Baptismal Sacramentalism* (Studies in Baptist History and Thought, 2; Paternoster Press: Carlisle, 2002), pp. 79-83.

[8] Grass and Randall, 'C.H. Spurgeon on the Sacraments', p. 75. This statement, I believe, does hold good for both baptism and the Lord's supper. Believers' baptism was crucial to Spurgeon's conception of the Christian life, acting, effectively, as a badge of full-blooded, radical, Christian discipleship. I hope to show this in a future paper.

[9] For a sample of some of the different definitions on offer, see A.E. McGrath, *Christian Spirituality* (Oxford: Blackwell, 1999), pp. 2-4.

spirituality also encompasses 'the way devotional lives are worked out in practice'.[10] The study of Christian spirituality can, therefore, include analysis of both the way in which a relationship with God through Christ is developed *and* the way that relationship is worked out, in private and in public.

I have sought to follow this broader, but still focused, approach, in particular adopting a framework for the study of spirituality proposed by Philip Sheldrake in *Spirituality and History*. Sheldrake understands spirituality as being concerned with the conjunction of theology, prayer and practical Christianity,[11] an 'analytical framework' adapted slightly by Ian Randall, who substitutes 'communion with God' for 'prayer'.[12] It ought to be noted that such an understanding of spirituality would have been alien to Spurgeon himself who, when he used the term, meant by it something akin to piety or devotion, thus focusing on the inner dimension of the spiritual life.[13] But this is not really the problem it might appear to be, and the adoption of this different, more recent, model for the study of spirituality is both legitimate and helpful, allowing as it does for an analysis of a wide range of Spurgeon's 'lived experience'.[14] What modern writers term 'spirituality' was vitally important to Spurgeon, and my own conviction is that his life and work cannot be adequately understood without reference to it. This essay will seek to highlight the different ways in which the Lord's supper was central to Spurgeon's spirituality.[15] The three different elements, the coming together of which constitute spirituality in Sheldrake's model, can each be analysed in turn, beginning with Spurgeon's theology.

---

[10] L. Wilson, *Constrained by Zeal: Female Spirituality Among Nonconformists: 1825–1875* (Paternoster Biblical and Theological Monographs; Carlisle: Paternoster Press, 2000), p. 4.

[11] P. Sheldrake, *Spirituality and History* (London: SPCK, 1991), p. 52.

[12] I.M. Randall, *What a Friend we Have in Jesus: The Evangelical Tradition* (Traditions of Christian Spirituality Series; London: Darton, Longman and Todd, 2005), p. 23; I.M. Randall, *Evangelical Experiences: A Study in the Spirituality of English Evangelicalism 1918–1939* (Paternoster Biblical and Theological Monographs; Carlisle: Paternoster Press, 1999), p. 2.

[13] Spurgeon, *Autobiography*, I, p. 145: 'Oh that my spirituality may be revived! My matchless Immanuel, let me see once more Thy face in the temple of my heart.' This quotation from Spurgeon's diary is not dated, but is probably from late 1850 or early 1851.

[14] S.M. Schneiders, 'Christian Spirituality: Definition, Methods and Types', in P. Sheldrake (ed.), *The New SCM Dictionary of Christian Spirituality* (London: SCM Press, 2005), p. 1; Randall, *Evangelical Experiences*, p. 2.

[15] Because Spurgeon's practice of celebrating the Lord's supper has been thoroughly analysed by Grass and Randall, 'C.H. Spurgeon on the Sacraments', pp. 71-74; M.J. Walker, *Baptists at the Table: The Theology of the Lord's Supper amongst English Baptists in the Nineteenth Century* (Didcot: Baptist Historical Society, 1992), pp. 167-70, this will not be rehearsed here. Spurgeon argued for open, as opposed to closed, communion, and for a simple, weekly and serious, although not sombre, celebration of the supper. Cf. Spurgeon, 'Fencing the Table', pp. 13-14.

Theology

Spurgeon was a theological conservative. He believed in the infallibility of the Bible, a position he was effectively content to state rather than argue for, and his rejection of nineteenth-century biblical criticism was almost wholesale.[16] The Calvinism of Spurgeon's early ministry is evidenced by sermon titles such as 'God's Sovereignty',[17] 'Particular Election'[18] and 'Free Will—A Slave'.[19] This last message, preached in 1855, contained a particularly fierce anti-Arminian polemic. But, as Mark Hopkins notes in his fine study of Spurgeon's theology, by the end of the 1850s Spurgeon's Calvinism was of a 'lower variety than in his earliest preaching', and he became content to let emphases that were considered 'Calvinistic' and 'Arminian' lie side by side, with minimal attempt at synthesis.[20] Writing in 1874, Spurgeon stated that he believed that the truth of God was wider than what he now called 'the two great systems' (i.e., Arminianism and Calvinism). It was not, Spurgeon continued, that he had thrown away the 'five points', rather that he 'may have gained (an)other five'.[21] Despite this shift in emphasis, Spurgeon remained essentially Calvinistic throughout his ministry, as the reference to the five points of the Synod of Dort in the previous sentence indicates. The chapter of his *Autobiography* entitled 'A Defence of Calvinism' represents his mature view.[22] The atonement was a particular focus of this conservative theology, and, as David Gillett

---

[16] As is evident in, e.g., C.H. Spurgeon, 'The Infallibility of Scripture', *MTP* 34, sermon number 2013, Isaiah 1.20, delivered 11 March 1888, pp. 145-56.

[17] C.H. Spurgeon, 'Notebook Containing Early Sermon Skeletons', Volume 1 (Spurgeon's College Heritage Room, K1.5), 'God's Sovereignty', sermon number 18, Psalm 10.16. Cf. 'Election', sermon number 10, Ephesians 1.4; 'Final Perseverance', sermon number 8, Psalm 94.14. These sermons were initially preached in 1851 in Cambridgeshire.

[18] C.H. Spurgeon, 'Particular Election', *NPSP* 3, sermon number 123, 2 Peter 1.10, 11, delivered 22 March 1857, pp. 129-36.

[19] C.H. Spurgeon, 'Free Will—A Slave', *NPSP* 1, sermon number 52, John 5.20, delivered 2 December 1855, pp. 394-402.

[20] M. Hopkins, *Nonconformity's Romantic Generation: Evangelical and Liberal Theologies in Victorian England* (Studies in Evangelical History and Thought; Carlisle: Paternoster Press, 2004), p. 140. The use of qualifiers such as 'lower' and 'higher' is fraught with difficulty in a debate about Calvinism, a term which in itself, along with Arminianism, can of course mean different things to different people. But Hopkins is surely correct in asserting that the end of the 1850s marked a change in Spurgeon's views, both in substance and in tone.

[21] C.H. Spurgeon, 'The Present Position of Calvinism in England', in C.H. Spurgeon (ed.), *The Sword and The Trowel: A Record of Combat With Sin and Labour For The Lord* (hereafter *ST*) (London: Passmore and Alabaster, 1865-92), February, 1874, pp. 49-53; cf. C.H. Spurgeon, 'High Doctrine and Broad Doctrine', *MTP* 30, sermon number 1762, John 6.37, undated, pp. 49-50.

[22] Spurgeon, *Autobiography*, I, pp. 167-78.

states, Spurgeon believed that this was the 'touchstone of all Christian doctrine'.[23] Writing in 1889 to his Metropolitan Tabernacle congregation from his winter retreat at Mentone in the south of France, Spurgeon declared that the 'substitutionary sacrifice of our Lord' lay 'at the heart of the Christian faith'. He continued: 'I do not conceive "substitution" to be an explanation of atonement, but to be of the very essence of it.'[24] Any attempt to water down penal substitution brought forth his strongest condemnation.[25] As Michael Walker states, Spurgeon believed that 'the vicarious, substitutionary and atoning death of Christ' was 'the central truth of the Christian faith'.[26]

Spurgeon's theology was always worked out from the standpoint of a participant rather than an observer, and nowhere is this more apparent than in his theology of the atonement. In a sermon entitled 'The Sacred Love Token', based on the phrase in Exodus 12.13, 'When I see the blood, I will pass over', Spurgeon defended penal substitution with all his might. 'The blood upon the lintel said, "someone has died here instead of us,"' he insisted. But he did not just 'hold' to this truth, he 'rested' in it. The use of the phrase 'the blood' in connection with the atonement was something which many in the nineteenth century shrank from. But for Spurgeon this was vital because, he stated, it brought out 'that fundamental truth which is the power of God unto salvation'. He continued: 'We dwell beneath the blood mark, and rejoice that Jesus for us poured out his soul unto death when he bare the sins of many.' Phrases such as 'we dwell', 'rejoice' and 'for us' bring out the fact that Spurgeon's theology of the atonement was deeply a part of him. For Spurgeon, these truths were 'precious'.[27] Similar emphases were present in a message, 'Redemption by Price', based on 1 Corinthians 6.19-20. Over and against those who objected to the 'idea of substitution and vicarious sacrifice', Spurgeon insisted that on the cross Christ bore 'divine wrath in our stead'. He continued: 'No truth within the circle of theology is so eminently consolatory to souls burdened with sin', adding dramatically, 'I nail my colours to the cross'.[28] Spurgeon was not committed to his views on the atonement in any abstract sense, rather he believed that a

---

[23] D.K. Gillett, *Trust and Obey: Explorations in Evangelical Spirituality* (London: Darton, Longman and Todd, 1993), pp. 68-73.

[24] C.H. Spurgeon, 'Letter from Mr Spurgeon', *MTP* 35, Mentone, 11 February 1889, p. 96. Cf. Spurgeon, *Autobiography*, I, p. 113, although he could also state, 'I feel...substitution does not cover the whole of the matter...no human conception can completely grasp the whole of the dread mystery.' Quoted by W.Y. Fullerton, *C.H. Spurgeon: A Biography* (London: Williams and Norgate, 1920), pp. 181-82. Cf. the discussion in Hopkins, *Nonconformity's Romantic Generation*, pp. 147-48.

[25] See C.H. Spurgeon, 'The Word of the Cross', *MTP* 27, sermon number 1611, 1 Corinthians 1.18, delivered 31 July 1881, pp. 425-36, for a particularly stinging rebuke.

[26] Walker, *Baptists at the Table*, p. 170.

[27] C.H. Spurgeon, 'The Sacred Love Token', *MTP* 21, sermon number 1251, Exodus 12.13, 22 August 1875, pp. 483-84.

[28] C.H. Spurgeon, 'Redemption by Price', *MTP* 26, sermon number 1554, 1 Corinthians 6.19-20, 22 August 1880, pp. 469-70.

conservative theology of the cross was essential to developing and maintaining a healthy spiritual life. As he famously put it, 'the coals of orthodoxy' were 'necessary to the fires of piety'.[29] Theology and experience were closely linked.

In fact, Spurgeon's experience was not only shaped and sustained by his theology; his experience helped give shape and validity to the theology itself. In a lecture given to students at the Pastor's College and first published in 1882, Spurgeon set out the following reasons for defending a conservative view of the atonement, stating: 'I cannot help holding that there must be an atonement before there can be pardon, because my conscience demands it, and my peace depends on it. The little court within my own heart is not satisfied unless some retribution be exacted for dishonour done to God.' Spurgeon brought forward similar arguments for holding to the doctrines of election ('I am quite sure that if God had not chosen me I would never have chosen him') and total depravity ('I find myself depraved in heart, and have daily proofs that there dwelleth in my flesh no good thing').[30] Spurgeon's *own experience* led to him to hold tenaciously to conservative understandings and approaches and reject the 'new theology' represented by men such as the Congregational leader J. Baldwin Brown.[31] Only what Spurgeon defiantly and proudly called the 'old theology' could provide a framework within which he could adequately interpret his spiritual experiences and continue to relate to God. Thus, as far as the atonement was concerned, although he defended traditional categories for understanding Christ's work on the cross, his approach was markedly different from that of, say, the Princeton theologians, Charles Hodge and his son, Archibald Alexander Hodge.[32] Whilst they tended to engage in more technical discussions on the death of Christ, Spurgeon's treatment was far less systematic and couched in

---

[29] Cited by J.M. Gordon, *Evangelical Spirituality: From the Wesleys to John Stott* (London: SPCK, 1991), p. 169. Cf. Spurgeon's *Autobiography*, I, p. 178: 'A man cannot have an erroneous belief without by-and-by having an erroneous life. I believe the one thing naturally begets the other.'

[30] C.H. Spurgeon, *Lectures to my Students: Second Series* (London: Passmore and Alabaster, 1882), p. 47. The Pastor's College was first established by Spurgeon in 1856. For the definitive history see I.M. Randall, *A School of the Prophets: 150 Years of Spurgeon's College* (London: Spurgeon's College, 2005).

[31] See D.A. Johnson, *The Changing Shape of English Nonconformity 1825-1925* (Oxford: Oxford University Press, 1999), pp. 125-62, for some of the views Spurgeon stood against, including those of Baldwin Brown. Cf. Hopkins, *Nonconformity's Romantic Generation*, pp. 17-45. For Spurgeon's own strictures on Baldwin Brown, see his *Autobiography*, II, pp. 279-80.

[32] For these men, see M.A. Noll, *Charles Hodge: The Way of Life* (New York: Paulist Press, 1987); P.J. Wallace, 'Hodge, Archibald Alexander', and 'Hodge, Charles', in T. Larsen (ed.), *Biographical Dictionary of Evangelicals* (Leicester: IVP, 2003), pp. 302-307. Spurgeon admired both father and son but this was because they reached similar conclusions to him on, for example, the infallibility of the scriptures. Their overall approaches were markedly different.

more poetic terms, in the 'language of the heart'. Crucially, the lead in his theological exploration was often taken by spiritual experience.[33]

Spurgeon's Theology of the Atonement and the Lord's Supper

Spurgeon's theology, then, can be described as both conservative and deeply rooted in his own experience, as well as having a special focus on the atonement. These emphases came together in his preaching at the Lord's supper. 'The Sin Bearer' was a message published in *Till He Come*, a book of Spurgeon's 'communion addresses and meditations' published after his death. In this particular address, Spurgeon defended his views on the atonement in some detail. The preacher's text was 1 Peter 1.24-25, and he was quite certain that the statement that Christ 'bare our sins in his own body on the tree' was a plain declaration of substitutionary atonement. Spurgeon set out a whole series of other scriptures which all pointed in the same direction, including Hebrews 9.28, 'Christ was once offered to bear the sins of many', and 2 Corinthians 5.21, 'Christ hath redeemed us from the curse of the law, being made a curse for us...'. In a comment which reflected his belief in an infallible Bible he stated, 'I cannot imagine that the Holy Spirit would have used language so expressive if He had not intended to teach us that our Saviour really did bear our sins, and suffer in our stead.' Those advocates of 'modern thought' who rejected substitution were, for Spurgeon, 'modern haters of the cross', so clearly were they denying what the 'word of God' taught about the death of Christ.[34]

Unsurprisingly, other addresses in *Till He Come* contain material in a similar vein. In 'The Memorable Hymn', Spurgeon concluded his message by declaring: 'Christ was punished in the room, place, and stead of every man and woman who will believe on Him. If you believe on Him...God cannot punish you, for he has punished Christ ahead of you, and He will never punish twice for the same offence.'[35] Spurgeon believed that the atonement was sufficient for all but efficient only for those who were the elect, for 'every man or woman who will believe'. In this he stood in line with the Calvinists of the Evangelical Revival, including the Baptists Andrew Fuller and William Carey. Spurgeon's language in 'A Defence of Calvinism' is sometimes very similar to Fuller's, who had in turn been profoundly influenced by Jonathan Edwards.[36] Preaching at the Lord's supper afforded Spurgeon particular opportunities to defend and expound his evangelical theology of the cross.

---

[33] Cf. Hopkins, *Nonconformity's Romantic Generation*, p. 141. Spurgeon's commitment to the infallibility of the scriptures was similarly grounded in spiritual experience. See pp. 137-38.

[34] 'The Sin Bearer', 1 Peter 2.24-25, 'A Communion Meditation at Mentone', in C.H. Spurgeon, *Till He Come* (London: Passmore and Alabaster, 1896), pp. 333-34.

[35] 'The Memorable Hymn', Matthew 26.30, in Spurgeon, *Till He Come*, p. 229.

[36] See, e.g., Spurgeon, *Autobiography*, I, p. 174, and the comment, 'There must be sufficient efficiency in the blood of Christ, if God had so willed it, to have saved not only all in this world, but all in ten thousand worlds...'. In 1787 Fuller had written that the sufferings of Christ were 'of infinite value, sufficient to have saved all the world, and a

But what is striking is how, once again, this theology is tied so closely to spiritual experience. Undoubtedly Spurgeon's theology was, in Eugene Peterson's terms, a *spiritual* theology, that is one that was 'lived', the antithesis of a theology 'depersonalised into information about God'.[37] In 'The Sin Bearer' this can be seen with particular clarity. In the introduction to his message Spurgeon stated that 'We ourselves now know *by experience* that there is no place for comfort like the cross.'[38] Later on in the sermon he declared,

> Beloved friends, we very calmly and coolly talk about this thing [the atonement], but it is the greatest marvel in the universe; it is the miracle of earth, the mystery of heaven, the terror of hell. Could we fully realise the guilt of sin, the punishment due to it, and the literal substitution of Christ, it would work in us an intense enthusiasm of gratitude, love, and praise. I do not wonder our Methodist friends shout, "Hallelujah!" This is enough to make us all shout and sing, as long as we live, "Glory, glory to the Son of God!"[39]

Again, it is clear that the 'literal substitution of Christ' was not an abstract concept to be debated but something living and vital, to be believed in ever more deeply. If the atonement were truly appreciated it would 'work in' the believer intense feelings of 'gratitude' and 'love' to God, feelings which could not help being expressed in praise. To Spurgeon's mind, for someone to discuss the atonement in a detached way was a sure sign that they had not understood it, and for a person to reject substitution was proof that they had not only an inadequate knowledge of their own sinfulness but also a shallow appreciation of God's majesty. For Spurgeon, who had a profound and deep sense of both, the work of Christ on the cross by which the guilty sinner and a holy God were reconciled was indeed a source of 'great comfort', as well as being a spur to heartfelt praise. In point of fact, to speak 'coolly and calmly' about the cross was quite beyond Spurgeon, and statements about its 'preciousness' for the

---

thousand worlds, if it had pleased God…to have made them effectual to this end'. The change from 'one thousand' to 'ten thousand' was a typical Spurgeonic flourish. See A.G. Fuller (ed.), J. Belcher (rev. ed.), *The Complete Works of the Rev Andrew Fuller…* (3 vols; Harrisonburg, VA: Sprinkle, 3rd edn, 1988 [1845]), II, p. 472. On Fuller's view of the atonement, and the influence of Edwards, see P.J. Morden, *Offering Christ to the World: Andrew Fuller (1754–1815) and the Revival of Eighteenth Century Particular Baptist Life* (Studies in Baptist History and Thought, 8; Carlisle: Paternoster Press, 2003), pp. 23-102, especially p. 71.

[37] E.H. Peterson, *Christ Plays in Ten Thousand Places: A Conversation in Spiritual Theology* (London: Hodder and Stoughton, 2005), p. 1. Elsewhere Peterson speaks of 'Spiritual Theology' as to do with 'prayer' and 'spiritual formation', linked with reading the Bible 'formationally, not just intellectually'. See E.H. Peterson, *Subversive Spirituality* (Vancouver, BC: Regent College Publishing, 1997), p. 259.

[38] Spurgeon, 'The Sin Bearer', p. 334. Italics mine.

[39] Spurgeon, 'The Sin Bearer', p. 338.

believer were never far away from any of his expositions of the atonement.[40] The Lord's supper, which 'set forth' so clearly the death of Christ, provided an important context for these reflections and was a focus for Spurgeon's spirituality.[41]

Communion with God

Union with Christ

This emphasis on experience points towards the second dimension of Spurgeon's spirituality to be examined, namely communion with Christ.[42] In a sermon entitled 'Love's Vigilance Rewarded', preached in 1877, Spurgeon declared, 'It is good to find sound doctrine, for it is very scarce nowadays. It is good to learn the practical precepts of the gospel, it is good to be in the society of the saints; but if you put any of these in the place of communion with your Lord himself, you do ill.'[43] Communion with Christ was absolutely vital to Spurgeon. Such communion was possible, and only possible, because of the union which existed between Christ and the believer, a union which was founded on God's grace in election. 'I was his before I knew him to be mine', Spurgeon stated,[44] and for him it was this that was the 'immovable basis of communion'.[45] The truth of a believer's election was also proved in his or her experience—in conversion and in conscious surrender to Christ on different occasions subsequently. 'We are his...to our own consciousness', said Spurgeon, 'because we have heartily...given ourselves up to him.'[46] Those who were truly elect would press on to make their calling and election sure, and spiritual

---

[40] For another example, see 'The Well Beloved', in Spurgeon, *Till He Come*, Song of Songs 5.16, pp. 104-105.

[41] Spurgeon repeatedly made the obvious point that observing the Lord's supper focused communicants minds on the atonement. See, e.g., Spurgeon, 'A Holy Celebration', *MTP* 19, sermon number 1092, undated, Exodus 12.42, pp. 1-2.

[42] Spurgeon's emphasis tended to be on 'communion with Christ', rather than communion with God the Father, although in 'Communion with Christ and His People', in Spurgeon, *Till He Come*, 1 Corinthians 10.16-17, 'A Communion Address at Mentone', p. 315, he stated that 'the Spirit Himself draws the heart of the renewed one... Truly our fellowship is with the Father, and with His Son Jesus Christ. Do *you* enjoy this charming converse?' Thus, Spurgeon's approach to communion with God was trinitarian.

[43] 'Love's Vigilance Rewarded', in C.H. Spurgeon, *The Most Holy Place: Sermons on the Song of Solomon* (London, Passmore and Alabaster, 1896), sermon number 2485, Song of Songs 3.4, delivered 4 October 1877, p. 228.

[44] 'The Interest of Christ and His People in Each Other', in Spurgeon, *The Most Holy Place*, sermon number 374, delivered Good Friday Evening, 29 March 1861, Song of Songs 2.16, p. 182.

[45] 'The Spiced Wine of My Pomegranate', in Spurgeon, *Till He Come*, Song of Songs 8.2; John 1.16, p. 117. Cf. 'Bands of Love; Or, Union to Christ', in Spurgeon, *Till He Come*, Hosea 11.4, pp. 181-83.

[46] 'A Song Among the Lilies', in Spurgeon, *Most Holy Place*, sermon number 1190, Song of Songs 2.16, delivered 30 August 1874, p. 191.

experience had a part to play in bringing full assurance that a believer belonged to Christ.

Nevertheless, the primary guarantee of assurance of this union was not a believer's experience, but what God had done and, once again, Spurgeon placed particular stress on the work of Christ on the cross. 'Christ has an absolute right to all that he bought with his blood', he stated. Because Christ had ransomed and redeemed his people they were in consequence 'eternally his'. Spurgeon emphasized that only a 'real' atonement could guarantee union with Christ, such was the justice of God and the sinfulness of humankind. It was this that was the objective and primary basis for assurance of union with Christ. Spurgeon wished that all his hearers 'could *feel* Christ' to be theirs.[47] But even if they could not, believers need have no doubts. 'We are his because he called us by his grace' and 'because he bought us with his blood'.[48] Union with Christ was thus based on God's decree and on Christ's work. From this basis of assurance, and through the indwelling power of the Holy Spirit, 'without whom we should never have had a spark of love to Jesus',[49] the earnest believer could press on to know Christ more deeply.

The Song of Songs and Communion with Christ

The survey of Spurgeon's views on the basis of union with Christ given in the previous two paragraphs is taken from a sampling of sermons he preached on the Song of Songs, a book which he interpreted allegorically as depicting the relationship between Christ and his church.[50] For Spurgeon, the Song was one of the 'high places of Scripture' because he believed it spoke of communion with Christ. For those not taught in this 'school of communion' the book was 'sealed', but for 'full grown Christians', who knew what it was to experience closeness to Christ, the spiritual meaning of the Song would be clear 'from the first verse to the last'.[51] Spurgeon's preaching on the Song illustrates the vital importance he attached to growing in communion with Christ, and helps to emphasize what a defining theme this was for him. One message in particular stands out.

This is a communion address given at Mentone and entitled 'The Well Beloved', in which Spurgeon expounded the phrase 'Yea, He is altogether lovely' from Song of Songs 5.16. As James Gordon states, 'The Well Beloved' is 'a sustained eulogy on the beauty of Jesus experienced by a man of powerful emotional capacity'.[52] It

---

[47] Spurgeon, 'The Interest of Christ and His People in Each Other', pp. 178, 181. Italics original.

[48] Cf. Spurgeon, 'A Song Among the Lilies', p. 191.

[49] 'The Church's Love to Her Loving Lord', in Spurgeon, *Most Holy Place*, sermon number 636, undated, Song of Songs 1.7, p. 66.

[50] 'The Lily Among the Thorns', in Spurgeon, *Most Holy Place*, sermon number 1525, delivered 29 February 1880, Song of Songs 2.2, p. 125.

[51] 'A Bundle of Myrrh', in Spurgeon, *Most Holy Place*, sermon number 558, delivered 6 March 1864, Song of Songs 1.13, pp. 89-90.

[52] Gordon, *Evangelical Spirituality*, p. 162.

expresses Spurgeon's desire for communion with Christ, and stands as a moving testimony of his sense of intimacy with, and love for, his Lord. In the course of the sermon, Spurgeon spoke of Christ in the following terms:

> His is an approachable beauty, which not only overpowers us with his glory, but holds us captive by its charms... He has within Himself an unquenchable flame of love, which sets our soul on fire. Put together all the loves of husbands, wives, parents, children, brothers, sisters, and they only make a drop compared with His great deeps of love, unexplored and unexplorable... It is a torrent which sweeps all before it when its founts break forth within the soul. It is a Gulf Stream in which all icebergs melt. When our heart is full of love to Jesus, His loveliness becomes the passion of the soul, and sin and self are swept away. May we feel it now![53]

The emphasis on personal experience is, once again, obvious, and expressed in terms which a number of writers have described as 'mystical'. Indeed, it was passages like these which led William Robertson Nicoll, the editor of the *British Weekly* from 1866, to bracket Spurgeon with Bunyan as one of the two greatest 'Evangelical mystics',[54] and J.C. Carlile to devote a whole chapter of his biography of Spurgeon to his subject's 'mysticism'.[55] These judgments were well founded. As Gordon points out, the imagery of flame, fire, ice, and ocean depths, together with the related verbs of burning, consuming, melting and flowing are 'the standard vocabulary of the mystic'.[56] One might add that the description of Christ's love as 'unexplored and unexplorable', and the vivid, emotionally charged nature of the description, taken as a whole, also point in this direction. Experience of communion with Christ was expressed in distinctly mystical vein.[57]

Communion with Christ and the Lord's Supper

Given that communion with God, most normally expressed as communion with Christ, was crucial to Spurgeon's spirituality, how closely did his theology and

---

[53] 'The Well Beloved', in Spurgeon, *Till He Come*, Song of Songs 5.16, 'A Communion Address at Mentone', pp. 101-102.

[54] T.H. Darlow, *W. Robertson Nicoll: Life and Letters* (London: Hodder and Stoughton, 1925), p. 402. Cf. W. Robertson Nicoll in the *British Weekly*, 27 June, 1907, p. 293, column 5, 'Maroon Bound Scrapbooks' 1-4 (Spurgeon's College, Heritage Room), Volume 1, p. 10, where Nicoll argued that Spurgeon had the rare gift of combining mysticism and popularity.

[55] J.C. Carlile, *C.H. Spurgeon: An Interpretative Biography* (London: Kingsgate Press, 1933), pp. 268-86. Cf. Fullerton, *Spurgeon*, pp. 181-82.

[56] Gordon, *Evangelical Spirituality*, p. 162.

[57] Spurgeon had a high regard for the writings of the seventeenth-century Roman Catholic mystic Madame (Jeanne) Guyon. See, e.g., 'The Church's Love To Her Loving Lord', in Spurgeon, *Most Holy Place*, sermon number 636, Song of Songs 1.7, undated, p. 72; 'Better than Wine', in Spurgeon, *Most Holy Place*, sermon number 2459, Song of Songs 1.2, delivered 2 June 1872, p. 3.

practice of the Lord's supper relate to this vital emphasis? In an address, 'Communion with Christ and His People', preached at a celebration of the Lord's supper at Mentone, Spurgeon set out a range of ways in which he believed communion could be enjoyed. These included prayer and the reading of God's word. As regards prayer, there was a particular focus in this message on silence and contemplation. 'We have intercourse with Jesus of a closer sort than any words could possibly express', he declared. This, he assured his hearers, was his 'own personal experience'.[58] This was a repeated stress for Spurgeon, and Gordon is mistaken when he says that 'Spurgeon had no patience with the more passive forms of devotion.'[59] Quiet meditation was a means to communion with Christ. Other ways communion could be known included in 'sorrows' for, as the believer suffered, he or she was able to 'readily enter the experience of the "man of sorrows"' himself. Once again, his comments here are shot through with autobiography. Spurgeon had experienced suffering through the criticism of others (as he noted here) and also through gout and depression.[60] Even so, Spurgeon had also experienced communion with Christ in times of joy, for 'Kind actions make us happy, and in such joys we find communion with the great heart of Jesus.' Practical action was, in and of itself, another route to communion, for wherever 'we cooperate with the Lord Jesus in His designs of love to men, we are in true and active communion with Him'.[61] Communion or, as he put it elsewhere, 'fellowship'[62] with Christ could be experienced in a number of different ways.

Spurgeon believed these different means of pursuing communion all represented 'windows of agate and gates of carbuncle' through which the earnest believer 'might come to the Lord'. Nevertheless, in 'Communion with Christ and His People' he declared that 'the ordinance of the Lord's Supper sets forth a way which surpasses them all'. It was the supper, Spurgeon stated, that was 'the most accessible and the most effectual method of fellowship'. The word 'accessible' was important. Spurgeon pictured a believer saying '"I do not feel that I can get near to Christ. He is

---

[58] 'Communion with Christ and His People', in Spurgeon, *Till He Come*, 1 Corinthians 10.16-17, 'A Communion Address at Mentone', p. 315. Cf. C.H. Spurgeon, *Lectures to My Students: First Series* (London: Passmore and Alabaster, 1875), p. 50. As the title 'Communion with Christ and His People' indicates, the corporate dimension of the Lord's supper was important to Spurgeon, although this is not a theme I have followed up in this essay. The supper was a place where believers could have fellowship with each other, and *together* have communion with Christ. For this, see Grass and Randall, 'C.H. Spurgeon on the Sacraments', p. 71. At the communion service which closed the annual Pastor's College conference, it was the usual custom of those present to link hands to sing the final song. See, e.g., The *Freeman*, 14 May 1886, 'Spurgeon's Scrap Folder', February–July 1886 (Spurgeon's College, Heritage Room, 2.F), p. 126; cf. *Christian World*, 13 May 1886, p. 128.

[59] Gordon, *Evangelical Spirituality*, p. 168.

[60] For this see Kruppa, *Spurgeon*, pp. 358, 387-88, 434-35 (gout and kidney disease); pp. 93-94, 416, 459-460 (depression).

[61] Spurgeon, 'Communion with Christ and His People', pp. 316-17.

[62] Spurgeon, 'The Spiced Wine of my Pomegranate', p. 118.

so high and holy, and I am a poor sinner".' Spurgeon could do nothing but approve of such an attitude, but this was precisely why the Lord's supper was such an important means to communion. For here Christ was presented as the saviour of sinners. The gulf separating the holiness of God and the sinfulness of men and women seemed impossibly wide, but in the atonement it had in fact been bridged, and God and the sinner could now be reconciled. Spurgeon declared that, 'This table sets before you His great sacrifice. Jesus has offered it; will you accept it? He does not ask you to bring anything, — no drop of blood, no pang of flesh; all is here, and your part is to come and partake of it.'[63] Here every repentant sinner, however wretched they might feel, could know communion with Christ. The ultimate means to communion, the grace of God in Christ, was especially magnified in the Lord's supper as the atonement was set forth in word and symbol.

The Lord's supper also spoke of how communion with Christ was, for the believer, 'eternal'. He stated,

> No power upon earth can henceforth take from me the piece of bread which I have just now eaten, it has gone where it will be made up into blood, and nerve, and muscle, and bone. It is within me, and of me. That drop of wine has coursed through my veins, and is part and parcel of my being. So he that takes Jesus by faith to be his Saviour has chosen the good part which shall not be taken away from him. He has received the Christ into his inward parts, and all the men on earth, and all the devils in hell, cannot extract Christ from him... By our sincere reception of Jesus into our hearts, an indissoluble union is established between us and the Lord, and this manifests itself in mutual communion.[64]

This is an astonishing passage, one which, yet again, shows Spurgeon's powerful imagination at work. The Lord's supper set forth with particular clarity the permanent nature of the believer's union with Christ, which was as certain as the fact that the bread and wine could not now be separated from the body of the individual believer. The taking of the bread and wine spoke of the reception of Christ into the 'inmost soul' of the believer, and the way the elements became an integral part of him or her pointed to the 'indissoluble' union between the communicant and Christ, one which manifested itself in present and felt communion. As Walker states, the bread and the wine were not just 'windows' through which Christ could be seen, important as this was. The elements, for Spurgeon, were also 'doors' through which the communicant 'might pass into a deeper experience of fellowship with Christ'.[65] Spurgeon's words indicate that he saw the closest possible connection between the symbols (of bread and wine) and the things signified (eternal union and present communion with Christ). Spurgeon enjoyed assurance of salvation and rich fellowship with Christ at the Lord's supper.

---

[63] Spurgeon, 'Communion with Christ and His People', pp. 318-19.
[64] Spurgeon, 'Communion with Christ and His People', pp. 319-20.
[65] Walker, *Baptists at the Table*, p. 177.

It should be abundantly clear by this point that, for Spurgeon, the supper was far more than a 'memorial'. He certainly believed it *was* a memorial, and could talk in these terms.[66] But he strongly resisted the drift towards what Timothy George describes as 'eucharistic minimalism'.[67] This trend towards viewing the supper as primarily a 'memorial to an absent saviour' had actually begun in the last quarter of the eighteenth century, even amongst Calvinistic Baptists.[68] But it was something Spurgeon resisted. In 'The Spiced Wine of my Pomegranate' he stated,

> The Lord's Supper is the divinely-ordained exhibition of communion, and therefore in it there is the breaking of bread and the pouring forth of wine, to picture the free gift of the Saviour's body and blood to us; and there is also the eating of the one and the drinking of the other, to represent the reception of these priceless gifts by us. As without bread and wine there could be no Lord's Supper, so without the gracious bequests of Jesus to us there would have been no communion between Him and our souls.[69]

To be sure, the bread and the wine 'picture' and 'represent' the reception of the grace-gift of Christ's body and blood but, once again, the symbol and the reality represented are closely tied together in Spurgeon's thought. Spurgeon believed that in the Lord's supper God took the initiative in manifesting his grace to all believers who would receive it by faith. The fellowship of receiving and being received by Christ which could be enjoyed at the Lord's supper was 'closer, more vital, more essential than any other'.[70] Spurgeon frequently spoke of the 'real presence' of Christ at the supper, and this has been well analysed by Grass and Randall, and before them by Michael Walker.[71] But some further exposition of Spurgeon's view of the real presence, especially as it relates to his views on communion with Christ, is

---

[66] For an example of Spurgeon speaking of the supper as a 'memorial', see 'The Lord's Supper', *MTP* 50, sermon number 2872, delivered 'on a Lord's-day Evening in the autumn of 1861', p. 98.

[67] T. George, 'Controversy and Communion: The Limits of Baptist Fellowship from Bunyan to Spurgeon', in D.W. Bebbington (ed.), *The Gospel in the World: International Baptist Studies* (Studies in Baptist History and Thought, 1; Carlisle: Paternoster Press, 2002), p. 56.

[68] See M.A.G. Haykin, '"His Soul Refreshing Presence": The Lord's Supper in Calvinistic Baptist Thought and Experience in the "Long" Eighteenth Century', in Cross and Thompson (eds), *Baptist Sacramentalism*, pp. 177-93.

[69] Spurgeon, 'The Spiced Wine of my Pomegranate', pp. 119-20.

[70] Spurgeon, 'Communion with Christ and His People', pp. 318-19.

[71] Walker, *Baptists at the Table*, pp. 174-81; Grass and Randall, 'C.H. Spurgeon on the Sacraments', pp. 55, 68-71, 75. H.F. Colquitt, 'The Soteriology of Charles Haddon Spurgeon Revealed in his Sermons and Controversial Writings' (PhD, University of Edinburgh, 1951), Appendix B, pp. 282-85, gives some attention to Spurgeon's theology and practice of the Lord's supper, but his comments are not incisive. That Spurgeon had a theology of Christ's 'real presence' at the supper is noted by a number of writers. See, e.g., C.W. Freeman, '"To Feed Upon by Faith": Nourishment from the Lord's Table', in Cross and Thompson (eds), *Baptist Sacramentalism*, pp. 204-205.

necessary before going on to finally consider how the Lord's supper links with Spurgeon's views on practical action.

The Real Presence of Christ at The Lord's Supper

First of all, it should be clear that, not withstanding his views on the 'real presence', Spurgeon vehemently rejected both the sacerdotalism of Roman Catholicism and the ritualism of the Oxford Movement in the Church of England.[72] The Roman Catholic doctrine of transubstantiation Spurgeon regarded with particular 'horror' and 'contempt'. He described it, in a sermon preached at the Metropolitan Tabernacle entitled 'The Witness of the Lord's Supper', as a 'foolish superstition' and an affront to both 'reason' and the 'spiritual nature'.[73] In another address, this time preached at a communion service at Mentone and given the title 'Mysterious Visits', Spurgeon asserted that although 'the Romish church' said much about the 'real presence' of Christ at the Mass, what they actually believed in was Christ's 'corporeal presence'.[74] This teaching was abhorrent to Spurgeon, and he never ceased to take opportunities to attack it, doing so throughout his ministry.[75]

As Walker notes, however, 'in the heat of battle' with Roman Catholicism Spurgeon 'surrendered nothing of his own deeply held beliefs',[76] refusing to capitulate to an eviscerated memorialism. Whilst fellow Baptists, such as John Clifford, left themselves 'hardly within reach of a viable eucharistic theology' in their own reaction against sacerdotalism, Spurgeon continued to affirm his belief in the 'real presence' of Christ at the supper.[77] This was true in both the messages cited in the previous paragraph. In 'The Witness of the Lord's Supper' he stated, 'We believe in the real presence... We believe that Jesus Christ spiritually comes to us and refreshes us.'[78] In 'Mysterious Visits' Spurgeon went on to expand on what he meant by the real presence, crucially with reference to his own experience:

> By spiritual we do not mean unreal... I believe in the true and real presence of Jesus with His people: such presence has been real to my spirit. Lord Jesus, thou Thyself

---

[72] For the Oxford Movement and the wider tradition of Anglican high churchmanship, see P.B. Nockles, *The Oxford Movement in Context: Anglican High Churchmanship 1760–1857* (Cambridge: Cambridge University Press, 1994). For high church spirituality, see D.W. Bebbington, *Holiness in Nineteenth-Century England* (Carlisle: Paternoster Press, 2002), pp. 7-28.

[73] C.H. Spurgeon, 'The Witness of the Lord's Supper', *MTP* 59, sermon number 3338, 1 Corinthians 11.26, undated, pp. 37-38.

[74] 'Mysterious Visits', in Spurgeon, *Till He Come*, Psalm 17.3, 'An Address to a Little Company at the Communion Table at Mentone', p. 17.

[75] See Spurgeon's exposition of Matthew 26.17-30 and 1 Corinthians 11.18-34 in *MTP* 50, pp. 22-24, for just one example of a sustained critique.

[76] Walker, *Baptists at the Table*, p. 193.

[77] Bebbington, *Dominance of Evangelicalism*, pp. 146-49; Walker, *Baptists at the Table*, pp. 193-94.

[78] Spurgeon, 'The Witness of the Lord's Supper', p. 38.

hast visited me. As surely as the Lord Jesus came really as to His flesh to Bethlehem and Calvary, so surely does He come really by His Spirit to His people in the hours of their communion with Him. We are as conscious of that presence as of our own existence.[79]

Although Christ's presence was not 'corporeal', it was nonetheless 'true' and 'real'. It was not that Spurgeon took a mediating position between the Roman Catholic and the memorialist views, a sort middle way between two extremes. As Gordon notes, for Spurgeon both Roman Catholic sacerdotalism and mere memorialism failed to take seriously enough 'the present reality of the indwelling Christ and all the potential for a communion of love which his real presence conveyed'.[80] In short, neither view of the eucharist was rich enough for Spurgeon. The passage from 'Mysterious Visits' is striking for the way Spurgeon directly addressed Christ with the words, 'Lord Jesus, thou hast visited me', in the context of this communion service. Spurgeon believed in, and *experienced*, the 'real presence' of Christ at the Lord's supper. Walker, who also cites this passage, suggests the influence of John Calvin on Spurgeon's theology of the supper.[81] Although it might be more strictly correct to say that Spurgeon was influenced by Calvin as mediated through his English Calvinistic and Puritan heritage, undoubtedly there was a link, and Walker's study was groundbreaking in pointing this out. But Randall and Grass are surely right to highlight the roles also played by reason (transubstantiation, said Spurgeon, made no sense to someone who was 'rational' and 'enlightened')[82] and, especially, experience in shaping and sustaining his view.[83] As Spurgeon put in a sermon preached in 1881, 'In heavenly things we see as much as we have within ourselves. He who has eaten Christ's flesh and blood spiritually is the man who can see this (truth) in the sacred Supper.'[84] Spurgeon's theology of the 'real presence' was grounded in his own experience of communion with Christ at the supper itself.

Spurgeon's views and experience of communion with Christ at the Lord's supper are in many ways summed up in the words of his hymn, 'Amidst us Our Belovèd Stands'. This was written in 1866 specifically for use in communion services, and included in the Metropolitan Tabernacle hymnal, *Our Own Hymn Book*, edited by Spurgeon himself and first published in that year. The first three verses are cited here:

AMIDST us our Belovèd stands,
And bids us view His piercèd hands;

---

[79] Spurgeon, 'Mysterious Visits', p. 17.
[80] Gordon, *Evangelical Spirituality*, p. 164.
[81] Walker, *Baptists at the Table*, pp. 174-75.
[82] Spurgeon, 'The Witness of the Lord's Supper', p. 38.
[83] Randall and Grass, 'C.H. Spurgeon on the Sacraments', p. 69.
[84] C.H. Spurgeon, 'Baptism—A Burial', *MTP* 27, sermon number 1627, Romans 6.3-4, delivered 30 October 1881, p. 618.

Points to His wounded feet and side,
Blest emblems of the Crucified.

What food luxurious loads the board,
When at His table sits the Lord!
The wine how rich, the bread how sweet,
When Jesus deigns the guests to meet!

If now with eyes defiled and dim,
We see the signs but see not Him,
Oh, may His love the scales displace,
And bid us see Him face to face![85]

The focus on the atonement, the description of Christ as the 'Belovèd' echoing the language of the Songs of Songs and, supremely, the presence of the risen Christ, spiritual but nonetheless real and tangible, are all apparent in this, the most enduring of Spurgeon's hymns. Spurgeon did not have an *ex opere operato* understanding of the supper. Christ had to 'deign' to meet with his people and the food was only 'luxurious' when Christ sat at the table. It was possible for the communicant to see only the 'signs' and miss the reality to which they pointed. But where the 'eye' of faith was able to look through the symbols of bread and wine, then Christ could be perceived and experienced as, by his grace, he met with his people. This, for Spurgeon, was the dominant theme of the Lord's supper, and a vital focus for his spirituality.

Practical Christianity

The third dimension of spirituality in Sheldrake's model is 'practical Christianity'. Spurgeon lived the Christian life with a passion, and he was self-evidently an activist. In this he was a typical Evangelical and many parallels could be adduced from eighteenth- and nineteenth-century Evangelicalism.[86] But it is tempting to suggest that Spurgeon took this particular aspect of evangelical piety to new heights. The two chapters in his *Autobiography* entitled 'A Typical Week's Work' give a flavour of the pace at which he operated.[87] He preached and led meetings, not only on a Sunday but often throughout the week, as well as revising his sermons for publication. He was the editor of the Tabernacle's monthly magazine the *Sword and Trowel* from its first issue in 1865 until his death, kept up a voluminous correspondence and wrote numerous books. This was all in addition to founding and maintaining such institutions as the boy's and girl's orphanages and the Pastor's

---

[85] C.H. Spurgeon (ed.), *Our Own Hymn Book* (London: Passmore and Alabaster, 1866), No. 939. Cf. Spurgeon, *Till He Come*, p. 359. In *Our Own Hymn Book* the hymn was headed 'Jesu's Presence Delightful'.

[86] For numerous examples, see Bebbington, *Evangelicalism*, pp. 10-12.

[87] Spurgeon, *Autobiography*, IV, pp. 63-92.

College.[88] Susannah Spurgeon recorded that for much of his ministry her husband found it almost impossible to keep a day off, and even when in Mentone and ostensibly resting he 'probably did as much as most men do when in full work'.[89] Spurgeon gave himself unstintingly to Christian activism. In the *Sword and Trowel* he frequently expressed a desire to 'do more' for Christ and urged his readers to cultivate the same attitude. The following comment, taken from the 'Preface' to the 1879 volume, is typical: 'O that we might do more for Jesus!', Spurgeon lamented, before appealing to his readers, 'do you not utter the same desire?'[90] This was a sentiment he echoed twelve months later: 'The sigh of last year', he wrote in the 'Preface' to the volume for 1880, 'is my inward groaning now'.[91] Activity in the cause of Christ was of vital importance to Spurgeon.

This activism relates to Spurgeon's spirituality in a number of different ways. As already noted, activity was, in itself, a form of communion with him.[92] A believer's actions could be a means in themselves to fellowship with Christ, not just an outworking of it. Activism was also the way to a 'happy' life, for just as 'unconsecrated strength' was unable to 'cheer' or 'exhilarate', so a 'religious life' was not 'joyful' unless it was worked out in vigorous service of Christ.[93] Practical activity was, additionally, an aid to assurance because 'active service brings with it warmth, and this tends to remove doubting, for our own works have become evidences of our calling and election.'[94] Activism, therefore, could be of great benefit a believer's spiritual life. But what Spurgeon stressed most often was simply the fact that a truly godly life simply *had* to be one where service of God was a key note. Activism was a vital horizon for the outworking of Spurgeon's spirituality. Authentic and continuing experience of communion with Christ would necessarily lead to a life of service.

The Lord's Supper and Practical Action

Did this emphasis on practical activity link with Spurgeon's theology and preaching at the Lord's supper in any way? *Till He Come* closes with a sermon entitled 'Swooning and Reviving at Christ's Feet'. This was unique in the collection in that it was delivered at the close of one of the college conferences, with the ministers present at the service about to return to busy pastorates. Although not dated in *Till He Come*, this message first appeared in the *Sword and the Trowel* in October 1882 and was in fact delivered at the close of the conference of that year, on the evening of

---

[88] For further detail, see M.K. Nicholls, *C.H. Spurgeon: The Pastor Evangelist* (Didcot: Baptist Historical Society, 1992), pp. 55-68, 74-96.
[89] Spurgeon, *Autobiography*, IV, p. 64.
[90] *ST*, 1879, Preface, p. iv.
[91] *ST*, 1880, Preface, p. iv.
[92] Spurgeon, 'Communion with Christ and His People', pp. 316-17.
[93] *ST*, 1876, Preface, p. iv.
[94] Spurgeon, *Autobiography*, II, p. 10.

Friday 21 April.[95] Spurgeon took as his text Revelation 1.17-18, and focused in particular on the picture of the apostle John first falling and then 'reviving' at the feet of the glorified Christ. Spurgeon sought to apply this image to those present in a number of ways which related to pastoral ministry. With the communion table set, Spurgeon believed that Christ was with them, and so the falling and reviving before Christ of which the text spoke could be the experience of all those who were present. First of all the importance of 'swooning' was emphasized. Those who were making progress in the life of holiness or experiencing success in ministry, needed to be brought back to the necessity of 'daily cleansing'. A right appreciation of the Lord's supper would do this, as well as engendering the humility Spurgeon believed simply had to be present if they rightly thought of 'Gethsemane and Calvary'. An experience of Christ granted at the supper would also show that a believer, let alone a pastor, 'could not live an hour spiritually without Him who is not only bread, but life'. Just as 'natural bread' was essential for daily living so, spiritually, none of them could ever grow out of their need of feeding on a 'present Christ'. Thus the supper spoke of the need for complete dependence on Christ, in ministry and life in general.[96] All those present should fall at the feet of Christ.

Spurgeon then proceeded to speak of the way Christ revived his people. The first, and primary, way by which it was possible to 'get alive again' spiritually was through being 'brought into contact' with Jesus, an unsurprising point given Spurgeon's repeated stress on communion with Christ. Spurgeon noted that in Revelation 1.17 Christ 'laid his right hand upon' the apostle. Thinking of this action in relation to himself and his hearers, Spurgeon asked why Christ did not 'lay his foot upon' them, treading them down 'as the mire of the streets?' As the image of the text combined with Spurgeon's fertile imaginative powers he had an answer, which was that the foot in question had been 'pierced for [them]'. Therefore it was inconceivable that it should 'trample them in His wrath'. Rather than trampling them down, Christ showed his love to his people by laying his 'right hand' upon them, and so his love could be felt, restoring and 'reviving' the 'fainting disciple'. This renewing power could be experienced at the Lord's supper because there the gracious self-giving of Christ in the atonement was set forth so clearly. Those present who entered into the 'true meaning' of what they were about to celebrate could expect to be 'revived and vitalized'. Indeed, there was the promise, in word and sacrament (although Spurgeon did not use this term), that Christ would be with the believer through every future 'dark hour'. Even the prospect of death should hold no fears for them because, as both text and supper proclaimed, Christ himself had died and risen again. 'Onward, soldiers of the cross', Spurgeon encouraged the conference members, 'for our immortal Captain leads the way'.[97]

---

[95] *ST*, October 1882, pp. 505-10; *The Christian World*, 27 April 1882, 'Spurgeon's Scrapbooks', Volume 6 (Spurgeon's College, Heritage Room), p. 47.

[96] 'Swooning and Reviving at Christ's Feet', in Spurgeon, *Till He Come*, Revelation 1.17-18, 'An Address Delivered at the Close of One of the Pastor's College Conferences', pp. 349-52.

[97] Spurgeon, 'Swooning and Reviving at Christ's Feet', pp. 353-56.

Another address printed in *Till He Come*, entitled 'The Well Beloved's Vineyard', was given in a quite different setting, in his 'own room' at Mentone, probably in the Hôtel Beau Rivage.[98] To the small group who had come together to celebrate communion Spurgeon spoke, in optimistic mood, of the many opportunities he saw all around them for fruitful Christian service:

> Each one of us may find work for the Master; there are capital opportunities around us. There never was an age in which a man, consecrated to God, might do so much as he can at this time. There is nothing to restrain the most ardent zeal. We live in such happy times that, if we plunge into a sea of work, we may swim, and none can hinder us. Then, too, our labour is made, by God's grace, to be so pleasant to us. No true servant of Christ is weary *of* the work, though he may be weary *in* the work: it is not the work that he ever wearies of, for he wishes that he could do ten times more.

How is this desire, and the activity itself, to be sustained? Yet again, part of the answer was the Lord's supper. Later on in his message, referring to the 'table of blessing', he stated, 'This hallowed ordinance, I am sure, is a spot where hopes grow bright, and hearts grow warm, resolves become firm, and lives become fruitful, and all the clusters of our soul's fruit ripen for the Lord.'[99] A way that a faithful believer was sustained for the work he or she had been called to do was, in part, through participating in the Lord's supper. As he put it elsewhere, just as people were renewed as to their 'bodily strength' by eating good food, so those who came to 'wait upon the Lord...by feeding upon the body and blood of Christ' would be renewed spiritually for active service.[100] In summary, flowing out of Spurgeon's theology of the 'real presence' was an emphasis that a direct encounter with Christ at the supper revitalized believers for practical activity in his cause, as well as strengthening them to face whatever might befall them along the way. Thus the Lord's supper links once again with a crucial aspect of Spurgeon's spirituality. As David Bebbington notes, for Spurgeon, the supper was undoubtedly a 'unique means of grace'.[101]

---

[98] In his early years of visiting Mentone, Spurgeon stayed at the *Hôtel des Anglais*. See Spurgeon, *Autobiography*, IV, p. 209.

[99] 'The Well-beloved's Vineyard', in Spurgeon, *Till He Come*, Isaiah 5.1, 'An Address to a Little Company of Believers in Mr Spurgeon's Own Room at Mentone', pp. 147-49.

[100] C.H. Spurgeon, 'Renewing Strength', *MTP* 29, sermon number 1756, Isaiah 40.31, undated, 'Suitable for the close of the year', p. 706. Cf. C.H. Spurgeon, 'The Blessing of Full Assurance', *MTP* 34, sermon number 2023, 1 John 5.13, delivered 13 May 1888, p. 269: 'Do you know the quickening, restoring, cheering, power of the precious blood of Christ which is set forth in the Lord's Supper by the fruit of the vine?'

[101] Bebbington, *Dominance of Evangelicalism*, p. 148.

Conclusion

As President of the 'Lambeth Auxiliary Sunday School Union' for 1882, Spurgeon led a communion service at the Metropolitan Tabernacle for the thousand or so teachers, from different churches and denominations, who were part of the Lambeth Union. As he presided on this occasion Spurgeon spoke of his 'intense joy' that those assembled had come 'not only to hear a little address from me but to see a sermon, for there is no sermon like the Lord's Supper'.[102] From one who had such a clear view of the importance of preaching, and who has been frequently styled by others the 'prince of preachers', this might seem a surprising statement, although less so in the light of the material surveyed in this essay.[103] Spurgeon's view of the Lord's supper was, as we have seen, extremely high. This was in part because of his Calvinistic and Reformed heritage, but due weight needs to be given to his experience at the supper itself. For Spurgeon, the Lord's supper was a vital focus for his spirituality. It provided the ideal context for the proclamation of Spurgeon's 'spiritual theology' of the atonement and a place where he, and others, could be renewed for daily Christian living. But most importantly the supper was where communion with Christ could be known in a way which surpassed any other. Spurgeon said that he enjoyed some of his 'happiest moments' around the communion table. This was because these were times spent with 'the King', for this was 'His table'.[104] It was in the Lord's supper that Spurgeon's deep desire for communion with Christ found its fullest expression.

Timothy George states that the 'vigorous theology of presence in the Supper of the Lord' which Spurgeon held in the nineteenth century would later 'be recovered by a new generation of Baptists'.[105] One might question the extent to which this is true. Certainly in my own, admittedly limited, British-based, experience, the view characterized in this essay as 'memorialism' tends to hold sway within the churches. Nevertheless, collections of essays such as this one, its predecessor and a number of other recent publications are perhaps harbingers of a new more 'sacramental mood'

---

[102] *The Sunday School Chronicle*, 17 February 1882, 'Spurgeon's Scrapbooks', Volume 6 (Spurgeon's College, Heritage Room), p. 8. Spurgeon's thoughts on this occasion focused on how the supper could be a uniting ordinance, bringing together those belonging to different denominations.

[103] Archibald Brown was possibly the first to use the phrase 'prince of preachers' in relation to Spurgeon, in his eulogy for his friend at Norwood cemetery in 1892. See Spurgeon, *Autobiography*, IV, p. 375. Timothy Larsen notes that at least nine different books about Spurgeon have been published with 'prince of preachers' in their titles or sub-titles. See T. Larsen, 'Charles Haddon Spurgeon's Reading of the Sermon on the Mount', in T. Larsen, J.P. Greenman and S.R. Spencer (eds), *Reading the Sermon on the Mount through the Centuries* (Grand Rapids, MI: Brazos, forthcoming).

[104] C.H. Spurgeon, 'The Blood Shed for Many', *MTP* 33, sermon number 1971, Matthew 26.28, delivered 3 July 1887, p. 377. Cf. 'The Lord's Supper: A Remembrance of Jesus', *MTP* 34, sermon number 2038, Luke 22.19, undated, p. 455.

[105] George, 'Controversy and Communion', p. 58.

amongst Baptists.[106] An awareness of Spurgeon's theology of the Lord's supper contributes to this debate, helping as it does to point the way to a richer, more biblical, estimate of one of the sacraments. Spurgeon's experience also suggests that if Baptists *were* able to recover this richer approach to the Lord's supper, they might also be able to discover a deeper spirituality.

---

[106] See, e.g., S.R. Holmes, *Tradition and Renewal in Baptist Life* (Oxford: Whitley Publications, 2003); J.E. Colwell, *Promise and Presence: An Exploration of Sacramental Theology* (Carlisle: Paternoster, 2006). Colwell describes *Till He Come* as 'deeply moving', p. xi.

CHAPTER 12

Southern Baptists, Sacramentalism, and Soul Competency[1]

Sean A. White

It was 9:45 a.m. and the congregation had gathered for Sunday school assembly. At the foot of the chancel stood the communion table draped in the familiar pall concealing the sacred elements of the Lord's supper. Quarterly we celebrated the meal, but no one knew for sure when the table would be set. It was always a surprise, and for some, a most unwelcome one. For, mostly, it meant that the service would last longer, and between Sunday school and worship many bailed out and opted for an early lunch. So it was, growing up in a Southern Baptist church. As far as I knew, everyone believed the words of *The Baptist Faith and Message*, Article VII,

> The Lord's Supper is a symbolic act of obedience whereby members of the church, through partaking of the bread and the fruit of the vine, memorialize the death of the Redeemer and anticipate His second coming.[2]

It was '*completely* symbolic [in] nature',[3] and, as explained by Herschel Hobbs, 'the elements *merely symbolize* the body and blood of Jesus, with no saving effect in partaking of them'.[4]

---

[1] This chapter is based on my doctoral research, 'Southern Baptist and British Baptist Contributions to a Theology of the Lord's Supper since 1948: Beyond a Theology of the Elements toward a Sacramental Theology of Enactment' (PhD dissertation, Union Theological Seminary and Presbyterian School of Christian Education, Richmond, Virginia, 2007).

[2] *The Baptist Faith and Message: A Statement Adopted by the Southern Baptist Convention June 14, 2000* (Nashville, TN: LifeWay Christian Resources of the Southern Baptist Convention, 2000), Article VII, p. 14. In the original 1925 confession, the Lord's supper is an act 'in which the members of the church, by the use of bread and wine, commemorate the dying love of Christ' (*Baptist Faith and Message* [1925], Article 13, in Robert A. Baker (ed.), *A Baptist Source Book: With Particular Reference to Southern Baptists* [Nashville, TN: Broadman, 1966], p. 202).

[3] Robert A. Baker, 'Baptist Sacramentalism', in *Chapel Messages* (Grand Rapids, MI: Baker Book House, 1966), p. 23. Emphasis added.

During this last decade, scholars have retrieved a lost sacramental heritage of Baptist liturgical thought and, in so doing, a rich strand of theology has been rediscovered. As early as 1677, 'the most significant of all Baptist statements of faith and practice', the *Second London Confession*, asserted a sacramental view of the Lord's supper.[5] Though shaped by the *Westminster Confession of Faith*, the writers deliberately avoided the use of sacrament, but they nonetheless adopted a modified Calvinism and asserted that worshipers spiritually receive Christ through partaking of the bread and wine. The *Second London Confession* declared,

> Worthy receivers, outwardly partaking of the visible Elements in this Ordinance, do then also inwardly by faith, really and indeed, yet not carnally, and corporally, but spiritually receive, and feed upon Christ crucified and all the benefits of his death: the Body and Blood of *Christ*, being then not corporally, or carnally, but spiritually present to the faith of Believers, in that Ordinance, as the Elements themselves are to their outward senses.[6]

Simultaneously, the elements are consumed and the spirit is fed. As the senses of sight and taste know the bread and wine, the spirit concurrently knows the One present at the table.[7] This immediate correspondence between physically eating and drinking and spiritually receiving the benefits of Christ's death make this statement undeniably sacramental. Despite the use of 'ordinance', the depth of this confessional theology bears the weight of a sacramentalism which conceives the supper as a means of grace and as an experience with the living Christ, and it establishes a paradigm which characterizes a strand of Baptist thought stretching into the twenty-first century. The description of the supper in *The Baptist Faith and Message* might

---

[4] Herschel H. Hobbs, *The Baptist Faith and Message* (Nashville, TN: Convention Press, rev. edn, 1996), p. 76. Emphasis added.

[5] John Brush, 'Baptists and the Lord's Supper', *Foundations* (October, 1958), p. 10. See also Robert C. Walton, *The Gathered Community* (London: Carey Press, 1946), p. 180, who asserts the *Second London Confession* 'is the most influential and important of all Baptist Confessions'; Philip E. Thompson, 'Seventeenth-Century Baptist Confessions in Context', *Perspectives in Religious Studies* 29 (Winter, 2002), p. 342, n. 38.

[6] *Second London Confession*, Article XXX.7, in William L. Lumpkin, *Baptist Confessions of Faith* (Valley Forge, PA: Judson Press, rev. edn, 1969), p. 293. Cf. with the *Westminster Confession of Faith*, Article XXIX.7, in *The Book of Confessions* (Louisville, KY: Office of the General Assembly Presbyterian Church [USA], 1999), p. 155. Of note is the replacement of 'sacrament' with the word 'ordinance' in the second line of the paragraph. The second usage of ordinance remains consistent with the *Westminster Confession*.

[7] Insight into the notion of simultaneity taken from Paul S. Fiddes, 'The Church as a Eucharistic Community: A Baptist Contribution', in Paul S. Fiddes, *Tracks and Traces: Baptist Identity in Church and Theology* (Studies in Baptist History and Thought, 13; Carlisle: Paternoster Press, 2003), p. 165.

suggest the absence of such a strand among Southern Baptists, but closer investigation reveals otherwise.

Throughout the latter half of the twentieth century Southern Baptists were embroiled in an intradenominational controversy that centered largely around divergent interpretations of the authority of scripture. In the process, Southern Baptists 'fixated so narrowly on inerrancy that doctrinal concerns in other areas were ignored or pushed to the sidelines'.[8] Namely, the concern for worship was peculiarly absent from Baptist leaders on both sides of this polarizing controversy. Reflecting on this void, Hugh T. McElrath observed that Southern Baptists had once

> agreed to place worship at the very top of the list [of essential functions of a local church] above proclamation, education, or ministry. The primary function of a church, we said, is the worship of God. However, neither denominational structures nor programs would seem to reflect this theoretical priority.[9]

Similarly, Franklin M. Segler insisted,

> The first order in the church's mission is worship. All other aspects of ministry are motivated by worship, and without worship the church will die... [It] is the motivating dynamic for the life and mission of the church...the life stream of the church.[10]

As the controversy raged, however, neither those on the right nor the left attended to the very aspect of ecclesial life which forms believers into the missional body of Christ, the celebration of the Lord's supper. Quietly, however, the sacramental strand of Baptist thought was being woven into the fabric of the Southern Baptist Convention (SBC).

In the eucharistic writings of Fred Howard, Frank Stagg, Eric Rust, John Carlton and Lewis Rhodes sacramental theologies of the Lord's supper were constructed, and the anemic theology of *The Baptist Faith and Message* was balanced with a more robust understanding of the meal. In their theologizing, they avoided what Curtis W. Freeman has called a 'theology of the elements', or an articulation of the supper's

---

[8] Timothy George, 'Toward an Evangelical Future', in Nancy Tatom Ammerman (ed.), *Southern Baptists Observed: Multiple Perspectives on a Changing Denomination* (Knoxville, TN: The University of Tennessee Press, 1993), p. 279. Emphasis original. See also David S. Dockery, 'Looking Back, Looking Ahead', in Timothy George and David S. Dockery (eds), *Theologians of the Baptist Tradition* (Nashville, TN: Broadman & Holman, 2001), pp. 338-60.

[9] Hugh T. McElrath, 'Perspectives on Public Worship in the 1970's', *Review and Expositor* 75 (Summer, 1978), p. 361.

[10] Franklin M. Segler, *Christian Worship: Its Theology and Practice* (Nashville, TN: Broadman, 1967), pp. 1-2.

significance by relating Christ's presence to the elements of bread and wine.[11] In its place, they formulated a 'theology of enactment' in which the actions of the meal rather the elements receive greater focus. Rather than theorizing about the transformation of bread and wine, they emphasized Christ's presence incarnate in the worshiping community.[12] In these little known writings from the 1960s, a eucharistic theology with profound implications for the formation of the Christian community takes shape.

Fred D. Howard

In 1966, the publishing house of the SBC published *Interpreting the Lord's Supper* by Fred D. Howard. In this work, Howard avoided calling the supper a sacrament but theologized about the meal in sacramental ways. Though mistaken in his broad claims about 'Baptist' theology, Howard correctly acknowledged the official *Southern* Baptist position when he explained,

> Historically, Baptists have rejected the sacramental concept of the Lord's Supper. Their position may be epitomized in the words of H.E. Dana: 'As presented by the New Testament, the significance of the Lord's Supper is purely and only symbolic.'[13]

Citing further 'restrictions' imposed upon the meaning of the Lord's supper, he quoted Harold W. Tribble who argued in the SBC publication, *Our Doctrines*,

---

[11] Curtis W. Freeman, '"To Feed Upon by Faith": Nourishment from the Lord's Table', in Anthony R. Cross and Philip E. Thompson (eds), *Baptist Sacramentalism* (Studies in Baptist History and Thought, 5; Waynesboro, GA: Paternoster Press, 2003), p. 201.

[12] For a similar British Baptist concern see, 'Baptist Union of Great Britain and Ireland', in Max Thurian (ed.), *Churches Respond to BEM: Official Responses to the 'Baptism, Eucharist and Ministry' Text: Volume I* (Faith and Order Paper 129; Geneva: World Council of Churches, 1986), p. 72.

[13] Fred D. Howard, *Interpreting the Lord's Supper* (Nashville, TN: Broadman, 1966), p. 21; H.E. Dana, *A Manual of Ecclesiology* (Kansas City, KS: Central Seminary Press, 1944), p. 294, quoted in Howard, *Interpreting the Lord's Supper*, p. 21. In 1966, Broadman also published a revised edition of *Baptist Church Manual*, and though the manual insists that the supper is a 'communion of the body and blood of Christ' it fails to explain the meaning of this claim. Its author, renowned Landmarkist, J.M. Pendleton, *Baptist Church Manual* (Nashville, TN: Broadman & Holman, rev. edn, 1966), p. 89, and for the fuller discussion pp. 63-99, essentially collapsed the discussion the Lord's supper into a discussion of baptism, church membership, and the terms of communion.

Strictly speaking, the ordinance is not a 'communion service' in any sense, but a memorial feast to be observed in obedience to Christ, and to keep alive the promise of his return to his people at the end of the age.[14]

For many Southern Baptists the meal 'has little or no meaning beyond the idea of a memorial to the death of Christ', but this narrow demarcation drove Howard to advance beyond the minimalism of Southern Baptist doctrine.[15]

In reconstructing a sacramental eucharistic theology, Howard reevaluated the traditional interpretations of Catholics, Lutherans, Calvinists, and Anglicans, and he retrieved their emphasis on Christ's presence. Predictably, he refuted transubstantiation, and, referring to the Lutherans, he insisted they too 'erred...in interpreting the Lord's Supper in terms of Aristotelian realism'. On the other hand, he affirmed the Lutheran and Catholic emphasis on Christ's 'unique presence' which proved to be 'the most favorable aspect' of their thought. Calvinist and Anglican doctrines of Christ's spiritual presence also appealed to Howard, but Christ's identification with the elements proved problematic.[16] He resisted the notion of a 'mystical, somewhat mechanical, impartation of grace' by virtue of simply consuming the elements which are in some sense Christ's body and blood.[17] On the other hand, the emphasis on Christ's unique presence apart from this identification with the bread and wine promised to advance Baptist theology.

Howard asked, 'Is Christ present at the Lord's Supper in a sense in which he is not present during other occasions of worship?' Answering in the affirmative, he built upon Markus Barth's claim that 'the Word is not substance but event'[18] and that *soma* refers to Christ's total person not just his fleshly body. Rather than 'confin[ing]' the divine presence to the elements, he emphasized the entire worship event as the medium through which Christ draws near.

At the Last Supper, Christ was present to his disciples within the context of the Passover, the anticipation of the cross, and the 'bond of table fellowship',[19] and at subsequent table gatherings he continues to meet his followers. As we remember Christ's death and resurrection, look forward to his coming, and proclaim the message of salvation in the context of this sacred meal, the Lord is present in our hearts. Howard argued,

> A combination of these factors, in varying degrees, creates a worship situation in which Christ seemingly is present in a unique sense. This totality of meaning

---

[14] Harold W. Tribble, *Our Doctrines* (Nashville, TN: The Sunday School Board of the Southern Baptist Convention, 1936), p. 117, quoted in Howard, *Interpreting the Lord's Supper*, p. 21.

[15] Howard, *Interpreting the Lord's Supper*, p. 22.

[16] Howard, *Interpreting the Lord's Supper*, pp. 12-18.

[17] Howard, *Interpreting the Lord's Supper*, p. 20.

[18] Markus Barth, *Das Abendmahl: Pasamahl, Bundesmahl und Messiasmahl* (Theologische Studien, Heft 18; Zollikon, Zürich: Evangelischer Verlag, 1945), p. 7, quoted in Howard, *Interpreting the Lord's Supper*, p. 57.

[19] Howard, *Interpreting the Lord's Supper*, pp. 57-60.

apparently is the distinctiveness of the Lord's Supper, which in many ways is the supreme act of worship.[20]

In no sense is the Lord's supper merely symbolic, and in every sense it is a communion service.

More than a sign which *stands for* or *represents* the fellowship of the Church with her Lord, the supper is, in Howard's words, a 'hypostatized symbol', or a symbol which *is* that fellowship. Building upon the analogy of faith as 'the *hupostasis* [or substance] of that for which one hopes', he argued that the Lord's supper is substantive of the unity between Christ and the church. 'Like faith', the meal 'is more than an abstraction or a symbol. It is a reified symbol, that is, a reality.'[21] It is part and parcel of the communion known in the 'existential presence of the living Christ'[22] experienced in the context of community.

Focusing upon Christ's communal presence, Howard described the unity of the worshiping community as *koinonia*, a community of 'sharing'.[23] Quoting John Macmurray, he argued that the community exists *only* to the extent that it 'is constituted by the sharing of a common life',[24] and there are no Christians in isolation, but only in relationship, relationship with God and with others. As the body of Christ, believers share the life of the risen Savior and together experience the Lord's presence. Referencing the Hebraic notion of 'corporate personality', Howard contended that though one stands responsible before God, he or she is also 'identified with the community' and exists in 'corporate solidarity' with those who believe.[25]

Advancing Southern Baptist theology beyond the limited view portrayed in *The Baptist Faith and Message*, Howard boldly struggled to conceptualize Christ's presence around the table. Though he never described the meal as a means of grace ,nor as a sacrament, he clearly centered his eucharistic theology around a communal

---

[20] Howard, *Interpreting the Lord's Supper*, pp. 59-60, 63 and 70. At one point, p. 69, Howard suggested that the promise of Christ's return repeated in the words of institution is fulfilled 'in a sense' with the coming of Christ to Christians each time they celebrate the Supper.

[21] Howard, *Interpreting the Lord's Supper*, p. 36. See also p. 70.

[22] See Howard, *Interpreting the Lord's Supper*, p. 70.

[23] Howard, *Interpreting the Lord's Supper*, p. 45.

[24] John Macmurray, *Conditions of Freedom* (London: Faber & Faber, 1950), p. 54; quoted in Howard, *Interpreting the Lord's Supper*, p. 52. Nine years earlier, John A. Wood, 'A Study of the Contemporary Southern Baptist Observance of the Lord's Supper in the Light of the New Testament' (ThM thesis, Southern Baptist Theological Seminary, 1957), pp. 51-52, also emphasized this aspect of *koinonia*. He argued, 'All Christians are one because they draw their life from a common source. They are bound together because they are bound to Christ... At the Lord's Table, the Christian has communion, not primarily in a human fellowship, but participates jointly with his fellow communicants in the life of Christ, as that life is imparted to the church.'

[25] Howard, *Interpreting the Lord's Supper*, pp. 51-52. On the concept of corporate personality, Howard cited Ernest Best, *One Body in Christ* (London: SPCK, 1955), pp. 203-207.

encounter with the living Lord. Avoiding the tendency of other traditions to link Christ's presence to the bread and wine, he located Christ in the hearts of those who worship, and the ritual of remembering, proclaiming, and eating becomes the means of a unique encounter between the risen Lord and the ecclesial community.[26]

Three years later, The Southern Baptist Theological Seminary dedicated an entire volume of the *Review and Expositor* to the Lord's supper, and Southern Baptist scholars continued the reconstruction of a sacramental theology of the Lord's supper.

Frank Stagg

In the winter 1969 *Review and Expositor*, Frank Stagg opened with 'The Lord's Supper in the New Testament'. Though retaining the use of 'ordinance', he affirmed the Lord's presence and the formative power of this ritual. In addition, he avoided an individualistic interpretation of communion with God and criticized the 'hyperspiritualists...at Corinth' for seeing the supper 'as a guarantee of their own *individual* salvation'.[27]

Countering an *ex opere operato* theology, Stagg argued that the apostle Paul combated a similar theology in the ancient church. Influenced by the paganism of mystery religions, some Corinthians presumed 'the Supper to be a sacrament offering a medicine or food of immortality'. They were 'pneumatic individualists who looked upon the food as itself able to work sacramentally'. Thus, at the table it was every person for himself, gorging on the guarantee of a right relation with God.[28] In response, Paul pointed to the Hebrews who had 'all eaten the same spiritual food' and 'drank the same spiritual drink' and yet God remained displeased and scattered many of 'their dead bodies...through the desert' (1 Cor. 10.3-4). Similarly, Stagg insisted the Lord's supper is neither a 'pledge against divine rejection' nor a 'pledge of security'. Apart from properly discerning the Body, the 'food of immortality' becomes the board of judgment (1 Cor. 11.10), for the salvation of individuals is inextricably caught up in the *community* eating in the name of the Lord.[29]

In scripture, Paul alone expounded the meaning of Jesus' words, 'This is my body', and he applied them specifically to the church. Thus, 'discerning' the Lord's body bears directly upon the worshiper's recognition of those around him or her. In an earlier work, Stagg argued,

---

[26] Howard, *Interpreting the Lord's Supper*, p. 24, see pp. 63 and 70, for specific reference to Christ's presence in the heart rather than the elements.

[27] Frank Stagg, 'The Lord's Supper in the New Testament', *Review and Expositor* (Winter, 1969), p. 6. Emphasis added.

[28] Stagg, 'The Lord's Supper in the New Testament'. Here Stagg cites the work of Ernst Käsemann, 'The Pauline Doctrine of the Lord's Supper', in Ernst Käsemann, *Essays on New Testament Themes* (Studies in Biblical Theology, 41; London: SCM Press, 1964), pp. 116 and 118; and Hans Conzelmann, *Grundriss der Theologie des Neuen Testaments* (München: Chr. Kaiser Verlag, 1967), p. 70.

[29] Stagg, 'The Lord's Supper in the New Testament', pp. 6-7.

Paul's *one purpose* in introducing the Lord's Supper into the discussion of I Corinthians had to do with its meaning as *koinonia*, affirming and expressing the oneness of the people of Christ... They had in common one life, that of Christ, in which together they participated: 'The cup of blessing which we bless, is it not the *koinonia* of the blood Christ?' (I Corinthians 10:16).[30]

Rather than connecting Christ's presence to the bread and wine and assuring the salvation of those who partake, Stagg contended that Christ is present and in *koinonia* with those who have gathered to share this meal.[31] To this extent it is truly the *Lord's Supper*.[32] He insisted,

The elements (bread and wine) are mere symbols, but the *koinonia* is no symbol; the *koinonia* is participation in 'the blood'—the life given—and 'the body'—the people of Christ.[33]

Discerning the body, therefore, bears a twofold significance which converges in the image of Christ's life continually incarnated in the community of believers. The community learns to see herself as the body of Christ and, in the communion of the blood, joins Christ in the fellowship of sacrificial living.[34]

As Christ poured out his life in 'complete self-denial and self-giving', the salvation effected in the cross and communicated in the Lord's supper becomes effectual in those who are crucified with him.[35] In the communion of sacrifice the new covenant is ratified, and Jesus' self-giving 'extend[s] into the one who has the faith which is openness to receive the living Christ into one's innermost being'. In this manner, the Lord is embodied in his church and 'redeem[s] it by drawing it into his kind of existence and life'.[36]

---

[30] Stagg, 'The Lord's Supper in the New Testament', p. 12, and his 'The Lord's Supper', in Frank Stagg, *New Testament Theology* (Nashville, TN: Broadman, 1962), p. 245. Emphasis upon 'one purpose' added.

[31] Stagg, 'The Lord's Supper in the New Testament', p. 14, and 'The Lord's Supper', pp. 245-46. Emphasis added.

[32] Stagg, 'The Lord's Supper in the New Testament', p. 14. Emphasis added. In 'The Lord's Supper', Stagg asserted, p. 239, '[I]n any true observance of the Lord's Supper one is in communion with Christ'.

[33] Stagg, 'The Lord's Supper', p. 247. Stagg also insisted, p. 239, 'The loaf and the cup are symbols, but Christ is not a symbol, and is not just symbolically present. He is actually present with and in his people.'

[34] See Stagg, 'The Lord's Supper', pp. 247 and 245; see also his 'The Lord's Supper in the New Testament', pp. 9 and 14.

[35] Stagg, 'The Lord's Supper in the New Testament', p. 11; see also 'The Lord's Supper', p. 249.

[36] Stagg, 'The Lord's Supper in the New Testament', pp. 13-14. Two years earlier, E. Glenn Hinson, *The Church: Design for Survival* (Nashville, TN: Broadman, 1967), pp. 65 and 69, argued that through worship the church 'grow[s] up...into Christ'. Ideally, all of its activities, he insisted, will transmit Christ's life to its members, and in particular,

Like Howard, Stagg consistently avoided the use of sacrament but nonetheless interpreted the meal sacramentally.[37] Around this table, would-be followers are drawn into Christ and united, and their idolatrous allegiances are surrendered to the exclusive claims of the Christ who calls communicants to the way of the cross.

Eric C. Rust

In 'The Theology of the Lord's Supper', Eric C. Rust noted the incongruity between Baptist worship and the worship of the church through the ages. While 'the Lord's Supper has [historically] shared the primary place with the preaching of the Word', Baptists have 'relegated the Lord's Supper to an infrequent observance'. Conceived as 'merely a remembrance feast' in obedience to the Lord's injunction, Baptists have forsaken church tradition and neglected a primary element of Christian worship.[38] In response, Rust reclaimed the Lord's supper as a sacrament through which Christ comes and reveals himself through the material media of a meal.[39]

Rather than arguing the finer points of whether to use the term 'sacrament', Rust simply acknowledged that Baptist aversion to the word is rooted in a reaction to Catholicism. In no sense, he argued, does it inherently suggest the transformation of the elements into the body and blood of Christ. Rather, it captures the truth that the elements 'point to the presence of the living Lord' whose grace, mercy, and forgiveness are appropriated in the celebration of the meal. But contrary to the individualism epitomized in the Baptist doctrine of soul competency, the grace extended in the supper requires the context of the faith community.[40]

Around the table, the community gathers and *together* experiences the Lord's presence. Thus, the supper not only 'points to', but actually *'involves us* in an experience' with Christ. We are drawn into something much larger than ourselves and enter a faith experience that transcends our individual relation with God. As Rust argued, this meal is a 'communal' sacrament

> whose meaning is shared by those who have a common faith, is validated by a common experience, and is transmitted within a common tradition. [It] require[s] more than an individual faith in God but one which is shared with others and nurtured within a historical community of faith... No man can be a Christian on his

---

baptism, the Lord's supper, and preaching 'involve us in [salvation history] in an unusual way'.

[37] See Stagg, 'The Lord's Supper in the New Testament', p. 14, and 'The Lord's Supper', p. 245.

[38] Eric C. Rust, 'The Theology of the Lord's Supper', *Review and Expositor* 66 (Winter, 1969), p. 35. In 1980, Paige Patterson specifically named Rust and five other professors as 'representative of the nature and extent of the problem' of liberalism in Baptist schools (*Baptist Press* 15 May 1980, quoted in Grady C. Cothen, *What Happened to the Southern Baptist Convention? A Memoir of the Controversy* [Macon, GA: Smyth & Helwys, corrected edn, 1993], p. 78).

[39] Rust, 'The Theology of the Lord's Supper', p. 35.

[40] Rust, 'The Theology of the Lord's Supper', p. 35.

own but is so in relationship to his fellows as well as to the Christ; such a redemptive experience has to be shared, interpreted, and developed within a believing community. To be 'in Christ' is never solitary involvement with the risen Lord. It takes place 'in the body of Christ', which is his Church.[41]

In no sense is there an *immediate* encounter between individuals and God apart from the body, and in the supper the Lord draws near through the media of a common meal.[42] Building upon Paul Tillich, Rust grounded his interpretation in the broader implications of living within a 'sacramental universe'.

In the Lord's supper 'we see the true end of all nature', for bread and wine point beyond their materiality toward 'the things of the spirit'.[43] Within the order of creation, 'God the Creator has chosen to disclose himself to us through and in the things he created', and all of creation bears the potential of becoming 'a sensible sign...of his presence'. In the Lord's supper, in particular, God's will is manifest, and the created order is 'drawn up into "salvation history"' as the bread and wine point beyond themselves to redemption in Christ.[44] As Tillich argued,

> Natural objects can become bearers of transcendent power and meaning, they can become sacramental elements... This is the basis for a Protestant rediscovery of the sacramental sphere.[45]

For Rust, it is the basis for a *Baptist* rediscovery of the sacrament of the supper.

As if the entirety of created realities can become the 'somatic aspects of [God's] personhood', human beings can know God through the natural order, and in the Lord's supper this is precisely what happens. Around this table, general and special revelation converge, and 'in the center of [the Christian] religion are set those elements which, in a peculiar way, are signs and symbols of his presence'.[46] But the

---

[41] Rust, 'The Theology of the Lord's Supper', pp. 35-36. Emphasis added.

[42] See Rust, 'The Theology of the Lord's Supper', p. 44, on the necessity of 'sacramental media' during this era of the Spirit, following Christ's ascension and prior to the final consummation of the kingdom of God. For an excellent essay on the issue of the mediation of grace see, Richard W. Harmon, 'The Mediation and Immediacy of Grace in the Community of Faith: A Baptist Perspective', *Southwestern Journal of Theology* 28 (Spring, 1986), pp. 35-41.

[43] Rust, 'The Theology of the Lord's Supper', pp. 37 and 36.

[44] Rust, 'The Theology of the Lord's Supper', pp. 36-37. In *Promise and Presence: An Exploration of Sacramental Theology* (Waynesboro, GA: Paternoster Press, 2005), pp. 55 and 45, British Baptist John E. Colwell warns against the general conception of creation as a 'sacramental universe', and though he strongly asserts belief in the 'mediate-ness of God's relatedness to creation', he labors to preserve the distinctiveness of Christ and to avoid 'undermin[ing] the sacramentality of specific signs within creation'.

[45] Paul Tillich, *The Protestant Era* (Chicago, IL: Chicago University Press, 1948), p. 102-103, quoted in Rust, 'The Theology of the Lord's Supper', p. 36.

[46] Rust, 'The Theology of the Lord's Supper', pp. 36-37. On the sacramental universe, see also Eric C. Rust, 'The Incarnation and a Sacramental Universe', in Eric C. Rust,

symbol of the Lord's supper does not simply point beyond itself to God. It actually embodies the presence of the Lord himself.

Drawing upon the Hebraic usage of *dabhar* (word), Rust related the Lord's supper to the prophets who both proclaimed and enacted the word of the Lord. Denoting both 'deed' and 'word', he explained,

> Realistically such a 'word' was envisaged as a substantial extension of the speaker himself, containing in itself his intention and the power to bring that intention to pass. Thus the *debar Yahweh* was an extension of Yahweh's own being, pregnant with his power and purpose.[47]

'The symbolic acts of the prophet were extensions of Yahweh's presence', and the prophetic enactment of the divine intention set God's purpose in motion. In Jeremiah wearing the yoke (Jer. 28.1-17), Ezekiel joining two sticks together (Ezek. 37.15-17), and Isaiah donning a slave's garb and walking through Jerusalem (Isa. 20.1-6), God's will was both proclaimed and 'initiat[ed]'. Similarly, in the Lord's supper the apostle Paul declared that we 'proclaim the Lord's death until he comes', and through the bread and the wine, 'the death of the Lord is acted out symbolically'. Rust contended,

> The reality of our redemption is set before our eyes as a present reality. As we eat, we do so in the presence of the Lord's atoning act... What has been achieved on Calvary becomes contemporaneous with those who worship. The forgiveness and mercy of the Cross become a present reality. In the *act of eating and drinking*, the believer *involves himself* by faith in the redemptive act, and the work of grace is carried out in his own life... The mercy of the Cross becomes a potent and recreative presence in the soul of the believer.[48]

While the bread and wine play key roles, Rust emphasized the entire ritual as a material *experience* through which Christ's presence in the power of the cross is known. In the communal actions of gathering, eating, and drinking, the word of the Lord's death is set in motion. Worshipers are drawn into the redemptive act completed in the faithful reception of those who believe. At the table, 'the host of the feast' gives bread and wine and offers *himself* to all who will receive.[49]

Uniting personal devotion and communal life as the body of Christ, Rust insisted that an 'existential decision' in the moment of eating and drinking fulfills the word of redemption initiated in the Lord's supper. Though Christ's sacrifice occurred once-for-all and remains 'forever constituent of God's own life', its meaning awaits fulfillment, contingent on the human response. At length, Rust asserted,

---

Science and Faith: Towards a Theological Understanding of Nature (New York: Oxford University Press, 1967), pp. 271-316.

[47] Rust, 'The Theology of the Lord's Supper', p. 37.
[48] Rust, 'The Theology of the Lord's Supper', pp. 37-38. Emphasis added.
[49] See Rust, 'The Theology of the Lord's Supper', pp. 38-39.

[T]he sacrifice in the heavenly order is meaningful only as, in our partaking of the elements, we offer ourselves. This is the sacrifice that we make at the Lord's Supper. We offer ourselves within the eternal sacrifice of our great High Priest, Jesus. Dietrich Bonhoeffer carefully differentiated between 'cheap grace' and 'costly grace.' He defined the former as a static acceptance of the means of grace in which the worshiper is not involved. So often that is what happens in the Lord's Supper! But 'costly grace' implies identification with the crucified and risen Lord. As the earthly elements are presented to us, we identify ourselves with the sacrifice of the Christ to which they point. We *become involved* with the passion of our Lord and so commit ourselves that we seek, in our own lives, to be crucified with Him, to take up our cross and follow him, to make up what is lacking in the sufferings of the Christ.[50]

Within the 'corporate setting' of the body, Christ 'forms himself in *us*', and our sacrifice acquires communal significance. We are 'bound to one another by the redeeming love which flows into our lives from his sacrifice'.[51]

John W. Carlton

In 'The Lord's Supper in Worship', John W. Carlton, purported to restore the Lord's supper to its proper place and at key points continued the trajectory of Rust's work. Noting the 'cavalier' attitude of those who have reduced the supper to 'an incidental addendum' to the service of the word, Carlton reminded his readers of the primacy of the meal in the early church and reclaimed the unity of the word and sacrament.[52]

Retrieving the meal from the vacuity of 'ordinance', Carlton set it alongside preaching as a means through which God communes with his people. More than a 'symbolic act of obedience' in memory of the One who died, the supper bears constitutive powers as the Lord draws near and forms worshipers into his body.[53] The church is 'a community of memory and understanding', and Carlton argued that the anamnetic nature of the word proclaimed and enacted in the Lord's supper mediates 'God's communion with his responsive people…[making him] contemporaneously present with them'.[54] Or, as he asserted in another place, it 'incarnates his presence with his faithful people'.[55] In the process, the faith community is reconstituted upon the foundational revelation of Christ's passion, and feeding upon Christ, worshipers are '*created* the Body of Christ'. They are 'renewed

---

[50] Rust, 'The Theology of the Lord's Supper', pp. 40-41. Emphasis added.

[51] Rust, 'The Theology of the Lord's Supper', pp. 41-42. Emphasis added.

[52] John W. Carlton, 'The Lord's Supper in Worship', *Review and Expositor* 66 (Winter, 1969), p. 67.

[53] *The Baptist Faith and Message*, Article VII, p. 14; Carlton, 'The Lord's Supper in Worship', pp. 69 and 72.

[54] Carlton, 'The Lord's Supper in Worship', pp. 69, 71 and 70.

[55] John W. Carlton, 'The New Emphasis on Worship and Liturgy', *Review and Expositor* 64 (Summer, 1967), p. 316.

and sent out as "men in whom the resurrection begun makes the resurrection credible.'"[56]

Through the 'prophetic symbolism' enacted in the upper room, another *dabhar* is set in motion. Reproducing these acts, the contemporary faith community is incorporated into the life of Christ, so that 'the work begun at "God's board" must be finished at ours'.[57] Thus, in addition to the unity of the word and sacrament, there is the unity of liturgy and life. In the Lord's supper, worshipers are swept into God's purposes begun in Christ, and through the ecclesial body, Christ's work continues.

Citing Paul's judgment against the Corinthian Christians for 'not discerning the Lord's body' (1 Cor. 11.29), Carlton asserted that the supper obligates the body formed around the table. He argued,

> Apparently [Paul] was not referring here to irreverence at the table, despite done to the consecrated elements, but primarily to the way they ate their own food beforehand, leaving those who had nothing in humiliation. They demonstrated no 'sense of the body', and it was a refusal to share bread *outside* communion that rendered it impossible for them truly to eat the Bread of life *at* communion. While this service begins with 'draw near with faith', it must conclude with 'arise, let us go hence', and both of these must be vital or the world will not be changed. When Jesus, said, 'Arise, let us go hence', in his discourse in the Upper Room, it was to go out and make real for mankind the sacrifice whose meaning he had expounded at the Supper.[58]

Taken up into Christ's sacrifice, communicants depart and complete that sacrifice in each new generation. They become one with Christ in the gift he offers, and quoting Henry Sloane Coffin, Carlton described this uniting

> as we receive his own chosen memorials and make them our own by eating and drinking, we offer ourselves to him. In the action there is both a memorial sacrifice of what Christ did for us and for the whole world and the presentation of ourselves 'a living sacrifice.'[59]

Partaking of the meal, worshipers enter the ongoing work of Christ and are transformed into his body offering themselves as Christ offered himself.

Reminiscent of Rust, Carlton concluded that bread and wine become 'bearers of transcendent value and meaning, [and are] restor[ed]... [to] what all matter was meant to be—the direct means of contact between God and man'. However, he carefully contended that the 'real eloquence' rests in the *acts* of breaking and pouring.[60]

---

[56] Carlton, 'The Lord's Supper in Worship', pp. 69 and 72. Internal quote is from Frederick W. Robertson. Original source not provided.

[57] Carlton, 'The Lord's Supper in Worship', pp. 73-74.

[58] Carlton, 'The Lord's Supper in Worship', pp. 71-72.

[59] Henry Sloane Coffin, *The Public Worship of God* (Philadelphia, PA: Westminster, 1956), p. 145, quoted in Carlton, 'The Lord's Supper in Worship', p. 72.

[60] Carlton, 'The Lord's Supper in Worship', pp. 73-74.

Emphasizing the actions over the elements and stressing God's transformative presence in the entire ritual, Carlton moved toward a theology of enactment. With the weight of his thought given to the formation of the body and the mediation of God's presence through the materiality of a communal meal, he also cast doubt on an unmediated relationship between God and individual souls. For ultimately, the Lord's supper constitutes a *community* of believers whose identity remains bound to the collective body.

Lewis E. Rhodes

In 'The Sacrament of Wholeness', Lewis E. Rhodes argued that a sharp delineation between word and sacrament has clouded the sacramental vision and relegated 'communicat[ive]' power to the proclamation of the word and placed the sacraments in a different category altogether.[61] Within this division of labor, Rhodes focused on the extreme practice in which the word assumes exclusive priority, and in Baptist churches this occurs in the cursory treatment of the Lord's supper. As Rhodes bemoaned,

> The Lord's Supper may be treated as an addendum, a P.S. to the order of worship, an afterthought, a white table cloth tent that reminds one that his noon meal will be late and causes a housewife anxiety because of food left cooking at home. It can be treated like a stepchild or in-law in the family of worship, denied the rights and privileges of sons and heirs. When the Supper is added to worship instead of made central to it, it says clearly the words of a minister are more important than its word.[62]

To provide balance, he argued that both the word and sacrament bear communicative power, and, rooted in the incarnation, he insisted that 'word may be person or event or both'. Thus, the sacrament is word, and like all words, it communicates.[63] But what does it communicate and how is its message conveyed?

The Lord's supper communicates grace defined as Christ's personal presence 'break[ing] into' the lives of those worshipping around the table, but this grace invades their lives as a personal encounter rather than as a commodity which can be simply handed on. Steering between two extremes, Rhodes, on the one hand, avoided

---

[61] Lewis E. Rhodes, 'The Sacrament of Wholeness', *Review and Expositor* 66 (Winter, 1969), p. 59. In his introduction of Southern Baptists to Roman Catholics, C. Brownlow Hastings, C. Brownlow Hastings, *Introducing Southern Baptists: Their Faith and Their Life* (New York: Paulist Press, 1981), p. 21, acknowledged that the Holy Spirit operates through certain media, but he failed to include the sacraments among his list of such means. 'The Spirit does not operate in a vacuum, nor apart from various means', he explained. 'He uses the Word of God, written and preached, the testimony of others, the situations and events of life.' As if the word communicates and the sacraments do not, he certainly placed them in a category outside of these means of the Spirit.

[62] Rhodes, 'The Sacrament of Wholeness', p. 62.

[63] Rhodes, 'The Sacrament of Wholeness', p. 59.

conceiving the supper as an 'objective sacrament' which automatically infuses grace by virtue of Christ's presence in the bread and wine. On the other hand, he resisted describing the supper as a 'mere symbol' which cannot possibly bear divine presence, for no symbol can be a 'mere' symbol. In fact, he insisted, a 'true' symbol bears the power to 'create the reality it symbolizes'. In the supper, that reality is grace, and grace is not 'a *thing* mediated to us by a means, but the Presence that mediates Himself to us because he is gracious'.[64] In the *event* of the Lord's supper, the word incarnates himself and worshipers encounter the living Christ.

Rhodes described the meal as a 'sacrament of wholeness', and, he contended,

> The Lord's Supper is a time, place, elements, liturgy, action, persons, and event. When the Lord's Supper is in action it is a happening, not an idea or subject for theological discussion. It is more than a symbol, for persons interacting cannot be a mere symbol. In some sense the Supper is the sacrament of wholeness. Sacrament used here is not an objective means of grace, but a time, condition, attitude, action, and experience in which wholeness comes. Wholeness is not an absolute to be achieved and held; is [*sic*] a condition like soundness and health. It is a quality of living, being, acting, becoming. Wholeness is not something one gets, but a way of living and relating.[65]

In short, the Lord's supper is a transformative event in the life of the church, and through perpetual observance it shapes participants into a certain kind of people by 'insinuat[ing] meaning and wholeness into life'.[66] Most importantly, the meal draws worshipers out of themselves and into relations with others. 'The Lord's Supper', argued Rhodes,

> is social, not individual. Persons are *with* persons; persons are with persons *for* persons. This is something of what it means to be a person, to be human, to be Christian. It means to be for persons, oneself and one's neighbor... Man is struggling to realize his destiny. He cannot find himself in tribalism or individualism. Now he must find himself to be a person in relationships with persons. Wholeness is not simply being but being related to others in love and trust.[67]

In 'The Marks of the Church: Sacraments', he continued this line of thought and contended

> The Lord's Supper stands nearer center to what the [*sic*] life is about than most other religious rites. For life is about life together. The Lord's Supper emphasizes and focuses on our corporate life. The 'mine and thine' are brought under the discipline

---

[64] Rhodes, 'The Sacrament of Wholeness', p. 61. Cf. Rhodes' relational understanding of grace to Colwell, *Promise and Presence*, p. 171.
[65] Rhodes, 'The Sacrament of Wholeness', p. 62.
[66] Rhodes, 'The Sacrament of Wholeness', p. 63.
[67] Rhodes, 'The Sacrament of Wholeness', p. 65.

of 'our', both to be judged and redeemed. We eat together because our lives are determined together.[68]

At the table, worshipers experience Christ in the community of faith where there is no '"me and Jesus" alone',[69] but only the shared story of walking with him.[70]

Worship is 'a community of faith celebrating its memory of Jesus', and the church's 'continual rehearsal' of Jesus' memory keeps it alive. More than that, it mediates Christ's living presence for those who celebrate. It brings the reality of the past into the experience of the present. In Rhodes' words,

> The more we rehearse the more we begin to feel like we were there. It becomes so much a part of the subconscious that the thereness of Jesus becomes more and more real... With a lifetime of rehearsing being there with Jesus it comes to mean Jesus is here with us... I find myself needing to rehearse the memory. I do this because I have no private memory. I am heir to the memory of the community of faith.[71]

As a participant in this larger community, he recognized his dependence on others, and he contended that even faith itself is actualized through the corporate memory of those who *were* with Jesus and who *are* with him now. In the celebration of the Lord's supper, Christ is present in the unity of the body worshiping in the oneness of the common loaf. In this moment, wholeness is 'nourished and exercised'.[72]

Far from connecting Christ's presence to the elements of bread and wine, Rhodes paved the way for a shift toward enactment as the entire 'happening' becomes a means of transforming grace. The various elements of the celebration converge in the mysterious mediation of Christ's graceful presence, a presence which, nonetheless, must be subjectively experienced. At the same time, in Rhodes' work, Christ's transforming presence has an autonomy not seen in other Baptist theologies, so that the 'effectual working' of the sacrament can occur independently of the cognizance of faith.[73] Within the community, each worshiper becomes a part of something much

---

[68] Lewis E. Rhodes, 'Marks of the Church: Sacraments', *Bulletin* 12 May 1974, Broadway Baptist Church, Knoxville, Tennessee.

[69] Lewis E. Rhodes, 'When and if Manipulation is Justified', *Bulletin* 18 July 1971, Broadway Baptist Church, Knoxville, Tennessee.

[70] Lewis E. Rhodes, untitled paper in the possession of Fred Watkins, to who I am grateful for allowing me access to this source, p. 42.

[71] Rhodes, untitled paper in the possession of Fred Watkins, p. 42.

[72] Lewis E. Rhodes, 'The Ties That Bind', *Bulletin* 23 January 1966, Broadway Baptist Church, Knoxville, Tennessee, and 'The Sacrament of Wholeness', p. 64.

[73] Rhodes, 'The Sacrament of Wholeness', p. 65. Cf. Elizabeth Newman's 'A Divided House?: Hospitality and the Table of Grace', in *Untamed Hospitality* (Grand Rapids, MI: Brazos, April 2007), p. 20 (pagination corresponds to a pre-published copy of this chapter provided to this writer by the author), where she quotes Ben Quash ('Drama and the Ends of Modernity', in Lucy Gardner, *et al.*, *Balthasar at the End of Modernity* [Edinburgh: T&T Clark, 1999], p. 170) and describes the Lord's supper as an experience

larger than herself, and Christ's influential presence breaks in and transforms in ways beyond our abilities to know or understand. Through the continual participation in the community which remembers and opens herself to the ongoing story of the risen Lord, worshipers can be made whole.

Baptists, Soul Competency, and Community

For Baptists laboring to reclaim their rich sacramental heritage, the theological stronghold of individualism and soul competency proves to be the most foreboding challenge. While these reconstructions invite Baptists beyond the paucity of the supper understood as a 'mere memorial', the communal focus penetrates to the heart of Baptist identity.

E.Y. Mullins' influence on twentieth-century North American Baptist thought is undeniable.[74] In particular, the wide distribution of Mullins' *Axioms of Religion* left an indelible mark on the Baptist family and gave them the common language of soul competency. In the *Declaration of Religious Liberty* adopted by the Baptist World Congress on 27 July 1939, the Baptist World Alliance asserted in its opening sentence, 'Worthy religion rests on the conviction that the *individual soul is competent* to deal directly with God, and has the right and the need of this direct dealing.'[75] Though it has been argued that belief in the soul's competency before God appeared in Baptist thought as early as the mid-seventeenth century,[76] Mullins coined a phrase that has become common idiom capturing a, if not the, foundational Baptist belief. As Baptists have reconstructed a sacramental theology of the Lord's supper, the emphasis has shifted away from this focus on the individual and toward the community.

Rather than asserting the right of an individual to deal directly with God, worshipers encounter the Lord *together* around a common table, and by the grace mediated through this communal practice, worshipers are constituted the body of Christ. In no sense does the isolated individual stand, as in the words of the *London*

---

in being 'conducted' and thus exercised in certain ways of being, of being within 'the loving movement of the Trinity itself'.

[74] See Harold Bloom, *The American Religion* (New York: Simon & Schuster, 1992), p. 199, quoted in James Dunn, 'Church, State, and Soul Competency', *Review and Expositor* 96 (Winter, 1999), p. 61; Timothy D.F. Maddox, 'E.Y. Mullins: Mr. Baptist for the 20th and 21st Century', *Review and Expositor* 96 (Winter, 1999), p. 87.

[75] *Declaration of Religious Liberty Adopted Unanimously by the Baptist World Congress in Atlanta, Georgia, on July 27, 1939, as Expressing the General Conviction and Position of Baptists throughout the World*, quoted in Henry Cook, *What Baptists Stand For* (London: Carey Kingsgate Press, 4th edn, 1961), Appendix III, pp. 248-49. Emphasis added.

[76] See Walter B. Shurden, 'The Baptist Identity and the Baptist *Manifesto*', *Perspectives in Religious Studies* 25 (Winter, 1998), pp. 329-31; Thomas Helwys, *A Short Declaration of the Mystery of Iniquity* (1611/1612) (ed. Richard Groves; Macon, GA: Mercer University Press, 1998); and *The Standard Confession* (1660), Article XXIV, in Lumpkin, *Baptist Confessions of Faith*, p. 232.

Confession (1644), 'naked' before God.[77] Instead, God's graceful presence draws near through the mediation of a common meal and makes one of the many. Rooted in soul competency, Baptist soteriology has drifted far from such a communal understanding of salvation and faith, but with this shift in their eucharistic thought, Baptists return to a New Testament understanding of the church as a body whose members always exist in relationship with God and with others. They reestablish the priority of community. The *body* is formed. The *people* are recreated. And an alternative community stands over against the world because of Christ's ways learned and instilled at the Lord's table.

In 'Re-envisioning Baptist Identity: A Manifesto for Baptist Communities in North America' (1997), both community and the Lord's supper stand at the heart of Baptist identity, and the way forward takes shape around this communal gathering. Characteristically, the shapers of this document assert their belief in 'freedom', a conviction 'celebrated' by Baptists from their beginnings, but such freedom is rightly understood only in connection with 'the fellowship of the Holy Spirit' who, among other things, 'incorporates us into the church'. It is the 'freedom of God's *people*', reflecting the Creator's freedom 'who does not will to be free in solitude but for creation'.[78] Thus, they boldly assert,

> We affirm *following Jesus as a call to shared discipleship* rather than invoking a theory of soul competency... We reject all accounts of following Jesus that construe faith as a private matter between God and the individual or as an activity of competent souls who inherently enjoy unmediated, unassailable, and disembodied experience with God.[79]

In place of such individualistic conceptions of faith, the Manifesto asserts that the church and its practices of proclamation, baptism, and the Lord's supper are intrinsic to our relationship with Christ and each other. Through the 'enactment' of these 'remembering practices',

> God's grace and Christian obedience converge in a visible sign of the new creation. By repeating these signs we learn to see the world as created and redeemed by God. The Spirit who proceeds from the Father through the Son makes the performance of

---

[77] This is the language of the *London Confession* (1644), Article XXV, in Lumpkin, *Baptist Confessions of Faith*, p. 163; See also Newman, 'The Lord's Supper: Might Baptists Accept a Theory of Real Presence?', in Cross and Thompson (eds), *Baptist Sacramentalism*, p. 213, who, highly critical of Baptist individualism, contends that 'the Lord's Supper, rightly understood, forms a people who can resist...a claustrophobic and privatized understanding of "religion"'. See also pp. 212, 214, 217-18, 225-26.

[78] Mikael Broadway, Curtis W. Freeman, Barry Harvey, James Wm McClendon, Jr, Elizabeth Newman and Philip E. Thompson, 'Re-Envisioning Baptist Identity: A Manifesto for Baptist Communities in North America', *Perspectives in Religious Studies* 24 (Fall, 1997), pp. 303-304. Emphasis added.

[79] Broadway, *et al.*, 'Re-Envisioning Baptist Identity: A Manifesto', p. 305. Italics is part of the original text.

these practices effectual so as to seal and nourish the faith and freedom of believers.[80]

Rather than emphasizing the individual in direct or immediate relation with God, the Manifesto envisions an economy of salvation in which the church and its practices mediate God's grace. Through the power of the Spirit, they effect the faithful response of a people perpetually learning what it means to be 'a distinctive community seeking to embody the reign of God'.[81] How far, however, can the influence of such emphases extend given the overarching belief in soul competency among many Baptists?

In his response to the Manifesto, Walter B. Shurden adamantly opposes this communal emphasis. While insisting upon a balanced approach to the 'individual-community motif', Shurden 'unhesitatingly' gives precedence to the individual.[82] Citing E.Y. Mullins and British Baptist, H. Wheeler Robinson, who asserted respectively that 'soul competency' and 'spiritual individualism' are the 'core value[s]' around which Baptist distinctives can best be understood, Shurden grants priority to 'individualism' as the governing hermeneutic for understanding the Baptist identity. The Manifesto's stress on 'community' as the 'core value', he insists, dangerously strikes at the heart of what it means to be Baptist.[83]

In *The Baptist Identity: Four Fragile Freedoms*, Shurden argues that freedom is the 'spirit' which pervades all Baptist distinctives, and regarding the 'freedom of the soul' he is unable to reconcile personal faith with faith mediated through the believing community. He contends,

> In the Baptist faith tradition, individualism in religious matters manifests itself at the very beginning of the Christian life. Baptists insist that saving faith is personal, not impersonal. It is relational, not ritualistic. It is direct, not indirect. It is a lonely, frightened, sinful individual before an almighty, loving, and gracious God.[84]

---

[80] Broadway, *et al.*, 'Re-Envisioning Baptist Identity: A Manifesto', p. 310; cf. pp. 306-07.

[81] Broadway, *et al.*, 'Re-Envisioning Baptist Identity: A Manifesto', pp. 308-309. On the 'Manifesto' and community, see Mikael Broadway, Curtis Freeman, *et al.*, '"Dangerous and Un-baptistic?" A Response from Supporters of the "Baptist Manifesto",' *Associated Baptist Press News* 1 February 2006, http://www.abpnews.com/806.article; and Greg Warner, '"Manifesto" Supporters Say Role of Community Misinterpreted', *Associated Baptist Press News* 1 February 2006, http://www.abpnews.com/810.article.

[82] Shurden, 'The Baptist Identity and the Baptist *Manifesto*', pp. 323-24.

[83] Shurden, 'The Baptist Identity and the Baptist *Manifesto*', pp. 322 and 324. For Robinson on individualism, see H. Wheeler Robinson, *The Life and Faith of the Baptists* (London: Kingsgate Press, rev. edn, 1946), reprint (Wake Forest, NC: Chanticleer, 1985), pp. v-vii, 69-81 and 123.

[84] Shurden, *The Baptist Identity: Four Fragile Freedoms* (Macon, GA: Smyth & Helwys, 1993), pp. 2 and 25. For another summery of Baptists and freedom, see Bill J.

It is personal, not sacramental.[85]

Interestingly, Tom Nettles insists that Shurden's individualism is an 'historical truncation of Baptist identity', an ecclesiology 'sever[ed] from the complete life of faith'.[86] In an uncharacteristic move for a mainstream Southern Baptist, Nettles also makes room for understanding grace as a mediated experience. Suggesting what he calls a synergistic conception of the operation of grace, he insists that grace is 'a cooperative venture', and with little detail he includes sacraments among the means through which grace happens.[87] Though such a position remains foreign to the stated theology of the SBC, Nettles' words invite Baptists beyond the 'Mullinsian' hold on Baptist thought.[88]

Along with Shurden, many Baptists with roots in the Southern Baptist family—including Grady C. Cothen, James M. Dunn, E. Glenn Hinson, Gary E. Parker, William Powell Tuck, and William D. Underwood—remain committed to the doctrine of soul competency. In their writings, the prevailing influence of E.Y. Mullins counters much that Baptist sacramentalists aim to accomplish, and the full

---

Leonard, 'Varieties of Freedom in the Baptist Experience', *Baptist History and Heritage* 25 (January, 1990), pp. 3-12.

[85] Shurden, *Baptist Identity*, p. 25. Interestingly, Bill J. Leonard, 'Southern Baptists and Conversion: An Evangelical Sacramentalism', in Gary A. Furr and Curtis W. Freeman (eds), *Ties That Bind: Life Together in the Baptist Vision* (Macon, GA: Smyth & Helwys, 1994), pp. 11 and 16, identifies personal conversion as 'evangelical sacramentalism', and he notes that Baptist worship has taken shape around the embodiment of this internal, individual experience. See also E. Glenn Hinson, 'Baptists and Spirituality: A Community at Worship', *Review and Expositor* 84 (Fall, 1987), p. 654. Here, Hinson refers to the 'sacrament...of the invitation.'

[86] Tom J. Nettles, *Ready for Reformation: Bringing Authentic Reform to Southern Baptist Churches* (Nashville, TN: Broadman & Holman, 2005), p. 101. On the polarity of the individual and community in Baptist life and thought, see Marv Knox, 'Baptist Scholars Point to Tension Between Individualism and Community Life', *Baptist Standard* 15 October 2004, http://www.baptiststandard.com, and 'Split Personality Compels Baptists to Fight, Historian Asserts', *Baptist Standard* 9 July 2004, http://www.baptiststandard.com; and Marv Knox and Greg Warner, 'Debate Over Believers' Priesthood Reveals Tension Between Individual, Community', *Associated Baptist Press News* 2 November 2004, http://www.abpnews.com/1132.article.

[87] Nettles, *Ready for Reformation*, pp. 78-89. Two other essays of note are Carl F.H. Henry, Timothy George, *et al.*, 'The *SBJT* Forum: The Current State of Worship', *Southern Baptist Journal of Theology* (Winter, 1998), http://www.sbts.edu/pdf/sbjt_1998winter7.pdf; and R. Albert Mohler, 'The Whole Earth is Full of His Glory' *Southern Baptist Journal of Theology* (Winter, 1998), http://www.sbts.edu/pdf/sbjt_1998winter2.pdf. Each takes shape around a corporate vision of worship and lacks an emphasis on individualism. However, neither makes substantive reference to the Lord's supper.

[88] In a personal phone conversation between this writer and Philip E. Thompson on 4 March 2004, Thompson noted the persistent emphasis on soul competency and the inconsistency of such with this revival of the communal, and he termed it 'Mullinsian'.

weight of the communal emphases seems compromised.[89] Without a doubt, the doctrine of soul competency encapsulated and divinely validated many of the Enlightenment principles embraced by the broader, modern Christian family.[90] However, Baptist individualism pre-dates the Enlightenment and, as noted by Glenn Hinson, can be rooted in the Puritan 'desire for immediate access to God'.[91] Thus, the advancement of a sacramental theology of the Lord's supper begun among Southern Baptists in the 1960s proves to be a radical re-visioning of Baptist identity balancing the historical emphasis on the individual with an understanding of spiritual formation within the community.

As direct heirs of the Mullins tradition, Southern Baptists would benefit from a broader reading of Mullins which reveals a kernel of communalism. In *The Christian Religion in Its Doctrinal Expression* (1917), Mullins briefly addressed 'The Holy Spirit and the Means of Grace'. Moving beyond faith as a direct encounter between an individual and God, Mullins argued that God has 'chosen to approach men

---

[89] See Grady C. Cothen and James M. Dunn, *Soul Freedom: Baptist Battle Cry* (Macon, GA: Smyth & Helwys, 2000); E. Glenn Hinson, *Soul Liberty: The Doctrine of Religious Liberty* (Nashville, TN: Convention Press, 1975), and 'The Theology and Experience of Worship: A Baptist View', *The Greek Orthodox Theological Review* 22 (Winter, 1977), pp. 417-27; Gary E. Parker, *Principles Worth Protecting* (Macon, GA: Smyth & Helwys, 1993); William Powell Tuck, *Our Baptist Tradition* (Macon, GA: Smyth & Helwys, 1993); and William D. Underwood, 'Baptist Summit Speech', 20 January 2006, http://www2.mercer.edu/President/BaptistSummitSpeech.htm. See also, Alan Neely, *Being Baptist Means Freedom* (Charlotte, NC: Southern Baptist Alliance, 1988).

[90] See Broadway, *et al.*, 'Re-Envisioning Baptist Identity: A Manifesto', pp. 309 10; Curtis W. Freeman, 'Can Baptist Theology Be Revisioned?', *Perspectives in Religious Studies* 24 (Fall, 1999), pp. 273-302; Philip E. Thompson, 'Re-envisioning Baptist Identity: Historical, Theological, and Liturgical Analysis', *Perspectives in Religious Studies* 27 (Fall, 2000), pp. 287-302; Gregory A. Wills, 'Are Southern Baptists in Danger of Losing Their Identity? A Historian's Perspective', a paper presented at the Baptist Identity Conference, Union University, 5 April 2004), pp. 7-9, and, 'Who are the True Baptists? The Conservative Resurgence and the Influence of Moderate Baptist Views of Baptist Identity', *The Southern Baptist Journal of Theology* 9 (Spring, 2005), pp. 18-20.

[91] E. Glenn Hinson, 'The Theology and Experience of Worship: A Baptist View', p. 420. See also Shurden, 'The Baptist Identity and the Baptist *Manifesto*', pp. 329-31; Knox and Warner, 'Debate Over Believers' Priesthood', p. 3; and Maddox, 'E.Y. Mullins', p. 100. On p. 100, Maddox affirms, that Baptists 'place the strongest historical emphasis on the individual among Christian churches at large'. Freeman, 'Can Baptist Theology be Revisioned?', p. 292, explains that 'the language of Baptist convictions and practices is much richer and more robust than accounts which simply connect timeless principles like beads on a string... [And in one sense], the language of liberal democratic individualism was added over time to the convictions of Baptist identity'.

through appointed means'.[92] Reminiscent of James Petigru Boyce in the nineteenth century, he included among these means preaching, the Bible, the church and its ordinances and officers, worship, and life experiences of fellowship, struggle, prayer, suffering, and loss. All of these are employed by the Holy Spirit as 'means of grace'. Rather than 'accomplishing his ends directly upon and within the human spirit', God has so ordained this economy of salvation.[93]

Rooted in the incarnation, each of these 'are simply means by which the Holy Spirit forms Christ within us' and continues 'creating his spiritual kingdom among men'. Rather than insisting the individual soul is competent before God in matters of religion and faith, Mullins made the individual dependent upon 'means of grace [which] are *necessary* for the effectual propagation of the gospel...'[94] In another place, Mullins asserted the inadequacy of individualism and maintained that 'man is more than an individual. He is a social being.' In this manner, he opened the possibility to understand Christian formation as a communal experience rather than an isolated journey of lonely individuals.[95]

Though Mullins himself never fully worked out the implications of these claims, he could not escape the fact that the individual remains dependent upon the community of faith. Through its practices, he admitted, God mediates himself and his grace to those who would believe and forms them into the body of Christ. May Baptists catch a glimpse of the light shining through this crack in the fortress of soul competency, and may they welcome this more balanced approach to understanding their life together—a life united in Christ around a common table. In addition, may they recognize, as Elizabeth Newman notes, that the individual herself stands within a particular social and communal context which forms the very 'assumptions about what it means to be an "individual."' Therefore, 'The deeper question is *which* communities are in fact forming us so that we can become more faithful disciples?'[96] May we hear the invitation to surrender ourselves to the discipline of the eucharistic community where the way of the cross perpetually forms us into a body prepared to die for the life of the world.

---

[92] Edgar Young Mullins, *The Christian Religion in Its Doctrinal Expression* (Nashville, TN: Sunday School Board of the Southern Baptist Convention, 1917), p. 362.

[93] Mullins, *Christian Religion*, p. 363; Timothy George, 'James Petigru Boyce', in George and Dockery (eds), *Theologians of the Baptist Tradition*, p. 78; James Petigru Boyce, *Abstract of Systematic Theology* (rev. F.H. Kerfoot; Philadelphia, PA: American Baptist Publication Society, 1899), pp. 331-34.

[94] Mullins, *Christian Religion*, pp. 364-65. Italics added. See also Harmon, 'The Mediation and Immediacy of Grace', pp. 35-41.

[95] Edgar Young Mullins, *The Axioms of Religion: A New Interpretation of the Baptist Faith* (Philadelphia, PA: American Baptist Publication Society, 1908), p. 51.

[96] Elizabeth Newman to Sean White, 2 April 2007; Elizabeth Newman, 'Formation and Malformation in the Church', *Associated Baptist Press News* 3 April 2007.

CHAPTER 13

Ex Opere Operato:
Re-thinking a Historic Baptist Rejection

Paul S. Fiddes

Nothing seems more Baptist than the rejection of the sacramental dogma of *ex opere operato*. Even where Baptist writers of past or present use the language of sacraments and affirm their function as 'means of grace', they seem obliged to distance themselves from any hint of the Roman Catholic understanding that the sacraments are effective 'through the act performed' (or 'by the very fact of the action's being performed').[1] It is assumed that the phrase *ex opere operato* stands for an automatic dispensing of grace through the actions of the administrant, regardless of the faith of the participants.[2] On these grounds, Martin Luther began the Protestant rejection of *ex opere operato*, declaring that a valid sacrament required more than the power of a priest.[3]

Moreover, the problem does not just lie with the apparent disregard of any need for human faith. Theologically, such a concept is found deficient in its apparent presumption that God's hand can be forced, or the Spirit of God manipulated, by ritual words and actions. The notion of grace coming *ex opere operato* is, suggests a modern Baptist sacramental theologian, 'effectively to imprison the Spirit within the

---

[1] *Catechism of the Catholic Church*, validated by Apostolic Constitution *Fidei Depositum* 11 October 1992 (available www.vatican.va/archive/catechism), 1128.

[2] E.g., J.H. Rushbrooke, 'Protestant of the Protestants', in J.H. Rusbrooke (ed.), *Faith of the Baptists* (London: Kingsgate Press, n.d. [1926]), p. 81; Christopher Ellis, 'The Sacramental Freedom of God', in Paul S. Fiddes (ed.), *Reflections on the Water: Understanding God and the World through the Baptism of Believers* (Regent's Study Guides, 4; Oxford: Regent's Park College/Macon, GA: Smyth and Helwys, 1996), p. 25; Brian Haymes, 'Towards a Sacramental Understanding of Preaching', in Anthony R. Cross and Philip E. Thompson (eds), *Baptist Sacramentalism* (Studies in Baptist History and Thought, 5; Carlisle: Paternoster Press, 2003), p. 269; and see especially John Colwell, below.

[3] Martin Luther, *Prelude on the Babylonian Captivity of the Church*, 2.62-63; *D. Martin Luthers Werke: Kritische Gesamtausgabe* (60 vols; Weimar: Hermann Böhlau, 1888), VI, p. 520.

human action', while 'no sacrament is God's prison'.[4] The notion of *ex opere operato* thus appears to be an assault on the very freedom of God. It seems to be saying that when the minister performs the action, God is bound to act.

In short, the first move in recovering a Baptist understanding of the sacraments as occasions for the gracious and transforming activity of God has often been to differentiate between what is regarded as truly sacramental theology and the *ex opere operato* dogma with which the former has been too often confused. In fact, however, modern Roman Catholic sacramental theology sets itself firmly against any understanding of 'automatic grace' while still affirming its coming to us as a sheer gift of God *ex opere operato*, and it claims to be in line with its historic tradition in taking this approach. It may well, then, be timely to identify Baptist misconceptions about this concept, but equally to tease out where the real Baptist unease with the dogma might still rightly remain.

The Primacy of God's Action

In his seminal book on the sacraments, the Baptist theologian John E. Colwell offers a definition of sacrament which he intends to be in contrast to an *ex opere operato* understanding: sacrament is 'a sign through which and in which God freely accomplishes that which is signified, not in a manner that can be presumed upon or manipulated, but in a manner that is truly gracious'.[5] Here Colwell draws attention both to the primacy of God's activity *through* the sacrament and to the character of divine activity as being free and gracious. The second aspect I want to leave for a moment, in order to focus on the action of God and its relation to human actions in the sacraments of baptism and Lord's supper.

Now, the *Catechism of the Catholic Church*, drawn up following the Second Vatican Council, explicitly relates the notion of *ex opere operato* to the action of God, which 'transforms' the merely human action into a means of grace. The 'work' (*opus*) which is primary is the saving work of Christ who acts through the sacrament in the power of the Holy Spirit. It is worth quoting two paragraphs fully, and we shall return to the wording of these several times in our discussion.

> Celebrated worthily in faith, the sacraments confer the grace that they signify. They are *efficacious* because in them Christ himself is at work:[6] it is he who baptizes, he who acts in his sacraments in order to communicate the grace that each sacrament signifies. The Father always hears the prayer of his Son's Church which, in the epiclesis of each sacrament, expresses her faith in the power of the Spirit. As

---

[4] John E. Colwell, 'The Sacramental Nature of Ordination', in Cross and Thompson (eds), Baptist Sacramentalism, p. 241; cf. John E. Colwell, *Promise and Presence: An Exploration of Sacramental Theology* (Carlisle: Paternoster, 2005), p. 9.

[5] Colwell, *Promise and Presence*, p. 11, in the context of a refutation of *ex opere operato* on p. 9; cf. p. 29.

[6] Christ is *auctor* of the sacraments, the 'author' and 'actor': Ambrose, *De sacramentis* IV.4.13; Augustine, *Contra Litteras Petitiani* 2.24.57.

fire transforms into itself everything it touches, so the Holy Spirit transforms into the divine life whatever is subjected to his power.

This is the meaning of the Church's affirmation that the sacraments act *ex opere operato* (literally: 'by the very fact of the action's being performed'), i.e., by virtue of the saving work of Christ, accomplished once for all. It follows that 'the sacrament is not wrought by the righteousness of either the celebrant or the recipient, but by the power of God.'[7] From the moment that a sacrament is celebrated in accordance with the intention of the Church, the power of Christ and his Spirit acts in and through it, independently of the personal holiness of the minister. Nevertheless, the fruits of the sacraments also depend on the disposition of the one who receives them.[8]

It can be claimed that this dynamic understanding of grace in the sacrament ('the power of Christ and his Spirit acts in and through it') is not just modern, but was originally intended by the Council of Trent. The Argentinian Dominican theologian Jorge Scampini argues that the Council was concerned to correct the view that sacraments were 'things' that people had at their disposal. The vocabulary of the Council, including *ex opere operato*, was intended to establish that the sacraments were (judges Scampini), 'ecclesial actions provided with a dynamism that comes from God and that human beings do not "produce" by themselves'.[9] In this it would be recalling the view of Thomas Aquinas that the 'matter' of the sacraments included the actions as well as the corporeal elements; also necessary were the words of the minister, declaring the gospel, which Aquinas regarded as the 'form' of the sacrament.[10] The very formula *ex opere operato* was intended, then, to affirm the primacy of God's action over the minister's action, and the corollary was that God acted despite the 'personal holiness' of the minister or the lack of it. The minister must intend to act in accord with the intentions of the church, as both Trent and the *Catechism* underline, but otherwise the action of God has an objectivity over against the worthiness of the human actor.

This doctrine did (and does) not necessarily entail an objectivity regardless of the faith of the *recipient* of the sacrament, but it is certainly a shortcoming of Trent to be virtually silent on the matter of faith, apart from stressing the need for the recipient not to 'place any obstacles' in the way of grace.[11] Here the Council shows its limitations, in shaping its statements in refutation of what it saw as the inadequate subjectivity of Luther's stress on faith. In face of Luther's personalistic and 'existential' approach to the sacraments, the Council responded with objective

---

[7] Here quoting from Aquinas, *Summa Theologiae* 3a.68.8.
[8] *Catechism of the Catholic Church*, 1127-28.
[9] Jorge A. Scampini, OP, 'Sacraments—Sacramentality: The "Crux" of the Doctrinal Disagreements in the Ecumenical Dialogue', unpublished paper given at the International Theological Conversations between the Baptist World Alliance and the Roman Catholic Church, Rome, 2-8 December 2007, p. 10. Used by permission of the author.
[10] Aquinas, *Summa Theologiae*, 3a.60.7.1.
[11] Council of Trent, Decree on the Sacraments, 6-8 (DZ-H 1606-8).

and ontological categories. We might say that the purpose of the Council was to make clear that justification comes only from the action of Christ rather than *from* human faith, echoing the Apostle Paul that we are justified by grace *through* faith. As we shall see, it took the Second Vatican Council and subsequent Catholic theology to restore the balance between the objective and the subjective, while not rejecting the *opus operatum*.

The doctrine of grace *ex opere operato* was thus intended to magnify the gracious action of God, and hence the irrelevance of the personal holiness of the minister, and not to deny the need for faith. This fact is shown by the origin of the phrase itself, which comes from the area of moral theology rather than sacramental theology.[12] The original context was discussion about the ceremonies of the old covenant and the works of the law, when Peter of Poitiers distinguished between the objective act (*opus operatum*: the work performed) and the moral intention of the action (*opus operans*: the performing of the work). The worthy nature of the Jewish ceremonies, he affirmed, lay in the intention with which the work was performed, for instance the spirit of charity (*ex opere operantis*) rather than the objective fact of the work (*ex opere operatum*). What really mattered, he stressed, was the intention and motives of the person doing the work.[13] When applied later to sacramental theology by Aquinas and Bonaventure, the opposite conclusion was drawn.[14] The effect of the Christian sacraments came from the action itself, not from the moral intention of the person acting, in baptizing or breaking bread. Significantly, a contrast was drawn here with the 'sacraments' of the old covenant such as animal sacrifice; *they* had an effect only because of the intentions of the heart of those performing them. The phrase *ex opere operato* was not then meant to point to any automatic effect of the sacraments, but to emphasize the grace of God received through them.

The Question of Causation

There ought then to be no quarrel with the doctrine of *ex opere operato* on the grounds that it supposedly elevates the action of the minister over the action of God and the saving work of Christ. Rather, it does just the opposite: God's work (*opus*) transforms the work (*opus*) of the minister, 'as fire transforms into itself whatever it touches'. Some traditional Baptist misconceptions therefore need to be swept away. However, there is still likely to be a Baptist objection to the notion of divine activity that it assumes, and we must identify carefully what it is. We see that the idea depends on a simultaneity of different kinds of causation. Grace is caused *both* by the action of the minister and by the action of God, although God's action is always more important and is the origin and cause of the human action. Here the

---

[12] For the following discussion, see Edward Schillebeeckx, *L'Économie Sacramentelle du Salut* (Freiburg: Academic Press, 2004), pp. 158-60; Scampini, 'Sacraments—Sacramentality', pp. 24-7.

[13] Petrus Pictaviensis, *Sententiarum Libri Quinque*, 5.6.

[14] See Aquinas, *Scriptum Super IV Libros Sententiarum*, 4.d.1.1.a5, cf. *Summa Theologiae*, 3a.64.5, 8; Bonaventure, *In IV Libros Sententiarum*, 4.d.1.5.

discussion of Aquinas is definitive, who distinguishes three actions happening at once in the action of the sacrament: there is the action of the triune God who causes grace in a primary way; there is the action of the humanity of Christ who obtained salvation for us; and there is the act of the minister who celebrates the sacrament.[15] Drawing on the four categories of cause in Aristotle (material, formal, efficient and final),[16] Aquinas affirms that all three actions in the sacrament are 'efficient causes'. That is, they are the origin of change or movement in something else; with regard to grace received through the sacrament, in their own way they all 'cause grace'.

We must however distinguish between the *kind* of efficient cause that these agents exert. Here Aquinas makes two further important distinctions. The first is that all causes in the world are only 'secondary', while God remains the 'primary' cause of everything that happens. Created things *are* really causal; for example, when a mother gives birth to a child it is indeed the mother who is causing the child to be born, but both mother and child exist and undergo change by virtue of God. God, he argues, 'works through intermediaries. For God governs the lower through the higher, not from any impotence on his part, but from the abundance of his goodness imparting to creatures also the dignity of causing'.[17] God is operative in every creaturely cause, so that the actions of creatures are always God's action: 'God is the cause of everything's action inasmuch as he gives everything the power to act, and preserves it in being...'[18] It is important to realize that Aquinas does not just mean that God gave this power to created things once upon a time, far back in a past creation; he gives the power here and now in continuous creative activity. This is a basic principle of *mediation* in creation to which I wish to return. So with regard to the sacrament, God is the primary cause of the minister's effective action. But more than this, with regard to efficient causes, Aquinas introduces a second distinction: that between 'principal' and 'instrumental' causes. While a principal efficient cause produces an effect because of its *own form*, an instrumental efficient cause makes an effect only because it is moved by another agent. So the sacrament causes grace, not because the created materials or the actions of the minister have in themselves power to produce grace, but because God uses them as an instrument to bring grace about.

> It is necessary to say that the sacraments of the New Law do cause grace in some way... *There are two kinds of efficient causes, principal and instrumental.* The principal cause produces its effect in virtue of its form, to which that effect is assimilated, as fire warms in virtue of its own heat. Now it belongs to God alone to produce grace in this way as its principal cause. For grace is nothing else than a

---

[15] Aquinas, *Summa Theologiae*, 3a.61.1; 62.5.
[16] The material cause is that from which something is made; the formal cause is the form or pattern of something which is expressed by its definition; the efficient cause is the origin of change in something, or the relation of a maker to what is made; the final cause is the end or purpose for which something is done: see Aristotle, *Metaphysics* V.765.
[17] Aquinas, *Summa Theologiae*, 1a.22.3.
[18] Aquinas, *De Potentia*, 3.7.

certain shared similitude to the divine nature... An instrumental cause, on the other hand, acts not in virtue of its own form, but solely in virtue of the impetus imparted to it by the principal agent. Here the effect has a likeness not to the instrument, but rather to the principal agent.[19]

Aquinas goes on to give the rather homely illustration that a bed does not resemble the axe that carved it (the instrument), but the design in the mind of the carpenter. So the grace produced by the sacraments does not have a likeness to the material of the sacraments or the action of the minister but only to God, or more exactly to the life, death and resurrection of Christ. Thus sacraments effect grace thanks to their instrumental virtue, as moved by Christ (*ex virtute Christi*), the only one who justifies. Only Christ elevates the instrument into a sacrament which gives grace, acting through it in the power of the Spirit. Timothy McDermott takes up the image of the axe, and comments,

> The rituals are tools, the cutting edge of which is their symbolic representation of Christ's sacrifice, tools actually being wielded in history by Christ...the sacraments are visible historical gestures of Christ in the present world. They are the outward bodily tools of the life of unity with God, just as kisses and embraces are the outward bodily tools of love between human beings.[20]

Now, a Baptist approach to the sacraments will certainly want to underline the language of instrumentality here. Recent Baptist writing on sacrament affirms that God *uses* the materials of bread, wine and water, and the actions of the minister in breaking, pouring and immersing, in order to meet with people in a way that transforms their lives.[21] God uses these created things as the means to embrace men and women and to deepen the love they have for God. God *uses* the water of baptism to plunge us more deeply into the death of Christ in order to raise us to newness of life. God *uses* the bread and wine of the Lord's supper to draw us more deeply into the nourishment of person and community that flows from the inner life of God. Baptists will, however, become uncomfortable with the idea that these instruments are an 'efficient cause' of grace, even within the complex distinctions that Aquinas

---

[19] Aquinas, *Summa Theologiae*, 3a.62.1, trans. by Brian Davies, *The Thought of Thomas Aquinas* (Oxford: Oxford University Press, 1993), p. 351; italics added.

[20] Timothy McDermott, *St Thomas Aquinas, Summa Theologiae: A Concise Translation* (Allen, TX: Christian Classics, 1989), p. 543.

[21] E.g., G.R. Beasley-Murray, *Baptism in the New Testament* (London: Macmillan, 1963), pp. 264-66; Stanley Grenz, *Theology for the Community of God* (Nashville, TN: Broadman and Holman, 1994), pp. 672-73; Paul S. Fiddes, *Tracks and Traces: Baptist Identity in Church and Theology* (Studies in Baptist History and Thought, 13; Carlisle: Paternoster, 2003), pp. 107-108; Timothy George, 'The Sacramentality of the Church: An Evangelical Baptist Perspective', in Cross and Thompson (eds), *Baptist Sacramentalism*, pp. 29-30; Stanley K. Fowler, *More Than a Symbol: The British Baptist Recovery of Baptist Sacramentalism* (Studies in Baptist History and Thought, 2; Carlisle: Paternoster Press, 2002), pp. 210-11.

introduces. For Aquinas, and for the doctrine of grace *ex opere operato*, the material elements and human actions are still efficient causes, even though they act *ex virtute instrumentali*. A typical Baptist reaction is to be found in the study of the sacraments by John Colwell, whose whole approach depends on distinguishing between 'efficient' and 'instrumental' means of grace, insisting that 'God and God alone is the *efficient* or *first* cause of grace in any sacrament',[22] and that 'all too easily we confuse an instrumental cause with an efficient cause'.[23] While Colwell writes appreciatively of Aquinas, the distinction he makes is not exactly Thomist, since Aquinas—as we have seen—clearly thinks that 'there are two kinds of *efficient* causes, principal and instrumental'.[24]

Here, I suggest, is the root of Baptist discomfort with all notions that the sacraments 'confer grace', 'impart grace', 'effect grace' or 'make grace present', language used by many sacramental theologians even when they do not subscribe to the principle of grace *ex opere operatum*. The *Catechism of the Catholic Church* uses this kind of language when it offers a definition of sacrament, after reminding us that the sacraments were instituted by Christ:

> The sacraments are perceptible signs (words and actions) accessible to our human nature. By the action of Christ and the power of the Holy Spirit they make present efficaciously the grace that they signify.[25]

Instead of the expression 'make present efficaciously', we will want to say that God uses the sacraments to *make God's self present*. Grace, indeed, is not a substance or charge of energy; it is nothing less than the gracious presence and activity of God, renewing and transforming created things, persons and communities. It is the gracious self-giving of Father, Son and Holy Spirit, a dynamic interaction of giving and receiving in love which God opens up to created beings so that we can participate in this flow of relations. Sacraments are places where this participation happens in a special way; to use the rather old-fashioned language of George Beasley-Murray about baptism, they are 'trysting-places' where lovers meet.[26] Resistance to the idea that sacraments 'cause' grace is not just a quibble about words, or a failure to understand a subtle and complex theory of causation. Of course, the doctrine that sacraments 'confer grace' intends to say that God is the 'primary' cause and the 'principal efficient' cause of this grace. The doctrine of grace *ex opere operato*, whether in Aquinas or the Council of Trent, intends to draw attention to the dynamic nature of divine activity, but it functions in a way that undermines such dynamism,

---

[22] Colwell, *Promise and Presence*, p. 8.

[23] Colwell, *Promise and Presence*, p. 60.

[24] Aquinas, *Summa Theologiae*, 3a.62.1. Aquinas explicitly rejects the view that sacraments 'are the cause of grace not by their own operation, but in so far as God causes grace in the soul when the sacraments are employed'—which would be an instrumental non-efficient cause. Aquinas dismisses this as a 'mere sign'.

[25] *Catechism of the Catholic Church*, 1084.

[26] Beasley-Murray, *Baptism in the New Testament*, p. 305.

by short-circuiting the necessary difference between divine and human activity. There must be a non-identity between the two in order to have the act of 'identification' of one with the other. To 'convey' grace[27] is not at all the same as to 'confer' grace.

There is nothing less than a vision of divine action in the world at stake here. The sacramental actions of breaking, pouring and immersing are held *within* the actions of the Trinity which are active movements of originating (Father), responding (Son) and opening up relations and the future (Holy Spirit) or passive movements of being glorified (Father), being sent (Son) and being breathed out (Holy Spirit). Human movements, whether ritual or everyday, cannot be said to *cause* the divine movements of self-giving (i.e., grace), but they can respond to them, reflect them and become carriers of them. God identifies God's self with them, as the pattern of human movements of self-sacrificial love fit over and match the divine pattern. While Hugh of St Victor (the first to write a treatise on the sacraments) defined a sacrament as 'a corporeal or material element set before the sense without…and *containing* by sanctification some invisible and spiritual grace',[28] we should rather say that the elements *are contained in* grace, sharing in the gracious outpouring of the triune persons. The actions are performative, but only in the sense that they are occasions for *God* to perform the work of salvation. Resistance to the language of sacramental efficacy is not to assert that the symbols merely signify, for God is present to make actual what is signified.

Calvin was perhaps reacting in a similar way to the scholastic theory of causation when he wrote the following against the notion of *ex opere operato*:

> It is here proper to remind the reader that all the trifling talk of the sophists concerning the *opus operatum* is not only false, but repugnant to the very nature of sacraments, which God appointed in order that believers, who are void and in want of all good, might bring nothing of their own, but simply beg. Hence it follows, that in receiving them they do nothing which deserves praise, and that in this action—which in respect of them is merely passive—no work can be ascribed to them.[29]

I hope it has become clear that the notion of *ex opere operato* is not at all 'repugnant' to the nature of sacraments, and precisely affirms that believers can only 'beg' and can do 'nothing which deserves praise'. But, beyond the polemic, Calvin is reaching towards the point that the action of the sacraments cannot be said to cause the 'good' that God offers. The seventeenth-century Baptist Benjamin Keach is surely moving in the same direction when he quotes with approval the words of the Puritan Stephen Charnock, 'Baptism is a means of conveying…Grace, when the Spirit is pleased to operate with it; but it doth not work as a physical Cause upon the Soul as a Purge doth upon the Humours of the Body: for 'tis the Sacrament of

---

[27] See Fiddes, *Tracks and Traces*, pp. 117-19.

[28] Hugh of St Victor, *De Sacramentis*, 1.9.2, italics added.

[29] Calvin, *Institutes*, 4.14.26, translation from John Calvin, *Institutes of the Christian Religion* (trans. J. Beveridge; 2 vols; London: James Clarke, 1949), II, p. 511.

Regeneration'.[30] I do want to take issue, however, with Calvin's view that the human action is 'merely passive'. It is both the active and the passive aspects of the ritual act that God takes and uses, taking up an obedient human response and making it the place for grace.

This discussion of causation opens up issues of God's action in the world beyond the sacraments of the church, that is, beyond the ritual acts that are claimed to be instituted by Christ—two in the view of the Reformers and seven according to the Catholic teaching of Trent. Those who affirm that sacraments 'cause' grace are usually nervous about extending this principle to objects and actions beyond the nominated sacraments. The Roman Catholic Church has distinguished sharply between the seven sacraments that 'cause' grace *ex opere operato*, other practices of the church (often called 'sacramentals'), and actions and things in the world that God may use to teach, instruct and encounter people. As we have already seen, in Scholastic thought the temple ceremonies of Old Testament worship, prefiguring Christ, were not truly sacraments as they only had an effect *ex opere operantis* (according to the spirit of love and charity with which they were performed). But if God acts through the sacraments which are materials of the created world we might expect to see a continuity of divine action between the dominical sacraments (whether two or seven), other 'sacramental' acts in the church, and objects in the wider world that God takes and uses as a medium for transforming power. The universe is sacramental in that God is present and active within it, taking the multiple and diverse bodies of the world as a means of encounter with created beings.[31] While God does not have a body in the way that we are embodied, God commits God's own self to bodies as a meeting-place with us.[32] Few poets have as eloquently expressed the sacramental body of the world than Gerard Manley Hopkins, finding both the lordship and the sacrifice of Christ in the swooping flight of a falcon, or greeting Christ with a *sursum corda* in the eucharistic grain of the harvest fields below and the drifting clouds above:

> Summer ends now; now, barbarous in beauty, the stooks arise
>   Around; up above, what wind-walks! what lovely behaviour
>   Of silk-sack clouds! has wilder, wilful-wavier
> Meal-drift moulded ever and melted across skies?

---

[30] Benjamin Keach, *Gold Refin'd: or Baptism in its Primitive Purity* (London, 1689), p. 173.

[31] See Leonardo Boff, *The Sacraments of Life, Life of the Sacraments* (trans. John Drury; Washington DC: Pastoral Press, 1987).

[32] Paul S. Fiddes, *Participating in God: A Pastoral Doctrine of the Trinity* (London: Darton, Longman and Todd, 2000), p. 279.

I walk, I lift up, I lift up heart, eyes,
Down all that glory in the heavens to glean our Saviour...[33]

In opposition to the Roman Catholic distinction between Christian sacraments and the temple ceremonies of old Israel, Calvin affirmed that the rites of the old dispensation as well as some natural signs recorded in the Old Testament (the rainbow, the burning bush) were equally sacraments because they were 'seals of the promises of God'.[34] We may go further and say that there is warrant in scripture for believing that God has promised to be present in the whole of nature and the human world, and that any object, act or word can become sacramental. To the objection that 'to presume the sacramentality of all creation is to undermine the sacramentality of specific signs within creation',[35] we may reply that signs signify in different ways and in different degrees. The signs instituted by Christ within the church are a 'focus' of God's presence and activity, which give us the necessary clue or key by which we can notice a sacramentality elsewhere. They form such a focus because the breaking of bread, pouring out of wine and immersion into water 'fit into' the movements of self-giving love within God in a particularly close way, recalling as they do the events of the life, death and resurrection of Christ. The 'match' is more exact than with other signs. It is from that viewpoint that we can go on to notice bread and wine in the sand and light of R.S. Thomas' eucharist of the sea,[36] or the eucharistic harvest in the fields of grain and the clouds of the sky with Gerard Manley Hopkins, or 'the mass on the world' of Teilhard de Chardin, who pours into his chalice 'all the sap which is to be pressed out this day from the earth's fruits'. We shall also notice, with Teilhard, the breaking and pouring out of self in the many acts of sacrificial care among people in society — 'all the labours and sufferings of the world'.[37]

A theory of causal efficacy in the sacraments requires a theology of agency, an identity of the ministerial agent with the agency of Christ, which is difficult to extend to a sacramentality of the whole world. Moreover, there are philosophical and moral problems with Aquinas' basic theory of double agency, which is the background for his distinction between primary and instrumental efficient causes. If all actions in the world have God as their primary cause, does this leave the created world with enough of its own freedom? If all actions are ultimately the work of God, is God implicated too directly in evil acts? It would be better to think of God's actions in the world as persuasive rather than coercive, enticing creation at all levels

---

[33] Gerard Manley Hopkins, 'Hurrahing in Harvest', in W.H. Gardner and N.H. Mackenzie (eds), *Poems of Gerard Manley Hopkins* (Oxford: Oxford University Press, 1967), p. 70.

[34] Calvin, *Institutes*, 4.14.23-26.

[35] Colwell, *Promise and Presence*, p. 55; William Cavanaugh, *Torture and Eucharist: Theology, Politics and the Body of Christ* (Oxford: Blackwell, 1998), p. 13.

[36] R.S. Thomas, 'In Great Waters', in *Frequencies* (1978), repr. in R.S. Thomas, *Collected Poems 1945-1990* (London: Phoenix Press, 2001), p. 351.

[37] Teilhard de Chardin, *Hymn of the Universe* (trans. S. Bartholomew; London: Collins, 1965), p. 14.

to respond to God's purposes of love.[38] As created things and created beings are held within the movements of the triune life, they are influenced by those movements, and so express well or poorly the grace of God. They signify, or fail to signify the salvation God offers, and so appear or fail to appear as sacraments. Theories of instrumental causation have their place in physical descriptions of the world. But when we are thinking of God's offer of grace, we need to replace these theories with a theology of participation. A vision of participation in God provides for both a continuity and a distinction between the sacraments of the church and sacraments in the world. By contrast, a theology of instrumental causes, on which *ex opere operatum* depends, is likely to restrict us to sacraments within the church.

God's Action and Faith

John Macquarrie accepts the teaching that Christ is the true minister of every sacrament and that this overrules any defect on the part of the human minister. However, he voices a typical objection when he goes on to write, 'I doubt if one should go on from this to the doctrine of *ex opere operato*...the view that the operation of a sacrament is entirely objective'.[39] He rightly urges that we must reject either a purely objective or purely subjective view of what is accomplished in the sacraments, and so must give an essential place to their reception in faith. As I have already suggested, however, the dogma does not *exclude* the necessity for faith in the recipient; the articulation of it by the Council of Trent is simply silent (or almost silent) on the issue, for reasons of its historical context. Faith is removed from the centre of the actual dynamic activity of the sacrament (*ex opere operato*) and demoted to a pre-condition which the individual needs for coming to the altar.[40] The Second Vatican Council has resoundingly broken this silence with its stress on the sacraments as 'sacraments of faith', affirming that

> The purpose of the sacraments is to sanctify men [sic.], to build up the body of Christ, and, finally, to give worship to God. Because they are signs they also instruct. They not only presuppose faith, but by words and objects they also nourish, strengthen and express it; that is why they are called 'sacraments of faith'. They do indeed impart grace, but, in addition, the very act of celebrating them most effectively disposes the faithful to receive the grace in a fruitful manner, to worship God duly, and to practice charity.[41]

Here the Council recalls Aquinas in his understanding of the sacraments as 'signs of faith', and adds that they also nourish and strengthen faith. However, faith is

---

[38] I have worked this out in detail in my *Participating in God*, pp. 131-48.
[39] John Macquarrie, *A Guide to the Sacraments* (London: SCM Press, 1997), p. 51.
[40] Council of Trent, *Decree on the Sacraments*, 11 (Dz-H 1611).
[41] Vatican II, *Sacrosanctum Concilium*, 59; translation from Austin Flannery, OP, (ed.), *Vatican Council II: The Conciliar and Post Conciliar Documents* (Dublin: Dominican Publications, 1977), p. 20.

understood as being necessary for 'receiving grace in a fruitful manner', an expression echoed by the *Catechism* when it affirms that 'the fruits of the sacraments depend on the disposition of those who receive them'. God acts, irrespective of faith, but faith is needed to receive this action in a way that bears fruit in the believer's life. This falls short of affirming that there can be no act (*opus*) of God at all without the presence of faith, that there can be no 'lovers' meeting' without both partners.

Here Karl Barth has a relevant insight about God's speaking of God's word. While, he affirms, God does not need human faith to speak the word, God never speaks into the world except where there *is* an effect in a human life. Revelation is always the act of the triune God: there is not only a revealer (God the Father) and a revelation (Jesus Christ) but a 'being revealed', the work of the Holy Spirit in a human person, evoking and creating faith.[42] Barth means that God does not speak out into the void, like an eternal radio broadcast which continues remorselessly whether there are listeners or not; God's speaking is always an encounter with human partners, for as the prophet says, 'My word shall not return to me empty' (Isa. 55.11). There can be no revelation without reception. Now, in the course of defending grace *ex opere operato* as grace that flows from the act (*opus*) of Christ, Edward Schillebeeckx at first distinguishes between the 'validity' and the 'fruitfulness' of the sacrament in the manner of Vatican II: 'the sacrament remains a real pledge of [Christ's] love even when man does not respond to it'. He then, however, takes a further step (though writing in advance of the Council's decree), based on understanding the sacrament as an encounter between the disciple and Christ:

> The sense and purpose of the whole sacramental event is to bring about the encounter with Christ. Since such an encounter must involve both parties, the religious intent of the recipient...*belongs to the essence of any authentic sacrament*; one, that is, which is a personal encounter with the living God.[43]

It is in line with this perception that Jorge Scampini proposes that 'Classical theology used to say, "There is no fruitful sacrament without the subject's faith", but contemporary theology says instead: "there is no sacramental event without faith".'[44] Again, he affirms that 'there cannot be a gift of grace without the exertion of faith'.[45]

Such statements see the necessity of faith as included within the very concept of *ex opere operato*, not just a subjective appendix to it. With such an understanding Baptists might well be pleased. Baptists should also agree that the faith in view is

---

[42] Karl Barth, *Church Dogmatics* (trans. and ed. G.W. Bromiley and T.F. Torrance; 14 vols; Edinburgh: T&T Clark, 1936–77), I/1, pp. 140-43, 329-32.

[43] Edward Schillebeeckx, *Christ the Sacrament of Encounter with God* (London: Sheed and Ward, 1963), p. 164, my italics.

[44] Scampini, 'Sacraments—Sacramentality', p. 28.

[45] Scampini, 'Sacraments—Sacramentality', p. 28.

both that of the individual person and the church, working alongside each other. But for a Roman Catholic theologian, the faith which is present in the sacrament might—in one case—*only* be the faith of the church. This is, of course, the case of infant baptism. However, it is significant that Roman Catholic doctrine insists on the 'completion'[46] of Christian initiation in the sacrament of confirmation, in which there is opportunity both for a personal confession of faith of the disciple himself or herself, and for the disciple to be enriched with a 'special strength' of the Holy Spirit to spread and defend the faith.[47] Through confirmation, believers share 'more completely' in the mission of Jesus Christ and the fullness of the Holy Spirit, are 'more deeply' rooted in the divine filiation and are united 'more firmly' to Christ.[48]

For at least the last thirty years, Baptists have been suggesting in various ecumenical conversations that baptism should not be treated as an isolated event, but should be placed in the context of a process of Christian initiation that is wider than the act of baptism itself.[49] It might then, it is urged, be possible to recognize that Christians of different confessions have all been engaged in a 'common initiation', where Baptists are resistant to affirming a 'common baptism'. In addition to the technical language of 'process' in discussing initiation, Baptists have also been promoting the phrase 'journey of Christian beginnings' which seems more accessible on a popular level. They have been insisting that baptism is only one point, though certainly the focal one, on the journey into faith and the Christian life. The image of 'journey' ought of course to be applied to the *whole* life of a Christian disciple, beginning from the prevenient work of the Spirit of God in the human heart and stretching forward into eternity; what is being suggested here is that there is an opening section of the journey which belongs appropriately to the phase of beginnings, or initiation. Such a journey of beginnings will include nurture within the Christian community, an act of conscious faith by the disciple, baptism itself, a receiving of the gifts of the Spirit, a commissioning to participate in God's mission in the world, and sharing in the eucharist or Lord's supper for the first time. For some—those coming to faith at a mature age—the journey will be relatively rapid, but for others—especially children who are brought up within the church—it will be

---

[46] Roman Ritual, *Rite of Confirmation* (OC), Introduction 1.

[47] Vatican II, *Lumen Gentium*, 11; cf. *Rite of Confirmation*, Introduction, 2.

[48] *Catechism of the Catholic Church*, 1303.

[49] See the Response of the Baptist Union of Great Britain in Max Thurian (ed.), *Churches Respond to BEM: Official Responses to the 'Baptism, Eucharist and Ministry' Text* (6 vols; Faith and Order Papers 129, 132, 135, 137, 143-44; Geneva: WCC Publications, 1986–88), I, p. 71; *Baptism and Church Membership, with particular reference to Local Ecumenical Partnerships*. A report of a working party to Churches Together in England (London: Churches Together in England, 1996), p. 13; *Conversations Around the World 2000–2005: The Report of the International Conversations between the Anglican Communion and the Baptist World Alliance* (London: The Anglican Consultative Council and the Baptist World Alliance, 2005), pp. 44-51; *Pushing at the Boundaries of Unity: Anglicans and Baptists in Conversation* (London: Church House Publishing 2005), pp. 31-57.

slow and gradual. The language of journey is in fact used in the *Catechism of the Catholic Church*:

> From the time of the apostles, becoming a Christian has been accomplished by a *journey and initiation in several stages*. This journey can be covered rapidly or slowly, but certain essential elements will always have to be present: proclamation of the Word, acceptance of the Gospel entailing conversion, profession of faith, Baptism itself, the outpouring of the Holy Spirit, and admission to Eucharistic communion.[50]

If, then, the language of grace *ex opere operato* is understood always to include reference to an act (*opus*) of faith, then it could be a support to the understanding that where infant baptism is concerned, confirmation (involving a personal profession of faith) is 'necessary for the completion of baptismal grace'.[51]

The Constancy of God, and the Church as Sacrament

The doctrine of grace *ex opere operato* assumes not only the faith of the disciple but the faithfulness of God. The *Catechism of the Catholic Church* affirms that 'The Father always hears the prayer of his Son's Church which, in the epiclesis of each sacrament, expresses her faith in the power of the Spirit'. Given that the *opus* referred to is primarily the work of God, a confidence is being expressed that God *will* graciously act in and through the sacraments in response to the faith of the church. Is there any difference here from the emphasis that Calvin laid on the faithfulness of God to fulfill the promise at the heart of the sacrament? Baptists will, I suggest, want to follow Karl Barth in asserting that we cannot presume on the promises of God, that God freely fulfills just as he freely promises, and that the promise never becomes our possession or our right.[52] We can recognize that *some* sacramental theology in the past has, unfortunately, forgotten this divine freedom and has presumed to manipulate God. But, on the other hand, would it not be unthinkable for Christ to refuse to come to his company of believing disciples at his table, or for God to leave disciples in the grave of baptism (forsaking them at the bottom of the baptistery, as it were), declining with regret to raise them to new life? When we read the words of institution of the Lord's supper we confidently expect that Christ will 'come and sit down to a meal' with his church (Rev. 3.20); we do not wait to see whether he will or not on any particular occasion. After all, Baptists, along with other Reformed groups, have held a virtually *ex opere operato* view of Christian proclamation, in line with the early declaration of the *Second Helvetic Confession* (1566) that 'the preaching of the Word of God *is* the Word of God' (chapter 1). There is a confident expectation that God will speak to the hearers through preaching based on scripture; can the confidence in God's use of bread, wine

---

[50] *Catechism of the Catholic Church*, 1229, italics added.
[51] Roman Ritual, *Rite of Confirmation* (OC), Introduction 1.
[52] Barth, *Church Dogmatics*, IV/4, pp. 108-109.

and water be less than in God's appropriation of the human word? Since God's freedom does not mean arbitrariness, is there really any difference between confidence in the faithfulness of God to fulfill divine promises and a doctrine of grace *ex opere operato*?

There is a difference, *if* the dogma is understood to imply that the church itself is somehow a guarantee of the gracious activity of God. This has certainly been deduced from the convergence of actions envisaged by the dogma—the actions of God and of the celebrant who holds a sacramental office in the church. Confidence in God has been supplemented or enhanced by the belief that Christ has given sacramental ministries to the church, and that Christ himself is present *with* the church as his bride, and *in* the church as his body. As Hans Urs Von Balthasar expresses it,

> The Church, as 'Bride', continually receives her being and life from the wellsprings of God-made-man; they are not her own creation. This is evident, according to the principle of incarnation, in the fact that it is the office instituted by Christ that imparts to the Church the life-giving substance in the sacrament of the eucharist.[53]

We should recognize that this is not a static view of an institution, as it is often accused of being. Von Balthasar here combines the abiding form and structure of the church with a dynamic sense of event; God is 'continually' giving God's own self to the church as a free gift, and this cannot be controlled by human beings.[54] 'God's arrival in the form of a covenant occurs freely', he stresses.[55] Covenant, he emphasizes, involves a free and gracious gift, unlike a contract. Likewise, Karl Rahner asserts that, despite Protestant criticism, there is an 'actualistic' element in the Catholic understanding of the being and action of the church; it is only an organism which 'dispenses grace' because of the continuous work of the unmerited grace of God which is 'not at man's free disposal'.[56] So let us ask again: is there really any difference between affirming that God gives God's self freely in the sacraments, and affirming that God freely gives God's self to the *church* whose ministry then guarantees God's further self-gift in the sacraments? Is it not in the end all a matter of confidence in God's faithfulness?

I suggest that there *is* a difference which Baptists will feel strongly. It would be unjust to conclude that the dogma of *ex opere operato* must inevitably encourage an attempt to 'manipulate' God. That some have misused it in this way does not mean that this is its true intent, and we should clear our minds of this accusation. But Baptists will always want to see the church as formed *by* the presence of Christ—in

---

[53] Hans Urs Von Balthasar, *Theo-Drama: Theological Dramatic Theory*: Volume 3. *Dramatis Personae: The Person in Christ* (trans. G. Harrison; San Francisco, CA: Ignatius Press, 1992), p. 355.

[54] Hans Urs Von Balthasar, *The Office of Peter and the Structure of the Church* (trans. André Emery; San Francisco, CA: Ignatius Press, 1986), pp. 288-89.

[55] Von Balthasar, *Theo-Drama*, III, p. 337.

[56] Karl Rahner, *Theological Investigations*: Volume 4. *Concerning Vatican II* (trans. K-H. and B. Kruger; London: Darton, Longman and Todd, 1974), p. 292.

the preaching of the word, in the sacraments and in the church meeting. The risen Christ stands in the congregation which is under his rule; it is his body, but he remains the head.[57] From the beginning Baptists have regarded the ordained ministry as a gift of Christ to his church, and have understood the administration of the sacraments *normally* to be the minister's Christ-given responsibility and privilege.[58] But to see the office as somehow *assuring* or *guaranteeing* the coming of Christ to his church in the sacraments reverses the direction of the rule of Christ, even when it is believed that the guarantee has been given by Christ in the first place. Baptists have understood that the congregation shares in the threefold ministry of Christ as prophet, priest and king, and so has the 'priestly' authority to administer the sacraments without sanction from other human powers,[59] but the ground for confidence that Christ acts in the sacraments relates to his priestly office alone. Emphasis on the freedom of God is essential to sacramental theology, as Baptists have made clear in recent years,[60] but it seems to be a misdirected critique of the concept of grace *ex opere operato*; the point is really to ask from where we draw our assurance that God will be faithful freely to fulfill the divine promise to be present.

It is in this context of the rule of Christ in the congregation that Baptists can affirm the sacramentality of the *church*. In recent years, the identification of the church with Christ, who is the primal sacrament, has led to the confession that the church itself is a sacrament. This can, of course, reinforce the idea that the institution of the church ensures the divine action in the sacraments, and it has certainly been appealed to in this way. Rahner, for instance, finds that the principle of the church as a sacrament of grace accounts for 'the connection between *opus operatum* and the causality of the sacraments in relation to grace'.[61] But the idea can equally make clear that Christ is using his church as a means of his ministry in the world. Baptist understanding of the Lord's supper has always stressed the overlap between the 'body of Christ' as held forth in bread, and the 'body of Christ' lived as the congregation. In some way, sharing in the Lord's supper deepens not only the

---

[57] In contrast to the Roman Catholic doctrine that 'the Church is the whole Christ, body and head'.

[58] E.g., *Second London Confession* (1677), ch. XXVI.8, in William L. Lumpkin (ed.), *Baptist Confessions of Faith* (Philadelphia, PA: Judson Press, rev. edn, 1959), p. 287; *An Orthodox Creed* (1679), Art. XXXIII, in Lumpkin (ed.), *Baptist Confessions*, p. 321. Ministerial administration of the sacraments is usually seen as normative practice and a matter of good order rather than a legal exclusiveness; see Michael J. Walker, *Baptists at the Table: The Theology of the Lord's Supper amongst English Baptists in the Nineteenth Century* (Didcot: Baptist Historical Society, 1992), pp. 131-37.

[59] See, e.g., *A Declaration of Faith* (1611), art. 9, in Lumpkin (ed.), *Baptist Confessions*, p. 119; the *London Confession* (1644), arts. X, XIII and XXIV, in Lumpkin (ed.), *Baptist Confessions*, pp. 159–60, 166; the *Second London Confession* (1677), ch. VIII.1, in Lumpkin (ed.), *Baptist Confessions*, p. 260.

[60] Ellis, 'Baptism and the Sacramental Freedom of God', pp. 33-35, 41-42; Colwell, *Promise and Presence*, pp. 9-10, 24-28.

[61] Karl Rahner, *The Church and the Sacraments: Quaestiones Disputatae 9* (Freiburg: Herder, 1963), p. 40.

relationship of Christ with the individual believer, but the presence of Christ in his gathered people. The real presence of Christ is manifested in the community of the church, as it becomes more truly the body of Christ broken for the life of the world. This was an insight firmly grasped by Zwingli, despite the popular view that he held to a 'mere memorialism'; commenting on the words of Paul in 1 Corinthians 10.17 that 'we who are many are one body because we all eat of the same bread', he affirmed that 'We eat bread so that we are made into one bread... What we become by this eating...is the body of Christ.'[62] Among the General Baptists, Grantham weaves together the supper, the church and the body of Christ:

> Yea, here Christ gathers his People together at his own Table, as one Family. And it is that Table, to which all Saints are to approach with such preparation as may render them fit for communion in that Mystical Body, the Church; which is also called Christ, because of that unity they have with him, and one another in him.[63]

Among the Particular Baptists, Hercules Collins answers the question, 'What is it to eat the Body of Christ?' in the Lord's supper, by bringing together the glorified body of Christ in heaven and the church as the body of Christ on earth into the closest identity:

> It is...more and more to be united to his sacred Body, that though he be in Heaven and we on Earth, yet nevertheless we are Flesh of his Flesh, and Bone of his Bones: and as all the Members of the Body are quickened by one Soul; so are we also quickend and guided by one and the same Spirit.[64]

Thus, as the members of the church share in bread and wine, Christ takes hold more firmly of their own bodies and uses them as a means of his presence in the world. As Christ uses the physical stuff of bread and wine as a meeting-place between himself and his disciples, so he uses their bodies as a means of encountering them through each other, and as a meeting-place with those outside the church.

The specific language of church as sacrament was expressed in the Dogmatic Constitution *Lumen Gentium* of Vatican II: 'The Church, in Christ, is in the nature of sacrament—a sign and instrument, that is, of communion with God and of unity among all men'.[65] But there is correspondence here with the Baptist emphasis that we become the body of Christ by eating the bread, and so participate bodily in the mission of God in the world. Bread, wine and water are 'visible words' of God, and

---

[62] H. Zwingli, *Letter to Matthew Alber*, 16 November 1524, translated in H. Wayne Pipkin (ed.), *Huldrych Zwingli: Writings* (2 volumes; Allison Park, PA: Pickwick, 1984), II, p. 141.

[63] Thomas Grantham, *Christianismus Primitivus* (London, 1678), 2.2.7, p. 89.

[64] Hercules Collins, *An Orthodox Catechism* (London, 1680), p. 39.

[65] *Lumen Gentium*, I.1, in Flannery (ed.), *Vatican Council II*, p. 350. See Günther Gassmann, 'The Church as Sacrament, Sign and Instrument', in Gennadias Limouris (ed.), *Church, Kingdom, World: The Church as Mystery and Prophetic Sign* (Faith and Order Paper, 130; Geneva: WCC, 1986), pp. 1–17.

in the same way the church as sacrament makes Christ visible and tangible in the world, allowing people to see and touch his body as 'flesh of his flesh and bone of his bones' (Collins, above). This must apply not only to the local congregation of 'visible saints', but to the wider church. Baptists have certainly always affirmed the 'invisible church' of all the company of the redeemed, past, present and future,[66] and this might be taken as a critique of the idea that the church is a sacrament whose character is visibility.[67] But the invisibility of the whole church universal is not in conflict with the idea that the church makes the body of Christ visible on more than the local level, and it does not undermine the hope that the *part* of the church universal which is present on earth might enjoy a visible unity. Early Baptists thought that the body of Christ was more than each individual local community; as 'distinct' congregations covenanted together, they were 'all to walk by one and the same Rule...as members of one body in the common faith under Christ their onely head'.[68] The language of body is about making Christ visible: the church as sacrament can make Christ visible on many levels of human society—local, regional, national and global.

Conclusion: Sacrament as Place of Mediation and Participation

The affirmation of grace *ex opere operato*, I have been arguing, is not in itself vulnerable to the criticisms of undermining the gracious action of God, of excluding faith, or of denying the freedom of God. From a Baptist point of view, it *can* be misleading if it is understood as making the human action the cause of grace rather than the opportunity for grace to be manifested, and if it shifts the confidence of the believer from the activity of God to the offices of the church. But it can be helpful in drawing attention to the faithfulness and constancy of God, in affirming the inseparability (though not confusion) of the human and divine acts in the sacrament, and so in portraying the church itself as a sacrament in the world.

I have already mentioned that the dogma, especially in the version of it in Thomas Aquinas, relies on a certain doctrine of creation. That is, the belief that the work (*opus*) of God is always performed (*operatum*) through the mediation of worldly actions and objects. In this way, the sacraments are part of the continuous creative activity of God. While I have taken issue with the 'two-cause' theory of divine action as formulated by Aquinas, we cannot take creation seriously unless we think that God always acts in and through worldly realities, and that God is always committed to the signs of the world. This is what Karl Rahner, in a lapidary phrase,

---

[66] See, e.g., the *Second London Confession*, ch. XXVI.1, in Lumpkin (ed.), *Baptist Confessions*, p. 285.

[67] So George, 'Sacramentality of the Church', pp. 24-27.

[68] The Particular Baptist *London Confession*, art. XLVII, in Lumpkin (ed.), *Baptist Confessions*, pp. 168-69; this is virtually identical to article 38 of *A True Confession* (1596), in Lumpkin (ed.), *Baptist Confessions*, p. 94.

calls the 'mediated immediacy' of God's presence.[69] We can find the same insistence in Karl Barth's thought. Despite his later detachment of the work of the Spirit from the sign of water in baptism, earlier he was emphatic about what he called the 'secularity of the Word of God': he writes that 'the speaking of God is and remains the mystery of God supremely in its secularity'.[70] Because the Word of God always 'meets us in the garments of creaturely reality' which is marked by sin and finitude, the Word will be 'veiled' even as it is 'unveiled'. In acting through the objects and events of the world, God hides God's self in the very moment when God is revealed to us through them.[71] Here is the theological basis, in revelation, for the many hymns of devotion which greet God as 'hidden' in the sacraments, as well as for finding Christ 'hidden' in the natural world and human society.

However, there is a way of thinking about mediation here which we should avoid. Notions of mediation have, in Christian tradition, been associated with a semi-Platonic view that Christ acts as a mediator between two completely separate realms of reality, a spiritual world in which God exists, and our own messy world of the everyday. This understanding derives from Plato's distinction between the realms of 'Being' and 'Becoming', the first being a sphere of immutable perfection and the second being our own world in which things change, decay and pass away. In Plato's thought the two were mutually exclusive, as pure Being could not participate in the lower world of Becoming. There needed therefore to be a 'bridge' principle between the two, which Plato conceived as the soul, both our individual souls and a soul of the whole world.[72] It was a fatally easy move for early Christian apologists to identify Christ with the Platonic mediatorial principle, and thereby to push God out of the world which we know. We can, of course, speak of Christ as a 'mediator' in terms of restoring a broken relationship between human beings and God (1 Tim. 2.5) or as the bringer of a new covenant (Heb. 8.6), but not as an ontological mediator, a bridge between two exclusive orders of being. Christian theology still suffers from this kind of world-view, which should not be confused with the sacramental principle of mediation, or integrated with it. The sacraments do not provide a kind of first stage in bridging a gap between the world and God, which is then completed by the mediation of Christ. They do not even offer a mediation in which a mediation of this kind by Christ is contained. The triune God needs no mediator to be involved in the secular world, but uses *the world itself* as a means or mediation to draw us into participation in God's own communion of life and love

God acts in the world by enticing and attracting created beings into the unfathomable personal relations that we call God—Father, Son and Holy Spirit. God makes room within this pattern or dance of relationships for us to dwell, and the material signs of the world can be the place where this happens. This is not surprising if the physical world is itself being shaped (as I suggest above) by being

---

[69] Karl Rahner, *Foundations of Christian Faith* (trans. W. Dych; London: Darton, Longman and Todd, 1978), pp. 83-84.
[70] Barth, *Church Dogmatics*, I/1, p. 165.
[71] Barth, *Church Dogmatics*, I/1, p. 169.
[72] Plato, *Timaeus*, 35A, 41D.

held within the relational movements of God's life. The dogma of grace *ex opere operato*, while potentially misleading in several ways, may still help to remind us that there needs to be no bridge between the actions of the world and the saving acts of God. There is an infinite difference between them, but still the gracious presence of God is there precisely through 'the act as performed'.

CHAPTER 14

The Sacramentality of the Word in Gregory of Nyssa's *Catechetical Oration*: Implications for a Baptist Sacramental Theology

Steven R. Harmon

I ask you, brothers and sisters—tell me: What seems greater to you, the word of God or the Body of Christ? If you will give a true reply, you surely must say that the former is no less than the latter. Therefore, with as great anxiety as we show when Christ's Body is ministered to us, lest nothing fall out of our hands onto the ground, with as great anxiety we should see to it that God's word which is dispensed to us may not perish from our hearts because we are thinking or talking about something else. The person who hears the word of God with inattention is surely no less guilty than one who allows Christ's body to fall on the ground through his carelessness.
Caesarius of Arles[1]

An essay on the fourth-century Cappadocian father Gregory of Nyssa might initially seem an odd fit for a book on Baptist sacramental theology. While it is true that the early English Baptists once held to more truly sacramental doctrines and practices of baptism and the Lord's supper than have prevailed in the past century and that these are not inconsistent with aspects of patristic sacramental theology, these earlier Baptists were most definitely not claiming patristic precedents as warrants for what they found taught clearly enough in the Bible. Gregory of Nyssa would have been a fine candidate for such an argument for Baptist continuity with elements of pre-medieval Christianity had these Baptists been so inclined, for Gregory's insistence in his *Catechetical Oration* that the waters of baptism have no power in and of themselves to save if they are not joined with personal faith that is evidenced in a regenerated life has much in common with the Baptist rejection of any sacramental theology that smacks of an *ex opere operato* dispensing of the grace of salvation.[2]

---

[1] Caesarius of Arles, *Sermo* 78.2 (ET, *Saint Caesarius of Arles: Sermons, Volume 1* [Fathers of the Church, 31; Washington, DC: The Catholic University of America Press, 1956], p. 361).

[2] Gregory of Nyssa, *Catechetical Oration* 40: 'If, then...when we undergo this sacramental "washing" we become "clean" in our wills and wash away "the iniquities" of our souls, we become better and are changed for the better. But if the washing has only

Yet it is not on account of any similarity between the Nyssene's baptismal theology and Baptist perspectives that I have chosen to connect Gregory and Baptist sacramentalism. I am interested rather in a set of curious phenomena regarding the use of scripture in the aforementioned *Catechetical Oration*, phenomena which point toward an implicit sacramentality of the word. After exploring this feature of the *Catechetical Oration*, I will return to the theme of Baptist sacramentalism by arguing that Baptists share a similar commitment to the sacramentality of the word. This commitment, even if unacknowledged, is the proper starting point for Baptist reflection on baptism, the Lord's supper, and anything else that might be regarded as a sacrament proper or sacrament-like.

The Use of Scripture in Gregory of Nyssa's *Catechetical Oration*

Gregory of Nyssa's *Catechetical Oration* was likely neither delivered to catechumens nor addressed orally to catechists, despite the connotations of its common titles in Latin and English.[3] Titled Λόγος Κατηχητικός in the best Greek manuscripts,[4] the

---

affected the body, and the soul has failed to wash off the stains of passion, and the life after initiation is identical with that before, despite the boldness of my assertion I will say without shrinking that in such a case the water is only water, and the gift of the Holy Spirit is nowhere evident in the action' (ET, 'An Address on Religious Instruction', in E.R. Hardy and C.C. Richardson [eds], *Christology of the Later Fathers* [trans. C.C. Richardson; Library of Christian Classics; Philadelphia, PA: Westminster Press, 1954], p. 324).

[3] *Oratio catechetica magna* is the standard Latin title as listed in M. Geerard (ed.), *Clavis Patrum Graecorum* (Corpus Christianorum; Turnhout: Brepols, 1974–87), II, §3150. G.W.H. Lampe (ed.), *A Patristic Greek Lexicon* (Oxford: Clarendon Press, 1961), p. xxvii, lists the work as *Oratio catechetica*. The titles of the two most prominent English translations also hint at oral catechesis: 'The Great Catechism', trans. W. Moore, in P. Schaff and H. Wace (eds), *Nicene and Post-Nicene Fathers*, 2nd series [NPNF²] (Peabody, MA: Hendrickson, 1994), V, pp. 473-509; 'An Address on Religious Instruction', in Hardy and Richardson (eds), *Christology of the Later Fathers*, pp. 268-325.

[4] According to the apparatus in E. Mühlenberg, *Gregorii Nysseni Oratio Catechetica* (Gregorii Nysseni Opera [GNO], vol. 3, pt. 4; Leiden: E.J. Brill, 1996), p. 5, codices Venetus Marcianus gr. 67 (11th cent.), Vaticanus gr. Pii II 4 (11th cent.), Cantabrigensis Trinity College B.9.1 (11th cent.), Escorialensis Ω.III.14 (AD 1285), Londinensis Musei Britannici gr. Old Royal 16.D.1 (12th cent.), and the *textus vulgatus* of the Migne edition (AD 1858, reprint of 1573 Paris edn. of G. Hervetus) all have λόγος κατηχητικός as the title; codex Patmensis 46 (11th cent.) reads λόγος περὶ κατηχήσεως, while codex Vaticanus gr. 1907 (12th-13th cent.) gives the same title sans λόγος; the *textus vulgatus* adds ὁ μέγας ἐν κεφαλαίοις τεσσαράκοντα διῃρημένος after κατηχητικός. On the manuscripts and textual history of the *Catechetical Oration*, see GNO vol. 3, pt. 4, pp. xi-cxxxix; J.H. Srawley, 'The Manuscripts and Text of the Oratio Catechetica of St. Gregory of Nyssa', *Journal of Theological Studies* 3 (1902), pp. 421-28. On the printed editions and translations of the *Catechetical Oration*, see also F. Mann and M. Altenburger,

work was probably an epitome of Gregory's own approach to catechesis, written to equip other catechists with a comprehensive theology and strategies for theological argumentation suitable for their task. Whether the *Catechetical Oration* was oral or written and whether it addressed catechists or catechumens, Gregory hoped that by means of such theologically grounded instruction, 'the church might be increased by the addition of those who are being saved, while the trustworthy word present in the teaching[5] approaches the hearing of unbelievers'.[6]

In light of this purpose, it is somewhat surprising to discover a paucity of explicit interaction with 'the trustworthy word' in the *Catechetical Oration*. In the 101 pages of Ekkehard Mühlenberg's edition of the text in *Gregorii Nysseni Opera*, there are only thirty-five citations of scripture. This feature of the *Catechetical Oration* seems more puzzling in light of a comparison with two other patristic works of similar length and content: Athanasius' *On the Incarnation* and Augustine's *On the Catechising of the Uninstructed*. Gregory's treatise contains thirty-five biblical citations in forty-seven columns in the Migne edition, for an average of one citation approximately every one-and-a-half columns of text. By contrast, Athanasius' *On the Incarnation* has ninety-three citations in fifty Migne columns for an average of roughly two citations per column, and Augustine's *On the Catechising of the Uninstructed* has forty-six citations in thirty-nine Migne columns, over one citation per column.[7] Athanasius and Augustine wrote these treatises for somewhat

---

Bibliographie zu Gregor von Nyssa: Editionen–Übersetzungen–Literatur (Leiden: E.J. Brill, 1988), pp. 265-66, and cross-references.

[5] Here I have translated κατὰ τὴν διδαχὴν distributively.

[6] Gregory of Nyssa, *Catechetical Oration* (GNO vol. 3, pt. 4, p. 5, lines 1-5): Ὁ τῆς κατηχήσεως λόγος ἀναγκαῖος μέν ἐστι τοῖς προεστηκόσι τοῦ μυστηρίου τῆς εὐσεβείας, ὡς ἂν πληθύνοιτο τῇ προσθήκῃ τῶν σωζομένων ἡ ἐκκλησία, τοῦ κατὰ τὴν διδαχὴν πιστοῦ λόγου τῇ ἀκοῇ τῶν ἀπίστων προσαγομένου (cf. 1 Tim. 3.16; Acts 2.47; Tit. 1.9). Although Moore's translation of ὁ τῆς κατηχήσεως λόγος ἀναγκαῖος μέν ἐστι τοῖς προεστηκόσι τοῦ μυστηρίου τῆς εὐσεβείας as 'The presiding ministers of the "mystery of godliness" have need of a system in their instructions' (NPNF[2] vol. 5, p. 473) is certainly consistent with the overarching purpose of the *Catechetical Oration* as providing catechists with a systematic theology proper to their task, λόγος is more naturally understood here as a reference to the oral discourse of catechetical instruction: thus I have translated this as 'The word of instruction is indeed indispensable for those who set forth "the mystery of piety"'; cf. C.C. Richardson, 'Address on Religious Instruction', p. 268: 'Religious instruction is an essential duty of the leaders "of the mystery of our religion"'.

[7] Gregory of Nyssa, *Catechetical Oration* (in J.-P. Migne [ed.], *Patrologiae Cursus Completus: Series Graecae* [PG] [Paris: Garnier, 1857–66], 45, cols. 11-105); Athanasius *De incarnatione* (PG 25, cols. 96-197); Augustine of Hippo *De catechizandis rudibus* (in J.-P. Migne (ed.), *Patrologiae Cursus Completus: Series Latina* [PL] [Paris: Garnier, 1844–64], 40, cols. 309-48). The inclusive column numbers for Gregory and Athanasius must be divided in half for these calculations, as they also include the facing columns of Latin translation. Citations in Athanasius, *De incarnatione*, are those noted in R.W. Thomson (ed. and trans.), *Athanasius: Contra Gentes and De Incarnatione* (Oxford:

different contexts and purposes than Gregory had in mind, but this comparison nevertheless highlights Gregory's apparent reticence to quote scripture directly to catechumens.

What might account for this comparative absence of direct appeals to scripture in the *Catechetical Oration*? Anthony Meredith attributes Gregory's different approach to the greater degree of attention he gives to pagan philosophical objections to the Christian conceptions of God as triune and incarnate, objections he counters with philosophical rather than biblical arguments.[8] This observation rings true, for one must read eight pages into Mühlenberg's text before encountering the first explicit biblical citation, the single Old Testament text adduced in the brief twenty-nine lines in which Gregory responds cursorily to Jewish objections before returning to matters primarily of Hellenistic concern.[9] Nevertheless, Gregory still cites scripture much less freely than does Athanasius in answering Greek objections to Christian doctrine with similar arguments. I will suggest three additional factors that may contribute to Gregory's distinctive strategy for the catechetical use of scripture.

Scripture and Mystagogical Catechesis

The first factor is related to the mystagogical context of the *disciplina arcani*, the 'discipline of secrecy' involving the exclusion of catechumens from the eucharistic portion of worship and the withholding of explanations of the sacramental mysteries until after baptism. The practice was common in the third through fifth centuries AD, and Gregory himself affirms it in his sermon *Against Those Who Postpone Baptism*.[10] With this practice in mind, it is interesting to note where Gregory's citations of scripture occur in the thematic structure of the *Catechetical Oration*. Table 1 below lists these citations, and the formulae that introduce them, by page and line number in Mühlenberg's *Gregorii Nysseni Opera* edition. The first column of the table places these citations in relation to the major sections of the thematic outline of the *Catechetical Oration* supplied by Cyril Richardson in the introduction to his Library of Christian Classics translation: (I) chapters 1-4, 'The Doctrine of God and the Trinity'; (II) chapters 5-7, 'The Creation of Humanity, the Nature of Evil, and the Fall'; (III) chapters 8-32, 'The Restoration of Humanity, the Incarnation and Atonement'; (IV) chapters 33-40, 'Baptism, Eucharist, Faith, and Repentance'.[11]

Clarendon Press, 1971), pp. 134-277; citations in Augustine *De catechizandis rudibus* are counted from the references printed as direct quotations in S.D.F. Salmond (trans.), 'St. Augustin: On the Catechising of the Uninstructed', in NPNF[1], III, pp. 283-314.

[8] A. Meredith, *Gregory of Nyssa* (The Early Church Fathers; London: Routledge, 1999), pp. 73-75.

[9] Gregory of Nyssa, *Catechetical Oration* 4 (GNO vol. 3, pt. 4, p. 14, lines 22-24).

[10] Gregory of Nyssa, *Adversus eos qui baptismum different* (GNO vol. 10, pt. 2, pp. 361-63).

[11] Richardson, 'Introduction to Gregory of Nyssa', in Hardy and Richardson (eds), *Christology of the Later Fathers*, p. 246. As the Mühlenberg text in GNO does not include

Table 1: Biblical Citations in the *Catechetical Oration*

Section	GNO pg./ln.	Biblical Passage	Citation Formula
I	14.22-24	Ps. 32.6 (LXX)	[14.19-20 ἐκ τῶν θεοπνεύστων...δείκνυται] φησίν
II	18.6	Gen. 1.27	λέγων
	22.8-9	1 Tim. 4.4	καθώς φησιν ὁ ἀπόστολος
	22.13-15	Gen. 2.7	φησί
	27.9-11, 15-16	1 Cor. 2.14-15	τὸν ἀπόστολον ...προστήσασθαι...φησίν
III	33.8-10	Mt. 9.2/par.	καθὼς λέγει τὸ εὐαγγέλιον...φησίν
	33.17-19	Ps. 38.12 (LXX)	καθώς φησί που ἡ προφητεία
	50.9-10	Ps. 30.20 (LXX)	καθώς φησὶν ἡ προφητεία
	51.5-6	Tit. 2.11	καθώς φησιν ὁ ἀπόστολος
	54.7-9	Ps. 106 (LXX)? Ps. 18.68 (LXX)?	καθώς φησιν ὁ Δαβίδ
	80.20-21	Eph. 3.18	ὁ μέγας...Παῦλος...διὰ τῆς διδασκαλίας
	81.3-4	Phil. 2.10	πρὸς Φιλιππησίους...φησιν ὅτι
IV	86.17-19	Heb. 2.10	καθώς φησιν ὁ ἀπόστολος
	89.18	Rom. 6.10	καθώς φησιν ὁ ἀπόστολος
	93.19-21	1 Cor. 5.6	καθώς φησιν ὁ ἀπόστολος
	97.8-9	1 Tim. 4.5	καθώς φησιν ὁ ἀπόστολος
	97.11-12	Mt. 26.26/par.	καθὼς εἴρηται ὑπὸ τοῦ λόγου ὅτι
	99.13	Mt. 28.19	ἐπεὶ οὖν ἐν τῷ εὐαγγελίῳ
	99.17-18	Jn 3.6	οὕτω γάρ φησι...τὸ εὐαγγέλιον
	99.18-19	1 Cor. 4.15	ὁ Παῦλος...
	99.19	Eph. 4.6	[ὁ Παῦλος...]
	102.2-3	Jn 3.3, 7	φησὶ δὲ τὸ εὐαγγέλιον
	103.1-4	Isa. 1.16	καθώς φησιν ὁ προφήτης
	104.2-3	Lk. 19.8	τὴν Ζακχαίου φησὶν ὅτι
	104.9-10	Gal. 6.3	ἀκουσάτω τῆς Παύλου φωνῆς ὅτι
	104.10-12	Jn 1.12	φησὶ...τὸ εὐαγγέλιον

the chapter divisions that have been supplied by the English translations, the second column in Tables 1 and 2 herein locates the passages in GNO by page and line number: thus 14.22-24 indicates p. 14, lines 22-24 of the Mühlenberg edition.

Table 1: Biblical Citations in the *Catechetical Oration* (continued)

Section	GNO pg./ln.	Biblical Passage	Citation Formula
IV (cntd)	104.18-19	Ps. 144.16 (LXX)	[105.3-4— καὶ ὅσα τοιαῦτα σποράδην παρὰ τῆς γραφῆς διδασκόμεθα]
	104.19	Mic. 7.18	[105.3-4—καὶ ὅσα τοιαῦτα σποράδην παρὰ τῆς γραφῆς διδασκόμεθα]
	104.19	Joel 2.13	[105.3-4— καὶ ὅσα τοιαῦτα σποράδην παρὰ τῆς γραφῆς διδασκόμεθα]
	105.1	Ps. 144.9 (LXX)	[105.3-4— καὶ ὅσα τοιαῦτα σποράδην παρὰ τῆς γραφῆς διδασκόμεθα]
	105.1-2	Ps. 7.12 (LXX)	[105.3-4— καὶ ὅσα τοιαῦτα σποράδην παρὰ τῆς γραφῆς διδασκόμεθα]
	105.2-3	Ps. 91.16 (LXX)	[105.3-4— καὶ ὅσα τοιαῦτα σποράδην παρὰ τῆς γραφῆς διδασκόμεθα]
	105.7-9	Ps. 4.3-4 (LXX); 81.6 (LXX)[12]	ἐρεῖ πρὸς σὲ ἡ προφητεία ὅτι
	105.13-14	1 Cor. 2.9	[no formula, but directly quoted]
	106.1-10	Mt. 3.12/par.; Mk 9.43, 48 (Isa. 66.24)	[ἀκούων...ἀκούσας... προσθήκη]

Gregory appeals to scripture only once in the first section in which he responds to Greek and Jewish objections to the Christian doctrine of God (GNO, pp. 5-15). There are four citations in the second section treating the creation of humanity, the nature of evil, and the fall (GNO, pp. 15-28) and seven citations in the third section on the restoration of humanity, the incarnation, and the atonement (GNO, pp. 29-82). In contrast to the scarcity of direct referencing of scripture in the first three sections, there are twenty-three citations in the fourth section on baptism, the eucharist, and faith and repentance (GNO, pp. 82-106). Twenty-three of the thirty-five citations appear in the final twenty-four pages of a 101-page text; these twenty-four pages deal with precisely those topics normally veiled from catechumens until their formal initiation into Christian community.

---

[12] Allusion not noted in GNO; suggested by Richardson (trans.), 'Address on Religious Instruction', p. 325 n. 66.

In light of this pattern, I cautiously suggest that Gregory regarded scripture as a mystery properly reserved for the faithful—or at least a mystery best appreciated by the faithful. Gregory certainly does not avoid scripture altogether prior to this final section. In addition to the handful of citations in these earlier sections, there is an abundance of indirect intertextuality in the form of biblical allusions, which will receive attention in the next subsection of this essay. As it was the norm in this period for catechumens to participate in the liturgy of the word prior to their dismissal before the liturgy of the table, the catechumens for whom this pattern of teaching was devised would have regularly heard the reading and exposition of scripture. Gregory, therefore, does not advocate the complete withholding of scripture from the catechumenate. Instead, Gregory's use of scripture in the *Catechetical Oration* hints at a mystagogical reluctance to offer explicit exegetical arguments in support of Christian doctrine until persons are better equipped for receiving them.

Scripture and the Role of Narrative in Catechesis

A second factor that may account for this use of scripture is Gregory's preference for summaries of biblical narratives, rather than the quotation of specific biblical passages, as a means of acquainting catechumens with the teachings of scripture.[13] Although there are only thirty-five citations of scripture in the *Catechetical Oration*, there are at least eighty-four allusions to scripture in the treatise. These are listed in Table 2 below, again in relation to the thematic sections outlined by Richardson.

Table 2: Biblical Allusions in the *Catechetical Oration*

Section	GNO pg./ln.	Biblical Passage
I	5.2	1 Tim. 3.16
	5.3	Acts 2.47
	5.3-4	Tit. 1.9
	6.2	Jn 1.18
	10.18	Gen. 1.31
II	15.22-23	Wis. 9.1-2; Ps. 103.4 (LXX); Prov. 8.22-26; Jn 1.3
	17.25-18.4	Wis. 2.23
	18.11-14	Gen. 2.8-10
	20.10-11	Js. 1.15[14]
	24.12-26.6	Wis. 2.24
	25.13-14	Gen. 1.28-30

---

[13] See S.R. Harmon, "'Doctrines in the Form of a Story': Narrative Theology in Gregory of Nyssa's *Oratio Catechetica Magna*', in F. Young, M. Edwards, and P. Parvis (eds), *Studia Patristica: Papers Presented at the Fourteenth International Conference on Patristic Studies Held in Oxford 2003* (Leuven: Peeters Press, 2006), pp. 327-32.

[14] Allusion not noted in GNO; suggested by Moore (trans.), NPNF², V, p. 479 n. 5.

Table 2: Biblical Allusions in the *Catechetical Oration* (continued)

II (cntd)	25.15	Wis. 2.24
III	29.18-19	2 Cor. 4.7
	29.19	Gen. 3.19
	30.3-6	Gen. 3.21
	33.21-22	1 Cor. 2.9
	36.21	Lk. 2.6
	36.22	Lk. 2.40, 52
	36.22	Mk 2:.6/Lk. 24.43
	36.22	Jn 4.6
	37.1	Mt. 8.24/Lk. 8.23
	37.1	Mt. 26.38
	37.1	Jn 11.35
	37.1	Mt. 26.59
	37.1	Mt. 27.27
	37.2	Mt. 27.38/par.
	37.2	Mt. 27.50/par.
	37.2	Mt. 27.57-60/par.
	40.6-7	1 Tim. 3.16
	41.18	Acts 2.31/Ps. 15.10 (LXX)
	42.13-18	Mt. 1.18-25
	42.18-19	Mt. 28.1-7
	44.12-13	Heb. 2.9
	47.10-11	1 Tim. 3.16
	48.21-24	Rom. 5.17
	55.17	Gen. 1.27
	58.18-19	Mt. 1.18, 25
	58.19	Lk. 11.27
	58.20-21	Lk. 2.14, 3.22/par., 9.35/par.
	58.21-59.1	Mt. 9.1-8
	59.1	Mt. 8.5-13
	59.1-2	Mt. 9.18ff/par.; Lk. 7.11-17; Jn 11.11-44
	59.2-3	Mt. 8.29/par.
	59.3	Mt. 8.23-27/par.
	59.4-9	Mt. 14.22-33/par.
	59.6	Ex. 14.19-29
	59.9	Mt. 4.2-4/par.
	59.10-17	Mt. 14.14-5.21/par., 15.32-39/par.
	59.11	Ex. 16.13ff; Num. 11.4-9
	59.16-19	Jn 6.1-13

Table 2: Biblical Allusions in the *Catechetical Oration* (continued)

Section	GNO pg./ln.	Biblical Passage
III (contd)	63.1-2	Lk. 19.10
	63.4-5	Phil. 2.7-8
	63.15	2 Cor. 7.1
	65.25	Gen. 3.6
	73.9-11	Gen. 3.1-6, 4.1-8
	73.11-12	Gen. 6.5ff
	73.12-13	Gen. 19.1-29
	73.13-14	Ex. 5-11
	73.14	Dan. 4.19 (LXX) or Isa. 37.23ff
	73.15	Mt. 23.29-39
	73.16	Mt. 2.16-18
	74.8-9	Gen. 3.15
	75.7-11	Acts 2.5-11
	75.20-22	Acts 2.41, 2.13
	78.10	Rom. 9.21; Gal. 5.9
	81.11-12	Jn 19.34
	81.14-15	Lk. 24.36?
	81.15-16	Jn 20.19, 26
	81.16-17	Jn 20.22
	81.17-18	Mt. 28.20
	81.19	Acts 1.9
	82.2-3	Tit. 3.5; Heb. 6.4
IV	84.16-17	Mt. 7.7; Jn 15.4-10
	84.17-18	Mt. 18.20
	87.14-15	Heb. 2.10
	87.15-16	Mt. 12.40, 16.21; 1 Cor. 15.4
	87.17	Rom. 6.5
	88.6	Jn 3.31; 1 Cor. 15.47[15]
	89.22	Rom. 6.4
	93.13	Gen. 3.6[16]
	97.1-2	Jn 1.14
	98.18-20	Jn 1.13, 3.6, 7[17]

---

[15] Allusion not noted in GNO; suggested by Richardson (trans.), 'Address on Religious Instruction', p. 315 n. 38.

[16] Allusion not noted in GNO; suggested by Richardson (trans.), 'Address on Religious Instruction', p. 318 n. 40.

IV (contd)	101.17	Jn 1.18
	101.19-23	Jn 3.4

Seventeen of these allusions are loose verbal echoes of biblical passages. Some of these allusions border on being paraphrased quotations without citation formulae, and others may not have been conscious recollections of specific texts. The remaining sixty-seven allusions tend to be references to events narrated in scripture, but with no accompanying quotation. Frequently these appear in clusters of narrative summary. These narrative summary allusions are perhaps the most significant feature of Gregory's catechetical use of scripture, even though they are rarely noted as biblical references in the English translations.

I offer four examples of these clusters of narrative summary allusions. In chapter 9 (GNO, pp. 36-37), Gregory anticipates objections to the distinctively Christian concept of God as incarnate, writing, 'I refer to the human birth, the advance from infancy to manhood, the eating and drinking, the weariness, the sleep, the grief, the tears, the false accusations, the trial, the cross, the death, and the putting in the tomb'.[18] It is not difficult to identify twelve specific passages in the Gospels that Gregory here summarizes with only a word or two (see the references in section III of Table 2 above).

In Gregory's familiar portrayal of the work of Christ as an ensnaring ransom in chapter 23 (GNO, pp. 58-59), he suggests with a cluster of fourteen narrative allusions why the devil was so attracted to the bait of Christ's flesh that he became ensnared.

> Among those whom history records from the beginning, he was aware of none who was connected with such circumstances as he was in His appearance. There was conception without sexual union, birth without impurity, a virgin suckling a child, and heavenly voices witnessing to his eminence. The healing of natural diseases was performed by him without technical skill, but by a mere word and act of will. There was the restoration of the dead to life, the rescue of the condemned, the fear inspired in demons, and authority over the elements. He walked across the sea so that the water was not parted to lay bare the bottom for those who passed over (as happened in Moses' miracle); but the surface of the water became like land to his tread, and supported his footsteps by offering a firm resistance. He ignored food as long as he wished. There were abundant feasts in the desert, which fed many thousands. Heaven did not rain down manna; nor did the earth naturally bring forth wheat to fill their need. But from the secret storehouses of God's power this abundance proceeded. Bread was produced ready-made in the hands of those who served it, and, indeed, increased as it satisfied those who ate of it. Then there were

---

[17] Allusions to John 1.13 and 3.7 are not noted in GNO; suggested by Richardson (trans.), 'Address on Religious Instruction', p. 321 n. 48.

[18] Gregory of Nyssa, *Catechetical Oration* 9 (Richardson [trans.], 'Address on Religious Instruction', p. 287).

the relishes of fish—not that the sea supplied their need, but He who sowed the sea with its different kinds of fish.[19]

A cluster of seven narrative allusions in chapter 29 (GNO, p. 73) summarizes the story of fallen humanity that is addressed by the incarnation.

> And so, when once the disease of wickedness had infiltrated human nature, the universal Physician waited until no form of evil remained concealed in our nature. In consequence, he did not apply his cure to man immediately on Cain's jealousy and murder of his brother. For the wickedness of those destroyed in Noah's time had not yet broken out. Nor had there come to light the terrible disease of Sodom's transgression, or the battle of the Egyptians with God, or the arrogance of the Assyrians, or the murder of God's saints by the Jews, or Herod's iniquitous slaughter of the children, or all the other things which history records or which were wrought by successive generations and left unrecorded. For the root of wickedness produced in men's wills a great variety of shoots. When, then, evil had reached its highest pitch and no form of wickedness had not been daringly attempted by man, he healed the disease.[20]

Near the end of the section on the incarnation, atonement, and restoration of humanity, in chapter 32 (GNO, p. 81) Gregory alludes to six passages in the Gospels and Acts in summarizing the story of Christ's resurrection and ascension.

> The succeeding events...in the gospel account are consistently of such a kind that even unbelievers would admit they involve no unfitting conception of God. He did not remain dead; and the wounds the spear inflicted on his body did not prevent his living. After the resurrection he appeared at will to the disciples. Whenever he wished, he was present with them, though unobserved. He came into their midst without needing doors to give him entrance. He strengthened the disciples by breathing on them the Spirit. He promised to be with them and that nothing would separate him from them. Visibly he ascended to heaven, but to their minds he was everywhere present. These facts, and whatever the gospel story contains of a similar nature, need no supporting arguments to prove their divine quality and their connection with sublime and transcendent power. I do not think it necessary to dwell upon them in detail. The mere mention of them at once indicates their supernatural character.[21]

---

[19] Gregory of Nyssa, *Catechetical Oration* 23 (Richardson [trans.], 'Address on Religious Instruction', pp. 299-300).

[20] Gregory of Nyssa, *Catechetical Oration* 29 (Richardson [trans.], 'Address on Religious Instruction', p. 307).

[21] Gregory of Nyssa, *Catechetical Oration* 32 (Richardson [trans.], 'Address on Religious Instruction', p. 312).

'The mere mention' of events in biblical salvation-history seems to be Gregory's preferred mode of referencing scripture to those who have not yet been baptized. All of these clusters of narrative allusions appear in the first thirty-two chapters of the *Catechetical Oration* (through GNO, p. 82). The final eight chapters (or twenty-four pages) deal with baptism, the eucharist, the Christian life, and the life of the age to come. In this final section there is a sudden increase in the frequency of direct biblical citations and an equally sudden decrease in the frequency of allusions. Prior to this point in the *Catechetical Oration* there are only twelve citations and seventy-two allusions, but from the discussion of baptism through the end of the document there are twenty-three citations and only twelve allusions.

This preference for narrative summary of scripture in pre-baptismal catechesis is by no means unique to Gregory. A similar pattern is commended in the *Apostolic Constitutions*, for example, and the two sample catechetical discourses in Augustine's *On the Catechising of the Uninstructed* are replete with summaries of salvation-history.[22] But unlike Gregory, Augustine and other patristic exemplars of catechetical methodology such as Cyril of Jerusalem do not refrain from direct quotation of scripture in the course of narrative summary.[23] Gregory's catechetical model remains distinctive in the subtlety with which it implicitly veils scripture from the uninitiated while still fulfilling its stated goal of bringing 'the trustworthy word' into 'the hearing of unbelievers' through summaries of biblical narrative.

Scripture and Progress in the Spiritual Life

A third factor which may account for this pattern is Gregory's concept of ἐπέκτασις, the progressive and ceaseless 'stretching forth' of the human soul toward God. This was an idea of great hermeneutical significance for Gregory.[24] Ἐπέκτασις provided Gregory with a key for understanding the spiritual significance of the structure of biblical passages, narratives, and even whole books of scripture. In the treatise *On the Inscriptions of the Psalms*, for example, Gregory discerns in the arrangement of

---

[22] *Apostolic Constitutions* 7.39 (ET J. Donaldson; 'Constitutions of the Holy Apostles', in A. Roberts and J. Donaldson [eds], *The Ante-Nicene Fathers* [Peabody, MA: Hendrickson, 1994], VII, pp. 475-76; Augustine of Hippo *On the Catechizing of the Uninstructed* (ET, 'St. Augustin: On the Catechising of the Uninstructed', in NPNF[1], III, pp. 283-314).

[23] Cyril of Jerusalem, *Procatechesis, Catecheses*, and *Mystagogical Catecheses*; ET, L.P. McCauley and A.A. Stephenson (trans.), *The Works of Saint Cyril of Jerusalem* (2 vols; Fathers of the Church, 61 and 64; Washington, DC: The Catholic University of America Press, 1969–70).

[24] M. Canévet, *Grégoire de Nysse et l'herméneutique biblique: Études des rapports entre le langage et la connaissance de Dieu* (Paris: Études Augustiniennes, 1983), pp. 253-54. On the eschatological implications of this aspect of Gregory's biblical interpretation, see S.R. Harmon, *Every Knee Should Bow: Biblical Rationales for Universal Salvation in Early Christian Thought* (Lanham, MD: University Press of America, 2003), p. 8.

the Psalter in five books five progressive steps in the ascent of humanity from sin to beatitude.[25] In the *Homilies on the Beatitudes* he finds in the sequence of Jesus' beatitudes a ladder of spiritual ascent, 'arranged in order like so many steps, so as to facilitate the ascent from one to another'.[26] The *Catechetical Oration* similarly presents a pattern of theological teaching in which catechumens are initially moved toward a grasp of the Christian faith through an appeal to its reasonableness rather than through an appeal to scripture; but it is only after catechumens have embraced Christian faith and undergone initiation into the community that they are ready to receive and appreciate the mystery that is scripture.

Accordingly the richest concentration of biblical citations is found in the final four pages of the text. In the brief paragraphs on the life that follows baptism and the life promised in the age to come, Gregory directly cites scripture fourteen times (roughly five times per Migne column, compared with an average of about one-half of a citation per column in the preceding portion of the work). In light of these observations, it seems appropriate to apply to the text of the *Catechetical Oration* and its intertextual connections the same hermeneutic of ἐπέκτασις that Gregory applies to the text of scripture. The *Catechetical Oration* functions not only as a pattern for catechesis but also as a pattern for progress in the spiritual life, from attraction to Christian faith through entry into the church and growth in the Christian life to the life of the age to come. The *Catechetical Oration* implies that a key component of progress in the spiritual life is a progressive appropriation of scripture by the convert. The broad outlines of the biblical story bring 'the trustworthy word' into 'the hearing of unbelievers' and attract them to Christian faith. After their formal entry into the church, believers are ready to make progress toward the life of the age to come through a more direct engagement with the details of the biblical story. In this pattern scripture functions not so much as the text of the catechumen; scripture is rather the text of the catechized candidate for baptism. Those who are ready to receive the sacraments proper, baptism and the eucharist, are also now ready to appreciate scripture as the sacrament-like sacred story that it

---

[25] Gregory of Nyssa, *In inscriptiones psalmorum* (GNO vol. 5, pp. 24-175); cf. M. Simonetti, *Biblical Interpretation in the Early Church: An Historical Introduction to Patristic Exegesis* (trans. J.A. Hughes; ed. A. Bergquist and M. Bockmuehl; Edinburgh: T&T Clark, 1994), p. 65; and J. Quasten, *Patrology* (Westminster, MD: Christian Classics, 1990), III, p. 265. This conclusion about the structure of the Psalter is discussed in detail in R.E. Heine, *Gregory of Nyssa's Treatise on the Inscriptions of the Psalms: Introduction, Translation, and Notes* (Oxford Early Christian Studies; Oxford: Clarendon Press, 1995), pp. 50-79 (section titled 'The Structure of the Psalter and the Stages of the Spiritual Life').

[26] Gregory of Nyssa, *Orationes viii de beatitudinibus* (PG 44, cols. 1193-1301); ET, H.C. Graef (trans.), *St. Gregory of Nyssa: The Lord's Prayer, The Beatitudes* (Ancient Christian Writers, 18; Westminster, MD: Newman Press, 1954), pp. 85-175. Cf. Quasten, *Patrology*, III, p. 268.

is—what Augustine of Hippo a few decades later encouraged the faithful to treat as 'the face of God' this side of heaven.[27]

Implications for Baptist Sacramental Theology

If the function of scripture in Gregory of Nyssa's *Catechetical Oration* points in the direction of a sacramentality of the word, then so does the function of scripture in the worship of Baptist churches.[28] Among Baptists, the Bible has a liturgical function that can best be expressed as the 'sacramentality' of the word, even if most of the Baptist faithful might find such an expression foreign to the Baptist grammar of faith. Modern Baptists may have tendencies toward a reductionistic Zwinglian 'mere symbolism' in their theology of baptism and the supper, but no Baptist would claim that a biblical sermon is 'merely symbolic'. Baptists believe that God is present in the preached word and that the faithful are transformed by their encounter with this presence. Some of them, such as British Baptist theologian John Colwell, have even explicitly named the ground of this expectation as the 'sacramentality of the word'.[29]

In the quotation that prefaced this essay, the sixth-century Gallican bishop Caesarius of Arles was able to assume that his hearers had the utmost reverence for the sacrament of the body and blood of Christ, showing 'great anxiety…lest nothing fall out of our hands onto the ground'. On the basis of this assumed regard for the presence of God in the sacraments proper, Caesarius could argue that the same regard should be extended to the hearing of the word of God in the public reading of the scriptures. The sacramentality of the word implicit in Baptist worship provides Baptist theologians and ministers with the opportunity to argue in the opposite direction: if we can acknowledge that God meets us by means of the aspects of materiality that are words printed with ink on paper and read with the voice and heard with the ears, then we can open ourselves to the possibility that there may be other acts of worship in which God meets us by means of aspects of the material order, beginning with water and bread and wine. The sacramentality of the word is the proper initial locus of a Baptist sacramental theology, and the extension of this

---

[27] Augustine of Hippo, *Sermon* 22.7 (ET, E. Hill [trans.], *The Works of Saint Augustine: A Translation for the 21st Century*, pt. 3, vol. 2, *Sermons [20-50] on the Old Testament* [Brooklyn, NY: New City Press, 1990], p. 46: 'So for the time being treat the scripture of God as the face of God. Melt in front of it. Repent when you hear all this about your sins.')

[28] See S.R. Harmon, 'Scripture in the Life of the Baptist Churches: Openings for a Differentiated Catholic–Baptist Consensus on Sacred Scripture', *Pro Ecclesia* 18 (2009, forthcoming).

[29] John E. Colwell, *Promise and Presence: An Exploration of Sacramental Theology* (Milton Keynes: Paternoster, 2005), ch. 4, 'The Sacramentality of the Word', pp. 88-105. *Promise and Presence* is Colwell's attempt to retrieve for his own Baptist (and more broadly Free Church/Protestant) tradition all seven sacraments identified as such in the medieval tradition, prefaced by chapter-length treatments of the sacramentality of creation, the sacramentality of the church, and the sacramentality of the word.

sacramentality of the word to the word-like qualities of baptism and the Lord's supper may lead Baptists toward a greater appreciation of the sacrament-like quality of these acts of worship—and maybe even toward an embrace of them as sacraments proper in which God does something for human beings. The discernment of the sacrament-like function of scripture in Gregory of Nyssa's *Catechetical Oration* offers Baptists a precedent, however indirect, for discerning the sacramentality of the word as it already functions in the first-order practices of Baptist congregations today as the first step in developing a theology of the sacraments that is both truly Baptist and fully sacramental.

CHAPTER 15

Baptists and Churches of Christ in Search of a Common Theology of Baptism

Stanley K. Fowler

Given their name, one would assume that Baptist churches would define their identity in terms of their theology of baptism. Surprisingly, this has not been the case to the extent that one would expect, but what can be said is that very often Baptist identity as it concerns baptism has been expressed in negative terms. So, for example, Baptist churches 'do not baptize infants', and they 'do not baptize by sprinkling or pouring'. For many Baptists, it is emphatically declared that they 'do not believe that baptism is sacramental'. In the Baptist context in which I received my early Christian nurture, one of the identity-statements would have been that 'we are not like the Churches of Christ'. However, in more recent years, a fascinating convergence has begun, and this is a story worth telling and celebrating.

Sources of the Conflict

The Churches of Christ have their origin in British and American renewal movements of the late eighteenth and early nineteenth centuries, all of which were in some way seeking to restore the primitive Christian church as they understood it. In Great Britain the precursors included Scots like John Glas (1695–1773), Robert Sandeman (1718–71), and Archibald McLean (1733–1812). In the USA, where the movement became numerically very significant, its earliest leader was Barton W. Stone, a former Presbyterian, but he was succeeded and eclipsed by the Scottish immigrant Thomas Campbell and especially his son, Alexander Campbell.[1] Alexander was for a few years a part of the Baptists in western Virginia, but it was an unstable relationship. Ultimately the Redstone Baptist Association withdrew fellowship from his Brush Run Church in 1824, and in 1832 the Dover Baptist Association excommunicated 'the Reformers' (as Campbell and his associates were called), largely due to his views of faith, baptism, and the remission of sins.[2]

---

[1] For a concise account of the British and American origins, see William Robinson, *What Churches of Christ Stand For* (Birmingham: Berean Press, 1959), pp. 11-24.

[2] For an historical and theological analysis of Campbell's experience among Baptists, see John Mark Hicks, 'The Role of Faith in Conversion: Balancing Faith,

Campbell's writings on baptism are voluminous and cover decades, and they are not entirely clear on the exact relationship between baptism and the remission of sins. In 1828 he wrote, 'He that goes down into the water to put on Christ...has when immersed the actual remission of his sins', but in 1843 he said that in baptism the individual 'formally receives what was at first received by faith in anticipation'. One of his sympathetic interpreters has admitted that '...Campbell's interpretation of what is achieved in the act itself is ambiguous'.[3] In other words, some of his assertions appear to make *actual* forgiveness of sins and a right standing with God dependent on a valid baptism, while in other places he seems to see only *formal* forgiveness of sins or *assurance* of this right standing as the effect of baptism. If he intended only this latter reference to assurance, then his view of baptismal efficacy was something like the traditional Reformed sense of baptism as a *seal* of union with Christ (as applied to confessing believers), but if he intended the former then he was clearly moving in a new and questionable direction.

Whatever may have been Campbell's final opinion, many of his descendants in the conservative portions of the movement tended to adopt the hard-core view. Thus they tended to say that apart from valid baptism with valid motives (i.e., baptism with the conscious intent to receive remission of sins through it), there is no remission of sins, or at least no basis on which one might consider a person to be in a right standing with God.[4] This drove a huge wedge between the Churches of Christ (who emphasized that we submit to baptism as a means to salvation) and Baptist churches (who jealously guarded the *sola fide* character of salvation and asserted that we submit to baptism because we have been saved).[5]

Over time both positions tended to harden, and the division became more important as an identity marker on both sides. I am sure that all along the way there have been charitable persons in both camps, but I know from experience that both sides have frequently questioned the Christian status of the other. I have had various conversations with zealous members of the Churches of Christ in which I have asked them about their understanding of my status. I confessed my faith in Jesus Christ via baptism by immersion (in running water, no less!), but in a Baptist context where it

---

Christian Experience and Baptism', in William R. Baker (ed.), *Evangelicalism and the Stone-Campbell Movement* (Downers Grove, IL: InterVarsity Press, 2002), pp. 91-110.

[3] This assertion and the preceding quotes are found in Royal Humbert (ed.), *A Compend of Alexander Campbell's Theology* (St. Louis, MO: Bethany Press, 1961), pp. 196 and 199.

[4] A concise account of the views of Campbell and his successors can be found in Joseph Belcastro, *The Relationship of Baptism to Church Membership* (St. Louis, MO: Bethany Press, 1963), pp. 21-38.

[5] For examples of the intensity of the Baptist reaction to Campbell and his associates, see James Robinson Graves, *The Relation of Baptism to Salvation* (Texarkana, TX: Baptist Sunday School Committee, 1881), pp. 16-56, and *The Act of Baptism* (Texarkana, TX: Baptist Sunday School Committee, 1881), pp. 44 and 56; and Jeremiah B. Jeter, *Campbellism Examined* (New York, NY: Sheldon, Lamport & Blakeman, 1855), pp. 191-281.

was interpreted as merely an act of obedience bearing witness to a previously completed union with Christ. Am I, therefore, to be considered a fellow Christian? The answer is No, according to many of my Church of Christ friends. I also heard the Baptist attacks on the Churches of Christ ('Campbellites' to many Baptists). One of the jokes was that while Baptists affirm 'power in the blood' of Christ, the Campbellites affirm that 'there is power in the tub', and that view of baptismal efficacy was assumed to imply salvation by works. Therefore, such persons would be considered to be purveyors of a false gospel, and thus under the anathema of God (Gal. 1). In my experience there was little contact between the two groups, and not much desire for it.

Apparently the divide has always been smaller in Great Britain for various reasons.[6] The Churches of Christ have never been a large group there, thus providing little basis for confidence in being a distinct group. In fact, most of the British congregations were received into the United Reformed Church in 1981. Both groups in England have existed as Dissenters over against a state church, and that would no doubt lead each to focus on their commonalities rather than their differences. Furthermore, Baptists in Great Britain have been much more open to a high view of baptismal efficacy than have their American counterparts, leading to less tension with their ecclesiastical cousins.[7]

This paper, then, will focus on the American context, where Baptist identity in relation to the Churches of Christ has been a major issue, and where in recent history there is evidence of theological convergence and warmer relations. At the outset I should make some comments about terminology in relation to the Churches of Christ. There are three streams of this movement in America: (1) the Christian Church (Disciples of Christ), which is ecumenically inclined and theologically diverse; (2) the a cappella Churches of Christ, so-called because of their rejection of musical instruments in corporate worship, which tend to be exclusivist in attitude; and (3) a mediating group variously called Christian Churches or Churches of Christ, which are theologically conservative but employ instruments in worship and are increasingly oriented toward the mainstream of Evangelicalism. All of these churches are considered to be part of the Stone-Campbell movement, which is also called by many the Restoration movement. Earlier literature sometimes referred to Stone, the Campbells, and their associates as 'the Reformers', but that rapidly leads to confusion for anyone familiar with the sixteenth century. Baptists have often used the label 'Campbellites', but that term is highly pejorative and dialogue-inhibiting.

---

[6] The relationship is explored in detail in E. Roberts-Thomson, *Baptists and Disciples of Christ* (London: Carey Kingsgate Press, 1948). See also R.L. Child, 'Baptists and Disciples of Christ', *Baptist Quarterly* 14.4 (October, 1951), p. 189.

[7] For a comprehensive survey of British Baptist perspectives on baptism, see Anthony R. Cross, *Baptism and the Baptists: Theology and Practice in Twentieth-Century Britain* (Studies in Baptist History and Thought, 3; Carlisle: Paternoster Press, 2000). For an analysis of the theology in greater detail, see Stanley K. Fowler, *More Than a Symbol: The British Baptist Recovery of Baptismal Sacramentalism* (Studies in Baptist History and Thought, 2; Carlisle: Paternoster Press, 2002).

In what follows I will use the terms 'Churches of Christ' (the label which reflects the desire for post-denominational Christian unity), 'Restorationists' (the label which reflects the primitivism inherent in the movement), and 'Stone-Campbell adherents' (the label which denotes the major founders of the movement) to denote individuals and congregations in any of the three streams which trace their origin to the work of Stone and the Campbells.

Theological Issues

There are several questions of biblical exegesis and theological synthesis which are at the heart of the distinction between Baptists and Restorationists. Among them would be the following.

1. What is the meaning of the actual baptismal texts of the New Testament? 'No creed but the Bible' is a slogan heard at times in both movements, so the interpretation of New Testament texts is clearly crucial. This involves, first of all, identifying which New Testament texts actually refer to water baptism, because some Baptists, in their fear of 'baptismal regeneration', argue that certain key texts are actually references to Spirit (and not water) baptism (e.g., Rom. 6.3-4; Col. 2.12; Gal. 3.27). In a crucial text like Acts 2.38, the debate is sufficiently fine-tuned to involve a dispute about the meaning of the Greek preposition εἰς.

2. What is the meaning of 'faith'? The Stone-Campbell tradition has often been accused of reducing faith to assent (believing 'that Jesus Christ is the Son of God', in line with Acts 8.37), but in the Baptist tradition saving faith has always been described in a way that emphasizes its fiducial character.

3. What is the place of subjective experience of grace prior to baptism? Baptist roots are found in English Puritanism, and Baptists have generally sought a Puritan-type conversion narrative, with a description of experienced grace, as a condition of baptism. Restorationists have tended to say that this reverses the biblical order and have asked only for a credible statement of faith in Jesus Christ, thus avoiding what they take to be the excessive subjectivism of Baptists and other heirs of the Puritans.

4. What does it mean to say that we are justified 'by faith alone'? This concept is a much greater concern for the Baptist side of the dialogue, and for many of them, to state the concern is to reject the Stone-Campbell perspective. But the Pauline writings which give rise to the 'faith alone' concept were addressed to a specific context in which Paul's concern was Torah versus Christ, not faith versus baptism. So one must ask whether the common Baptist concerns are the same as the apostle's concerns.

5. If, as the Stone-Campbell tradition asserts, baptism is done in order to experience salvation, does this imply that those who are not validly baptized are not saved? This inference is drawn for their opponents by most Baptists, I

think, and also by many in the Stone-Campbell movement, but most persons find it difficult to apply it to the humans they actually know.

6. Is baptism fundamentally about human action, divine action, or both? Restorationists have normally said that it is both, with the divine action contingent upon the human action, while Baptists have tended to say that it is human action alone.

7. Is there a consistent Restorationist or Baptist tradition on this question? Both sides would say that this is a very secondary question, because what matters is what the Bible teaches. However, both sides would agree that their labels are not infinitely elastic, so that at some point one's conclusions about biblical teaching would put one outside the tradition. But is there a monolithic tradition on either side? To assume that such exists is not to make it so.

Steps toward Convergence

Convergence between Baptists and Churches of Christ could occur only if Baptists were willing to grant baptism status as some sort of instrument in the application of redemption. Baptists in America have not been the source of much teaching along that line, but they have been the recipients of such from other parts of the Baptist world. British Baptists, in particular, have recovered a sacramental understanding of baptism in the twentieth century and have articulated this in print. Without doubt the most widely acclaimed contribution has been George Beasley-Murray's 1962 classic, *Baptism in the New Testament*, which was published by Eerdmans in the USA as well as Macmillan in England and continues to be widely read. In addition to the presence of this literature in America as a stimulus to Baptist thought, Beasley-Murray taught at Southern Baptist Theological Seminary from 1973 to 1980. Therefore, the stimulus to a higher view of baptismal efficacy was clearly present among Baptists in America from about 1960 on, but it must be admitted that the British reformulation did not easily take root in American soil.[8]

Ultimately, near the end of the last century, some Baptist scholars in the USA did begin to admit that the biblical witness demands that baptism be thought of as a means of grace and an integral part of Christian conversion. Some of these moves are very tentative and modest, but there is evidence of a growing recognition that the purely symbolic, anti-sacramental view of baptism does not arise naturally from the biblical language about baptism. For example, Wayne Grudem explicitly describes baptism as a 'means of grace' which is used by the Holy Spirit 'to increase our

---

[8] When I began research for my doctoral thesis on the twentieth-century reformulation by British Baptists, I was surprised to discover that there was virtually no serious interaction with the British literature by Baptists in America. The biography of Beasley-Murray by his son indicates that his baptismal theology was a source of controversy more than a means of persuasion in the Southern Baptist context. See Paul Beasley-Murray, *Fearless for Truth: A Personal Portrait of the Life of George Beasley-Murray* (Carlisle: Paternoster Press, 2002), p. 180.

experiential realization of death to the power and love of sin in our lives' and 'to give additional assurance of union with Christ'. He writes,

> Although we must avoid the Roman Catholic teaching that grace is imparted even *apart from* the faith of the person being baptized, we must not react so strongly to this error that we say that there is no spiritual benefit at all that comes from baptism, that the Holy Spirit *does not* work through it and that it is *merely symbolic*.[9]

One of the more creative Baptist theologians of the recent past, Stanley J. Grenz of Carey Theological College in Vancouver, Canada, has indicated an awareness of the British restatement, which in his view 'offers a basis for us to reaffirm a sacramental significance for the acts of commitment, while retaining the primacy of the designation "ordinances"'.[10] He recognizes the problem of viewing baptism (and the Lord's supper) as *mere* ordinances or symbols:

> Viewing the acts of commitment as merely ordinances can be as inappropriate as the magical understandings that the change in terminology was intended to avoid. Under the rationalistic impulse, use of the term 'ordinance' has led some thinkers to reject any connection between the sacred practices and divine grace. In so doing, they attach less significance to the ordinances than is present in the New Testament itself. And by reducing these rites to mere symbols, they risk devaluing them.[11]

Clark Pinnock, clearly one of the most creative pioneers among contemporary Baptists, enthusiastically affirms the sacramental significance of baptism, in particular as the normal context for the bestowal of the Spirit to indwell and empower the individual. He writes,

> The Spirit is normally given with water in response to faith. This makes baptism a sacrament and means of grace. Proper initiation is water baptism coupled with Spirit baptism. Earlier encounters with the Spirit call for a fresh infusion in water baptism, and later encounters should be viewed as occasions of release of the potentials of grace bestowed in the sacrament.[12]

Pinnock's sacramentalism is informed to a great degree by the perspectives of Roman Catholic and Orthodox theology (as is clear from a survey of the endnotes in his book), nevertheless, he still affirms the Baptist pattern of dedicating infants and

---

[9] Wayne Grudem, *Systematic Theology* (Grand Rapids, MI: Zondervan, 1994), pp. 953-54, italics original.

[10] Stanley J. Grenz, *Theology for the Community of God* (Nashville, TN: Broadman & Holman, 1994), p. 671.

[11] Grenz, *Theology for the Community of God*, p. 670.

[12] Clark H. Pinnock, *Flame of Love: A Theology of the Holy Spirit* (Downers Grove, IL: InterVarsity Press, 1996), p. 124.

reserving baptism for a later stage of personal confession, in part because baptism is an event 'in which the Spirit comes and we respond'.[13]

Robert H. Stein, of Southern Baptist Theological Seminary, has written a significant article in that school's journal defending the following thesis:

> In the New Testament, conversion involves five integrally related components or aspects, all of which took place at the same time, usually on the same day. These five components are repentance, faith, and confession by the individual, regeneration, or the giving of the Holy Spirit by God, and baptism by representatives of the Christian community.[14]

Stein proceeds in the rest of the article to demonstrate that his thesis makes sense of the New Testament language about baptism, and then he argues that various Christian traditions tend to separate what scripture ties together. But this is not a Baptist pointing fingers just at Paedobaptists, for he comments,

> Baptist theology also deviates from the New Testament pattern. Although repentance, faith, confession, and regeneration are associated with baptism, baptism is separated in time from these four components. Thus baptism is an act which witnesses to a prior experience of repentance, faith, confession, and regeneration. As a result such passages as Romans 6:4, 1 Peter 3:21, Titus 3:5, John 3:3ff., and others, which associate baptism with the experience of conversion, are embarrassing to many Baptists and often receive a strained exegesis at their hands.[15]

It would be overstating the case to say that Baptist theologians such as these are launching an aggressively sacramental movement, but clearly there is a growing recognition that inherited forms of baptismal theology may be inadequate.[16]

Compelling evidence of this Baptist reformulation has recently appeared in a multi-author book published by the Southern Baptist publishing house.[17] The editors unfortunately continue to use the label 'sacramental' as if it applied only to something like a traditional Catholic perspective, arguing that, 'Sacramental theology clearly compromises the gospel since it teaches that infants enter God's kingdom by virtue of the sacramental action.'[18] Nevertheless, the baptismal theology

---

[13] Pinnock, *Flame of Love*, p. 129.

[14] Robert H. Stein, 'Baptism and Becoming a Christian in the New Testament', *Southern Baptist Journal of Theology* 2.1 (Spring, 1998), p. 6.

[15] Stein, 'Baptism', p. 16.

[16] Further evidence of the positions of Grenz and Pinnock, as well as contributions by several other Baptists, can be found in Anthony R. Cross and Philip E. Thompson (eds), *Baptist Sacramentalism* (Studies in Baptist History and Thought, 5; Carlisle: Paternoster Press, 2003).

[17] Thomas R. Schreiner and Shawn D. Wright (eds), *Believer's Baptism: Sign of the New Covenant in Christ* (Nashville, TN: B&H Academic, 2006).

[18] Schreiner and Wright, 'Introduction', in Schreiner and Wright (eds), *Believer's Baptism*, p. 2.

actually developed within the book must be described as sacramental in content if not in terminology. This is nearly affirmed in a footnoted reference to my book that admits that my view may be congruent with the editors' view, since I agree 'that those who are unbaptized but believers may still be saved'.[19] I could wish for a better understanding of the nuances of sacramentalism, but still the conceptual framework of the authors asserts what may be lacking in their terminology, as the following summary will demonstrate.

Andreas Köstenberger surveys the baptismal texts of the Gospels, including the crucial baptismal language of Matthew 28.19. Traditionally, many Baptists have argued that this text indicates via the order of the verbs that individuals are first made disciples, and then after becoming confirmed disciples they are to be baptized, thus refuting both paedobaptism and baptism as an instrument of union with Christ. Köstenberger, on the other hand, argues that the participle βαπτίζοντες indicates the manner or means by which persons are made disciples.[20] This instrumental function, therefore, marks out baptism as an essential part of Christian discipleship.[21]

Baptism in Luke-Acts is handled by Robert Stein, who continues to press the points which I have noted above. Baptists have tended to use John the Baptist's words about his baptism in water versus the messianic baptism in the Holy Spirit to drive a conceptual and temporal wedge between the two. The effect of that dichotomy is to relate Spirit-baptism to conversion and water-baptism to a post-conversion act of sheer obedience, but Stein rejects this construction of the matter. Instead he suggests that this is an instance not of 'antithetical parallelism' but of 'step parallelism', in which the second element (Spirit-baptism) builds on and expands the first element (water-baptism). Christian baptism, then, mediates both repentance (as in John's baptism) and the gift of the Spirit (the new reality of the messianic age), which is to say that for Luke baptism is part of becoming a Christian.[22]

Acts 2.38 has been a longstanding point of controversy between Baptists and Restorationists, the latter quoting it continually and the former often resorting to exegetical gymnastics to explain it away. Baptists have sought to blunt the natural force of the verse in at least two ways, many following A.T. Robertson's suggestion that the prepostition εἰς should be translated 'because of' here, and others arguing that the phrase 'for the forgiveness of sins' modifies only 'repent' and not 'be baptized'.[23] Stein argues that each of these approaches is a tendentious interpretation of the text rooted in false assumptions about the implications of Peter's words, and he asserts that the text clearly sees baptism as leading to the forgiveness of sins.[24]

---

[19] Schreiner and Wright, 'Introduction', p. 2 n. 4.

[20] Andreas Kostenberger, 'Baptism in the Gospels', in Schreiner and Wright (eds), *Believer's Baptism*, p. 23.

[21] Kostenberger, 'Baptism in the Gospels', p. 33.

[22] Robert Stein, 'Baptism in Luke-Acts', in in Schreiner and Wright (eds), *Believer's Baptism*, pp. 35-36.

[23] For an analysis of the exegetical debate, see Fowler, *More Than a Symbol*, pp. 166-70.

[24] Stein, 'Luke-Acts', p. 36.

In Thomas Schreiner's chapter on baptism in the Epistles, the author argues at length that baptism is for the apostles 'an initiation event, representing the boundary between the old life and the new'.[25] Whereas many Baptists have wanted to find Spirit-baptism as opposed to water-baptism in texts that seem to say too much for Baptist sensitivities (e.g., Rom. 6.3-4; Gal. 3.27; Col. 2.11-12; 1 Cor. 12.13), Schreiner is content to read the texts as a natural reference to conversion-baptism in which water and the Spirit are both present, recognizing that such references to baptism could hardly fail to bring to mind the water-baptism of the Epistles' recipients. Beyond the explicitly baptismal texts, Schreiner also accepts a baptismal allusion in texts that speak of a spiritual 'washing' connected to regeneration (e.g., 1 Cor. 6.11; Eph. 5.26; Tit. 3.5).[26]

1 Peter 3.21, with its statement that 'baptism now saves you', has always forced Baptists to think hard about their anti-sacramental perspective, but Schreiner simply accepts the instrumental force of baptism that is clearly present. As he notes, the text itself makes clear that the instrumental power does not lie in the physical ritual itself, but in the 'appeal to God for a good conscience' that is expressed in the event, but it is still true that baptism is a kind of acted prayer in which forgiveness of sins and a clear conscience are understood as the effects of the event, not the conditions of the event.[27]

Jonathan Rainbow argues for 'confessor baptism' as seen in the early Anabaptists, notably Balthasar Hubmaier in his conflict with Ulrich Zwingli. He laments the fact that Baptists have often overreacted to the baptismal theology of the various paedobaptist groups and have thus propounded a baptismal theology that is both unbiblical and disconnected with the best of their tradition, a perspective that is 'often the fruit of misunderstanding on the part of baptists'.[28] Rainbow writes,

> our look at the 1520s may help Baptists to recover a full-bodied doctrine of baptism instead of the minimalistic view that is often heard in baptist circles today... So what is usually left as the compulsion for baptism among baptists? Obedience. Why do it? Because Jesus did it and the NT commands it. So baptism, instead of being a cataclysmic gateway from death to life, becomes merely the first of many acts of discipleship. The sense of drama is gone, the sense of baptism having some real contact with salvation is gone, and baptism has been reduced to an act of sheer obedience. The real drama is elsewhere, in the private enclave of the heart.[29]

---

[25] Thomas R. Schreiner, 'Baptism in the Epistles: An Initiation Rite for Believers,' in Schreiner and Wright (eds), *Believer's Baptism*, p. 92.

[26] Schreiner, 'Baptism in the Epistles', pp. 83-86.

[27] Schreiner, 'Baptism in the Epistles', pp. 70-71 and 92.

[28] Jonathan H. Rainbow, '"Confessor Baptism": The Baptismal Doctrine of the Early Anabaptists', in Schreiner and Wright (eds), *Believer's Baptism*, p. 205. Rainbow uses the lower-case 'baptists' to describe all those who affirm that baptism is limited to confessing believers, whether they use the 'Baptist' label or not.

[29] Rainbow, '"Confessor Baptism"', p. 205.

The baptismal doctrine of the Swiss Anabaptists was forged in their controversy with Ulrich Zwingli concerning infant baptism, and, as Rainbow notes, Zwingli's defense of infant baptism was grounded in a separation between faith and baptism and a purely symbolic view of baptism. This was a Zwinglian innovation over against both medieval Catholics and Martin Luther, who posited some sort of infused faith as the experience of infants. Ironically, then, modern Baptists tend to side with Zwingli against the radical reformers, but Rainbow rejects this, saying,

> we are dealing with the same bifurcation of matter and spirit that we saw in the baptismal doctrine of Ulrich Zwingli. Among Baptists today, as with Zwingli, there is a fear of allowing water baptism to come too close to the work of grace in the sinner's heart; there are raised eyebrows and puzzled looks at the NT texts that closely associate baptism with salvation; many would rather not baptize at all than leave room for the impression that baptism is an integral part of the conversion experience.[30]

Rainbow concludes his chapter thus:

> For Zwingli, baptism was a *mere* sign. For Hubmaier, it was *more than a sign*. Baptists historically belong in the high baptismal tradition which sees baptism as the expression and embodiment of the saving work of God, the *sacramentum fidei*, not just an act of obedience tacked on. Baptists historically have known how to embrace Peter's declaration, 'Baptism now saves you' (1 Peter 3:20 [*sic*]), not because they ascribe a crude, magical saving power to the rite as such, but because they consider, on the basis of an open and personal confession, that the person coming to the water believes in Jesus Christ, and that there is an inner reality to which the baptism corresponds. Baptism is not magic, but it is more than a sign.[31]

For my purposes in this study, the most significant chapter in the book may be A.B. Caneday's analysis of 'Baptism in the Stone-Campbell Restoration Movement'. There he seeks to explain the diverse statements on baptism by Alexander Campbell in the foundational era of the movement, and also surveys some of the updated statements by contemporary Stone-Campbell scholars. Caneday asserts that Baptists must recognize that while sacerdotally-oriented views of baptism must be rejected, baptism is 'not a bare symbol'.[32] Over against those Baptists who feel it necessary to explain away the language of the New Testament baptismal texts which routinely seem to say too much, he argues for a straightforward reading of those texts. A standard proof-text for Restorationists is Acts 2.38, a text that has been a major battleground in the ongoing debate between Baptists and Churches of Christ. Caneday indicates that Baptists must simply accept the fact that the

---

[30] Rainbow, '"Confessor Baptism"', p. 205.
[31] Rainbow, '"Confessor Baptism"', p. 206. For another defense of this reading of the baptismal theology of earlier Baptists, see Fowler, *More Than a Symbol*, pp. 10-32.
[32] A.B. Caneday, 'Baptism in the Stone-Campbell Restoration Movement', in Schreiner and Wright (eds), *Believer's Baptism*, p. 285.

Restorationist interpretation that understands the forgiveness of sins as the result of baptism is 'the obvious sense of the verse'.[33]

Ultimately the question debated between these two Christian traditions is whether baptism looks forward or backward toward salvific union with Christ. Baptists in general have found it difficult to understand baptism as a causal factor in salvation, even though numerous biblical texts seem to say this, but Caneday argues cogently that this is rooted in a failure to distinguish between two senses of causality, the instrumental and the efficient. Baptists tend to say that *faith* (and not baptism) is the cause of salvation, but Caneday suggests that a more biblical approach would emphasize that even faith is only an instrumental cause of salvation, while God is the efficient cause. Viewed in this way, one could say that faith and baptism are related to salvation in virtually the same way, i.e., as instrumental causes in the application of salvation, with God as the efficient cause.[34] This view of the matter, written by a Baptist, appears to be clearly in line with the most careful statements of the Restorationist tradition, and Caneday notes with appreciation this rapprochement that is developing among scholars in these two traditions.[35]

It is very significant that this important new book has been produced by self-described conservatives in the Southern Baptist Convention. Up to this point, most of the Baptist literature that has used the language of 'sacrament' to describe baptism has come from those described as 'on the left' by conservative Baptists.[36] Now that some connected to the conservative resurgence among Southern Baptists have articulated their dissatisfaction with common Baptist rhetoric about baptism and have suggested that baptism is in fact not a mere symbol pointing backward to an already complete conversion, it will be impossible to describe this debate among Baptists as one of right versus left.

Factors other than baptismal theology forced some Baptists to rethink what they meant by the phrase 'faith alone'. I am thinking here of the intra-evangelical debate over what is called 'Lordship salvation', which was touched off by John MacArthur's *The Gospel According to Jesus* and the critical response by Zane Hodges and others in the Grace Evangelical Society.[37] MacArthur's contention was that saving faith cannot be disconnected from repentance and the acknowledgement that Jesus is both the source of forgiveness and justification on the one hand and the Lord of life on the other hand, but Hodges and his associates argued vehemently that introducing any kind of commitment to lifestyle change into conversion is to essentially teach

---

[33] Caneday, 'Baptism in the Stone-Campbell Restoration Movement', p. 311.

[34] Caneday, 'Baptism in the Stone-Campbell Restoration Movement', pp. 312-13.

[35] Caneday, 'Baptism in the Stone-Campbell Restoration Movement', pp. 326-27.

[36] See, e.g., Malcolm B. Yarnell, III, 'The Heart of a Baptist', a paper published by The Center for Theological Research, p. 7 (available online at www.BaptistTheology.org), who specifically refers to the previously noted Cross and Thompson (eds), *Baptist Sacramentalism*.

[37] See John F. MacArthur, Jr, *The Gospel According to Jesus* (Grand Rapids, MI: Zondervan, rev. edn, 1994); and Zane C. Hodges, *Absolutely Free! A Biblical Reply to Lordship Salvation* (Grand Rapids, MI: Zondervan, 1989).

works-salvation. Hodges' view has never received wide acceptance, largely because others recognize that the Pauline Epistles, which demand the *sola fide* affirmation, set faith in Christ over against a misuse of the Mosaic Law, but not over against repentance and commitment to discipleship. Once this specific focus of *sola fide* is admitted, it can also be seen that Paul does not oppose faith to baptism any more than faith to repentance. Either 'faith' or 'repentance' can be used as a synecdoche to describe Christian conversion, because they are just two aspects of one act of turning to Jesus as Lord, and it is not a great leap to say as well that baptism is the normative way in which this penitent faith comes to tangible, fully personal expression. That would explain those biblical texts which speak of union with Christ in terms of being 'baptized into Christ'.[38]

For Restorationists, one critical factor in the convergence has been increased personal contact with other evangelical traditions, including Baptists. Several scholars in the Stone-Campbell movement have studied at mainstream evangelical schools and thus created greater understanding across the divide. For example, both William Baker of Cincinnati Bible Seminary and Robert Kurka of Lincoln Christian College earned degrees at Trinity Evangelical Divinity School. Robert Lowery of Lincoln Christian Seminary is a graduate of Gordon-Conwell Theological Seminary. Perhaps the greatest leap across the divide, given the resolutely Arminian nature of Restorationism, is seen in John Mark Hicks of Lipscomb University, who earned his PhD at Westminster Seminary. Baker has noted that this exposure brought the realization of belonging to a wider Christian community and shattered stereotypes on both sides.[39]

This study in institutions outside the Stone-Campbell orbit forced Restorationists to recognize the obvious presence of the Spirit of God in other Christians, including Baptists who held to a purely memorial view of baptism as obedient witness to a previously completed and validated conversion. This, in turn, forced a second look at their own tradition, notably the writings of Alexander Campbell. Among other things they found there that Campbell himself had affirmed the presence of the Spirit among those who had never been baptized according to his paradigm, and, therefore, he affirmed the genuinely Christian status of those persons. For example, Campbell wrote

> I cannot, therefore, make any one duty the standard of Christian state or character, not even immersion into the name of the Father, of the Son, and of the Holy Spirit, and in my heart regard all that have been sprinkled in infancy without their own knowledge and consent, as aliens from Christ and the well grounded hope of heaven... It is the image of Christ the Christian looks for and loves and this does

---

[38] An illuminating treatment of the Lordship salvation controversy and its implications for the way in which faith and baptism are related can be found in Jack Cottrell, 'The Role of Faith in Conversion', in Baker (ed.), *Evangelicalism and the Stone-Campbell Movement*, pp. 75-84.

[39] William R. Baker, 'Christian Churches (Independent): Are We Evangelical?', in Baker (ed.), *Evangelicalism and the Stone-Campbell Movement*, pp. 29-31.

not consist in being exact in a few items, but in general devotion to the whole truth as far as known.[40]

In this particular passage, Campbell is discussing the status of paedobaptist Christians, but if he is prepared to consider them as genuine disciples of Christ, then quite clearly he would affirm the same of Baptists who had been immersed with an intention somewhat different from that of the Restoration.

But what about Campbell's assertion that immersion as a confessing believer is the only divinely-ordained means to the remission of sins? A fresh look at Campbell's writings revealed that he did not necessarily speak with the kind of dogmatism and exclusivism which had become common among his spiritual offspring. I have shown above that there is evidence to support the thesis that for Campbell baptism is the God-given, objective means by which God conveys the *assurance* rather than the *fact* of forgiveness. If the two ideas are not always clearly distinguished in Campbell's writings that is not surprising, because when baptism is understood to be in itself the initial confession of faith in Christ (not a witness to a prior confession) fact and assurance for all practical purposes coincide. It became clear that the Stone-Campbell movement was by no means the monolith that many people, insiders and outsiders, thought it to be.

The Stone-Campbell Study Group within the Evangelical Theological Society has helped to strengthen connections both between the a cappella Church of Christ stream and the independent Christian Church stream of the Restoration movement, and also between Stone-Campbell adherents and other Evangelicals (many of whom would be baptistic if not Baptist). The study group first met at the annual ETS meeting in November 1996, and it has met almost every year since, incorporating papers by Restorationists and scholars from outside the movement, including Baptists like Craig Blomberg of Denver Seminary and Stanley Grenz of Carey Theological College in Vancouver, Canada. The published papers of this study group give some of the clearest evidence of the refinements of Restorationist thinking that signify a convergence with Baptist thought.[41]

One sign of convergence is an increased emphasis on the divine activity in baptism and the corresponding willingness to use the term 'sacrament'. Historically,

---

[40] Alexander Campbell, 'Any Christians Among Protestant Parties?', *Millennial Harbinger* (1837), p. 412. This assertion by Campbell is quoted and affirmed by John Mark Hicks, 'Balancing Faith', p. 113. See also John Mark Hicks, 'Alexander Campbell on Christians Among the Sects', in David Fletcher (ed.), *Baptism and the Remission of Sins* (Joplin, MO: College Press, 1990), pp. 171-202; and Gary Holloway, 'Not the Only Christians: Campbell on Exclusivism and Legalism', *Christian Studies* 15 (1995–96), pp. 46-54.

[41] The previously cited volume edited by Baker, *Evangelicalism and the Stone-Campbell Movement*, is a collection of the papers given at the Stone-Campbell Study Group Meetings from 1996 to 2000. Another significant contribution is Robert C. Kurka, 'The Stone-Campbell Understanding of Conversion: A Misunderstood "Sola Fide"' (unpublished paper given at the Evangelical Theological Society, Colorado Springs, Colorado, 15 November 2001).

the Stone-Campbell tradition has emphasized baptism as a human act of obedience, the final human condition to be met in order to secure forgiveness from God. As such, they have not felt the need to talk in sacramental terms, thinking that such language minimizes the importance of the human response to the gospel and opens the door to a magical understanding of the rite. Without denying the free and responsible character of the human act in baptism, there is a new willingness to speak of baptism as God's act of bringing the penitent sinner into experiential union with Christ, and not just of baptism as the act by which the sinner appropriates Christ and his benefits. In other words, the focus falls on grace more than obedience. Hicks puts it this way:

> It is preferable to see baptism as a 'sacramental' moment where God gives his Spirit to believers through faith in God's work at the cross. It is not sacramental in a Roman Catholic sense but sacramental in that it is a 'holy moment' where God acts to unite us to himself in the baptismal symbolism of the death and resurrection of Jesus Christ. It is a divine means of grace. God truly does something gracious in the moment of baptism.[42]

Once baptism is conceived as a sacrament in which God is active from start to finish and is not just waiting for the human conditions to be met, then it is possible to reformulate baptism as the normative way that God works to seal both human faith and divine bestowal of salvation, without asserting that it is an absolute necessity. To put it another way, it is recognized that God has bound himself to baptism in such a way that the sign, rightly used, leads to the thing signified, but this does not imply that God is bound by baptism in the sense that he cannot convey grace in another way. It is one thing to say that baptism is the normative way in which the sinner turns to Christ for salvation, but quite another thing to say that there can be no salvation unless the move toward Christ occurs in this specific way. This distinction should not seem foreign to Baptists who are acquainted with the 'altar call' methodology. Many Baptist preachers have exhorted their listeners to come to the front of an auditorium in order to be saved without in any way implying that apart from such an act there can be no salvation.

A remarkable evidence of the developing paradigm shift among scholars in the Churches of Christ is the recent book, *Down in the River to Pray: Revisioning Baptism as God's Transforming Work*, co-authored by John Mark Hicks and Greg Taylor. The first sentence of the book (which recurs frequently within the volume) says, 'Baptism is more important than you think, but not for the reasons you suppose.'[43] The book proceeds, then, to argue that no tradition, not even their own Restorationist tradition, has articulated the importance of baptism in a thoroughly adequate way. Looking in several directions, they write,

---

[42] Hicks, 'Balancing Faith', p. 116.
[43] John Mark Hicks and Greg Taylor, *Down in the River to Pray: Revisioning Baptism as God's Transforming Work* (Siloam Springs, AR: Leafwood Publishers, 2004), p. 11.

> Many believe baptism is simply the sign of salvation already received. Others believe it is an indispensable command that legally divides those heading to heaven from those going to hell. Baptism is more important than either think.
>
> Baptism is a performative, or effectual, sign through which God works by his Holy Spirit to forgive, renew, sanctify and transform. It is a symbol by which we participate in the reality that it symbolizes. We must not reduce it to a mere symbol or sign that only looks to the past without any present power or reality. Baptism is more important than that.
>
> Neither is baptism, however, the technical line between heaven and hell. It is not primarily a loyalty test or a command satisfied by legal performance of the rite. We must not reduce baptism to a line in the sand. Such a reading of baptism's function reduces its significance to a technical legal requirement. Baptism is more important than that.
>
> While baptism is both a sign and a command, it is more. Baptism points beyond itself and effectually participates in God's transforming work. God is at work through baptism to transform fallen humanity into his own image, to transform the fallen human community into a people who share the life of the divine, triune community.[44]

This disavowal of baptism as a loyalty test or line in the sand indicates with some clarity that the book is moving away from a major part of the Restorationist tradition, but this becomes clearer yet in the crucial chapter, 'Transformed Unimmersed Believers?' The authors retain their tradition's emphasis on baptism as an instrument in the experience of the forgiveness of sins and the reception of the Holy Spirit, and they face squarely the question of how to view others who do not share that perspective. They argue, contrary to much of their tradition, that the answer is 'not found in a narrow treatment of the biblical texts regarding baptism', but 'must arise out of the heart, intent and goal of God'.[45] Assuming that God's purpose for fallen humans is salvation in its comprehensive sense of renewal in the image of God, baptism is then conceived of as a means of that relational transformation. But a crucial qualifier is that while baptism is an important means, it is only a means and not the end, and the end is more important than the means.[46]

The authors illustrate this superiority of spiritual reality over divinely ordained ritual by reference to Hezekiah's irregular observance of the Passover one month late (2 Chron. 30) and by reference to Jesus' defense of his disciples' activity on the Sabbath (Mt. 12.1-15). The application to baptism follows:

> Baptism is no less important than sacrifice and Sabbath in Israel's faith. But it is no more necessary than sacrifice and Sabbath were in Israel's faith. Jesus teaches us to choose mercy over sacrifice without devaluing the significance of sacrifice.

---

[44] Hicks and Taylor, *Down in the River to Pray*, pp. 11-12.
[45] Hicks and Taylor, *Down in the River to Pray*, pp. 182-83.
[46] Hicks and Taylor, *Down in the River to Pray*, pp. 184-85.

Consequently, we acknowledge that faith is more important than baptism without devaluing the significance of baptism.[47]

So then, while affirming that baptism is the normative occasion for the experience of forgiveness and the gift of the Spirit, thus assuming a unity of water and Spirit in spiritual rebirth, the authors accept that 'the Spirit is free to blow wherever God wills' (Jn 3:8), even in the lives of persons who 'have misunderstood God's immersion ritual'.[48] This distinction between 'normative instrument' and 'necessary condition' is true both to the best instincts of Alexander Campbell and, more importantly, to scripture, and it deals effectively with the crucial point of division between Baptists and the Churches of Christ.

Conclusion

It does not take a huge paradigm shift on either side to effect a convergence of Baptists and Churches of Christ in the area of baptismal theology. For Baptists it means being prepared to admit that baptism is the climax of conversion and the act of a penitent sinner, not of a confirmed saint, so that the baptizand is turning to Christ for the conscious experience of salvation. For the Churches of Christ, it means admitting that while the grace of entrance into union with Christ is normatively mediated through baptism, it is not the exclusive means, so that the negative inference, 'No valid baptism implies no salvation', is invalid. Both of these conceptual shifts are in process, and this is cause for celebration and continued dialogue.

---

[47] Hicks and Taylor, *Down in the River to Pray*, p. 192.
[48] Hicks and Taylor, *Down in the River to Pray*, pp. 193, 197.

Index

absolution 129, 130, 133
  priestly absolution 121
activism 192
admonition 122, 124
  private admonition 121
adoption 162, 169
aesthetics 12
agape feasts 67, 68
agency
  double agency 228
  efficient agent 119
  principal agent 224
  theology of agency 228
altar 20, 21, 22, 23
Anabaptism 18, 57
Anabaptists 56, 150, 262
  Dutch Mennonites 57
  Swiss Anabaptists 263
Andronoviene, Lina 33
Anglo-Catholicism 61
Anglo-Catholics 118, 133
Angus, Joseph 1
anthropology xxiii, 40, 41, 42
antiliturgica xviii, xxiii
antithetical parallelism 261
Apostolic Constitutions 250
Apostolic Fathers, the 159, 160
apostolicity of the church 59, 60
appeal 66, 170
architectural space 11
architecture 135, 141
Aristotelian realism 201
Aristotelianism 33
Aristotle 223
Arminianism 153, 178, 265
  anti-Arminianism 178
Arminius, Jacobus 57, 153
assent 257
assurance 255, 266
Athanasius 241, 242
  On the Incarnation 241
atonement 34, 37, 84, 140, 179, 180, 181-83, 187, 191, 207, 242, 244, 249
  penal substitution 179
  substitutionary atonement 179, 181

  vicarious atonement 179
Aubrey, M.E. 94
  A Minister's Manual 94
Augustine xxii, 138, 163, 164, 165, 241, 250, 252
  On the Catechising of the Uninstructed 241, 250
auricular confession 121, 125
Austin, J.L. 119, 134
autonomy 58

Bailey, Kenneth E. 108, 109
Baillie, D.M. 138
Baker, William 265
baptism xxi, xxii, xxiv, 1, 3, 5, 6, 7, 9, 12, 17, 19, 25, 26, 28, 29, 30, 31, 33, 36, 53, 55, 56, 58, 59, 61, 62-67, 75, 76, 80, 81, 85-87, 90, 91, 93, 94, 98, 103, 104, 105, 112, 113, 115, 118, 119, 121, 140, 142, 149-74, 154, 155, 156, 157, 159, 160, 161, 162, 167, 168, 169, 170, 171, 172, 173, 174, 176, 200, 214, 219, 225, 231, 232, 237, 239, 242, 244, 250, 251, 252, 253, 254, 255, 257, 258, 260, 261, 262, 263, 264, 265, 266, 267, 268, 269
  administration of baptism 64
  age of baptism 63
  baptism in/with the Spirit 33, 63, 104
  baptism on behalf of the dead 64
  baptismal efficacy 256, 258
  baptismal grace 232
  baptismal hymn 166, 168
  baptismal liturgy 166
  baptismal pool 14
  baptismal practice 6-9, 91
  baptismal regeneration xxiv, 149-74, 257
    anti-baptismal regeneration 164
  baptismal sacramentalism xxi
  baptismal services xxii
  baptismal theology 157, 162, 164, 240, 260, 262, 264, 269
  Baptist baptismal theology 149

bath 66
believers' baptism 2, 9, 81, 88, 90, 91, 150, 173, 174, 176
common baptism 231
eschatological sign 113
faith-baptism 165, 167, 173, 174
messianic baptism 261
minister of baptism 150
one baptism 79
post-baptismal sin 126, 129
reform of baptism 173, 174
second baptism 91
Spirit baptism 257, 259, 261, 262
theology of baptism 172, 173, 254
unbaptized believers 261
unimmersed believers 268
valid baptism 255
vicarious baptism 64
water 225, 228, 233, 235, 237
water baptism 104, 162, 168, 169, 170, 257, 259, 261, 262
baptistery 232
Baptists xvii, xviii, xix, xx, xxi, xxiii, xxiv, 1, 2, 3, 4, 9, 11, 17, 18, 19, 29, 31, 56, 57, 61, 62, 63, 67, 77, 78, 79, 85, 87, 88, 89, 90, 91, 92, 105, 110, 117, 119, 121, 123, 125, 129, 132, 133, 135, 136, 137, 148, 149, 151, 152, 153, 154, 162, 163, 164, 165, 166, 171, 172, 181, 189, 198, 205, 213, 214, 219, 220, 222, 224, 225, 230, 231, 233, 234, 236, 252, 253, 254-69, 255, 256, 257, 259, 260, 261, 262, 263, 265, 266, 267, 269
  Baptist Association in Charleston, South Carolina 124
  Baptist community 152
  Baptist distinctives 215
  Baptist ecclesiology 57, 151
  Baptist history 152
  Baptist identity 214, 216, 217
  Baptist individualism 217
  Baptist life xxii
  Baptist liturgical thought 198
  Baptist modality xxiii, xxiv
  Baptist practices xxiii
  Baptist sacramental theology 239, 252-53
  Baptist sacramentalists xviii, 216, 219
  Baptist theologians 252, 260
  Baptist theology/thought xviii, 22, 25, 93, 117, 149, 154, 159, 165, 168, 198, 199, 201, 212, 213, 216, 219
  Baptist tradition 151, 154, 257, 258
    evangelical Baptist tradition 61
    North American Baptist thought 213
  Baptist Union of Great Britain (and Ireland) 2, 7, 8, 78, 91, 93, 94, 95
  Baptist World Alliance xxiv, 213
  Baptist World Congress 213
    Declaration of Religious Liberty 213
  Baptist worship 252
Berkshire Association Records 125
British Baptists 7, 57, 90, 92, 116
Brush Run Church 254
Calvinistic Baptists 188
Catholic Baptists 153
conservative Baptists 264
Dover Baptist Association 254
English Baptists 239
General Baptists 6, 54, 57, 121, 152, 153, 154, 235
Loughwood Baptist Church 122, 123
Mill Yard Seventh Day Baptist Church 125
Particular Baptists 57, 92, 93, 153, 155, 235
Philadelphia Association, the xxi
Redstone Baptist Association 254
Speldhurst and Penbury Baptist Church 122
Spilshill General Baptist Church, Kent 125
White Alley's church, London 125
baptized believers 27
baptized community 113, 114
baptizers 120
Barrett, C.K. 73
Barth, Karl 52, 136, 145, 230, 232, 237
Barth, Markus 201
Bauckham, Richard 44
Bearborn, Kerry 144
Beasley-Murray, George R. 2, 63, 87, 107, 165, 166, 167, 168, 171, 173, 225, 257
  Baptism in the New Testament 258
  Christian Baptism 171
Beasley-Murray, Paul 62, 111, 112, 258

Index 273

Bebbington, David 175, 194
Becoming 237
becoming a Christian 261
Beeson Divinity School of Samford University 173
Being 237
being-sent-ness of the church 59
Bell, Rob 141
  Velvet Elvis 141
Berger, Peter xviii
biblical criticism 178
Bird, Michael F. xviii, xxiii
Blomberg, Craig L. 152, 266
body language 15
body of Christ 6, 7, 28, 31, 36, 37, 38, 40, 44, 46, 52, 67, 72, 75, 158, 202, 208, 239, 234, 235
Bolyer, Ryan 142
Bonaventure 222
Bonhoeffer, Dietrich 208
born again 160, 162, 170, 174
boundaries 68, 69, 99, 104, 105, 114
Boyce, James Petigru 218
bread and wine 1, 6, 11, 15, 29, 56, 58, 62, 68, 72, 97, 99, 100, 105, 106, 116, 127, 138, 144, 187, 191, 197, 198, 203, 204, 207, 225, 235
breaking of bread 67, 113, 125
Brown, Archibald 195
Brown, David 145
Brown, J. Baldwin 180
Bugnini, Annibale 117, 118
Bunyan, John 93, 185
Butler, Basil 51

Caesarius of Arles 239, 252
Calvin, John 12, 30, 50, 113, 119, 199, 138, 153, 156, 163, 164, 172, 190, 226, 227, 228, 232
Calvinism 57, 122, 164, 178, 190, 195, 201
Calvinists 181, 201
Campbell, Alexander 254, 255, 257, 263, 265, 266, 269
Campbell, Thomas 254, 257
Campbellites 256
Caneday, A.B. 263, 264
Cappadocian Fathers 39
Carey Theological Seminary 266
Carey, William 181
Carlile, J.C. 185
Carlton, John W. 199, 208-10
Carlyle, Thomas 175

catechesis xxiii, 241, 248, 250
  pre-baptismal catechesis 162
catechetical stataments 18
catechists 241
catechumenate 161, 245
catechumens 240, 241, 242, 244, 245, 251
catholicity 59, 60
catholicity of the church 59
causality 234
causation 227
  efficient causes 50, 223, 224
  first cause 225
  instrumental cause 50, 223, 224, 225
  instrumental efficient causes 228
  instrumental non-efficient cause 225
  material cause 223
  primary cause 223, 225, 228
  principal cause 223, 225
  secondary cause 223
Celtic spirituality 136
Celtic writing 144
ceremonial meals 25
ceremonial washings 19, 20
charismatic renewal 3, 145
charismatics 34
Charnock, Stephen 154, 226
children 111, 112, 160, 163, 164, 231
  children and communion 111
Christendom 34, 74, 75, 113, 120
  post-Christendom 43, 116
Christian baptism 29
Christian community 231
christology xxiii
church buildings 11, 140
church growth movement 142
church meeting 132
church membership 200
Church of England 90, 91, 116, 189
  Anglican Church 143
  Anglican communion 115
  Anglicanism xix, xx, 61, 201
  Anglicans 91, 172, 201
  evangelical Anglicans 156
Church of Scotland 128
church unity 58
church, the 32, 33, 51, 58, 60, 89, 120, 121, 202, 206, 231, 234, 235, 236, 241
  church as sacrament 18, 29, 32, 33, 34, 39, 48-60, 236
  church universal 236

Churches of Christ/Disciples of Christ xxiv, 151, 254-69
Cincinnati Bible Seminary 265
circumcision 70
Clark, Neville 2, 4, 5, 149, 157
Clarke, Anthony xviii, xxii, xxiii, xxiv
cleansing 19, 65, 170
   washing 19, 65, 156, 161, 167, 168, 239, 262
Clement of Alexandria 160
Clifford, John 1, 189
Coffin, Henry Sloane 209
Collins, Hercules 235, 236
Colwell, John E. xxii, xxiii, 42, 43, 87, 103, 107, 110, 111, 112, 113, 119, 127, 128, 206, 220, 225, 252
   Promise and Presence 110
command 268
common meals 28
communal actions 207
communalism 217
communion xx, xxiv, 56, 59, 67-74, 75, 76, 93, 94, 94, 103, 104, 105, 109, 110-14, 113, 114, 115-16, 127, 183, 184, 185, 186, 187, 188, 190, 192, 193, 201, 202, 203, 204, 208, 209, 237
communion table 193
community 13, 14, 15, 17, 23, 28, 30, 33, 35, 37, 39, 41, 71, 72, 75, 89, 105, 111, 112, 113, 117, 121, 203, 206, 212, 213, 215, 217, 244, 251
   community of believers 210
   community of faith 4, 205, 212, 218
   eschatological community 72
   sacred community 75
Community of the Holy Transfiguration, Geelong, Australia 129
condemnation 75
confession 116, 121, 131, 133, 170, 260
   confession of faith 55, 61, 231, 266
   confession of sin(s) 126, 127
   personal confession 263
   private confession 127
confessors 120
confirmation 231
Congregationalists 1
conscience 65, 118, 127, 170
contrition 133

conversion 62-67, 75, 115, 116, 167, 168, 169, 170, 173, 174, 183, 232, 258, 260, 261, 263, 265, 265
conversion narrative 257
conversion-baptism 173, 174, 262
conversion-initiation process 64
Cothen, Grady C. 216
Council of Trent, the 32, 221, 225, 227, 229
covenant 26, 56, 57, 79, 82, 83, 98, 103, 104, 105, 113, 114, 143, 233
   new covenant 71, 72, 204
   old covenant 19, 20, 26
covenant community 80, 115
   new covenant community 74
covenant identity(ies) 69, 80
covenantal unity 57
Cox, Benjamin 92
Cranmer, Thomas 129
creation 6, 49, 82, 120, 138, 139, 140, 145, 146, 236, 242
   creation, theology of 143
   creation, trinitarian theology of 146, 147
credobaptist traditions 151
creedal statements 18
cross and resurrection 157
Cross, Anthony R. xviii, xxii, xxiii, 2, 19
   Baptist Sacramentalism xvii, xviii, 17, 117, 176, 240
cross, the 10, 11, 21, 22, 23, 24, 26, 36, 111, 179, 180, 181, 182, 201, 204, 207, 218, 248
cultural modernism 152
Cyprian 161
Cyril of Jerusalem 162, 250

Dana, H.E. 200
Day of Atonement, the 24, 26
de Chardin, Teilhard 228
death 66
death and resurrection 158
death and resurrection of Christ 9, 36, 39, 70, 86, 109, 167, 224, 267
death of Christ 14, 21, 24, 29, 66, 73, 82, 84, 101, 106, 163, 183, 207, 248
   death, burial and resurrection of Christ xxi
decisionism 44
deconstruction 31

Index

deism 146, 147
democratic individualism 217
demonic activity 142
Denver Seminary 266
discipleship 25, 113, 176, 262, 265
discipline 121-25
Disraeli, Benjamin 175
Dissenters 256
divine acts 76
divine economy, the 41, 63
divine–human acts 76
divine–human encounter 4, 137, 141, 148
docetism 11
doctrine of God 244
Donatists 150
Dowley, T. 121, 125
dualism 139
Dunn, James D.G. 40, 80, 81
Dunn, James M. 216
dynamism 225

ecclesial body 209
ecclesial community 203
ecclesiology 8, 48, 60, 135
　antihierarchical ecclesiology xix
　evangelical ecclesiology 144
　Free Church ecclesiology 48, 54, 56, 58
ecumenism 3, 55, 93
　ecumenical dialogue 77, 78
　ecumenical hermeneutics 90
Edwards, Jonathan 181
efficacy 64, 156, 163, 165, 220, 224, 225
elect, the 164
election 79, 183
elements 210, 211, 232
Eliade, Mircea 136
Ellis, Christopher J. xviii, xxii, xxiii
embodiment 12-16, 29
　embodied grace 3, 4, 5, 12, 15
　embodied worship 9 12
emerging church, the 142, 148
emotionalism 141
enactment xxiv
encounter, theology of 148
Enlightenment, the 3, 58, 217
　Enlightenment Rationalism 152
　Enlightenment thought 43
epiclesis xxi, 232
Episcopal Church of the United States of America, the 115

eschatology 34
Esler, Philip 88
eternal life 163, 166
ethical purification 158
ethical purity 103
ethics 44
eucharist, the 12, 19, 28, 33, 36, 56, 67, 68, 73, 74, 75, 126, 127-29, 233, 242, 250, 251, see also Lord's supper
　eucharistic communion 53, 232
　eucharistic community 114
　eucharistic liturgy 58, 100
　eucharistic minimalism 188
　eucharistic presidents 120
　eucharistic sacramentalism 201
　eucharistic theology 189, 202
　eucharistic thought 214
Evangelical Revival, the 181
Evangelical Theological Society 266
evangelical tradition 152
Evangelicalism 3, 61, 152, 153, 191, 256, 265
Evangelicals 18, 154, 158, 165, 172, 266
evangelism 8, 142
evil 242, 244
ex opere operantis 222, 227
ex opere operato xxiii, xxiv, 159, 165, 166, 168, 172, 173, 191, 203, 219-38, 239
ex opere operatum 222, 229
excommunication 123, 124
exorcists 143
experience, theology of 145
experientialism 42

faith 3, 4, 8, 13, 25, 37, 55, 59, 61, 63, 73, 74, 79, 80, 81, 83, 84, 85, 86, 90, 93, 96, 97, 113, 138, 156, 157, 158, 159, 161, 163, 164, 166, 168, 170, 172, 174, 208, 214, 215, 222, 229, 230, 232, 236, 239, 242, 254, 257, 259, 260, 263, 264, 265, 269
　infused faith 263
　vicarious faith 158
faith alone 264
　sola fide 165, 255, 265
Faith and Order 3
　Baptism, Eucharist and Ministry 77
fall, the 242, 244
fasting 121, 159

feast 109, 205
fellowship 18, 56, 57, 70, 71, 72, 75, 89, 103, 124, 125, 186, 202, 203, 218
Fiddes, Paul S. xxii, xxiii, 40, 57, 88
final consummation 146
food laws 88, 89
footwashing 6, 18, 20, 30
forgiveness xxii, xxiv, 36, 37, 58, 115, 126-27, 129, 132, 134, 163, 167, 207, 255, 261, 262, 264, 266, 267, 268, 269
foundationalism 31, 32
Fowler, Stanley K. xviii, xxiv, 87, 156
Free Church tradition 11, 56, 60
Free Churches, the 7, 30, 48, 55, 58
free will 178
freedom 214, 215, 228
freedom of God, the 11, 145, 234
freedom of the Spirit 63
Freeman, Curtis W. 199, 217
full assurance 184
Fuller Theological Seminary 142
Fuller, Andrew 181

Garrett, J.L. 125
gathered community 12, 34, 110, 111, 114
Gathering for Worship 98
general confession 126, 127, 128, 129-31
George, Timothy 173, 195
Gibbs, Eddie 142
Gibson, David 74
Gillett, David 178
Gladstone, W.E. 195
Glas, John 254
God's ontic actuality 42
God's transcendence 143, 144
Gordon, James 184, 185, 186, 190
Gordon-Conwell Theological Seminary 265
gospel, the 32, 49, 62, 65, 67, 76, 80, 81, 82, 83, 85, 87, 111, 173, 174
gospel, false 256
Gould, G.P. 94
A Manual for Free Church Ministers 94
grace xix, xxi, xxiii, 9, 14, 15, 20, 23, 26, 28, 31, 34, 36, 42, 49, 50, 54, 76, 80, 84, 85, 90, 105, 107, 108, 111, 113, 118, 119, 120, 130, 133, 155, 156, 163, 166, 169, 176, 188, 205, 208, 215, 216, 222, 223, 224, 225, 226, 227, 229, 230, 233, 234, 236, 238, 239, 257, 263, 267
automatic grace 220
falling from grace 123
transforming grace 59
Grace Evangelical Society, the 264
Grantham, Thomas xix, 154, 235
Grass, Tim 176, 188, 190
Great Commission, the 64, 147, 173, 261
greeting 18
Gregory of Nyssa xxiv, 239-53
  Against Those Who Postpone Baptism 242
  Catechetical Oration 239, 240, 241, 242, 253, 245, 250, 251, 252
  Homilies on the Beatitudes 251
Grenz, Stanley J. 259, 260, 266
Gruden, Wayne 258
Gunton, Colin E. 146
Gushee, David P. 44
Guthrie, Donald 168

Hall, Robert 1
Harmon, Steven R. xxiii, xxiv
Hays, Richard 71
Helwys, Thomas 57
hermeneutics 215
Hicks, John Mark 265, 267
  Down in the River to Pray: Revisioning Baptism as God's Transforming Work 267
hiddenness of God 60, 237
hierarchized communion 51
hierarchy 58, 59, 60
hierophanies 136
Hinson, E. Glenn 216, 217
Hippolytus 161
Hobbs, Herschel 197
Hodge, Archibald Alexander 180
Hodge, Charles 180
Hodges, Zane 264, 265
holiness xxiv, 54, 60, 65, 75, 121, 187
holy kiss, the 18
holy, the 137
Honiton, Devon 122, 123
Hopkins, Gerard Manley 17, 227, 228
Hopkins, Mark 178
Horne, C. Sylvester 1
Howard, Fred D. 199, 200-203, 205
Hubbard, R.L. Jr 152

Hubmaier, Balthasar 56, 57, 262, 263
Hugh of St Victor 226
hymnbooks 8
hymns xxi, xxii, 16, 190
hypostatized symbolism 202

iconoclastic controversy 10
iconography 32, 145
identification 86
idolatry 71
illumination 19, 63, 160
immanence 138, 139, 142, 144, 147
immediacy 32, 43
immersion 63, 87, 149, 150, 151, 228, 266, 269
immortality 160, 203
imputation of righteousness 163
incarnation, the 5, 6, 9, 10, 11, 15, 18, 32, 34, 35, 36, 37, 41, 42, 139, 140, 141, 146, 147, 148, 218, 233, 242, 248, 249
incorporation into Christ 87
independence 58
individualism 174, 205, 211, 213, 214, 216, 218
infallibility 178, 180
infant baptism 9, 77, 78, 79, 85, 87, 88, 90, 91, 112, 113, 159, 160, 161, 163, 164, 168, 172, 232, 254, 263, 263, see also paedobaptism
infant dedication 259
infant sprinkling 149
Inge, John 139, 146
initiation 19, 33, 91, 149, 167, 231, 232, 244, 251, 259
  Christian initiation 19, 231
  sacrament of initiation 113
instruction 18
instrumentality 49, 59, 104, 224, 262
  instrument 18, 51
  instrumental cause 50, 223, 224, 225
  instrumental efficient causes 228
  instrumental means 119
  instrumental non-efficient cause 225
insulae 87-90
interconnectedness 40
interdependence 13
International Baptist Theological Seminary 165
inward cleansing 66
Iona 136
Irenaeus 49, 160

Jenson, Robert 51, 52
Jewett, Robert 67, 88, 89
John Chrysostom 15
John of Damascus 10
Jones, Keith G. 93
journey 232
justification 65, 70, 80, 84, 85, 86, 165, 167, 168, 169, 264
Justin Martyr 19, 159, 160

Kant, Emmanuel 40
Käsemann, Ernst 81
Keach, Benjamin 154, 226
kingdom of God 34, 44, 107, 109, 143, 206
Klein, W.W. 152
Köstenberger, Andreas 261
Kruppa, Patricia 175
Kurka, Robert 265
Kyrie eleison 130, 131

Lambeth Union, the 195
Lampe, P. 101
Landmarkists 200
Larsen, Timothy 195
Lash, Nicholas 40
Last Supper 68, 72, 99, 100, 105, 106, 107, 111, 201
Lathrop, Gordon xviii, xix, xx, xxiv
laying on of hands 4, 6, 161
legalism 70
lex credendi xxi, 8
lex orandi 8
lex supplicandi xxi
liberalism 205
Lincoln Christian Seminary 265
Lindisfarne 136
Lipscomb University 265
liturgical practice(s) xxiii, 4, 7, 8, 94-99
  liturgical rites 51
liturgical theology 4, 6
liturgy xvii, 5, 32, 211, 245
  liturgy of the table 245
local church 45, 150
local congregation 37, 44, 58
Lombard, Peter 6
London Confession, The (1644) 92, 213, 214
Lord's supper xvii, xix, xx, xxiv, 1, 2, 3, 5, 6, 17, 18, 19, 21, 22, 25, 26, 27-29, 30, 31, 36, 55, 56, 57, 61, 62, 67-74, 75, 76, 92, 93, 94, 95,

96, 97, 99, 100, 101, 102, 103, 104, 105, 107, 110, 111, 112, 114, 115, 116, 150, 152, 155, 156, 175-96, 197, 199, 200, 201, 202, 203, 204, 205, 207, 208, 209, 210, 211, 212, 213, 214, 219, 224, 231, 232, 234, 235, 239, 240, 252, 253, 259, see also eucharist
  converting ordinance 116
Lord's table 14, 67, 92, 96, 98, 102, 113, 114, 205, 207, 212, 214
  open table 115
  theology of communion 116
  theology of the elements 199
Lordship salvation controversy, the 265
love-feast 36
loving acts 18
Lowery, Robert 265
lustration(s) 158
Luther, Martin 50, 80, 81, 85, 163, 219, 221, 263
Lutheranism 18, 80
Lutherans 51, 52, 201

MacArthur, John 264
  Gospel According to Jesus, The 264
Macmurray, John 202
Macquarrie, John 229
Maddox, Timothy D.F. 217
magic 61, 62
Manchester Cathedral 136
martyrdom 25
martyrs 135
mass, the 30, 67, 189
material media 4, 5, 11, 15
materiality 9, 10, 206, 252
matter 51
McBeth, H. Leon 153
McClendon, James W. Jr 43, 165
McDermott, Timothy 224
McElrath, Hugh T. 199
McFague, Sallie 138, 139
McLaren, Brian 142
McLean, Archibald 254
meals 68, 71
means of grace 2, 9, 14, 42, 61, 76, 110, 111, 113, 128, 133, 202, 208, 218, 219, 220, 235, 258, 267, 268
mediation xxi, 42, 50, 51, 52, 54, 57, 60, 65, 120, 145, 146, 210, 211, 215, 216, 237
  mediated immediacy 49, 237

mediated presence 53
mediating efficacy 34
mediating function of the Holy Spirit 49, 50
mediation of the Spirit 52
mediation(s) of grace 31, 32, 42
mediatorial principle 237
unmediated immediacy 50
unmediated presence 54, 55
unmediated, the 42, 43
Meltio of Sardis 25
membership 7, 8, 9, 70, 76, 121, 124
memorial 188
memorialism 56, 57, 189, 201
  mere memorialism 235
  Zwinglian memorialism 31
memorialists 190
Mennonites 30
Mentone 179, 184, 186, 189, 192, 194
Meredith, Anthony 242
messianic banquet 109, 115
metaphor 13, 25, 27, 52, 74, 104, 139, 158, 169
  synecdoche 167
Methodism 18
Metropolitan Taberncle, the 179, 189, 190, 191, 195
Michaels, J. Ramsey xxiii, 169
Migne, J.-P. 241, 251
Milton, John 124
minimalism 201
minister(s) 59, 222, 224, 229, 252
ministry 46, 199
mission 59, 142, 144, 147, 148, 199, 231
missionary candidates 149, 150
missionaries 149, 150
Mitchill, William 155, 156, 157
modernity 75
Moltmann, Jürgen 49, 113, 115, 146
monasticism 136
Mönnich, C.W. xviii
Morden, Peter J. xxii, xxiii, xviii, xx
Morgan-Wynne, John E. 159
mortification 163
Moynagh, Michael 137
Mühlenberg, Ekkehard 241, 242
Muir, Edwin 11
Mullins, E.Y. 213, 215, 216, 217, 218
  Axioms of Religion 213
  Christian Religion in Its Doctrinal Expression, The 217
Mullinsianism 216

Murphy, Nancey 40
music 145
mystagogical catechesis 242-45
mystagogy 4, 245
mysteries 15
mystery 12, 26, 51, 59, 60, 245, 251
mystical experiences 14
mysticism 11, 141

neo-paganism 62, 147
neo-pentecostals 34
Nettles, Tom J. xvii, 216
new birth 157, 161, 169, 170
new creation 140, 166
New Perspective on Paul 80
Newman, Elizabeth 218
Nicene theology 41 42
Nicoll, William Robertson 185
Noel, Baptist Wriothesley 156, 157
Nonconformists 34
Northumbria Community, the 136

O'Connor, Flannery 17
obedience 61, 66, 75, 81, 113, 150, 155, 156, 165, 170, 197, 208, 214, 256, 261, 262, 267
objectivity 221
objects 29
omnipresence 146, 147, 148
ontological mediator 237
opus operatum 222, 226, 234
ordinance(s) xix, xx, 1, 3, 30, 61, 62, 75, 116, 123, 150, 151, 155, 176, 194, 198, 203, 208, 259
dominical ordinances 6
ordination 17, 133
ordination of women 70
ordo salutis 63
original sin 161, 165
Orthodox Creed, The (1679) 152
Orthodox theology 259
Orthodoxy 10, 32, 55
Russian Orthodoxy 8
orthodoxy 40, 43, 44
orthopathy 40, 43, 44, 45-46
orthopraxis/orthopraxy 40, 43, 44, 45-46
Otto, Rudolf 136
Oxford Movement, the 1, 61, 189
Tractarians 61

paedobaptism 77, 103, 113, 162, 167, 261, see also infant baptism

Paedobaptists 88, 153, 158, 260, 266
pagan philosophy 242
paganism 203
Pahl, Jon 138, 139
panentheism 146, 147
pantheism 139, 146, 147
Parker, Gary E. 216
participation 28, 71, 76, 86, 166, 167, 213, 237
participation in Christ 58, 91, 103
partnership 70, 71
Passover 24, 68, 69, 110, 111, 112, 268
Pastor's College 180
pastoral care 133
pastoral theology 129
Patterns and Prayers for Christian Worship 95, 96, 97
Patterson, D. Tait 94, 95
Call to Worship, The 94, 97
Patterson, Paige 205
Payne, Ernest A. 7, 95
Orders and Prayers for Church Worship 95, 96, 97, 99
peace, the 14, 58
Pelagianism 56, 57
penance xxiv, 117-34
private penance 132-34
Pendleton, J.M. 200
penitence 118
penitential rites 121
Peretti, Frank 143
perfection 160
perichoresis 40, 42, 49
perichoretic oneness 58
persecution 29, 114
personology 41
Peter of Poitiers 222
Peterson, Eugene 137, 182
phenomenology 31
Philo 19
physicalism 41, 42, 47
physicality 38, 39, 40-41, 43, 44, 45
piety 180
pilgrimage(s) xxiv, 128, 137, 144
Pinnock, Clark H. 17, 18, 117, 259, 260
Plato 237
Platonism 237
pledge 66, 170
pluralism 62, 74, 75
pneumatology 159
postmodern culture 45

postmodern world 62
postmodern culture 136
postmodernity 31
post-Nicene theology 42
praise 18
Praise God 95
prayer 23, 59, 60, 121, 140, 155, 159
prayer of confession 115
preaching xviii, xix, xx, 17, 218
predestinarianism 57
predestination 164
pre-existence of the Logos 39
pre-Nicene theology 41
Presbyterian Church of Scotland, the 30
Presbyterians 154, 254
presence of Christ 59, 72, 201, 203, 211, 233, 235
  unique presence 201
priestcraft 120, 132
priesthood 23
priesthood of all believers 118, 132
Princeton College 180
proclamation 73, 199, 210, 214, 232
profession of faith 232
promise 50, 51, 59, 60, 138
propitiation 169
Protestantism 33, 55, 81, 90, 233
  Protestant churches 62
  Protestant liberalism 145
  Protestant tradition 136
Protestants 169
  evangelical Protestants 135
Puritanism 57, 190
Puritans 154, 172
  English Puritanism 257
Purves, Jim xxii, xxiii

Quakers 122, 123

radical reformers 263
Rahner, Karl 52, 233, 234, 236
Rainbow, Jonathan 174, 262, 263
Randall, Ian M. 176, 177, 188, 190
ransom 248
rationalism 3
Ratzinger, Joseph 54
re-baptism xxiv, 78, 91, 150, 151
rebirth 162, 174
reconciliation 37, 117, 169
redemption 49, 84, 115, 157, 179, 207, 258
  general redemption 123
  particular redmption 178

reductionism 3, 4
'Re-envisioning Baptist Identity: A Manifesto for Baptist Communities in North America' 214, 215
Reformation, the 3, 6, 67, 117, 118, 120, 126
Reformed groups 232
Reformed tradition, the 138, 139, 195, 255
reformers, the 227, 254, 256
  magisterial reformers 163
regeneration 63, 150, 154, 155, 156, 157, 158, 159, 160, 161, 162, 163, 164, 165, 166, 167, 168, 169, 170, 172, 174, 227, 260, 262
relativism 31
religious art 145
remembering practices 214
remission of sins 162, 254, 255
Renaissance, the 3
renewal 158, 162, 167, 168
repentance 116, 118, 124, 156, 158, 160, 170, 242, 260, 265
restoration 249
Restoration movement 256, 266
Restoration(ist) tradition 264, 267, 268
Restorationism 264
Restorationists 257, 258, 261, 265, 266
resurrection xxii, 9, 10, 11, 35, 38, 39, 43, 150, 170, 209
  bodily resurrection 38
  resurrection and ascension of Christ 249
  resurrection of Christ 65, 66, 67, 163, 228
revelation 237
  special revelation 17
revivalism 31
Rhodes, Lewis E. 210-13
Richardson, Cyril 242
righteousness 75, 81, 82, 83, 84, 165
rite(s) xxi, xxii, 211, 268
ritual(s) xvii, xxiv, 13, 20, 29, 88, 210
ritual action(s) 4, 11
ritualism 189
Robertson, A.T. 261
Robinson, H. Wheeler 215
Roman Catholic Church 18, 118, 120, 227
  Catechism of the Catholic Church 220, 221, 225, 230, 232

Index 281

Lumen Gentium 18, 51, 235
Roman Catholicism 18, 21, 33, 55, 189, 190, 205, 219, 228, 233, 259, 260
   Roman Catholic theology 117, 222, 259
   quasi-Catholicism 61
Roman Catholics xxiv, 5, 51, 52, 133, 172, 201, 231
   medieval Catholics 263
Romanticism 152
Ross, J.M. 149
Rust, Eric C. 199, 205-208, 209

sacerdotalism 52, 263
sacrament of continuation 113
sacrament(s) xvii, xviii, xix, xx, xxiii, 2, 3, 4, 5, 6, 9, 12, 15, 14, 17, 25-27, 26, 27, 28, 30-32, 31, 32, 34, 35, 36, 37, 42, 43, 46, 47, 48, 50, 51, 53, 55, 61, 62, 67, 76, 93, 105, 110-14, 115, 117, 118-20, 133, 138, 140, 144, 155, 161, 163, 176, 196, 200, 205, 210, 216, 219, 220, 221, 223, 224, 225, 226, 227, 228, 229, 230, 231, 232, 233, 234, 235, 236, 240, 252, 259, 264, 266, 267
   dominical sacraments 6
   ecclesial sacraments 17
   first covenant sacraments 26
   gospel sacraments 84
   natural sacraments 17
   objective sacrament 211
   one sacrament, Jesus Christ 62
   primal sacrament, the 35-36, 51, 235
   primary sacrament 32, 33, 35, 36, 37, 38, 41, 43, 44
   primordial sacrament 5, 6, 11, 18
   sacraments of faith 229
   sacramentum fidei 263
   quasi-magical view of sacraments 119
   secondary sacraments 36, 43, 46, 47
   seven sacraments 252
   theology of the sacraments 253
   visible sacrament 51
sacramental theology xvii, xx, xxii, xxiii, xxiii, 1, 2, 3-6, 10, 12, 31, 32, 37, 48, 61, 159, 203, 213, 217, 219, 234, 239, 260
   pre-Reformation sacramental theology 67
   Roman Catholic sacramental theology 220

sacramental action(s) 88, 260
sacramental acts 227
sacramental efficacy xxiv, 138
sacramental elements 14-15, 206
sacramental embodiment 90
sacramental encounter(s) 140, 144
sacramental events 12
sacramental grace 33
sacramental identity 60
sacramental means 86
sacramental mediation 54, 55, 58, 59
sacramental moment 267
sacramental mysteries 242
sacramental offices 233
sacramental participation 56, 59
sacramental practice xxii, 3, 104
sacramental principle 237
sacramental realism 87
sacramental union 156
sacramental universe 206
sacramentalism xvii, xviii, xxiii, xxiv, 18, 19, 25, 29, 61, 142, 150, 153, 156, 171, 198, 259
   anti-sacramentalism 61, 164, 258, 262
   biblical sacramentalism 62
   Calvinistic sacramentalism 157
sacramentalists 153
sacramentality 3-6, 48, 50, 52, 137, 138, 140, 206, 228
   sacramentality of creation 18, 252
   sacramentality of the church 252
   sacramentality of the word 239-53
sacramentally mediated holiness 59
sacramentals 227
sacred space 135-48
   holiness of place xxiv
sacredness 144
sacrifice(s) 1, 13, 19, 20, 21, 22, 23, 24, 25-27, 28, 84, 132, 187, 204, 207, 208, 209, 227, 268
   atoning sacrifice 37
sacrificial meals 28
salvation xxii, 6, 10, 20, 36, 55, 62, 63, 64, 66, 74, 79, 80, 83, 84, 85, 86, 91, 115-16, 150, 151, 155, 157, 158, 163, 167, 169, 170, 179, 187, 201, 203, 214, 239, 255, 257, 262, 263, 264, 267, 268, 269
   economy of salvation 218
   universal salvation 161
   works/works salvation 85, 265
Salvation Army, the 42, 112

salvation history 206, 250
sanctification 15, 38, 53, 54, 65, 85, 165, 229
sanctifying grace 59
Sandeman, Robert 254
Sanders, E.P. 81
satisfaction 133
Scampini, Jorge 221, 230
scepticism 31, 43
Schillebeeckx, Edward 5, 6, 11, 230
Schleiermacher, F.D.E. 55
Schmemann, Alexander 4, 5, 8
Schneider, Johannes 159
Scholasticism 118
Schoolmen, the 119
Schreiner, Thomas R. 167, 168, 173, 174, 262
seal 50, 160, 162, 255
Second Helvetic Confession, The (1566) 232
Second London Confession, The (1677/89) 61, 93, 152, 198
secularism 74
Segler, Franklin M. 199
self-examination 102, 116
Separatism 90
Separatists 172
shadows 26
Shakespeare, J.H. 94
  A Manual for Free Church Ministers 94
Sheldrake, Philip 177, 191
Sheppy, Paul xviii, xxiii, xxiv
Shurden, Walter B. 215, 216
  The Baptist Identity: Four Fragile Freedoms 215
sign(s) xxi, 18, 51, 118, 119, 120, 140, 154, 156, 176, 220, 225, 228, 235, 263 267, 268
  effectual sign 268
  figure 154
  initiatory sign 163
  outward sign 86
  performative sign 268
  signification 119, 134
  sign of regeneration 164
  signs of faith 229
sin xxi, 37, 38, 62, 79, 86, 97, 117, 118, 119, 120, 121, 126, 127, 130, 150, 155, 158, 159, 160, 161, 163, 167, 169, 170, 182, 184, 251, 254, 261, 262, 268
singing 18

Smyth, John xix, 54, 55, 57, 58
  Paralleles: Censures: Observations xix
Society of Friends, the 42
soteriology xxiii, 159, 174
soul competency 205, 213-18
Southern Baptist Convention 149, 151, 199, 216, 264
  International Mission Board 149, 151, 152, 159, 173
Southern Baptist doctrine 201
Southern Baptist theology/thought xxiv 202
Southern Baptist Theological Seminary, The 165, 167, 168, 203, 258, 260
Southern Baptists xvii, 125, 150, 151, 196-218, 258, 260
  Baptist Faith and Message, The 150, 199, 197
  Review and Expositor 203
sovereignty of God 63, 82
speech-events 119
spiritual cleansing 19
spiritual direction 128
spiritual efficacy 162
spiritual gifts 29
spiritual individualism 215
spiritual union 57
spirituality 3, 9, 10, 11, 176-77
Spurgeon, Charles Haddon 175-96
  Sword and Trowel 192
  Till He Come 181, 192, 194
Spurgeon, Susannah 192
Spurr, Frederic C. 94
Stackhouse, Ian 31, 32, 43
Stagg, Frank 199, 203-205
Stassen, Glen H. 44
state church xx
Stein, Robert H. 166, 167, 260, 261
Stone, Barton W. 254, 257
Stone-Campbell movement 256, 257, 258, 263, 265, 266, 267
Stone-Campbell Study Group 266
subjectivism 50, 257
subordinationism 41
symbol(s) xx, xxi, 21, 25, 26, 67, 154, 140, 169, 187, 188, 191, 204, 206, 207, 211, 226, 259, 268
  effective symbol(s) 62, 67, 75, 76
  mere symbol 61
  symbols of the gospel 67

symbolism 2, 56, 63, 65, 68, 72, 73, 87, 91, 107, 109, 119, 142, 150, 151, 161, 162, 164, 166, 197, 200, 202, 207, 211, 258, 259, 263, 267
  effective symbolic events 18
  mere symbolism xvii, 252
  prophetic symbolism 209
  symbolic act(s) 207, 208
  symbolic enactment 67
Synod of Dort, the 178

table fellowship 98, 99, 105-107, 111, 201
  fenced table 95, 99, 101, 110
Tarwater, Francis Marion 17
Taylor, Greg 267
  Down in the River to Pray: Revisioning Baptism as God's Transforming Work 267
teaching 18
Temple, William 138
Tennyson, Alfred (Lord) 175
terms of communion 200
  closed communion xxiv
  open communion 93, 115
territorial spirits 142, 143
Tertullian 159, 160
thanksgiving 18
Theodore of Mopsuestia 161
Theology of the Sacraments 138
theophany 37, 45
Theophilus of Antioch 160
Thiselton, Anthony C. 103
Thomas Aquinas 50, 52, 119, 133, 163, 221, 222, 223, 224, 225, 228, 229, 236
  Thomism 225
Thomas, R.S. 228
Thompson, Philip E. 154, 155, 216
  Baptist Sacramentalism xvii, xviii, 17, 117, 176, 240
Tidball, Derek 152
Tillich, Paul 206
total depravity 180
transcendence 32, 42, 138, 139, 147
transformative event 211
transforming work of God 65
transubstantiation 189, 190
Tribble, Harold W. 200
  Our Doctrines 200
Trinity, the xxiii, 11, 37, 39, 40, 41, 42, 48, 49, 54, 58, 144, 147, 226, 230, 237

  economic Trinity, the 41
  immanent Trinity, the 41, 42
  trinitarian formula 64
Trinity Evangelical Divinity School 265
Tuck, William Powell 216
Turner, Philip 115

Underwood, William D. 216
union with Christ 67, 167, 183-84, 187, 255, 259, 264, 267
United Reformed Church 256

Vanier, Jean 33
Vatican II 117, 118, 220, 222, 229, 230, 235
Vatican, the xxiv
via negativa 63
vivification 169
Volf, Miroslav 48, 54, 55, 55, 56, 57, 58
voluntarism 56, 57
Von Balthasar, hans Urs 233

Wagner, C. Peter 142
Walker, Michael J. 179, 188
Watts, Graham xxii, xxiii, xxiv
Webster, John 85
weddings 140
Wesley, John 116
Westminster Confession of Faith (1647) 153, 172, 198
Westminster Seminary 265
White, R.E.O. 2, 157, 158
White, Sean A. xvii, xviii, xxiii
Wilson, Linda 176
Winter, Sean F. xxiii, xxiv
Winward, Stephen F. 7, 95
  Orders and Prayers for Church Worship 95, 96, 97, 99
word and sacrament(s) 30, 96, 208, 210
World Council of Churches 3, 77
worship 12, 13, 14, 15, 20, 22, 23, 24, 27, 29, 44, 137, 139, 199, 204, 205, 212, 253
worship music 70
Wright, David F. 63, 165
Wright, Nigel G. 112, 114

Zizioulas, John 54
Zwingli, Huldrych/Ulrich 56, 164, 235, 262, 263
Zwinglianism 31, 164, 252

Studies in Baptist History and Thought

(All titles uniform with this volume)
Dates in bold are of projected publication
Volumes in this series are not always published in sequence

David Bebbington and Anthony R. Cross (eds)
Global Baptist History
(SBHT vol. 14)

This book brings together studies from the Second International Conference on Baptist Studies which explore different facets of Baptist life and work especially during the twentieth century.

2006 / 1-84227-214-4 / approx. 350pp

David Bebbington (ed.)
The Gospel in the World
International Baptist Studies
(SBHT vol. 1)

This volume of essays from the First International Conference on Baptist Studies deals with a range of subjects spanning Britain, North America, Europe, Asia and the Antipodes. Topics include studies on religious tolerance, the communion controversy and the development of the international Baptist community, and concludes with two important essays on the future of Baptist life that pay special attention to the United States.

2002 / 1-84227-118-0 / xiv + 362pp

John H.Y. Briggs (ed.)
Pulpit and People
Studies in Eighteenth Century English Baptist Life and Thought
(SBHT vol. 28)

The eighteenth century was a crucial time in Baptist history. The denomination had its roots in seventeenth-century English Puritanism and Separatism and the persecution of the Stuart kings with only a limited measure of freedom after 1689. Worse, however, was to follow for with toleration came doctrinal conflict, a move away from central Christian understandings and a loss of evangelistic urgency. Both spiritual and numerical decline ensued, to the extent that the denomination was virtually reborn as rather belatedly it came to benefit from the Evangelical Revival which brought new life to both Arminian and Calvinistic Baptists. The papers in this volume study a denomination in transition, and relate to theology, their views of the church and its mission, Baptist spirituality, and engagements with radical politics.

2007 / 1-84227-403-1 / approx. 350pp

July 2005

Damian Brot
Church of the Baptized or Church of Believers?
A Contribution to the Dialogue between the Catholic Church and the Free Churches with Special Reference to Baptists
(SBHT vol. 26)

The dialogue between the Catholic Church and the Free Churches in Europe has hardly taken place. This book pleads for a commencement of such a conversation. It offers, among other things, an introduction to the American and the international dialogues between Baptists and the Catholic Church and strives to allow these conversations to become fruitful in the European context as well.

2006 / 1-84227-334-5 / approx. 364pp

Dennis Bustin
Paradox and Perseverence
Hanserd Knollys, Particular Baptist Pioneer in Seventeenth-Century England
(SBHT vol. 23)

The seventeenth century was a significant period in English history during which the people of England experienced unprecedented change and tumult in all spheres of life. At the same time, the importance of order and the traditional institutions of society were being reinforced. Hanserd Knollys, born during this pivotal period, personified in his life the ambiguity, tension and paradox of it, openly seeking change while at the same time cautiously embracing order. As a founder and leader of the Particular Baptists in London and despite persecution and personal hardship, he played a pivotal role in helping shape their identity externally in society and, internally, as they moved toward becoming more formalised by the end of the century.

2006 / 1-84227-259-4 / approx. 324pp

Anthony R. Cross
Baptism and the Baptists
Theology and Practice in Twentieth-Century Britain
(SBHT vol. 3)

At a time of renewed interest in baptism, *Baptism and the Baptists* is a detailed study of twentieth-century baptismal theology and practice and the factors which have influenced its development.

2000 / 0-85364-959-6 / xx + 530pp

Anthony R. Cross and Philip E. Thompson (eds)
Baptist Sacramentalism
(SBHT vol. 5)
This collection of essays includes biblical, historical and theological studies in the theology of the sacraments from a Baptist perspective. Subjects explored include the physical side of being spiritual, baptism, the Lord's supper, the church, ordination, preaching, worship, religious liberty and the issue of disestablishment.
2003 / 1-84227-119-9 / xvi + 278pp

Anthony R. Cross and Philip E. Thompson (eds)
Baptist Sacramentalism 2
(SBHT vol. 25)
This second collection of essays exploring various dimensions of sacramental theology from a Baptist perspective includes biblical, historical and theological studies from scholars from around the world.
2006 / 1-84227-325-6 / approx. 350pp

Paul S. Fiddes
Tracks and Traces
Baptist Identity in Church and Theology
(SBHT vol. 13)
This is a comprehensive, yet unusual, book on the faith and life of Baptist Christians. It explores the understanding of the church, ministry, sacraments and mission from a thoroughly theological perspective. In a series of interlinked essays, the author relates Baptist identity consistently to a theology of covenant and to participation in the triune communion of God.
2003 / 1-84227-120-2 / xvi + 304pp

Stanley K. Fowler
More Than a Symbol
The British Baptist Recovery of Baptismal Sacramentalism
(SBHT vol. 2)
Fowler surveys the entire scope of British Baptist literature from the seventeenth-century pioneers onwards. He shows that in the twentieth century leading British Baptist pastors and theologians recovered an understanding of baptism that connected experience with soteriology and that in doing so they were recovering what many of their forebears had taught.
2002 / 1-84227-052-4 / xvi + 276pp

Steven R. Harmon
Towards Baptist Catholicity
Essays on Tradition and the Baptist Vision
(SBHT vol. 27)

This series of essays contends that the reconstruction of the Baptist vision in the wake of modernity's dissolution requires a retrieval of the ancient ecumenical tradition that forms Christian identity through rehearsal and practice. Themes explored include catholic identity as an emerging trend in Baptist theology, tradition as a theological category in Baptist perspective, Baptist confessions and the patristic tradition, worship as a principal bearer of tradition, and the role of Baptist higher education in shaping the Christian vision.

2006 / 1-84227-362-0 / approx. 210pp

Michael A.G. Haykin (ed.)
'At the Pure Fountain of Thy Word'
Andrew Fuller as an Apologist
(SBHT vol. 6)

One of the greatest Baptist theologians of the eighteenth and early nineteenth centuries, Andrew Fuller has not had justice done to him. There is little doubt that Fuller's theology lay behind the revitalization of the Baptists in the late eighteenth century and the first few decades of the nineteenth. This collection of essays fills a much needed gap by examining a major area of Fuller's thought, his work as an apologist.

2004 / 1-84227-171-7 / xxii + 276pp

Michael A.G. Haykin
Studies in Calvinistic Baptist Spirituality
(SBHT vol. 15)

In a day when spirituality is in vogue and Christian communities are looking for guidance in this whole area, there is wisdom in looking to the past to find untapped wells. The Calvinistic Baptists, heirs of the rich ecclesial experience in the Puritan era of the seventeenth century, but, by the end of the eighteenth century, also passionately engaged in the catholicity of the Evangelical Revivals, are such a well. This collection of essays, covering such things as the Lord's Supper, friendship and hymnody, seeks to draw out the spiritual riches of this community for reflection and imitation in the present day.

2006 / 1-84227-149-0 / approx. 350pp

Brian Haymes, Anthony R. Cross and Ruth Gouldbourne
On Being the Church
Revisioning Baptist Identity
(SBHT vol. 21)

The aim of the book is to re-examine Baptist theology and practice in the light of the contemporary biblical, theological, ecumenical and missiological context drawing on historical and contemporary writings and issues. It is not a study in denominationalism but rather seeks to revision historical insights from the believers' church tradition for the sake of Baptists and other Christians in the context of the modern–postmodern context.

***2006** / 1-84227-121-0 / approx. 350pp*

Ken R. Manley
From Woolloomooloo to 'Eternity': A History of Australian Baptists
Volume 1: Growing an Australian Church (1831–1914)
Volume 2: A National Church in a Global Community (1914–2005)
(SBHT vols 16.1 and 16.2)

From their beginnings in Australia in 1831 with the first baptisms in Woolloomoolloo Bay in 1832, this pioneering study describes the quest of Baptists in the different colonies (states) to discover their identity as Australians and Baptists. Although institutional developments are analyzed and the roles of significant individuals traced, the major focus is on the social and theological dimensions of the Baptist movement.

*2 vol. set **2006** / 1-84227-405-8 / approx. 900pp*

Ken R. Manley
'Redeeming Love Proclaim'
John Rippon and the Baptists
(SBHT vol. 12)

A leading exponent of the new moderate Calvinism which brought new life to many Baptists, John Rippon (1751–1836) helped unite the Baptists at this significant time. His many writings expressed the denomination's growing maturity and mutual awareness of Baptists in Britain and America, and exerted a long-lasting influence on Baptist worship and devotion. In his various activities, Rippon helped conserve the heritage of Old Dissent and promoted the evangelicalism of the New Dissent

2004 / 1-84227-193-8 / xviii + 340pp

Peter J. Morden
Offering Christ to the World
Andrew Fuller and the Revival of English Particular Baptist Life
(SBHT vol. 8)

Andrew Fuller (1754–1815) was one of the foremost English Baptist ministers of his day. His career as an Evangelical Baptist pastor, theologian, apologist and missionary statesman coincided with the profound revitalization of the Particular Baptist denomination to which he belonged. This study examines the key aspects of the life and thought of this hugely significant figure, and gives insights into the revival in which he played such a central part.

2003 / 1-84227-141-5 / xx + 202pp

Peter Naylor
Calvinism, Communion and the Baptists
A Study of English Calvinistic Baptists from the Late 1600s to the Early 1800s
(SBHT vol. 7)

Dr Naylor argues that the traditional link between 'high-Calvinism' and 'restricted communion' is in need of revision. He examines Baptist communion controversies from the late 1600s to the early 1800s and also the theologies of John Gill and Andrew Fuller.

2003 / 1-84227-142-3 / xx + 266pp

Ian M. Randall, Toivo Pilli and Anthony R. Cross (eds)
Baptist Identities
International Studies from the Seventeenth to the Twentieth Centuries
(SBHT vol. 19)

These papers represent the contributions of scholars from various parts of the world as they consider the factors that have contributed to Baptist distinctiveness in different countries and at different times. The volume includes specific case studies as well as broader examinations of Baptist life in a particular country or region. Together they represent an outstanding resource for understanding Baptist identities.

2005 / 1-84227-215-2 / approx. 350pp

James M. Renihan
Edification and Beauty
The Practical Ecclesiology of the English Particular Baptists, 1675–1705
(SBHT vol. 17)

Edification and Beauty describes the practices of the Particular Baptist churches at the end of the seventeenth century in terms of three concentric circles: at the centre is the ecclesiological material in the Second London Confession, which is then fleshed out in the various published writings of the men associated with these churches, and, finally, expressed in the church books of the era.

2005 / 1-84227-251-9 / approx. 230pp

Frank Rinaldi
'The Tribe of Dan'
A Study of the New Connexion of General Baptists 1770–1891
(SBHT vol. 10)

'The Tribe of Dan' is a thematic study which explores the theology, organizational structure, evangelistic strategy, ministry and leadership of the New Connexion of General Baptists as it experienced the process of institutionalization in the transition from a revival movement to an established denomination.

2006 / 1-84227-143-1 / approx. 350pp

Peter Shepherd
The Making of a Modern Denomination
John Howard Shakespeare and the English Baptists 1898–1924
(SBHT vol. 4)

John Howard Shakespeare introduced revolutionary change to the Baptist denomination. The Baptist Union was transformed into a strong central institution and Baptist ministers were brought under its control. Further, Shakespeare's pursuit of church unity reveals him as one of the pioneering ecumenists of the twentieth century.

2001 / 1-84227-046-X / xviii + 220pp

Karen Smith
The Community and the Believers
A Study of Calvinistic Baptist Spirituality in Some Towns and Villages of Hampshire and the Borders of Wiltshire, c.1730–1830
(SBHT vol. 22)

The period from 1730 to 1830 was one of transition for Calvinistic Baptists. Confronted by the enthusiasm of the Evangelical Revival, congregations within the denomination as a whole were challenged to find a way to take account of the revival experience. This study examines the life and devotion of Calvinistic Baptists in Hampshire and Wiltshire during this period. Among this group of Baptists was the hymn writer, Anne Steele.

2005 / 1-84227-326-4 / approx. 280pp

Martin Sutherland
Dissenters in a 'Free Land'
Baptist Thought in New Zealand 1850–2000
(SBHT vol. 24)

Baptists in New Zealand were forced to recast their identity. Conventions of communication and association, state and ecumenical relations, even historical divisions and controversies had to be revised in the face of new topographies and constraints. As Baptists formed themselves in a fluid society they drew heavily on both international movements and local dynamics. This book traces the development of ideas which shaped institutions and styles in sometimes surprising ways.

2006 / 1-84227-327-2 / approx. 230pp

Brian Talbot
The Search for a Common Identity
The Origins of the Baptist Union of Scotland 1800–1870
(SBHT vol. 9)

In the period 1800 to 1827 there were three streams of Baptists in Scotland: Scotch, Haldaneite and 'English' Baptist. A strong commitment to home evangelization brought these three bodies closer together, leading to a merger of their home missionary societies in 1827. However, the first three attempts to form a union of churches failed, but by the 1860s a common understanding of their corporate identity was attained leading to the establishment of the Baptist Union of Scotland.

2003 / 1-84227-123-7 / xviii + 402pp

Philip E. Thompson
The Freedom of God
Towards Baptist Theology in Pneumatological Perspective
(SBHT vol. 20)

This study contends that the range of theological commitments of the early Baptists are best understood in relation to their distinctive emphasis on the freedom of God. Thompson traces how this was recast anthropocentrically, leading to an emphasis upon human freedom from the nineteenth century onwards. He seeks to recover the dynamism of the early vision via a pneumatologically-oriented ecclesiology defining the church in terms of the memory of God.

2006 / 1-84227-125-3 / approx. 350pp

Philip E. Thompson and Anthony R. Cross (eds)
Recycling the Past or Researching History?
Studies in Baptist Historiography and Myths
(SBHT vol. 11)

In this volume an international group of Baptist scholars examine and re-examine areas of Baptist life and thought about which little is known or the received wisdom is in need of revision. Historiographical studies include the date Oxford Baptists joined the Abingdon Association, the death of the Fifth Monarchist John Pendarves, eighteenth-century Calvinistic Baptists and the political realm, confessional identity and denominational institutions, Baptist community, ecclesiology, the priesthood of all believers, soteriology, Baptist spirituality, Strict and Reformed Baptists, the role of women among British Baptists, while various 'myths' challenged include the nature of high-Calvinism in eighteenth-century England, baptismal anti-sacramentalism, episcopacy, and Baptists and change.

2005 / 1-84227-122-9 / approx. 330pp

Linda Wilson
Marianne Farningham
A Plain Working Woman
(SBHT vol. 18)

Marianne Farningham, of College Street Baptist Chapel, Northampton, was a household name in evangelical circles in the later nineteenth century. For over fifty years she produced comment, poetry, biography and fiction for the popular Christian press. This investigation uses her writings to explore the beliefs and behaviour of evangelical Nonconformists, including Baptists, during these years.

2006 / 1-84227-124-5 / approx. 250pp

Other Paternoster titles relating to Baptist history and thought

George R. Beasley-Murray
Baptism in the New Testament
(Paternoster Digital Library)

This is a welcome reprint of a classic text on baptism originally published in 1962 by one of the leading Baptist New Testament scholars of the twentieth century. Dr Beasley-Murray's comprehensive study begins by investigating the antecedents of Christian baptism. It then surveys the foundation of Christian baptism in the Gospels, its emergence in the Acts of the Apostles and development in the apostolic writings. Following a section relating baptism to New Testament doctrine, a substantial discussion of the origin and significance of infant baptism leads to a briefer consideration of baptismal reform and ecumenism.

2005 / 1-84227-300-0 / x + 422pp

Paul Beasley-Murray
Fearless for Truth
A Personal Portrait of the Life of George Beasley-Murray

Without a doubt George Beasley-Murray was one of the greatest Baptists of the twentieth century. A long-standing Principal of Spurgeon's College, he wrote more than twenty books and made significant contributions in the study of areas as diverse as baptism and eschatology, as well as writing highly respected commentaries on the Book of Revelation and John's Gospel.

2002 / 1-84227-134-2 / xii + 244pp

David Bebbington
Holiness in Nineteenth-Century England
(Studies in Christian History and Thought)

David Bebbington stresses the relationship of movements of spirituality to changes in their cultural setting, especially the legacies of the Enlightenment and Romanticism. He shows that these broad shifts in ideological mood had a profound effect on the ways in which piety was conceptualized and practised. Holiness was intimately bound up with the spirit of the age.

2000 / 0-85364-981-2 / viii + 98pp

July 2005

Clyde Binfield
Victorian Nonconformity in Eastern England 1840–1885
(Studies in Evangelical History and Thought)

Studies of Victorian religion and society often concentrate on cities, suburbs, and industrialisation. This study provides a contrast. Victorian Eastern England—Essex, Suffolk, Norfolk, Cambridgeshire, and Huntingdonshire—was rural, traditional, relatively unchanging. That is nonetheless a caricature which discounts the industry in Norwich and Ipswich (as well as in Haverhill, Stowmarket and Leiston) and ignores the impact of London on Essex, of railways throughout the region, and of an ancient but changing university (Cambridge) on the county town which housed it. It also entirely ignores the political implications of such changes in a region noted for the variety of its religious Dissent since the seventeenth century. This book explores Victorian Eastern England and its Nonconformity. It brings to a wider readership a pioneering thesis which has made a major contribution to a fresh evolution of English religion and society.

2006 / 1-84227-216-0 / approx. 274pp

Edward W. Burrows
'To Me To Live Is Christ'
A Biography of Peter H. Barber

This book is about a remarkably gifted and energetic man of God. Peter H. Barber was born into a Brethren family in Edinburgh in 1930. In his youth he joined Charlotte Baptist Chapel and followed the call into Baptist ministry. For eighteen years he was the pioneer minister of the new congregation in the New Town of East Kilbride, which planted two further congregations. At the age of thirty-nine he served as Centenary President of the Baptist Union of Scotland and then exercised an influential ministry for over seven years in the well-known Upton Vale Baptist Church, Torquay. From 1980 until his death in 1994 he was General Secretary of the Baptist Union of Scotland. Through his work for the European Baptist Federation and the Baptist World Alliance he became a world Baptist statesman. He was President of the EBF during the upheaval that followed the collapse of Communism.

2005 / 1-84227-324-8 / xxii + 236pp

Christopher J. Clement
Religious Radicalism in England 1535–1565
(Rutherford Studies in Historical Theology)

In this valuable study Christopher Clement draws our attention to a varied assemblage of people who sought Christian faithfulness in the underworld of mid-Tudor England. Sympathetically and yet critically he assess their place in the history of English Protestantism, and by attentive listening he gives them a voice.

1997 / 0-946068-44-5 / xxii + 426pp

July 2005

Anthony R. Cross (ed.)
Ecumenism and History
Studies in Honour of John H.Y. Briggs
(Studies in Christian History and Thought)

This collection of essays examines the inter-relationships between the two fields in which Professor Briggs has contributed so much: history—particularly Baptist and Nonconformist—and the ecumenical movement. With contributions from colleagues and former research students from Britain, Europe and North America, *Ecumenism and History* provides wide-ranging studies in important aspects of Christian history, theology and ecumenical studies.

2002 / 1-84227-135-0 / xx + 362pp

Keith E. Eitel
Paradigm Wars
*The Southern Baptist International Mission Board
Faces the Third Millennium*
(Regnum Studies in Mission)

The International Mission Board of the Southern Baptist Convention is the largest denominational mission agency in North America. This volume chronicles the historic and contemporary forces that led to the IMB's recent extensive reorganization, providing the most comprehensive case study to date of a historic mission agency restructuring to continue its mission purpose into the twenty-first century more effectively.

2000 / 1-870345-12-6 / x + 140pp

Ruth Gouldbourne
The Flesh and the Feminine
Gender and Theology in the Writings of Caspar Schwenckfeld
(Studies in Christian History and Thought)

Caspar Schwenckfeld and his movement exemplify one of the radical communities of the sixteenth century. Challenging theological and liturgical norms, they also found themselves challenging social and particularly gender assumptions. In this book, the issues of the relationship between radical theology and the understanding of gender are considered.

2005 / 1-84227-048-6 / approx. 304pp

David Hilborn
The Words of our Lips
Language-Use in Free Church Worship
(Paternoster Theological Monographs)
Studies of liturgical language have tended to focus on the written canons of Roman Catholic and Anglican communities. By contrast, David Hilborn analyses the more extemporary approach of English Nonconformity. Drawing on recent developments in linguistic pragmatics, he explores similarities and differences between 'fixed' and 'free' worship, and argues for the interdependence of each.

2006 / 0-85364-977-4

Stephen R. Holmes
Listening to the Past
The Place of Tradition in Theology
Beginning with the question 'Why can't we just read the Bible?' Stephen Holmes considers the place of tradition in theology, showing how the doctrine of creation leads to an account of historical location and creaturely limitations as essential aspects of our existence. For we cannot claim unmediated access to the Scriptures without acknowledging the place of tradition: theology is an irreducibly communal task. *Listening to the Past* is a sustained attempt to show what listening to tradition involves, and how it can be used to aid theological work today.

2002 / 1-84227-155-5 / xiv + 168pp

Mark Hopkins
Nonconformity's Romantic Generation
Evangelical and Liberal Theologies in Victorian England
(Studies in Evangelical History and Thought)
A study of the theological development of key leaders of the Baptist and Congregational denominations at their period of greatest influence, including C.H. Spurgeon and R.W. Dale, and of the controversies in which those among them who embraced and rejected the liberal transformation of their evangelical heritage opposed each other.

2004 / 1-84227-150-4 / xvi + 284pp

Galen K. Johnson
Prisoner of Conscience
John Bunyan on Self, Community and Christian Faith
(Studies in Christian History and Thought)
This is an interdisciplinary study of John Bunyan's understanding of conscience across his autobiographical, theological and fictional writings, investigating whether conscience always deserves fidelity, and how Bunyan's view of conscience affects his relationship both to modern Western individualism and historic Christianity.

2003 / 1-84227- 151-2 / xvi + 236pp

R.T. Kendall
Calvin and English Calvinism to 1649
(Studies in Christian History and Thought)
The author's thesis is that those who formed the Westminster Confession of Faith, which is regarded as Calvinism, in fact departed from John Calvin on two points: (1) the extent of the atonement and (2) the ground of assurance of salvation.

1997 / 0-85364-827-1 / xii + 264pp

Timothy Larsen
Friends of Religious Equality
Nonconformist Politics in Mid-Victorian England
During the middle decades of the nineteenth century the English Nonconformist community developed a coherent political philosophy of its own, of which a central tenet was the principle of religious equality (in contrast to the stereotype of Evangelical Dissenters). The Dissenting community fought for the civil rights of Roman Catholics, non-Christians and even atheists, on an issue of principle which had its flowering in the enthusiastic and undivided support which Nonconformity gave to the campaign for Jewish emancipation. This reissued study examines the political efforts and ideas of English Nonconformists during the period, covering the whole range of national issues raised, from state education to the Crimean War. It offers a case study of a theologically conservative group defending religious pluralism in the civic sphere, showing that the concept of religious equality was a grand vision at the centre of the political philosophy of the Dissenters.

2007 / 1-84227-402-3 / x + 300pp

Donald M. Lewis
Lighten Their Darkness
The Evangelical Mission to Working-Class London, 1828–1860
(Studies in Evangelical History and Thought)

This is a comprehensive and compelling study of the Church and the complexities of nineteenth-century London. Challenging our understanding of the culture in working London at this time, Lewis presents a well-structured and illustrated work that contributes substantially to the study of evangelicalism and mission in nineteenth-century Britain.

2001 / 1-84227-074-5 / xviii + 372pp

Stanley E. Porter and Anthony R. Cross (eds)
Semper Reformandum
Studies in Honour of Clark H. Pinnock

Clark Pinnock has clearly been one of the most important evangelical theologians of the last forty years in North America. Always provocative, especially in the wide range of opinions he has held and considered, Pinnock, himself a Baptist, has recently retired after twenty-five years of teaching at McMaster Divinity College. His colleagues and associates honour him in this volume by responding to his important theological work which has dealt with the essential topics of evangelical theology. These include Christian apologetics, biblical inspiration, the Holy Spirit and, perhaps most importantly in recent years, openness theology.

2003 / 1-84227-206-3 / xiv + 414pp

Meic Pearse
The Great Restoration
The Religious Radicals of the 16th and 17th Centuries

Pearse charts the rise and progress of continental Anabaptism – both evangelical and heretical – through the sixteenth century. He then follows the story of those English people who became impatient with Puritanism and separated – first from the Church of England and then from one another – to form the antecedents of later Congregationalists, Baptists and Quakers.

1998 / 0-85364-800-X / xii + 320pp

Charles Price and Ian M. Randall
Transforming Keswick

Transforming Keswick is a thorough, readable and detailed history of the convention. It will be of interest to those who know and love Keswick, those who are only just discovering it, and serious scholars eager to learn more about the history of God's dealings with his people.

2000 / 1-85078-350-0 / 288pp

Jim Purves
The Triune God and the Charismatic Movement
A Critical Appraisal from a Scottish Perspective
(Paternoster Theological Monographs)

All emotion and no theology? Or a fundamental challenge to reappraise and realign our trinitarian theology in the light of Christian experience? This study of charismatic renewal as it found expression within Scotland at the end of the twentieth century evaluates the use of Patristic, Reformed and contemporary models (including those of the Baptist Union of Scotland) of the Trinity in explaining the workings of the Holy Spirit.

2004 / 1-84227-321-3 / xxiv + 246pp

Ian M. Randall
Evangelical Experiences
A Study in the Spirituality of English Evangelicalism 1918–1939
(Studies in Evangelical History and Thought)

This book makes a detailed historical examination of evangelical spirituality between the First and Second World Wars. It shows how patterns of devotion led to tensions and divisions. In a wide-ranging study, Anglican, Wesleyan, Reformed and Pentecostal-charismatic spiritualities are analysed.

1999 / 0-85364-919-7 / xii + 310pp

Ian M. Randall
One Body in Christ
The History and Significance of the Evangelical Alliance

In 1846 the Evangelical Alliance was founded with the aim of bringing together evangelicals for common action. This book uses material not previously utilized to examine the history and significance of the Evangelical Alliance, a movement which has remained a powerful force for unity. At a time when evangelicals are growing world-wide, this book offers insights into the past which are relevant to contemporary issues.

2001 / 1-84227-089-3 / xii + 394pp

Ian M. Randall
Spirituality and Social Change
The Contribution of F.B. Meyer (1847–1929)
(Studies in Evangelical History and Thought)

This is a fresh appraisal of F.B. Meyer (1847–1929), a leading Free Church minister. Having been deeply affected by holiness spirituality, Meyer became the Keswick Convention's foremost international speaker. He combined spirituality with effective evangelism and socio-political activity. This study shows Meyer's significant contribution to spiritual renewal and social change.

2003 / 1-84227-195-4 / xx + 184pp

July 2005

Geoffrey Robson
Dark Satanic Mills?
Religion and Irreligion in Birmingham and the Black Country
(Studies in Evangelical History and Thought)
This book analyses and interprets the nature and extent of popular Christian belief and practice in Birmingham and the Black Country during the first half of the nineteenth century, with particular reference to the impact of cholera epidemics and evangelism on church extension programmes.
2002 / 1-84227-102-4 / xiv + 294pp

Alan P.F. Sell
Enlightenment, Ecumenism, Evangel
Theological Themes and Thinkers 1550–2000
(Studies in Christian History and Thought)
This book consists of papers in which such interlocking topics as the Enlightenment, the problem of authority, the development of doctrine, spirituality, ecumenism, theological method and the heart of the gospel are discussed. Issues of significance to the church at large are explored with special reference to writers from the Reformed and Dissenting traditions.
2005 / 1-84227330-2 / xviii + 422pp

Alan P.F. Sell
Hinterland Theology
Some Reformed and Dissenting Adjustments
(Studies in Christian History and Thought)
Many books have been written on theology's 'giants' and significant trends, but what of those lesser-known writers who adjusted to them? In this book some hinterland theologians of the British Reformed and Dissenting traditions, who followed in the wake of toleration, the Evangelical Revival, the rise of modern biblical criticism and Karl Barth, are allowed to have their say. They include Thomas Ridgley, Ralph Wardlaw, T.V. Tymms and N.H.G. Robinson.
2006 / 1-84227-331-0

Alan P.F. Sell and Anthony R. Cross (eds)
Protestant Nonconformity in the Twentieth Century
(Studies in Christian History and Thought)

In this collection of essays scholars representative of a number of Nonconformist traditions reflect thematically on Nonconformists' life and witness during the twentieth century. Among the subjects reviewed are biblical studies, theology, worship, evangelism and spirituality, and ecumenism. Over and above its immediate interest, this collection provides a marker to future scholars and others wishing to know how some of their forebears assessed Nonconformity's contribution to a variety of fields during the century leading up to Christianity's third millennium.

2003 / 1-84227-221-7 / x + 398pp

Mark Smith
Religion in Industrial Society
Oldham and Saddleworth 1740–1865
(Studies in Christian History and Thought)

This book analyses the way British churches sought to meet the challenge of industrialization and urbanization during the period 1740–1865. Working from a case-study of Oldham and Saddleworth, Mark Smith challenges the received view that the Anglican Church in the eighteenth century was characterized by complacency and inertia, and reveals Anglicanism's vigorous and creative response to the new conditions. He reassesses the significance of the centrally directed church reforms of the mid-nineteenth century, and emphasizes the importance of local energy and enthusiasm. Charting the growth of denominational pluralism in Oldham and Saddleworth, Dr Smith compares the strengths and weaknesses of the various Anglican and Nonconformist approaches to promoting church growth. He also demonstrates the extent to which all the churches participated in a common culture shaped by the influence of evangelicalism, and shows that active co-operation between the churches rather than denominational conflict dominated. This revised and updated edition of Dr Smith's challenging and original study makes an important contribution both to the social history of religion and to urban studies.

2006 / 1-84227-335-3 / approx. 300pp

David M. Thompson
Baptism, Church and Society in Britain from the Evangelical Revival to *Baptism, Eucharist and Ministry*

The theology and practice of baptism have not received the attention they deserve. How important is faith? What does baptismal regeneration mean? Is baptism a bond of unity between Christians? This book discusses the theology of baptism and popular belief and practice in England and Wales from the Evangelical Revival to the publication of the World Council of Churches' consensus statement on *Baptism, Eucharist and Ministry* (1982).

2005 / 1-84227-393-0 / approx. 224pp

Martin Sutherland
Peace, Toleration and Decay
The Ecclesiology of Later Stuart Dissent
(Studies in Christian History and Thought)

This fresh analysis brings to light the complexity and fragility of the later Stuart Nonconformist consensus. Recent findings on wider seventeenth-century thought are incorporated into a new picture of the dynamics of Dissent and the roots of evangelicalism.

2003 / 1-84227-152-0 / xxii + 216pp

Haddon Willmer
Evangelicalism 1785–1835: An Essay (1962) and Reflections (2004)
(Studies in Evangelical History and Thought)

Awarded the Hulsean Prize in the University of Cambridge in 1962, this interpretation of a classic period of English Evangelicalism, by a young church historian, is now supplemented by reflections on Evangelicalism from the vantage point of a retired Professor of Theology.

2006 / 1-84227-219-5

Linda Wilson
Constrained by Zeal
Female Spirituality amongst Nonconformists 1825–1875
(Studies in Evangelical History and Thought)

Constrained by Zeal investigates the neglected area of Nonconformist female spirituality. Against the background of separate spheres, it analyses the experience of women from four denominations, and argues that the churches provided a 'third sphere' in which they could find opportunities for participation.

2000 / 0-85364-972-3 / xvi + 294pp

Nigel G. Wright
Disavowing Constantine
Mission, Church and the Social Order in the Theologies of John Howard Yoder and Jürgen Moltmann
(Paternoster Theological Monographs)

This book is a timely restatement of a radical theology of church and state in the Anabaptist and Baptist tradition. Dr Wright constructs his argument in dialogue and debate with Yoder and Moltmann, major contributors to a free church perspective.

2000 / 0-85364-978-2 / xvi + 252pp

Nigel G. Wright
Free Church, Free State
The Positive Baptist Vision

Free Church, Free State is a textbook on baptist ways of being church and a proposal for the future of baptist churches in an ecumenical context. Nigel Wright argues that both baptist (small 'b') and catholic (small 'c') church traditions should seek to enrich and support each other as valid expressions of the body of Christ without sacrificing what they hold dear. Written for pastors, church planters, evangelists and preachers, Nigel Wright offers frameworks of thought for baptists and non-baptists in their journey together following Christ.

2005 / 1-84227-353-1 / xxviii + 292

Nigel G. Wright
New Baptists, New Agenda

New Baptists, New Agenda is a timely contribution to the growing debate about the health, shape and future of the Baptists. It considers the steady changes that have taken place among Baptists in the last decade – changes of mood, style, practice and structure – and encourages us to align these current movements and questions with God's upward and future call. He contends that the true church has yet to come: the church that currently exists is an anticipation of the joyful gathering of all who have been called by the Spirit through Christ to the Father.

2002 / 1-84227-157-1 / x + 162pp

Paternoster:
thinking faith

Paternoster
9 Holdom Avenue,
Bletchley,
Milton Keynes MK1 1QR,
United Kingdom
Web: www.authenticmedia.co.uk/paternoster

July 2005